TRAVELLERS SURVIVAL KIT

Sri Lanka

TRAVELLERS
SURVIVAL KIT

Sri Lanka

John & Colette Leak

Published by Vacation Work, 9 Park End Street, Oxford
www.vacationwork.co.uk

TRAVELLERS SURVIVAL KIT: SRI LANKA

by John & Colette Leak

Editor: Ian Collier

Copyright © Vacation Work 1999

ISBN 1 85458 222 4

No part of this publication may be reproduced or transmitted in any form or by any means without the prior written permission of the publisher.

Cover Design:
Miller Craig & Cocking Design Partnership

Maps by Andrea Pullen

Chapter headings by Becky Blake

Cover photograph
High Buddha at Wewurukannala
by John Leak

Printed by Unwin Brothers Ltd, Old Woking, Surrey, England.

Contents

SRI LANKA AND ITS PEOPLE — 11
The land 11
Climate 14
History — A brief chronology — The civil war 15
Government and politics — Central government — Politics 20
The economy 22
The people — Ethnic background — Women in Sri Lanka —
  Marriage in Sri Lanka — Sex in Sri Lanka —
  Homosexuality in Sri Lanka 22
Meeting people — Dodgy characters — Women travellers 25
Religion — Buddhism — Hinduism — Islam — Christianity 26
Art and architecture — Buddhist architecture — Painting —
  Hindu architecture 33
Language 36
Reading 37

PRACTICAL INFORMATION

GETTING THERE — 38
Independent travel — Flying — Sea routes 38
Package tours 40
Insurance 41

RED TAPE — 42
Passports and visas — Major Sri Lankan Legations 42
Customs 43
Security 43

MONEY — 44
What money to take — Living costs 44
Money in Sri Lanka — Rupees — Changing money — The black
  market — Transfers — Caution 44
Tipping 45

WHAT TO TAKE — 46
Baggage — Oddments — Dress — Nudity — Cameras 46

COMMUNICATIONS — 48
Telephone — International calls from Sri Lanka — Calling Sri Lanka
  from abroad — Mobile phones — Fax 48
Telegrams 49
Mail — Poste Restante 49
Media — Newspapers — Magazines — Radio — Television 49

GETTING AROUND 50
Planning — Maps — Festivals — Stars 50
Flying 51
Railways — Route planning — Classes — Reservations — Tickets —
   Facilities — For the enthusiast 51
Bus 53
Car hire 53
Self-Drive Car Hire 54
Motorcycle hire 55
Hitching 55
Local transport — Three-wheelers — Taxis — Fares — Bicycles 55
Guided tours 56

ACCOMMODATION 56
Hotels and Guest Houses 56
Rest Homes 57
Other Accommodation — Tea estate Bungalows — National Park
   Bungalows — Retiring Rooms 57
Special Places — Seasons 57
Prices and Taxes 58

EATING AND DRINKING 58
Restaurants 59
Sri Lankan Specialities 59
Snacks — Sweets — Ice cream 60
Drinking — Soft drinks — Water — Tea and coffee — Other drinks 60
Hardstuff — Imported liquor — Beer — Local drinks 61
Smokes and paan 61

EXPLORING 62
Museums and art galleries 62
The great outdoors — Flora and fauna — National Parks and nature
   reserves 62
Recreation — Sport and adventure — Scuba diving and
   snorkelling — Angling — Walking and trekking — Running —
   Golf — Yachting — Other ideas — Beaches — Swimming pools... 63

ENTERTAINMENT 65
Cinema and theatre 65
Music and dance — Classical music — Popular music — Dance 65
Nightlife 66
Spectator sports 66
Festivals — *Buddhist* — Poya — *Hindu* — Pongal — Maha
   Shivaratri — Dussehra — Deepavali — *Muslim* — *Christian* —
   Secular festivals — Dates and details 67

SHOPPING 69
Opening hours — Shopping 69

HEALTH AND HYGIENE 70
Natural hazards — Heat — Sun — Insects — Snakes 70
Diseases and other health hazards — Inoculations — Rabies —
   Malaria — Gastric problems — AIDS 71
Medical treatment — Pharmacies 72
Everyday health — Cuts — Women's health — Toilets 73
Insurance 73

CRIME AND SAFETY	**73**
Black market — Crime against visitors — How to avoid robbery — Violence — Police — Drugs — Photography	73
HELP AND INFORMATION	**75**
Children	75
Travellers with disabilities	75
Electrical equipment	75
Youth and student concessions	75
Time	76
Weights and measures	76
The Internet	76
Tourist information — Tourist offices abroad — Tourist offices in Sri Lanka	76
Embassies, High Commissions and Consulates in Sri Lanka	77

COLOMBO

History	79
Exploring — Fort — The Pettah — Harbour and churches — Galle Face and Slave Island — Modern Colombo	79
Further afield	86
Shopping	87
Entertainment	88
Practical information — Arrival and departure — Trains and buses — Local transport	88
Accommodation — At Mount Lavinia	90
Eating and drinking	92

WEST COAST BEACHES

North of Colombo	95
Negombo — Negombo beach	95
North from Negombo — Mahawewa — Chilaw — Puttalam — Kalpitiya — Wilpattu National Park	99
South of Colombo: Colombo to Hikkaduwa — Ratmalana — Kalutara — Beruwela — Aluthgama — Bentota — Induruwa — Ambalangoda	100
Hikkaduwa — Beaches — watersports — Dodanduwa	104
Galle — History — Walls and bastions — The Old Town — The New Town	108

THE SOUTH

Unawatuna	114
Unawatuna to Weligama — Koggala — Kataluwa — Ahangama — Weligama — Mirissa — Polhena	117
Matara — The Dutch Forts	121
Matara to Tangalla — Weherehena Temple — Dondra Head — Dikwella — Wewurukannala Temple — Mulkirigala Cave Temples — Mawella Blowhole	122
Tangalla	125
Tangalla to Tissamaharama — Hambantota — Bundala National Park — Kirinda	127
Tissamaharama — Exploring — Practical information	130

Yala West National Park	131
Kataragama — The sacred area — Devotions and festivals	132
Uda Walawe National Park	135

THE HILL COUNTRY

Colombo to Kandy — Henerathgoda Botanic Gardens — Pasyala — Alawwa — Dedigama	137
Pinnewala Elephant Orphanage — Balana — Mawanella — Kadugannawa	138
Kandy — History — Planning and architecture — Temple of the Tooth Relic — Royal Palace — The four devales — The lake — Around town — Walks — Entertainment — Festivals — Shopping	141
Practical information	152
Accommodation — Eating and drinking	153
Excursions — Peradeniya Botanic Gardens — Historic temples	156
Kandy towards the East Coast — Victoria Dam — Hanguranketa — Kirindu Oya Falls — Mahiyangana	159
Kandy to Adam's Peak and Nuwara Eliya by rail — Gampola — Hatton — Bogawantalawa — Maskeliya	160
Adam's Peak — Dalhousie and the ascent — The holy footprint — The catch	161
Nuwara Eliya — Exploring — Other attractions — accommodation	163
Excursions — Hakgala Botanic Gardens	168
Nuwara to Badulla by rail	168
Horton Plains — World's End and Baker Falls — Around the Plains	168
Haputale — Walks — Visiting a Tea Factory — Diyatalawa	171
Bandarawela	174
Ella — Ella Gap — Rawana Ella Rock Temple	175
Badulla — Bogoda bridge and cave temple — Dunhinda Falls — Namunkulla	178
Wellawaya — Buduruvagala Buddhist statues — Handapanagala elephants — Maligawila — Bat cave — Diyaluma Falls — Belihul Oya — Kurugala Caves	179
Sinharaja Biosphere Reserve	182
Ratnapura — Gem Bureau and Museum	183
Ratnapura to Colombo — Avissawella — Kelani Valley Railway	185

THE ANCIENT CAPITALS

The Cultural Triangle	188
Kandy to Dambulla — Matale — Hunas Falls — Aluvihara — Nalanda — Wahakotte	189
Dambulla — Spectacular Cave Temples	192
Sigiriya — History — Planning — Fortifications and gardens — Boulder Garden — Frescoes and Mirror Wall — Lion Platform — The palace — Pidurangala	196
Sigiriya to Polonnaruwa — Habarana — Minneriya Giritale Sanctuary	204
Polonnaruwa — Southern group — Rest House group — The Ancient City — Inner Citadel — Sacred Quadrangle — More dagobas and temples — Alahana Parivena — Galvihara — Outer Garden	205
Further afield — Dimbulagala — Medirigiriya	216

Polonnaruwa to Anuradhapura — Ritigala Strict Natural
Reserve — Kalawewa — Aukana — Sasseruwa — Yapahuwa 218
Anuradhapura — Southern dagobas and monasteries —
Mahavihara — Jetavanaramaya — Citadel — Uttaravihara —
Elsewhere.. 221
Excursions — Induarane 232
Mihintale — Around town — The holy hill.................................... 233
Anuradhapura to Colombo — Kurunegala — Ridigama Vihara —
Panduvasnavara — Dambadeniya.. 236

THE EAST

Trincomalee — Fort Frederick — Excursions 239
Beach resorts — Uppuveli — Nilaveli — Passekudah — Kalkudah Bay 241
Batticaloa 242
Gal Oya National Park 243
Arugam Bay — Pottuvil 243
Lahugala-Kitalan National Park 244

THE NORTH

The Jaffna Peninsula — Elephant Pass — Jaffna Town 245
Adam's Bridge — Mannar — Talaimannar 246

APPENDICES

Glossary... 247
Place Names 250
Bibliography... 250
Index 253

MAPS

Sri Lanka	12–13	Kandy	142–143
Colombo	80	Kandy Excursions	157
Colombo (Fort)	82	Nuwara Eliya	165
Negombo Town & Beach	98	Horton Plains	170
Hikkaduwa & Wewala Beach .	105	Haputale	172
Galle	110	Ella	176
Unawatuna	115	Ratnapura	185
Welligama & Mirissa	119	Dambulla	192
Matara	122	Sirigiriya	198
Tangalla	127	Polonnaruwa	207
Hambantota	128	Anuradhapura	223
Tissamaharama	130	Mihintale	234

While every effort has been made to ensure that the information contained in this book is as up-to-date as possible, some details are bound to change within the lifetime of this edition, and readers are strongly advised to check facts and credentials themselves.

The *Travellers Survival Kit: Sri Lanka* will be revised regularly. We are keen to hear comments, criticisms and suggestions from both natives and travellers. Please write to the authors at Vacation Work, 9 Park End St, Oxford OX1 1HJ. Those whose contributions are used will be sent a complimentary copy of the next editon.

Preface

Serendipity is the art of making happy discoveries by accident. Horace Walpole, the novelist, had heard accounts of Sri Lanka's beauty and coined the word from Serendib, the old Arab name for the island. Earlier writers had linked the island with the biblical Tarshish, a place of great wealth, with its 'gold and silver, ivory, apes, and peacocks'. The local name Lanka means the 'Resplendent', a very fair description. For the modern traveller Sri Lanka offers stunning beaches, blue mountains, manicured tea gardens, rain forest, and remarkable temples and palaces.

Sri Lanka may technically be a Third World country. The fact is that to anyone used to other parts of Asia or most of Africa, Sri Lanka simply does not feel like a Third World country. It is an orderly place, unusually quiet for Asia, where most things work as they should. The people are relaxed, welcoming, and tolerant.

Nor should one fall into the trap of thinking of Sri Lanka as just an appendage of India. Its adherence to Buddhism and its legal code, introduced by the Dutch, put it a very different position from India where the British by and large used the institutions they had inherited from the Mughals. The British acknowledged this distinction by administering Ceylon quite separately from their Indian Empire — and with a rather lighter hand.

Sri Lanka was a new experience for us as we researched this book, despite all the time we had spent in India, and we were knocked out. It is simply a lovely, fascinating, relaxed place to visit.

Safety

The continuing troubles in Sri Lanka prompt many would-be visitors (or, more often, their mothers!) to worry about their safety there. The short answer is that (with only one exception in 1986) the insurgents have never targeted foreign visitors. The risk of being caught up in a terrorist incident is generally no greater than in a western city.

The occasional bomb attack does indeed occur in Colombo or Galle, but it must be stressed that, for all the attention from the world's media, these incidents are extremely rare. Few visitors spend much time in these places anyway.

At the time of going to press, elections were provoking considerable unrest. For an up-to-date report on the current security situation contact either the British Foreign Office or the US State Department — for details see p.43.

John and Colette Leak
April 1999

Telephone area code changes: As of June 1st, 1999 there are to be a number of changes to certain area telephone code prefixes in the UK. The most important of these is that the current 0171- and 0181- prefixes for London will both be replaced by the prefix 020- followed by 7 for current 0171 numbers and 8 for current 0181 numbers. Also affected will be Cardiff (numbers will begin 029 20), Portsmouth (023 92), Southampton (023 80) and Northern Ireland (028 90 for Belfast); contact directory enquiries for other numbers in Northern Ireland.

In addition, as from the same date, the numbers for various special services including freephone and lo-call numbers will begin with 08 and all mobile phone numbers will begin with 07. Telephone operators are planning to ease the transition by running the current 01 numbers in parallel with the new 02 numbers until April 22nd, 2000.

SRI LANKA AND ITS PEOPLE

Sri Lanka, formerly known as Ceylon, is an island at the tip of the Indian subcontinent. Its area of 66,000sq km (25,330sq miles) places it quite low in the world ranking of islands, being only about two-thirds the size of Iceland for instance, or four-fifths of Ireland. The population at present is a little under 20 million.

THE LAND

The extremes of Sri Lanka are near enough 430km/270 miles north to south and 224km/140 miles east to west. Point Pedro, the northernmost part of Sri Lanka is 10° north of the equator and Matara in the south 6°N.

Unlike its giant neighbour India, which has large climatic variations Sri Lanka is thus an entirely tropical land. The landscape is nevertheless very varied, offering beautiful beaches, rain forest, tea and coffee plantations, and forested mountains.

Geologically Sri Lanka is part of Gondwanaland, the great proto-continent which broke up to form South America, Africa, India, Australasia, and Antarctica. Sri Lanka is an extension of the Western Ghats, the rocky escarpment which runs down the whole seaboard of western India. Indeed, until comparatively recently it was solidly connected to India. The Archaean rocks which make up most of the island are among the oldest on Earth, several hundred million years old. These are crystalline rocks similar to those of Madagascar and eastern Africa; they appear always to have been above sea level. Around Jaffna are sedimentary limestones laid down under the sea around 27 million years ago.

Geographically Sri Lanka divides into four areas: the south-west, the central highlands or Hill Country, the east, and the northern lowlands.

The **south-west**, together with much of the Hill Country, constitutes the Wet Zone, and the other two areas the Dry Zone, these expressions being fully explained in the next section on climate. Much of the south-west is an extension of the Hill Country. In its natural state this a place of jungly ridges, though since the population drift to the Wet Zone the level land has been mostly cleared for agriculture and plantations. The coastal area is similar and, apart from the immediate surroundings of Jaffna, has the highest population density on the island.

The central highlands, known as the **Hill Country**, have an average

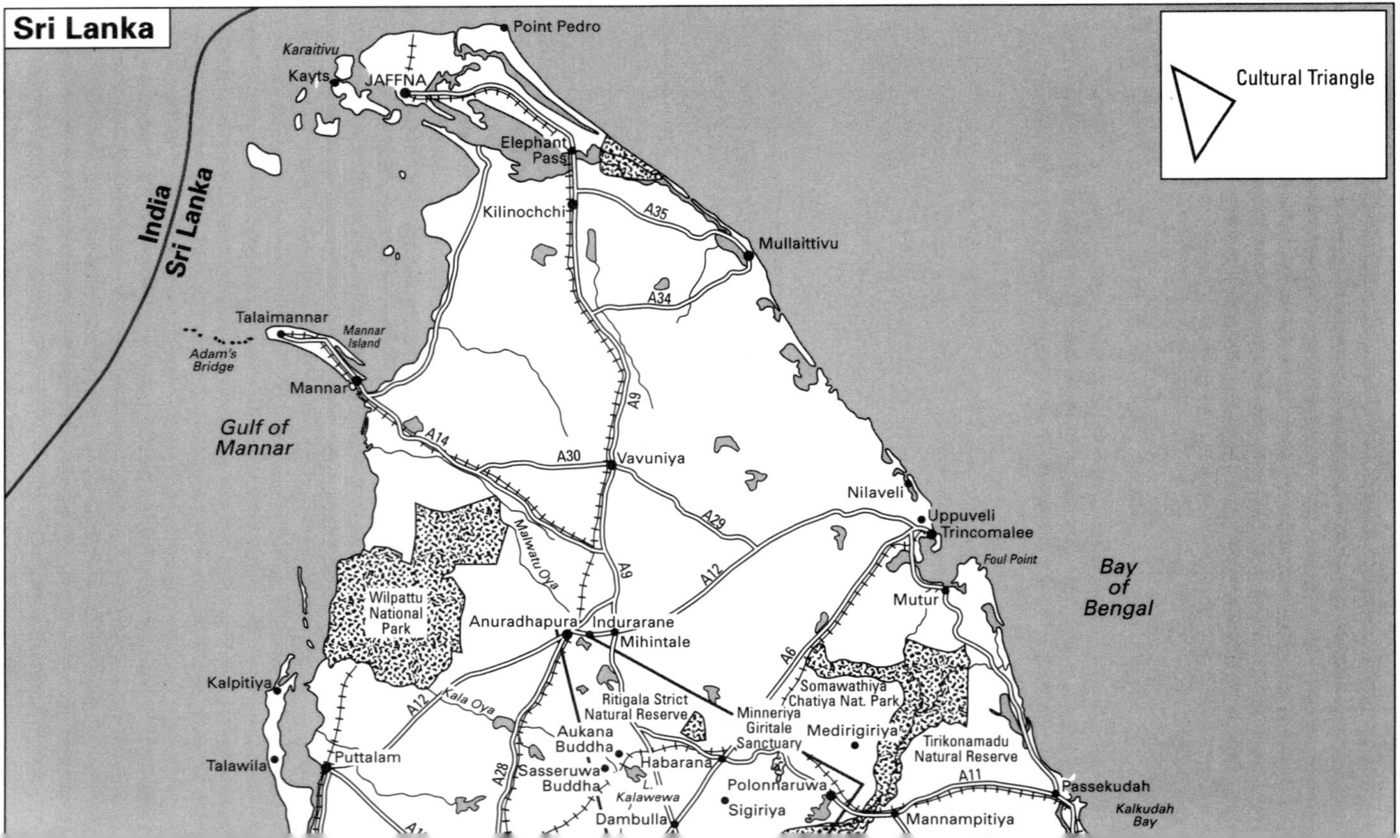
Sri Lanka
Cultural Triangle
India
Sri Lanka
Point Pedro
Karaitivu
Kayts
JAFFNA
Elephant Pass
Kilinochchi
A35
Mullaittivu
A34
Talaimannar
Mannar Island
Adam's Bridge
Mannar
A9
Gulf of Mannar
A14
A30
Vavuniya
Nilaveli
A29
Uppuveli
Trincomalee
Malwatu Oya
A12
Foul Point
Bay of Bengal
Mutur
Wilpattu National Park
Anuradhapura
Indurarane
Mihintale
A6
Somawathiya Chatiya Nat. Park
Kalpitiya
Kala Oya
Ritigala Strict Natural Reserve
Minneriya Giritale Sanctuary
Medirigiriya
Aukana Buddha
Tirikonamadu Natural Reserve
Talawila
Puttalam
Habarana
A28
Sasseruwa Buddha
L. Kalawewa
Polonnaruwa
A11
Passekudah
Sigiriya
Dambulla
Mannampitiya
Kalkudah Bay

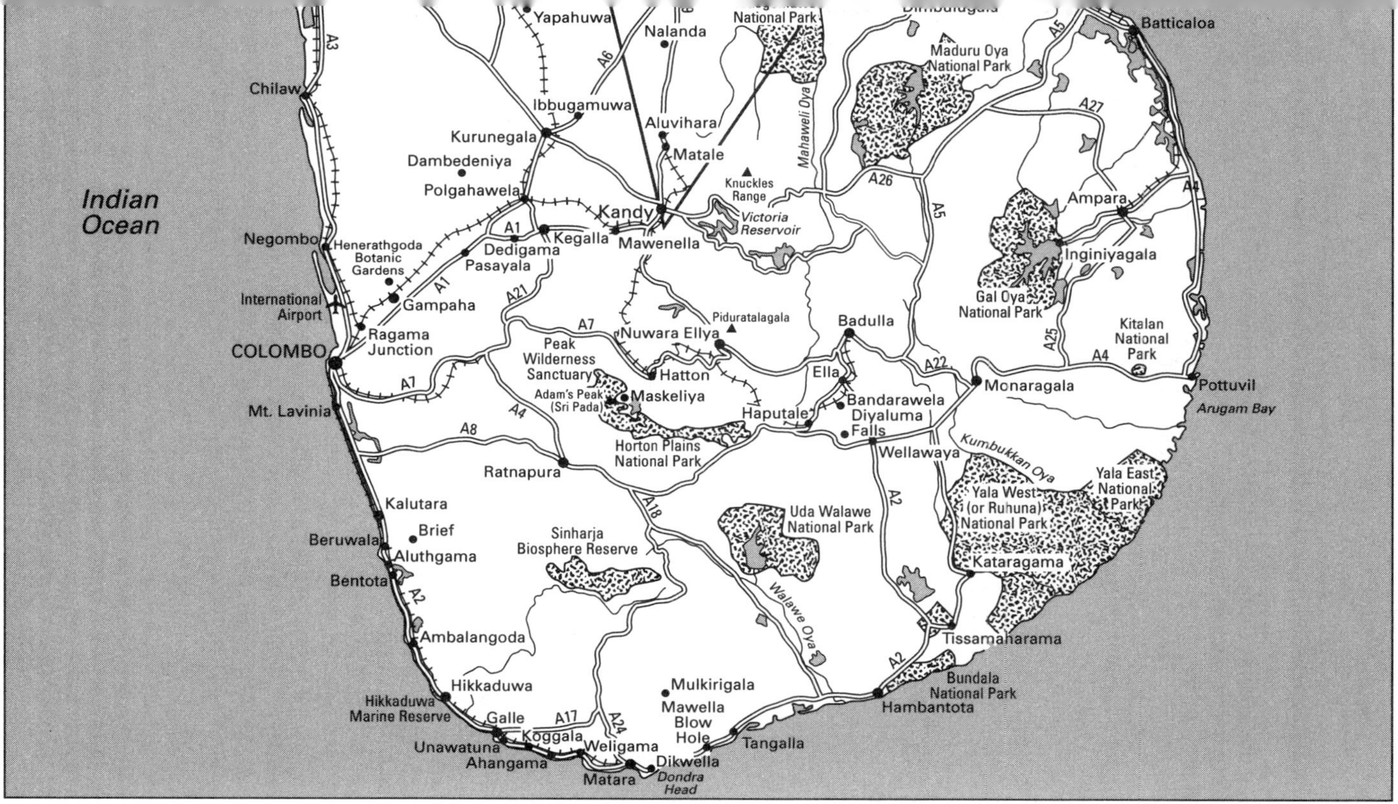
Indian Ocean
Chilaw
Negombo
International Airport
COLOMBO
Mt. Lavinia
Yapahuwa
Nalanda
National Park
Batticaloa
Maduru Oya National Park
Ibbugamuwa
Kurunegala
Dambedeniya
Polgahawela
Aluvihara
Matale
Knuckles Range
Kandy
Victoria Reservoir
Mawenella
Kegalla
Dedigama
Pasayala
Henerathgoda Botanic Gardens
Gampaha
Ragama Junction
Mahaweli Oya
Ampara
Inginiyagala
Gal Oya National Park
Kitalan National Park
Pottuvil
Arugam Bay
Piduratalagala
Nuwara Ellya
Badulla
Peak Wilderness Sanctuary
Hatton
Adam's Peak (Sri Pada)
Maskeliya
Ella
Bandarawela
Diyaluma Falls
Haputale
Monaragala
Wellawaya
Horton Plains National Park
Ratnapura
Kumbukkan Oya
Yala East National Park
Yala West (or Ruhuna) National Park
Kataragama
Uda Walawe National Park
Kalutara
Brief
Beruwala
Aluthgama
Bentota
Sinharja Biosphere Reserve
Walawe Oya
Tissamaharama
Ambalangoda
Hikkaduwa
Hikkaduwa Marine Reserve
Galle
Unawatuna
Koggala
Ahangama
Weligama
Matara
Dikwella
Dondra Head
Mulkirigala
Mawella Blow Hole
Tangalla
Hambantota
Bundala National Park
A1
A2
A3
A4
A5
A6
A7
A8
A17
A18
A21
A22
A24
A25
A26
A27

heightover 1500m/5000ft, although only one sixth of the country as a whole is over 300m/1000ft. The highest point is Pidurutalagala Peak at 2524m/8281ft, whilst the better known Adam's Peak is 2243m/7362ft. Rivers rising in the hills flow all year.

The **east** is undulating country, still quite heavily wooded. Rainfall is low, and agriculture dependent on irrigation.

The **northern lowlands** are flat, fertile plains through which flows the Mahaweli, Sri Lanka's largest river, and one of the few in this area to flow all year. This has now been harnessed for both hydro-electric power and irrigation. In the extreme north, around, Jaffna, agriculture depends on water from very deep wells.

The waters around Sri Lanka are an extension of the Indian continental shelf. This is shallow, as little as 9m/20ft deep in the Palk Strait between Sri Lanka and India, and generally around 60m/200ft. The shelf, however, is narrow, and after 19km/12miles at the most the sea-bed drops sharply to 900m/3000ft. This shallow warm sea is a prolific fishery, augmented by fish and shellfish farming in the many lagoons around the coast.

CLIMATE

The climate in Sri Lanka is equatorial with little seasonal variation in temperatures. Average afternoon temperatures vary from 29°C/85°F to 33°C/92°F in the lowland areas to around 21°C/70°F in the hills. Humidity tends to be high all year round and regardless of location. Rainfall varies from less than 100cm/40in to 500cm/200in.

Because of its closeness to India Sri Lanka's rainfall does not follow a typically equatorial pattern. Instead it experiences both of the monsoons which affect India. The **south-east monsoon** blows from May to October bringing heavy rain to the Wet Zone and making the sea rough on the western and southern beaches. The **north-east trade winds** blow from December to March bringing rain to the Dry Zone and making the beaches on the north and east unsafe for swimming. In the Wet Zone rainfall, mist, and cloud are far from uncommon outside the monsoon period, especially as you go into the hills. This means that once the political situation has settled down the traveller can always find a beach that is safe and pleasant. Travel, both surface and air, can be disrupted by the monsoons.

A combination of the central mountain area and differences between the two monsoons divides Sri Lanka into two basic climatic areas. The south-eastern quarter of the island is the Wet Zone, and the other three-quarters the Dry Zone. There are gradations between the two, and in the south and west there are actually small areas classified as arid. The difference between the two zones is very marked and has had a major influence on the social history of Sri Lanka. The great ancient capitals of Anuradhapura and Polonnaruwa could only exist in the Dry Zone because the Sinhalese developed one the world's most effective and extensive irrigation systems. When warfare disrupted this the population had little choice but to move to the better watered south-east.

Despite Sri Lanka's small size considerable variations do occur. Mannar, on the promontory leading to Adam's Bridge, has an annual rainfall of only 100cm/40 inches compared with 230cm/90 inches 250km away in Colombo, both places having an average temperature of 28°C/82°F. At the other end of the scale 550cm/218 inches fall on Watwala in the highlands where the average temperature is 18°C/62°F. In any given place the temperature variation around the year or day and night is very small, around only 4°C or 8°F. Humidity everywhere is high all through the year, though it rarely feels oppressive in the Hill Country.

HISTORY

Firstly, let's sort out the name. Vijaya, leader of the Aryan settlers, was from the Simhalas or Lion tribe. They named the island Simhaladvipa (dwipa is Sanskrit for land or continent), from which is derived the Arabic Serendib. The Greeks and Romans had extensive trade links with the island by the start of the Christian era, but had known about it, as Taprobane, much earlier. The Portuguese Ceilão, like the Dutch Zeylan, is said to come from the Arabic, but the Chinese were calling the island Si-Lan long before that. The name most used by the local people was Lanka, or Ilanki to the Tamils, and the official name changed from the British Ceylon to Sri Lanka in 1972.

Our knowledge of Sri Lanka's early history is based on two chronicles, the Mahavansa (sixth century AD) and the Culavansa (13th century AD). Whilst these reflect the bias of their Buddhist compilers and aggrandise the Buddhist rulers they are a source without parallel in the rest of south Asia.

A brief chronology

Prehistory Evidence of habitation around 500,000 years ago. The inhabitants before the arrival of Aryan settlers were the Veddahs, related to the aborigines of India and probably diluted by Dravidians (in this case from Orissa) who had supplanted their counterparts in southern India around 1500BC.

483BC Death of Buddha. Legendary arrival of Indo-Aryan settlers under Vijaya, possibly from southern Gujarat, more likely from Orissa, who evolved into the Sinhalese.

377BC Foundation of Anuradhapura. Scattered settlements with no central control, but already dependent on irrigation.

273BC Accession of the Emperor Ashoka to the Indian Maurayan empire. Buddhism adopted as state religion and exported to Sri Lanka by Ashoka's son Mahendra and daughter Sanghamitra in 246BC.

177BC Tamils seize Anuradhapura and rule there for 22 years.

145BC Anuradhapura again taken by Tamils. Ruled for 44 years by Elara, eventually defeated by Dutthagamani, who for the first time brought northern Lanka under one rule.

44BC Tamils again in control (to 29BC).

AD

274 King Mahasena (to 301). Arrival of the Tooth Relic in Lanka.

455 King Dhatusena evicts Tamils (to 473).

473 Capital at Sigiriya under regicide Kassapa. Defeated by his brother Mogallana, whose Tamil mercenaries had great influence, in effect the start of the present Tamil presence (to 491).

500 Resurgence of Hinduism in southern India leading to rise of Pallava (Kanchipuram), Pandya (Madurai), and Chola (Thanjavur) empires. Constant raids and invasions with control constantly

	changing hands (to 1500).
1000	Anuradhapura sacked and Polonnaruwa occupied by the Cholas.
1055	King Vijayabahu I evicts Tamils from whole island. Start of new Sinhalese golden age (to 1110).
1153	King Parakramabahu I. Anuradhapura and Polonnaruwa at their height (to 1186).
1213	Fresh Tamil incursions, this time the Pandyas. Start of collapse of irrigation civilisations and consequent drift of population to fertile southwest. Growth of spice trade and establishment of Tamil kingdom based on Jaffna. Origin of Kandyan kingdom (to 1600).
1235	Sinhalese reassert control and initiate religious and cultural renaissance.
1288	Final abandonment of Polonnaruwa and Anuradhapura.
1409	Chinese invasion in retaliation for refusal to hand over Tooth Relic. Royal family taken to China as hostages for five years.
1505	First Portuguese reconnaissance of Sri Lanka.
1518	Portuguese fort built in Colombo. After siege in 1524 Portuguese base moved to Kotte.
1538	Invasion by Zamorin of Calicut foiled by Portuguese thus preventing Muslim takeover of island.
1541	Sinhalese embassy to Lisbon and friendly trading relations.
1556	King Dharmapala and his queen baptised as Christians. Possibility of converting whole population spoiled by fundamentalist approach of Catholic priests.
1559	Open war between Sinhalese and Portuguese who shift their base to Colombo (-1565).
1565	Sporadic warfare sees Portuguese influence extended to most maritime areas (-1597)
1597	Philip II (Portugal being under Spanish rule at the time) declared king of Ceylon.
1600	Founding of (English) East India Company.
1602	Dutch visit Batticaloa (not then occupied by Portuguese) and Kandy.
1638	Dutch, with connivance of king of Kandy, take Batticaloa from Portuguese; start of twenty year battle for supremacy. Dutch generally in command of seas by this time and looking to expand from their Indonesian bases.
1640	Negombo and later Galle taken by Dutch. Portugal independent of Spain again, so truce between Dutch and Portuguese.
1640	English occupy Madras.
1644	Portuguese cede Negombo and Galle and with them part of the lucrative cinnamon trade.
1655	In wake of Portuguese defeat of Dutch in Brazil Dutch launch all-out assault on Colombo, aided by king of Kandy.
1657	Dutch expel Portuguese from Mannar and, in following year, from their last stronghold in Jaffna.
1668	English establishment at Bombay.
1672	French in Pondicherry.
1736	Rebellion against corrupt and inefficient Dutch rule.
1746	Hostilities between British and French in India leave Britain dominant foreign power there. Unlike the Portuguese and Dutch

the British had up to this time concentrated on trade achieved by friendly relations with local rulers rather than evangelising or conquering territory (-1761).

1760 War between Dutch and king of Kandy (encouraged by British). Kandy sacked but king restored by new treaty in 1766 which gave Dutch complete control of coast.

1782 War between British and Dutch. British take Trincomalee but lose it to French who eventually restore it to Dutch.

1795 Hostilities between Britain and France in wake of French revolution (Dutch allied to French). The Swiss regiment which constituted much of the garrison of Colombo was suborned and the Dutch commander surrendered with scarcely a shot fired. The rest of coastal Ceylon was soon occupied. Ceylon administered by East India Company (whose troops had captured it). Kingdom of Kandy remains independent.Sri Lanka and Its People

1797 Sinhalese revolt against insensitive rule and imposition of land revenues by Madras Presidency.

1798 Ceylon made a Crown Colony ruled by a governor appointed from London.

1802 Treaty of Amiens ending French Revolutionary War leaves Ceylon in British hands, though other French and Dutch possessions are returned.

1803 British intrigues with prime minister and pretenders to throne of Kandy leads to massacre of British garrison in Kandy.

1814 Excesses of the king, notably slaughtering the family of the prime minister in a very unpleasant fashion, leads to rebellion of nobles.

1815 King deposed with British help and exiled to Vellore (in Tamil Nadu), he died in 1832. British impose treaty giving them control of kingdom of Kandy.

1817 Major rebellion, put down in following year.

1833 Formal constitution introduced. Progressive changes between then and 1924 give gradually increasing local representation.

1931 Donoughmore Commission produces new constitution which, with important exceptions, makes the island largely self-governed by elected representatives.

1939 Second World War. Ceylon vital base for Allies, especially after capture of Singapore by Japanese in 1941 (to 1945).

1942 British government concedes principle of total self-government soon after end of war. Tamils less than enthusiastic because of dangers to them of a Sinhalese majority, exactly as the Muslims felt about the Hindus in India.

1945 Negotiations with British government (Soulbury Commission) lead to curtailment of British governor's powers and hence effective self-government.

1947 Partition of British Indian Empire to form self-governing dominions of India and Pakistan.

1948 Ceylon becomes a self-governing dominion on 4 February. Peaceful transfer of power, unlike India and Burma. United National Party (UNP) form government with D.S. Senanayake as prime minister. Senanayake staunchly secular in outlook, but sowed seeds of ethnic conflict by removing citizenship and voting rights of Indian (plantation) Tamils. Economic problems caused by over-ambitious welfare programmes and food subsidies (to 1952).

1951 S.W.R.D. Bandaranaike leaves UNP to form Sri Lanka Freedom Party (SLFP) adopting opportunistic Sinhalese/Buddhist slant.

1952 Death of D.S. Senanayake, succeeded by his son Dudley who wins general election on sympathy vote.

1953 Severe economic problems. Riots prompted by reduction of rice subsidy. Dudley resigns in favour of Sir John Kotelewala. Government still in hands of western looking elite, and administration largely run by English speaking Tamils.

1955 Both government and SLFP cave in to popular agitation and promise a Sinhalese only language policy.

1956 General election, landslide defeat of UNP orchestrated by Buddhist monks. Coalition government led by SLFP, S.W.R.D. Bandaranaike prime minister. End of multi-racial principles. Official Language Act makes Sinhalese only government and administrative language. Race riots. Extension of nationalisation and state control of business.

1959 Bandaranaike assassinated by Buddhist monks resenting lack of progress towards Sinhalese domination. Succeeded by his widow Mrs Srimavo Bandaranaike.

1960s Period of financial instability coupled with rapid growth of population and unemployment.

1961 Sinhala Only policy enforced and Christian schools taken over by state. Further discrimination against Tamils and arrangements with India for repatriation of over 500,000 (to 1964).

1965 General election. UNP back at head of coalition under Dudley Senanayake. Some concessions to Tamils, monks appeased by adoption of Buddhist calendar which created chaos, no-one knowing which day of the week was their day off!

1970s Period of social unrest and moves towards authoritarian government. Continuing economic and unemployment problems.

1970 General election. SLFP, leading leftist United Front, win on wildly optimistic manifesto.

1971 Rebellion by Janatha Vimukthi Peremuna (JVP), an ultra-left anti-Tamil grouping of unemployed and disillusioned youth with suspected North Korean backing. Put down by government with maybe 10,000 dead, many 'disappeared'.

1972 UF produces new constitution severely curtailing civil liberties, and giving itself another two years in power. Tamils further disadvantaged. Ceylon becomes a republic and assumes name of Sri Lanka on 22 May. Curbs on freedom of press. Balance of payments crisis leads to food shortages.

1975 Left-wing parties leave coalition, and UF takes sharp turn to the right. Start of agitation for separate Tamil state.

1976 Amidst widespread public disorder the government again attempts to increase its term. It fails, and the coalition collapses.

1977 Landslide win for UNP in general election (140 out of 168 seats). J.R. Jayawardene prime minister. Conciliatory approach to Tamils

	and promise of free market economics. Serious race riots soon after election.
1978	New less authoritarian constitution with J.R. Jayawardene as executive president. Free trade policies but rampant inflation.
1982	Jayawardene re-elected president.
1983	Referendum, allegedly fixed, cancels the general election due this year. Start of Tamil insurrection with ambush of army patrol. Perhaps 2000 Tamils killed and huge damage done in rioting all over the island.
1985	Insurrection builds up to full-scale civil war. Random acts of ethnic violence by Tamil guerillas and retaliation by armed forces. Severe economic disruption.
1987	Agreement between Rajiv Gandhi, PM of India, and Sri Lanka to settle insurgency. Joint council to rule Northern and Eastern Provinces. Indian Peace Keeping Force (IPKF) of 3000 men deployed, compromised by inability to cut off Indian support and training of Tamil separatists for political reasons. Chaos as different Tamil groups attack one another and provoke action by IPKF against them. Fighting worsens, heavy casualties on all sides. IPKF eventually grows to 70,000 and more or less pacifies north of island.
1988	New JVP rebellion, government members assassinated, and havoc in south of island; put down with heavy casualties. Sri Lankan pressure for withdrawal of IPKF. Jayawardene retires, replaced by Ranasinghe Premadasa of UNP.
1989	Premadasa undermines IPKF by negotiating with Tigers, and allegedly supplies them with arms!
1990	IPKF finally withdrawn from Sri Lanka; violence flares up again.
1991	Rajiv Gandhi assassinated in Tamil Nadu by Tamil partisans whilst campaigning for Indian general election.
1993	Premadasa assassinated, replaced by Gamini Dissanayake of UNP.
1994	Peoples Alliance (incorporating SLFP) wins general election. Dissanayake assassinated. Mrs Chandrika Kumaratunga wins presidential election. Her mother, Mrs Srimavo Bandaranaike, PM.
1995	Cease-fire and negotiations between government and Tigers. Failure followed by major government offensive against north.

The civil war

Trying to condense Sri Lanka's civil war and the events which led up to it into a few paragraphs is bound to upset both sides. Neither side has clean hands, and Indian involvement, official and otherwise, has not helped.

The first, and very important point, is that Tamils have been living in Sri Lanka as long as the Sinhalese have. They were in conflict with the Sinhalese, not always their fault, from the very beginning and remained so for nearly two thousand years until the successive Dutch and British colonial governments imposed peace on them.

Within months of independence in 1948 the Sinhalese majority government had imposed discriminatory laws on the Tamils. They also tried to persuade

India to repatriate half a million Tamils who, they said, were stateless. In fact, they had been living peacefully in Sri Lanka for a long time and making a useful contribution to the economy. Discrimination worsened during the following thirty years, the result of opportunism by Sinhalese politicians egged on by Buddhist religious leaders. At times there were outbreaks of vicious rioting. The violence was not spontaneous, the only victims were Tamils, and the finger was pointed at senior figures in the government. This was the background to the rise of the various Tamil resistance groups demanding, inter alia, a separate state consisting of Sri Lanka's Northern and Eastern Provinces.

The Tamil Tigers are the most aggressive and successful of the many different Tamil insurrectionists. A classic Marxist organisation, they started by terrorising their own people before attacking the government. Initially weak, they deliberately provoked the ill-trained Sri Lankan armed forces into acts of retaliation against Tamil civilians. In time, and with the connivance of the Indian government which declined (for its own narrow political reasons) to close down their training camps in the southern Indian state of Tamil Nadu, they grew into a formidable army. They slaughtered their Tamil rivals and anyone else who dared speak against them.

You get an idea of the problem facing the Sri Lankan armed forces by looking at the young soldiers, male and female, who guard buildings and man the road blocks. They wear their neatly pressed combat kit like the latest modes and their AK47s and M16s like costume jewellery. Charming young people, always smiling, but they simply do not look like real soldiers in the way that a British squaddie or a French bidasse does. As an exasperated colonel put it to us; 'Two thousand years of Buddhism, and now we expect them to be soldiers'.

The Sri Lankan armed forces are now more or less on top of the situation with military aid from Israel and South Africa (when that was a pariah state) and the even more dubious support of a variety of mercenaries.

The Sri Lankan government has offered concessions over the years, but never as much as it had already taken away, and always too late. The present prime minister, Mrs Srimavo Bandaranaike, has been making conciliatory noises, but there is at present no sign of a general shift in opinion. Far too many Sinhalese, in fact, think that the prospects, at last in sight, of military success will end the problem. It will not, of course. The silent majority may be ready for concessions; there is little sign that their politicians and religious leaders are.

As usual, of course, it is the ordinary people who have suffered most. Perhaps 60,000 have been killed in the war, most of them innocent civilians. Over a million people have been driven from their homes, many to Tamil Nadu where they are unemployed and destitute.

GOVERNMENT AND POLITICS

Except for a brief (and unhappy) period shortly after the British took Ceylon in 1795 the government of the island was not associated, as one might have expected, with that of the British Indian Empire. Before independence in 1948 the British ruled Ceylon as a Crown Colony in the nominal charge of a Governor. This meant that it was under a greater degree of control from London than was India, and its governance was generally more progressive.

The British regarded Ceylon as the most advanced of their colonies (as opposed to the dominions with their predominantly European populations) and used it to experiment with involving the local people in their own governance. The process started in 1833 when a Legislative Council was set up, six of the fifteen members being Ceylonese. The numbers of Ceylonese members increased over the years until, in 1920, they were not only in a majority but elected by a limited suffrage. Further negotiations with the Donoughmore Commission resulted in the establishment in 1931 of a State Council elected by universal suffrage, including women. This meant that Ceylon was effectively self-governing. This peaceful progress was very different from India, where there was also a core of well educated western-looking professional people. Whilst the British did make more concessions in India than they are usually given credit for the process was accompanied by thirty years of agitation and bloodshed.

Central government

Ceylon became independent with a bicameral parliamentary system. The House of Representatives was directly elected, and the Senate a mixture of indirectly elected and nominated.

The 1972 constitution, a product of the dirigiste United Front government, and a reaction to the JVP insurrection of the previous year, abolished the Senate and increased executive authority. No longer could the courts declare legislation invalid or rescue the victims of state maladministration or oppression. The name of the House of Representatives was changed to the appropriately Soviet sounding National State Assembly.

Politics

Politics in Sri Lanka are the usual messy business that one expects in this part of the world. Belying the peaceful image of the country as a whole, rough stuff and corruption are common, and assassination far from unknown. The electoral system tends to lead to a plethora of small parties and coalition governments. The government frequently uses a name, United Front for instance, different from that of any of the parties which constitute it. This is very confusing to the outsider, but two parties dominate the scene.

The **United National Party** grew out of the Ceylon National Congress. Initially it was an essentially conservative grouping which oversaw the smooth transition to independence.

The radical **Sri Lanka Freedom Party** was set up by S.W.R.D. Bandaranaike in 1951; he had previously been a member of the UNP government. Whilst the UNP had already shown disturbing signs of Sinhalese chauvinism and a tendency to insupportable welfare policies, the SLFP greatly accelerated this process. The expectations of the Sinhalese majority in the electorate were raised to an unrealistic level and, ever since then, it has been virtually impossible for either party to backpedal.

The smaller parties range from unreformed Marxists to ultra-conservative Buddhist groups, and are important because they often hold the balance of power when it comes to forming a government.

General elections traditionally lead to a change of government. This may seem a good thing. The trouble is that the parties are well aware of this, and it encourages them to make ever more extravagant promises.

THE ECONOMY

Sri Lanka has a mixed economy in which the state and private enterprise play a part. State industries have been heavily subsidised by the International Monetary Fund and other agencies, but job creation has not kept pace with population growth, and unemployment is a major problem, especially among the educated young.

At present Sri Lanka is very like India in that 80% of the population live in the countryside and only 20% in the cities, though this is expected to change radically in the next century. About 40% of the population work in agriculture, though they account for only about 20% of GNP in the process. Sri Lanka's agriculture is mainly a traditional plantation economy producing large quantities of tea, rubber, spices, and coconut derivatives for export. The economy is thus at the mercy of world markets and suffers severely when prices fall. The staples, almost entirely rice, were and are grown on smallholdings. Productivity has been increased in recent years by the use of artificial fertilisers, but Sri Lanka still has to import rice. Recent land reform has seen an increased proportion of the tea and rubber grown by small producers.

Manufacturing is somewhat more efficient than agriculture in that the 10% of the population so employed account for 20% of the GNP. Virtually all large scale enterprises producing basic materials are in government hands, whilst the private sector concentrates on consumer goods. Sri Lanka was advanced in introducing a tax-free enterprise zone for foreign businesses in the late 1970s.

The largest part of GNP is services, which employ 33% of the work force. Foreign banks have been encouraged to set up offshore units since 1979.

Sri Lanka has limited natural resources including iron and titanium ores, kaolin, and a wide variety of gemstones, the latter found mostly around Ratnapura and described in that section. The island is the largest producer of graphite in the world.

The trade balance has been pretty disastrous since the mid-1970s, and the conflict with the Tamils and consequent disproportionate defence spending makes any early improvement unlikely. Tourism, which was a major earner, has suffered.

THE PEOPLE

The population of Sri Lanka is estimated to be 19.3 million in the year 2000, which is five times the population at the beginning of the 20th century. Interestingly, this was the same as the estimated four million at the height of the Anuradhapura civilisation, more than a thousand years before.

The population is still increasing at a modest rate. The well educated people of Sri Lanka generally limit themselves to two children. Unlike many other Asian countries they have no hang-ups over girls, and there is no compulsion to have a son.

Population density over the country as a whole is 292 per km^2, not very different from India, and roughly half that in Britain. The population is not evenly distributed, mainly because of the difficulties facing agriculture in the dry northern and eastern parts of the island.

Sri Lanka's literacy is high in Asian terms, reflecting universal education and one of the best pupil to teacher ratios in the world. The overall figure is almost

90% (males 93%, females 84%). Life expectancy is similarly high, 70 years for men and 74 for women.

Ethnic background

The present day population of Sri Lanka consists of around 75% Sinhalese, 17% Tamils, and 7% Muslims.

The native population of Sri Lanka was the **Veddahs**, related to the aborigines of India (the Adivasis) and to the peoples of Sumatra and Australia. They survive in small groups in the hills and jungles, though diluted by both Sinhalese and Tamil blood.

It would be logical to assume that the major part of Sri Lanka's population would be related to that of southern India, but this is not the case. The peoples of southern India are Dravidians, descendants of tribes who probably moved into northern India from western Asia in around 2500BC, supplanting the indigenous population. The Dravidians in turn were pushed south by successive waves of Aryans who took over the northern part of India from about 1500BC onwards.

The majority community in Sri Lanka, the **Sinhalese**, are Aryans, descendants of north Indian invaders and traders who first arrived in serious numbers in the sixth century BC. This process is discussed more fully on p36 *Language.*

The **Tamil** population has two distinct elements. As can be seen from the chronology above it is no exaggeration to say that Tamils have probably been in Sri Lanka for as long as the Sinhalese. These long established communities, which form the majority in much of the North and East are referred to as **Sri Lankan Tamils**. The other group is the **plantation Tamils**. The ambition of the hill country Sinhalese was traditionally to have his own plot of land, grow his own food, and generally enjoy a quiet life. Jolly nice too, as you will appreciate when you have seen the beauty of the country — and experienced its enervating climate. Hard work and wages held no appeal at all. Thus, as the plantations expanded, there was a serious shortage of labour. The answer was to import Tamil workers, both men and women, from the Madras Presidency of South India. Conditions were pretty brutal, but so they were for just about everybody in the early 19th century, and at least they were paid in cash. A key factor in this migration, often overlooked, is that in the early days it was not permanent. Coffee, which predominated at that time, is a seasonal crop, and the Tamils used to travel to and from Ceylon each year. Around 1875 the coffee plantations were wiped out by blight and gradually replaced by tea. Tea cultivation is highly labour intensive, and picking is carried out all year round. So Ceylon suddenly found itself with a large and permanent addition to its Tamil population.

There is little social contact between the two Tamil groups. They are geographically separated, and the plantation Tamils seem to have no great interest in a self-governing Tamil region. Like, indeed, the hill Sinhalese, they prefer to keep their heads down and prosper quietly. In return, the Sri Lankan Tamils look down on the plantation workers as parvenus, and low caste ones at that.

The **Muslims** of Sri Lanka, though usually lumped together, are not a single racial group. The popularly used terms Moors or Moros are equally misleading. Sri Lanka's Muslim population is long established and has a variety of origins. Some are descended from Arab seafarers and traders, some from Malay fishermen, and others are Sinhalese or Tamils who freely converted to Islam as a way out of the caste system.

The **Burghers** are people of mixed race. The name implies a mixture of Dutch and Sinhalese or Tamil, but has come to be used more generally. The community these days numbers about 50,000. Very active in business and the arts, they have rarely suffered any discrimination.

The Gipsies of Sri Lanka are known as **Ahikuntakaya** in Sinhalese and **Kuraver** in Tamil. They are an offshoot of numerous similar South Indian groups. Each clan has an Aratchi, or leader, who combines the functions of judge, priest, and registrar. Most are nomadic because of the belief that a campsite used too long will become infested by maggots. Popular ways of earning a living include snake charming, animal training, fortune telling, and so on. They are a lively and outgoing lot, and Diwali sees a major get-together somewhere in North-Central Province.

Women in Sri Lanka

Women in Sri Lanka seem to suffer very few of the disadvantages so common in the rest of Asia. On a social level, and in all walks of life, you see them mixing freely with one another and with their menfolk. Seeing couples together you get an impression of familiarity and equality. Particularly telling is the treatment of girl children. They receive just the same amount of fuss and attention from their fathers as do boys; there are not many countries in this area where you see fathers carrying girl children.

Unlike other South Asian countries, where the idea would be totally unacceptable, large numbers of mostly young Sri Lankan women work and live away from home. Many of these are in the free trade and industrial zones of Colombo, where, by all accounts, they have to put up with considerable harassment. Others work in the Arab Gulf states where conditions vary a lot. The newspapers often carry horror stories of their treatment.

Most people are familiar with the fact that India was the first major country in the world to have a woman prime minister, Indira Gandhi. It is often overlooked that six years before Mrs Gandhi's elevation Ceylon became the very first state to choose a woman as head of its government. There was a dynastic element in each case. Mrs Gandhi got the job partly because she was daughter of Pandit Jawaharwal Nehru, the man who steered India to independence, and partly due to the very mistaken belief of the party hierarchy that as a woman she would be malleable. Mrs Srimavo Bandaranaike succeeded to the post after the assassination of her husband Solomon. Still on the political scene forty years later, she has proved even more radical than her late husband.

Marriage in Sri Lanka

Seemingly contradicting the liberal impressions expressed above, marriage in Sri Lanka is still a very formal and serious business, and the vast majority of marriages are arranged ones. The Sunday papers every week carry many matrimonial notices where parents advertise for a match for their children. The requirements are very detailed, going into caste and sub-caste, education, employment, and domestic attainments. As yet there is little sign of Sri Lankan parents using the expression 'No bars', now quite common in the same advertisements in India, to signify that a match from a different caste would be considered. An interesting indicator of the underlying conservatism of an outwardly westernised country.

The wedding celebrations tend to be quieter and more modest than the Indian equivalents.

Sex in Sri Lanka

Sri Lanka has something of a reputation for sexual tourism. Prostitution, though illegal, exists in both Colombo and the resort areas. The police frequently crack down on this, but have their difficulties. A police inspector complained to us that he knew of a family (mother, father, and three children) who were all on the game and who earned an awful lot more than he did. He ran them in, they paid the fines, and were back at work the next day.

The nastiest aspect of sexual tourism is paedophilia. Recent laws allow offenders to be pursued and tried in their own countries where there is no risk of a court being suborned, and the police are making enthusiastic use of these new powers.

Male visitors can forget any fantasies about affairs with respectable Sri Lankan girls. Western women will find that whilst they have no shortage offers, the men are less pushy than in other Asian countries.

Homosexuality in Sri Lanka

Homosexuality is illegal in Sri Lanka, and it is by no means unknown for the law to be enforced. And that includes foreign visitors. Homosexuality does, of course, exist, but affairs are very discreet. Trying to buck the system is asking for trouble. Contacts, whether for money or fun, are made mostly in the beach resorts.

MEETING PEOPLE

Guide books invariably devote the most space to descriptions of temples, museums, and so on. Some, in fact, are written as if there were no local population. Yet meeting people is one the most rewarding aspects of travel. Friendships are quickly formed with fellow travellers; learning about Sri Lanka the best way, by speaking to the locals, requires a conscious effort.

Travelling in other Asian countries you soon become used to being the centre of attention and bombarded with conversation. Something that can become too much of a good thing. Yet this does not happen in Sri Lanka. This seems to be because Sri Lankans of all backgrounds are self-confident and self-sufficient people. They do not have the lingering inferiority complex (or the aggression which succeeds it) found in other former colonial countries. In fact their self-confidence, allied to a natural reserve, can make it seem very hard even to get into conversation with Sri Lankans. They are very polite and affable, but they do not readily open up to strangers.

We eventually decided that this is because they see themselves as people of the world, hence visiting Westerners are nothing special. Certainly in all but the most out of the way places nobody will take the slightest notice of you. Very, very different from India and Pakistan and, however much easier, slightly unnerving. It's a funny thing, but you never feel a total alien in Sri Lanka. It feels more like southern European country than an Asian one. In a way it has the same feel as Tunisia, where people tell you they are not really

Arabs or Africans but Europeans who somehow fetched up on the wrong side of the Mediterranean.

Dodgy characters

Robbery of foreigners, especially with menaces or violence, is unheard of in Sri Lanka. There is, however, no shortage of con-men who will try to sweet-talk you out of your money. Watch out for friendly souls who approach you claiming to collect money for schools, orphanages, or any other charity or good cause. Particularly, take no notice of any credentials they may present; a rascally printer can produce anything.

The other people to watch out for are hotel touts and unofficial guides. These are invariable personable and friendly young men whose sole interest is the commissions they can earn through you. Read the section on crime against visitors (p73).

Women travellers

Sri Lanka is probably the most relaxed of Asian countries for a woman travelling on her own or with another woman.

You may not think it from their free and easy behaviour and the couples kissing in the parks, but association with the opposite sex before marriage is not common in their society. Sri Lankan men generally do have a much better understanding of western lifestyles than elsewhere in Asia, but there is a belief, however, that western women are much more likely to say yes than Sri Lanka ones.

This does not mean that you have to refuse every friendly approach, just be cautious. The safest way is to make sure that there are always other women present. It is not common in Sri Lanka for women to shake hands with men.

Physical sexual harassment is very rare in Sri Lanka. Modest clothing will reduce the risk even further.

Most medication, make-up, tampons, sanitary towels, and so on can be found in all but the smallest towns. Western brands are fairly readily available in supermarkets in the cities.

RELIGION

Religion is one of the major forces in the Sri Lankan way of life. The dominant religion, followed by 70% of the people, is Buddhism.

Buddhism has been the main religion of Sri Lanka for over two thousand years. It has had many ups and downs, and at times it has been necessary to bring priests over from Siam or Cambodia to lead the Samgha, the community of monks in Sri Lanka, back on to the straight and narrow.

Sri Lankan Buddhism saw a remarkable self-generated revival in the nineteenth century, and this became a major focus in the campaign for independence. An unfortunate aspect of this is the way in which religion has become politicised. Buddhist religious leaders have considerable clout, and have often not been shy in using it. There are a lot of Buddhist monks in Sri Lanka, and they have a great deal of influence on secular life.

As in India there is a certain blurring of divisions between the different religions. The Buddhists, for instance, respect Hindu deities and use them as guardians for their own temples. Caste, which supposedly has no place in Buddhism, is certainly a factor in family relationships and marriage.

Buddhists can be remarkably pragmatic in a way that eludes Hindus. They believe that killing animals for meat is wrong but, if a Muslim butcher has killed one anyway, what's wrong with helping to ensure that the meat is not wasted?

Buddhism

The life of Buddha. Siddhartha Gautama, the Buddha, like Christ, is a historical figure. His father, Suddodana Gautama, is popularly referred to as a king; his actual status was more probably akin to a squire. The gods, wishing to send a guide to relieve the suffering of mortals, chose Buddha's mother, the saintly Queen Maya. She dreamt that she was taken up to heaven on a cloud, and that there Prince Siddhartha was conceived as the result of a six-tusked elephant thrusting one of its tusks into her side. The birth took place in 563BC at Lumbini in present day Nepal. The child emerged from his mother's right side, as often depicted in sculpture. The stated reason for the earthly birth was that thus mere mortals could aspire to his ideals, difficult for a heaven-born leader. The comparison with the story of the Annunciation is obvious, and some of the jatakas (folk tales of Buddha's birth and early life) found their way into the fables of Aesop and La Fontaine.

Siddhartha lived a cossetted life up to the age of twenty-nine. Then, on an illicit journey out of his father's palace he encountered for the first time poverty, disease, and death. Shocked, he renounced his comfortable life (including a wife and young child) and devoted himself to achieving enlightenment. Six years of austerity proved fruitless. Breaking his fast, an act which alienated him from five fellow ascetics, he settled down to meditate for seven days under a pipal (fig) tree at Bodh Gaya in northern India. Here he became The Enlightened One, The Buddha. Afterwards he walked the 200km to Benares, then as now the most important religious centre in northern India. There he was reunited with his five followers, and preached his first sermon in the Deer Park at Sarnath. A ministry of forty-five years followed, ending with Buddha's death at Kushinagar in 483BC.

According to local legends, Buddha himself visited Sri Lanka on three occasions. There is no historical basis for this belief; it is probably symbolic of earlier, failed Buddhist missions.

Growth and eclipse. Buddhism spread rapidly and, as state religion under the Emperor Ashoka (second century BC), covered almost all of India and reached as far west as Afghanistan. It was Ashoka's brother Mahinda who brought Buddhism to Sri Lanka. Other missionaries carried it eastwards to South-East Asia, China, and eventually Japan.

By around AD500 Buddhism was already dwindling in India by a process of re-absorption into the mainstream of Hinduism. An aggressive Hindu revival quickly saw off Buddhism in the south of India, and the effects of this spilled over into Sri Lanka. Buddhism lingered longer in northern India, as a monastic order rather than a popular religion, as it had started. The Muslim invasions of northern India completed the job by destroying Buddhism's holy places, notably the great monastic university of Nalanda in the 12th century.

Basic concepts. There is no god in Buddhism; one can even argue that it not really a religion at all. The reverence of Buddha himself is a development of the Mahayana sect aimed at providing a more popular appeal. In the early days there were no images of Buddha, and devices such as an empty throne or a riderless horse were used instead. The footprints seen in many places are a throwback to this practice.

The basic Buddhist belief is in the **Four Noble Truths**:

  (i) life is suffering (*dukkha*)
 (ii) suffering is caused by desire
(iii) by ending desire man can end his suffering
 (iv) there is a way of ending desire.

The way to end desire is to follow the **Eight-fold Path**:

   (i) perfect understanding of the Four Noble Truths
  (ii) perfect detachment from worldly things
 (iii) perfect speech free from lies and malice
  (iv) perfect conduct in obeying ten monastic rules
   (v) perfect living to avoid harm to others
  (vi) perfect effort to achieve good karma
 (vii) perfect mindfulness
(viii) perfect concentration in meditation.

The Mahayanists see this as too self-centred and selfish, and interpret the Path much more liberally. Either way, by following the Path one can ultimately achieve nirvana, or freedom from the cycle of death and rebirth, the ideal of the serious Buddhist.

Here we should mention the concept of the Boddhisatva, which means different things to different sects. To the Mahayanists a Boddhisatva is one who has achieved enlightenment but forgone the benefits of Nirvana to give help and leadership to less fortunate souls. For the Therevadans a Boddhisatva is simply a form that Buddha took in earlier lives.

Sects. Not surprisingly Buddhism has evolved in different ways in the various countries where it has taken root. The Tantric Buddhism of Tibet and the Zen of Japan, for instance, have moved a long way from what many regard as orthodox Buddhism.

In India and Sri Lanka the basic split is between the Mahayana and the Hinayana or Therevada.

Mahayana translates literally as Great Vehicle. Mahayana tones down the agnostic asceticism of earlier, purer teachings, and holds out the hope of salvation to the layman.

Hinayana means Lesser Vehicle; although widely used this term is not exactly complimentary, and the followers of this way prefer the word **Therevada** (Teachings of the Elders). The main principle here is that the only way to salvation is through a monastic life, that being the only way to follow properly the Eightfold Path. This is the form followed by the monks of South-East Asia and Sri Lanka, and its adherents regard it as closest to Buddha's original teachings. In Sri Lanka, Therevada is divided into a number of lesser sects who get on together pretty amicably.

You may also come across the term **Vajrayana**, a sect which absorbed ideas from Tantric Hinduism, and is much influenced by magic rituals in which female sexual power plays a major part.

Caste. In theory Buddhism does not acknowledge caste. In practice, in Sri Lanka, caste certainly did and does exist. This is not the all-pervading and crushingly discriminatory affair it still is in rural India. The only time the visitor might be aware of a caste system is when reading the matrimonial advertisements in the newspapers. In this instance, and among the middle class who use these advertisements, caste seems to count for more than it does in India these days. In everyday life caste among the Sinhalese is more like old-fashioned snobbery, with the hereditary landowners looking down on tradesmen and everyone else. These landowners (some of whom are little more than peasant farmers) are the *goyigamas*, hardly an exclusive lot as they comprise nearly half the population. The sub-castes of *radala* and *mudali*, who equated to the peerage and landed gentry certainly were exclusive. The interesting thing, and very different from India, is that there was no rigid pecking order of castes below the goyigamas, nor were there any untouchables.

Hinduism

The word Hindu is synonymous with Indian, and it is the dominant force in religion, culture, and behaviour in its home country. Because a Big Brother complex could cause hackles to rise old guide books to Ceylon used to prefer the pedantic term Brahmanist to Hindu. The fact is, though Buddhists will not thank you for saying it, that Buddhism is in effect a reformed Hinduism. As, and equally the adherents will not be pleased to hear it, are Jainism and Sikhism.

Hinduism is the religion of most of the Tamils living in Sri Lanka. The Sri Lankan Buddhists, mostly Sinhalese, have learned to live with Hinduism, and its influence is strong.

Hinduism is not only a religion, it is a social system, a philosophy, a whole way of life. It is much older than all other major religions having its origin in the Vedism, or nature worship, brought to India by the Aryans in about 1500BC. The verses called *Vedas* which explain this are still a basis of Hindu belief. Around 1000BC Brahmanism introduced the concept of a universal god or Brahman, and a class of priests, or Brahmins, whose duties are laid down in the Brahmanas. The following thousand years saw the writing of many other holy works including the Upanishads and the great epic poems, the *Mahabharata* (tenth century BC) and the rather later *Ramayana*. The former includes the *Bhagavad Gita* which is probably the best known of these works. The *Ramayana* is of special relevance as much of the action takes place in Sri Lanka. The most influential, however, was the Law Book of Manu (third century BC) which codified the caste system and the rigid social law which still binds most Hindus.

Concepts. There are three basic concepts in Hindu belief, *samsara*, *karma*, and *dharma*, which also apply (more or less) in Buddhism and Jainism. Samsara is belief in the principle of reincarnation. The idea is that as one body dies the soul migrates to a new one. Whether this new body is higher or lower in the social scale (it can be the body of an animal or insect) depends upon karma.

Karma means action or deeds, and here signifies the belief that one's behaviour in this life determines the status of the soul's new body. Karma, in this sense, is how dharma is followed.

Dharma is the law which governs a Hindu's every action. It is basically a matter of caste, the mode of life being determined by the caste into which one is born. The Gita teaches that it is less harmful to follow your own dharma badly than to excel in some other life-style. The only way to progress up the social scale is to fulfil your dharma and achieve a good reincarnation. Eventually, with good karma and countless incarnations one can achieve moksha, oneness with god and freedom from the cycle of death and rebirth. This may be interpreted as leading to a certain degree of social inertia.

The practicalities of dharma are far-reaching. For each caste rituals are laid down for washing, the preparation of food, what to wear, and how to avoid every caste Hindu's greatest fear – pollution by someone lower in the system. A Brahmin could be polluted by an untouchable venturing within 40m of him. Things are generally less extreme now, and the system is rapidly breaking down in urban areas. You will still, however, see plenty of Hindus who carry their own cups and packed meals rather than risk contact with something handled by a person lower in the order.

The Gods. Despite the apparent profusion of gods Hinduism is, in effect, a monotheism. As already mentioned Brahman is the all-pervading God, the Atman within each soul. The many different gods are just aspects of Brahman who is symbolized as the **trinity** of Brahma, Shiva, and Vishnu.

Brahma, the creator, is depicted as having four heads (five until Shiva lopped one off), and his wife **Sarasvati** is goddess of music. Brahma is not worshipped as such, and it is said that there only two temples to him in the whole of India.

Shiva, the destroyer and reproducer, has a much wider appeal. You will always be able to spot one of his shrines by the symbols: tridents and lingams. The lingam is a stylized phallus representing Shiva's role as reproducer. In front of most Shiva temples you will find the bull Nandi which is also revered.

Shiva's consort **Parvati** is the goddess of beauty, but also has a more sinister aspect as **Kali**, or **Durga**, who carries out most of Shiva's destructive function.

Ganesh (Ganapati in southern India), the elephant-headed god of wisdom and enterprise, is one of their two sons.

The other, much more common in Sri Lanka, is the god of war, known by a variety of different names. In the north of India he is **Kartikkeya**, and in the south **Skanda** or **Subrahmanya**. Much more common though is the peculiarly Sri Lankan form of **Kataragama**, regarded as one of the four guardians of Buddhism.

Vishnu, the preserver, is notable for his nine visits to earth. In each case Vishnu has taken an earthly form to help him rescue mankind from great danger. The inspiration for this belief, which had been adopted in its final form by the 11th century AD, comes from a variety of sources, some quite possibly not Indian. Recognising the avatars makes temple visits more interesting:

1. *The Fish (Matsya)* rescued Manu, a figure analogous to both Adam and Noah, from a flood which engulfed the earth.
2. *The Tortoise (Kurma).* Among the things lost in this flood was the amrit, or nectar of the gods. Vishnu took the form of a giant tortoise to retrieve

the amrit from the bottom of the primeval ocean.
3. *The Boar (Varaha)* killed the demon who had thrown the earth back into the ocean, and raised it up again on his tusks.
4. *The Man-Lion (Narasimha)* killed an otherwise invincible demon.
5. *The Dwarf (Vamana)* dealt with another demon which had taken over the earth. Granted one wish by the demon, Vamana demanded as much ground as he could cover in three paces. His three steps encompassed not only earth, but also heaven and the middle air.
6. *Parasurama (Rama with axe).* Vishnu made his first incarnation in human form to avenge a Brahmin robbed and later murdered by Kshatriyas. The story goes that he killed twenty-one generations of male Kshatriyas – not a popular theme as the princes who endowed most temples came from this caste.
7. *Rama*, perhaps based on a real prince of the eighth century BC, is best known as the hero of the epic poem, the **Ramayana**. Helped by Hanuman, the monkey-faced demigod, he rescued his wife Sita from the demon king Lanka. He took this incarnation, however, to rescue the world from the demon Ravana. Rama is usually depicted with a dark face and carrying a bow and arrow.
8. *Krishna* is the most popular figure in the Indian pantheon. Best known as a lover of the countryside and patron of herdsmen (and especially herdswomen), he is also the hero of the **Mahabharata**. In this epic he vanquishes the forces of evil all over the country and delivers the seminal message of Hinduism, the **Bhagavad Gita**. The huge body of Krishna stories is obviously based mainly on the exploits of a number of real Indian folk heroes, but seems also to draw on themes from as far away as the Near East and Greece. It has even been conjectured that the child-god form derives from missionaries' tales of Jesus.
9. *Buddha* is a comparatively late addition to the list. Traditionally Vishnu took this form to save animals from the ritual slaughter associated with Brahmanical worship. The real reason is probably more prosaic: to encourage Buddhists, who could be seen as nonconformist Hindus, to return to the fold.
10. *Kalkin* will be the next avatar. Vishnu will appear on a white horse and bearing a flaming sword to end the present age of evil and to deliver judgment on all men. This apocalyptic vision has Christian and Parsi parallels, but probably owes more to Buddhist and Jain belief in teachers yet to come.

The two most important figures, apart of course from Buddha, are Rama and Krishna. Rama is the hero of the epic *Ramayana*, much of which takes place in Sri Lanka. Krishna, most approachable of all the Hindu gods, has a very wide following, especially among the Tamils. In paintings Krishna is most often depicted with a blue face and playing a flute. A frequent image is of him lifting a mountain to shelter peasants from the Vedic rain god Indra. His consort Radha was a milkmaid. Vishnu's wife is **Lakshmi**, goddess of wealth.

Caste. The word caste comes from the Portuguese (and Latin) *casta* meaning pure. The term a Hindu uses is *Varna* or colour. There are four of these varnas:

1) *Brahmins*, or priests and pundits.
2) *Kshatriyas*, warriors, landowners, and aristocrats. Generally speaking Rajputs belong to this caste.
3) *Vaisyas*, farmers and tradesmen.
4) *Sudras*, labourers and servants.

There is a racial aspect to this division. The first three castes were Aryan, but the Sudras were Dravidian. Outside the caste system altogether were the untouchables (the preferred term these days is *Dalits*), who got all the really unpleasant jobs.

In fact, unless one of the upper two castes were bragging, he would not refer to himself as a Brahmin or a Rajput. He would describe himself by his *jati* or *gotra*, the clan or sub-caste, of which there are thousands.

Among the Sri Lankan Tamils there are effectively no Rajputs. Their rank below the Brahmins is taken by the *Vellalas*, a group of farmer-landlords analogous to the Sinhalese *Goyigamas*. Some of the castes in Sri Lanka, fishermen for instance, have a much higher place in society than their counterparts in India. They have achieved this over a long period of time by adopting the practices of their peers. In theory this can happen in India, but it is very unusual.

The whole business of caste among the Sri Lankan Hindus has been stood on its head by the Marxist Tamil Tigers. It will be interesting to see what the position is when everything settles down.

Islam

About 7% of the population is Muslim. In the century following the foundation of the faith in AD622 it spread rapidly to Spain in the west, and India in the east. By the end of the thirteenth century conquest had carried it over all of India except the very south. Sri Lanka escaped this process, but communities of Arab traders brought Islam to Sri Lanka very early on. They lived on friendly terms with their neighbours and, as with Christianity, attracted converts hoping to escape the caste system.

The very word Islam means total submission to God, and Muslim religious practices though few are well defined. A devout Muslim will pray five times a day facing Mecca and will try to visit Mecca at least once in his lifetime. Islam is the one religion, apart from Christianity, which requires its adherents actively to propagate its teaching.

Islam is purely monotheistic, with Allah as the one God, and Mohammed his principal prophet.

Christianity

As with the Muslims, about 7% of the population is Christian. Christianity arrived early in this area, Thomas the Apostle ('Doubting Thomas') reaching Madras in AD52. He was martyred on the outskirts of the city, but the church he founded remains strong. The Portuguese were surprised to find Christians in India, and not at all pleased that they should follow the Syriac tradition. Partly as a result of their interference, a schism occurred resulting in part of the church becoming an Eastern Catholic one whilst the remainder held to the Syrian Orthodox tradition.

The Malabar Christians may have made some slight impression in Sri Lanka, but little evidence remains. The advent of Christianity on a large scale had to await the arrival of the Portuguese in the 16th century. Their brand of Christianity has prevailed, and virtually all Christians in Sri Lanka are Roman Catholics.

The Dutch encouraged conversion to their Reformed Church as the Dutch East India Company would employ only Christians. This led to many jokes about 'Company Christians', and all the evidence is that people stuck to the old faith at home, and openly reverted to it as soon as they retired.

The British suffered their usual dichotomy over missionaries, balancing Christian obligations against a desire not to stir up religious trouble. Because pressure could more readily be brought to bear in London, missionaries were far more active in Ceylon than in India. Their efforts went mainly into education, setting an example that Sri Lanka has never lost sight of. Paradoxically, the main effect of this missionary zeal was a revival of Buddhist education and Buddhism itself. As in England Anglicanism had its main influence on the ruling elite, an influence which became a liability with the rise of Sinhalese nationalism in the 1950s.

ART AND ARCHITECTURE

Not surprisingly art and architecture in Sri Lanka have always been heavily influenced by Buddhism. Patronage was in the hands of Buddhist kings and monks who were inclined to austerity, in keeping with Buddha's principles. It follows that there was very little in the way of secular painting, sculpture, or literature.

The western education and liberal regime of the British period stimulated both painting and literature, though it was the 20th century before the abilities of Sri Lankans became really apparent.

Buddhist architecture

Initially the Buddhist architecture of Sri Lanka drew on North Indian themes, but after that was largely free of outside influences. Thus the true arch and dome, brought to India by Muslim invaders, are absent.

Buddhist architecture in Sri Lanka is essentially religious architecture. The only large secular buildings of which anything remains are the palaces at Polonnaruwa. After the abandonment of that city in AD1293 the evidence is that whilst a fair amount of effort and expense still went into religious buildings the kings and nobles lived in much simpler, one might say reduced, circumstances. The palace buildings of Kandy, for instance, have charm but are far from grand.

Looking at Buddhist religious buildings one must bear in mind that they are not places of worship in the Christian, Muslim, or Hindu sense. Similarly, the images in them are not objects of veneration (though they are highly respected). Their purpose is to act as a focus, an aid to concentration on the path to salvation.

Dagobas. These distinctive circular structures occur in various forms all over the Buddhist world, and they vary in size from the tiny to the huge. They began as memorials to house the remains of Buddha and his disciples. Later, they proliferated as building them came to be seen as a way of gaining merit.

The dagoba developed over time from the simple burial mound, and is called by different names according to location. Dagoba, cetiya, stupa, thupa, tope, and chorten are all variations on the theme, the first two the most commonly used in Sri Lanka. Dagoba is one of the suggested origins of the word pagoda. Cetiya, or chaitya, is a bit confusing as it covers a number of different things. In the early days of Buddhism it was simply a relic dagoba. When, around the beginning of the Christian era, the cult of worshipping Buddha images began it came also to mean a chapel or image house.

The first large construction of this kind was the Great Stupa at Sanchi in Central India, built by Ashoka in the third century BC. The early Sri Lankan dagobas followed the same form of a rather flattened hemisphere, called by their builders egg-shaped or 'water bubble'. The core was usually of unfired brick, the outer skin of fired brick plastered over. Inside would be one or more relic chambers, sometimes with murals, and often containing beautiful caskets and items of jewellery. Thus far, the parallel with the pyramids of Egypt is obvious. Around the base of the dagoba would be a fence marking the devotional circumambulatory (always done clockwise). On top of the dagoba, and taking various forms, was a ceremonial umbrella. The umbrella was a general mark of respect and, in the early days, a symbol of Buddha himself. The circular dagoba was set in a square enclosure to symbolise the transformation from one state to another.

The shape of the dagoba later evolved into the hemisphere, and in this form the dagobas of Sri Lanka surpassed in size those anywhere else in the Buddhist world. Later, the shape changed to that of a bell, a precursor of the spires of Thailand where the original form is all but lost. At the cardinal points around the dagoba are the *vahalkadas*, projections marking the flower altars. In later dagobas these sometimes have Buddha figures.

Image houses come in two forms. The first, the circular **vatadage**, is closely related to the dagoba and unique to Sri Lanka. This is a dagoba with its circumambulatory enclosed by a solid wall. Rings of stone pillars supported a light roof over the whole structure. None of these roofs has survived, and they are hard to visualise, but there is a good model in the museum at Anuradhapura. The **pilimage** is a more conventional rectangular building, of which two spectacular examples have survived at Polonnaruwa.

Architectural details. The entrances to many buildings, secular as well as religious, are flanked by guardian figures. These **doratupalas** (the dwarapalas of northern India) are occasionally free-standing, more often carved in relief. They are commonly variations on the theme of Vishnu, the Hindu god seen as a defender of Buddhism. Behind or above these are the makaras. Strictly speaking a **makara** is a sea-beast resembling a crocodile. In Sri Lanka it can be a lot more elaborate, incorporating elements of up to eight different animals. It is another guardian figure, with additional connotations of virility. A makara-torana, rare in Sri Lanka, is these beasts formed into an arch or as bracket figures in a doorway. Supporting the steps, and elsewhere, you may see dwarves. These are thought to be a throwback to some pre-Buddhist, maybe even pre-Hindu beliefs.

Moonstones are placed at the entrances of major shrines to help worshippers concentrate their minds as they enter. The idea came from India but evolved in Sri Lanka from a plain semicircular slab to the magnificent specimen at the entrance of the so-called Queen's Pavilion in Anuradhapura. The outermost carving is a ring of flames symbolising desire and purification. The four animals in the next ring are the Buddhist perils of birth, disease, old age, and death. The way they endlessly chase one another represents the cycle of death and rebirth, which the Buddhist (and Hindu and Jain) strives to escape. The vines next are the clinging to life. The geese with lotuses in their beaks are the wise people who have renounced the pleasures of life to achieve the purity of the lotus. The goose is a Hindu symbol, as Hans or Hamsa it is the vehicle of Brahma and a sign of wisdom and discrimination. At the centre is the lotus of Nirvana.

Another common device is the **chakra**. This circular device derives from the sun, and represents not only the wheel of the law but also the universal monarch, in other words Buddha's preeminence.

Buddha images. Images of the Buddha are not intended to be true likenesses, nor do they stem from the artistic whim of the sculptor. Sakyamuni, a disciple of Buddha, provided artists with measurements and proportions to work from, and in Sri Lanka these are enshrined in a work called the Sariputra. In this system the face is used as the unit of measure. The height of a standing figure is nine units, the trunk being three, the thigh and lower leg two each, and so on. Even more precise rules apply to the face itself and the head.

The images come in three general forms, standing, sitting, and reclining. Standing figures are mostly upright, more occasionally relaxed. Sitting figures are in the lotus position and, as with the standing figures, the hands will be in a variety of mudras or positions, each signifying an activity (or lack of it):

Abhaya mudra: the right hand is held up with the palm outwards. This is the fearless position.
Asisa mudra: as above but the palm is turned sideways in blessing.
Vitarka mudra: the thumb and forefinger of the right hand touch in the teaching or discourse mode.
Bhumisparsha mudra: on seated figures the right hand is on the ground. Buddha is calling on the earth to witness his resistance to temptation.
Dhyani or *samadi mudra*: on seated figures the right hand is on top of the left in the lap signifying meditation.

The position of the hands is always the same in reclining figures. Although the Buddha is occasionally represented in other positions different poses imply that the figure is someone other than Buddha.

The style of the figures seen in Sri Lanka holds close to the old rules. There is none of the Greek influence so evident in contemporary North Indian works.

Painting

The only ancient truly secular paintings to be seen in Sri Lanka are the remarkable frescoes on the rock face at Sigiriya (late sixth century). These are in the same style as the contemporary frescoes in the Ajanta cave temples, themselves the earliest surviving examples of painting in India. In some of the temples the paintings are on the threshold between religious and secular. At Kataluwa, for instance, many of the fascinating murals are narrative of everyday life, and even include Queen Victoria. These are the nearest thing stylistically to Indian miniature painting.

In this century Sri Lankan artists, notably George Keyt, have produced some original and lively work.

Hindu architecture

Hindu building in Sri Lanka closely follows the example of Dravidian (south Indian) architecture in Tamil Nadu, albeit on a less grandiose scale. Many of the devales, Hindu shrines associated with Buddhist places of worship, are Dravidian in style.

The Portuguese used their control of the Tamil areas of Ceylon to destroy most of the Hindu (and Buddhist) temples. Whilst the Dutch and British restored freedom of worship they did not restore the temple lands, so there were never funds for rebuilding on a lavish scale. When you look at the gopuram, the sculpted and brightly painted doorway of a Tamil temple, you have to bear in mind that in India the same thing would be four or five times as high.

LANGUAGE

The official languages of Sri Lanka are Sinhala (or Sinhalese) and Tamil. English, whilst not performing the vital link role it has in India, is widely spoken.

Not surprisingly, we have to look to India for the origin of Sri Lanka's languages. There most of the many, many languages fall into two main groups. In the south are the Dravidian tongues, stemming from a people who arrived in northern India around 2500BC from the area of the Ural Mountains. These Dravidian languages may well be related to those European misfits, Hungarian, Finnish, and Estonian. **Tamil** is in many ways the most developed of the Dravidian languages, having a large literature and attendant culture.

In northern India are many Indo-Aryan languages including Gujarati, Punjabi, Urdu, Hindi, and Bengali. These all developed from the language (a proto-Sanskrit) of a later wave of invaders who began to arrive around 1500BC and pushed the Dravidians to the south. Almost all the European languages, including English, also belong to the Indo-Aryan group.

On a geographical basis one might assume that **Sinhala** would be related to the adjacent Dravidian languages, but this is not the case. The Sinhalese people came from Orissa and Gujarat in northern India and brought an early version of their language with them. Because of the lack of continuing North Indian influence Sinhala has stayed much closer to its Vedic roots than other Indian languages. Long association, friendly and otherwise, with the Tamils has led to a certain Dravidian influence. One might think from its curly elegance that the distinctive Sinhala script came from this source. In fact, it developed locally and for the same reason. Writing in Sri Lanka and southern India was traditionally done with a sharp metal stylus on dried and polished palm leaves. The grain of these leaves simply does not suit straight lines. You can see the preparation of palm leaves and the writing process at Aluvihara Monastery (see p190).

Not surprisingly Sinhala has drawn on the languages of its European invaders. Most of the Sinhala vocabulary relating to buildings and construction derives from Portuguese, *ispiritale* (hospital) and *iskola* (school) clearly derived, like Portuguese itself, from Latin. By contrast, many household items have Dutch names. The law is based on Dutch Roman law and uses some of its terms; *notaris* and *advakat*, for example, need little explanation. The creole still spoken by a few Portuguese Burghers is not dissimilar to modern Portuguese.

Nor is Sinhala quite the southern limit of the Indo-Aryan languages, as Maldivian is a dialect of Sinhalese.

Note. Because of the difficulty of transcription there is considerable disagreement over the spelling of personal and place names. The spellings of kings' names are taken from de Silva's *A History of Sri Lanka*, as are their dates, another contentious issue. Place names are generally spelt according to modern usage, but be prepared for variations.

READING

We have fitted all we can into this book. There is, of course, an awful lot more to know. And the more you do know the more you will enjoy Sri Lanka. Your local library and second-hand bookshops are a good place to start hunting.

The best history is K.M. De Silva's *A History of Sri Lanka* (OUP). This is a highly readable book which covers related subjects such as architecture, religion, and so on.

Assignment Colombo. The author, J.N. Dixit, was India's high commissioner (ambassador) in Colombo from 1985 to 1989, the period of the Indian government's involvement in the Sinhalese-Tamil conflict. The book is as wordy as you would expect from an Indian diplomat, but it gives a unique insight into the troubles. Particularly clear, and depressing, is the duplicity with which both sides entered into their negotiations.

Tigers of Lanka - From Boys to Guerillas, by M.R. Narayan Swamy is a journalist's exhaustive account of the civil war, and especially the savage infighting of the many different Tamil groups.

Nor Iron Bars a Cage, by Penelope Tremayne, is the perceptive story of five weeks spent as a captive of the Tamil Tigers. This remarkable woman, in her sixties at the time, deliberately ignored the advice to butter up ones captors in such a situation. She got away with it, learned far more than she might otherwise, and wrote an inspirational book.

Modern Sri Lankan literature in English is of a very high standard. Look for the authors Romesh Gunesekhere (*Monkfish Moon* and others), Michael Ondaatje (*Running in the Family* and others), and J. Vijayatunge (*Grass for my Feet*). Carl Muller, a member of the Burgher community, has written a rollicking trilogy, starting with *The Jam Fruit Tree*, about their way of life. Two good anthologies are *The Penguin New Writing in Sri Lanka*, edited by D.C.R.A. Goonetilleke, and *An Anthology of Sinhalese Literature of the 20th Century*, edited by C.H.B. Reynolds.

Once you are in Sri Lanka you can pick up copies of the free publications *Travel Lanka*, *Explore Sri Lanka*, and *The Linc*. Details in the Colombo 'Information' section. Two books of great use to the long stayer or expat are *Culture Shock! Sri Lanka*, by Robert Barlas and Nanda P. Wanasundera, and *Colombo Handbook*, edited by the American Women's Association. The Cultural Triangle Office, Ministry of Cultural Affairs, 212 Bauddhaloka MW, Colombo 7, (Tel 01-587 912) sells inexpensive handbooks to the historic sites and some very attractive coffee table books on Sri Lankan art and architecture.

Other books are detailed in the text. There are good bookshops in Colombo and Kandy which are well worth a browse, and second-hand bookstalls near Maradana station. Sri Lanka has an active publishing industry which, in addition to new books by local authors, also produces inexpensive hardback reprints of relevant books long out of print in the West.

PRACTICAL INFORMATION

Getting There

INDEPENDENT TRAVEL
Independent travellers to Sri Lanka tend to fall into two groups: those who visit only Sri Lanka, and those for whom Sri Lanka is a side trip from India, perhaps as part of an even longer journey.

Flying
Here are a few thoughts on air tickets. Bucket shops (clearing houses for airlines' surplus seats) offer the cheapest fares, but do make sure you understand the restrictions which can be very tight indeed. If making a multiple stop journey consider the advantages of a full-price economy ticket. This gives you far more flexibility than a cut-price ticket as the mileage allowed is rather more than the direct route, and it can be extended by paying a modest supplementary fare. Full-price tickets allow you to visit off-route destinations and change your plans as much as you like. Round the world fares seem popular at the moment; again check the restrictions very carefully.

Surplus seats are not limited to economy class. Airlines sometimes offer a free upgrade to business or even first class if economy is overbooked. Ask when you check in. Preference is given to holders of full price economy tickets, but it is always worth asking. You need to be smartly dressed to stand a chance.

The only airport in Sri Lanka to accept scheduled international flights is Bandaranaike Airport at Katunayake, 30km north of Colombo. Ratmalana Airport only 12km from central Colombo is rarely, if ever, used these days.

Scheduled flights from Europe. None of the major European airlines flies to Colombo, and the only non-stop services are by Sri Lanka's flag carrier Air Lanka. They fly from London five days a week (via Amsterdam two days), and also have less frequent services from Zurich, Rome, Paris, and Frankfurt. Air Lanka is a good airline with a sound safety record; its recent operational tie-up with Emirates promises even better service.

All the other airlines stage through the Middle east, involving a change of flight. Except around Christmas time most have surplus seats which they unload at substantial discounts. High street travel agents sell these tickets, but the best deals are from the bucket shops. Air Lanka's economy return fare to Colombo is £425, yet you can buy the same comfort and standard of service for between £300-400 from a bucket shop. Bucket shops advertise in the Sunday papers and magazines like *Time Out* and *TNT*; you can also try page 236 on ITV Teletext. Always make sure before handing over your money that you have either the ticket or a receipt with an ATOL number. Probably not the very cheapest, but certainly highly reliable are Trailfinders, 46 Earls Court Road, London W8 6FT (Tel 0171-938 3366).

The choice of airline is important. The airlines probably most favoured by budget travellers are Gulf and Emirates, and others are equally safe. Kuwait Airways tends to be the cheapest (around £380), but there are two things to bear in mind; it's dry (though you arrive feeling better for not drinking alcohol), and the Kuwait-Colombo leg is in fiendishly uncomfortable tightly packed seats.

Charter flights from Europe. Whilst package tourism is at a low ebb there are few charter flights, the package companies using scheduled flights instead. In fact, only two charter flights, by Caledonian and Monarch from London, show in the schedules. On the other hand, except at peak times, you can get a return flight and two weeks basic bed and breakfast for less than the price of just a fare to Colombo. The problem is persuading them to let you stay more than two weeks, and spending eight hours with your knees under your chin. The charter market may improve as tourism picks up. Try Teletext page 224. Dutch, German, and Austrian charter airlines also operate.

Scheduled flights from the USA and Canada. None of the American airlines serves Colombo, so the only convenient option from the east coast is with an airline like Gulf, Emirates or Singapore staging through London and the Middle East. Discounted fares are around $1300 return; check the weekend papers, internet or STA Travel for sources. It may be possible to save a little money by taking a cheapie from New York or Toronto to London, and getting a bucket shop ticket there. Hardly worth it unless you want to spend a few days in London.

From the west coast you have to stage through Hong Kong, Singapore, or Bangkok, fares being around $1380 return. Thai, Singapore, and Cathay Pacific fly right through on these routes, and Air Lanka also does the final legs.

Scheduled flights from Australia and New Zealand. As with the US there are no direct flights at the time of writing; you will need to change flights in Singapore, Kuala Lumpur, or Bangkok. Contact STA Travel or try Yellow Pages, but start well in advance. You may only be able to save much money by buying an advance-purchase excursion (APEX) ticket. Expect to pay around

A$1400 or NZ$1900. Some airlines offer good student discounts to anyone under 26.

Flights from India. Air Lanka has at least one flight daily to Madras (two or three some days, around £100/$160 return fare) and three flights a week to Trivandrum, Trichy and Delhi. Allowing for changes to their schedules the flights to Trivandum (£70/$110) are on Monday, Tuesday and Friday; to Trichy (Tiruchirapalli, £70/$110) on Wednesday, Friday and Saturday and to Delhi (£230/$360) on Wednesday, Friday, and Sunday. There are also two flights per week to Bombay (£210/$335) on Friday and Sunday.

Indian Airlines flies daily to Madras, and on Wednesday only to Trivandrum, similar fares to Air Lanka. In addition there are frequent flights to Male in the Maldives.

Onward and return travel. Generally speaking, it is best to go to Sri Lanka with a return or onward ticket.

Don't forget the airport tax of Rs500 levied as you leave the country.

Sea routes

There are no longer any regular passenger ship links to Sri Lanka, not even the ferry from Rameswaram in southern India. Sri Lanka does have a considerable amount of overseas trade, and it follows that cargo ships from all over the world call at Colombo. Some of these freighters carry a small number of passengers. Information on scheduled services will be found in ABC Shipping or from local agents. You travel more or less as a personal guest of the captain and officers, so do not expect any bargains.

A few cruise ships call at Sri Lanka, often as part of a very expensive cultural lecture tour.

In the not too distant past it was possible to travel between South India (usually Tuticorin) and Sri Lanka, sometimes under sail. Tightened security has made this effectively impossible. There are very real dangers in trying to use unofficial routes (see p245 Jaffna).

PACKAGE TOURS

Despite the troubles a number of companies still arrange package tours to Sri Lanka. These vary in cost, mainly according the quality of the hotels, and are centred mostly on the beach resorts. Some divide the time between the beach, the Hill Country, and the ancient cities. Organised tours to these places can also be taken from the beach resorts, though they tend to be too rushed. Many package operators allow you to stay an extra week or two very reasonably thus giving you a measure of independence. At the time of writing two week packages were advertised on Teletext for £449. The best source of information is a high street travel agent.

More interesting and adventure tours are arranged by smaller, more specialised companies. Most of the better operators belong to the Association of Independent Tour Operators who will provide an index to the tours organised by their members. Contact: AITO Ltd, 133a St. Margaret's Road, Twickenham, TW1 1RG (Tel 0181-744 9280 Fax 0181-744 3187).

INSURANCE

It is absolutely essential, whether you are an independent or package visitor, that before you leave home, you take out insurance to cover medical expenses, repatriation, and baggage and belongings. Consider carefully the cost of replacing all your gear and add something for souvenirs and other acquistions.

Every airline, tour operator and travel agent will be delighted to sell you insurance, but shopping around can save money or get you better cover for the same premium, especially as the definitions of what constitutes a hazardous activity may vary between companies. The Travel Insurance Club Ltd (0800-163518) offers insurance packages aimed at the young traveller starting at £20 for 31 days, going up to £180 for a year. This includes access to a 24-hour medical emergency helpline and cover for a range of hazardous activities as standard.

For any insurance claim, the golden rule is to amass as much documentation as possible to support your application. In particular, compensation is unlikely to be paid for lost baggage or cash unless your claim is accompanied by a police report of the loss.

Red Tape

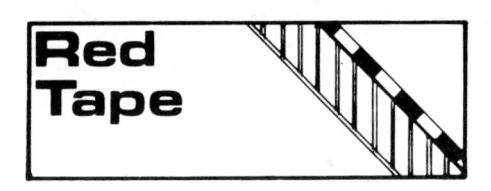

PASSPORTS AND VISAS

A full passport is obviously essential; make sure that it is valid for a minimum of three months beyond the planned duration of your trip. Few bucket shops will warn you of this, but you could find yourself denied entry to Sri Lanka or even not allowed to board the plane. Check that there enough blank pages for visas and stamps.

Visas. Nationals of many countries notably Australia, New Zealand, and the USA do not need a visa at all. Nationals of of Canada, Japan, and EU countries (including unfortunately the UK) do. In fact this makes no great difference because it is not necessary to apply for a visa before your trip. The difference is that the first group are allowed to stay for an initial 90 days whilst it is only 30 days for the second group.

Visa extensions. The Immigration Department is now at the bottom of Station Road, Bambalapitiya right next to the station (it used to be in Fort). This place is open 0830-1530 but best visited early in the morning or after 1400hrs. Get an application form, fill it in and join the queue at Counter 2 (for starters). Take your passport, travellers cheques, encashment certificates, and air ticket. Fees for a further two months cost nothing for New Zealanders up to Rs2775 for British citizens, and others in between. Anything over three months costs Rs5000.

Major Sri Lankan legations:

Britain   Sri Lankan High Commission
13 Hyde Park Gardens, London W2 2LU
Tel 0171-262 1841 Fax 0171-262 7970

USA   Sri Lankan Embassy
2148 Wyoming Ave. NW, Washington DC 20008
Tel 202 483 4026 Fax 202 483 8017

Canada   High Commission
Suite 1204, 333 Laurier Ave. West, Ottawa K1P 1C1
Tel 613 233 84409 Fax 613 238 8448

Australia   High Commission
35 Empire Circuit, Forrest, Canberra ACT 2600
Tel 06 239 7041 Fax 06 239 6166

South Africa   High Commission
410 Alexander Street, Brooklyn, Pretoria 0181
Tel 012 467 690 Fax 012 467 702

India	High Commission 27 Kautilya Marg, Chanakyapuri, New Delhi 110021 Tel 301 0201 Fax 301 5295
Consulate	Sri Lanka House, 34 Homi Modi St., Bombay 400023 Tel 022 206 5861 Fax 287 6132
Consulate	9D Nawab Habibullah Ave., Anderson Road, Chennai (Madras) 600006 Tel 827 0831 Fax 827 2387
Thailand	Embassy No 89 Soi 15, Sukhumvit Road, Bangkok 10110 Tel 261 1934 Fax 651 0059

In countries where Sri Lanka has no representation the British embassy or high commission may be able to help.

Driving licence. You need a temporary Sri Lankan licence to drive any vehicle in Sri Lanka, hire car or otherwise. The easiest way of obtaining this is to get an International Driving Licence in your own country and then have this endorsed (quickly and for free) by the Automobile Association of Ceylon, 40 Sir Macan Markar Mawatha, Galle Face, Colombo 3 (Tel 01-421 528). The office is open Monday to Friday excluding the many public holidays. The car hire company may do this for you.

All is not lost if you have only your home driving licence. Take it (and Rs600) to the Registrar of Motor Vehicles, Elvitigala Mawatha, Colombo 5, and they will issue a one month permit.

Airport tax. The airport departure tax is currently Rs500.

CUSTOMS

Customs clearance for foreigners on arrival is very relaxed, and you are most unlikely to have your baggage examined. Just head for the Green Channel. Duty-free allowance is the usual litre-and-a-half of spirits and 200 cigarettes.

Export regulations. Any item more than 100 years old requires an export permit. Export of animal and snake skins, coral, and tortoise and turtle shell is forbidden.

SECURITY

Although the troubles in Sri Lanka are not yet over, with one exception in 1986, the insurgents have never targeted foreign visitors. Therefore the risk of being caught up in a terrorist incident is no greater than in a western city. However, that does not mean that you should not be prudent during your visit and it is always advisable to check the security situation before you travel. Both the UK Foreign Office (Travel Advice Unit, Consular Division, Foreign & Commonwealth Office, 1 Palace Street, London, SW1E 5HE; tel 0171-238 4503/4504) and the US State Department (2201 C Street, NW, Washington DC 20520, USA; tel 202-647 4000 24 hr service) have travel information offices offering free advice on various countries; these departments also have comprehensive online travel advisory pages (http://www.fco.gov.uk/travel and http://travel.state.gov).

WHAT MONEY TO TAKE

Living costs. At the present time a return air ticket from London to Colombo costs in the region of £400-600. Once you have landed in Sri Lanka you need to budget anything from £50 per person per week upwards.

Expenditure will depend on your style of travel. At the bottom of the scale younger backpackers cover all their expenses, including travel by bus or 3rd class rail, hotels, and food, on £50-70 per week.

Staying and eating in four and five star hotels, and making use of chauffeured hire cars for sightseeing runs to around £500-700 per week for two people. Perhaps a better guide is that the authors spent £200 a week when working on this book. For the two of them that covered rail travel (first class when available), spartan but clean and comfortable hotels, good food, three wheelers and public taxis for sightseeing, and beer whenever they felt like it. It is worth noting that single hotel rooms in all price brackets are hard to find, and that there is often no reduction for single occupancy of a double room. This means that it is substantially cheaper for two people to travel together.

MONEY IN SRI LANKA

Rupees. The Sri Lankan monetary unit is the rupee (abbreviated to Rs), which consists of 100 cents. Notes (bills) are in denominations of Rs10, 20, 50, 100, 500, and 1000. Some of these come in two different patterns, both legal. Coins smaller than 25 cents are no longer in regular use.

Sri Lanka is a relatively cheap country for the foreign visitor (though nothing like as cheap as India, for instance); it most certainly not cheap for the locals. To understand this try to 'think rupees' rather than converting prices into your own currency. If you find this difficult just remember that Rs7000 is a fairly normal monthly salary for a school teacher or civil servant, and that a tea plantation worker earns Rs101 a day. A basic rice and curry meal can be bought for Rs40; short eats are even less. Western style bread, of which the Sri Lankans eat a great deal, is a highly subsidised Rs5 a loaf. The standard offering to a beggar is Rs1 or Rs2.

Changing money. As a rough guide at the time of writing the exchange rate was:

Stg £1 = Rs113	Rs1 = 0.8 pence
US $1 = Rs69	Rs1 = 1.5 US cents
Aus $1 = Rs44	Rs1 = 2 Aus cents
NZ $1 = Rs37	Rs1 = 2 NZ cents

The rupee is fixed against a basket of currencies in which the US dollar predominates. Its value against sterling and other currencies depends on their strength or weakness against the dollar. The current exchange rate can be found from a bank or Sri Lanka tourist office. The rupee is not a fully convertible currency and not legally available outside Sri Lanka. Always change back surplus currency (apart from the Rs500 airport tax) before checking in. If you can change it at all in another country the rate may be discounted 25% or more.

The only way to carry your money is as **traveller's cheques**. Get them from a well-known bank and have them in US dollars or sterling; they are often easier and quicker to cash. Before purchasing check carefully with the bank the terms on which they replace lost or stolen cheques. The cost of cashing a traveller's cheque varies surprisingly from bank to bank; the Hatton National Bank is well represented and usually cheapest. Major **credit cards** are accepted in top-range hotels and the better shops. They can also be used to obtain cash from the cash dispensers (**ATMs** or Automatic Teller Machines) at some of the banks.

Banking hours are 0900-1400 Monday to Friday, though you will find local variations. Banks are always closed on Poya days (the full moon each month), and there are numerous other holidays throughout the year, so try not to run low on cash. Changing money is a relatively quick process.

When you change money always make sure that the bank gives you a receipt and keep it. Bank receipts are needed to re-convert surplus rupees.

The black market. It may be worth carrying a small amount of dollars or sterling which can be changed when banks are closed. It is emphatically not worth trying to play the black market. There isn't one, and anybody who offers over the bank rate is bound to be a rip-off artist. Further, the banks give a better rate for travellers' cheques than currency notes.

Transfers. It is best to take the money you will need with you. Transfers can be made reasonably quickly; the best bet is an international agency such as Thomas Cook. An alternative is to write or cable to your bank asking them to send an International Money Order to where you are staying or to the nearest Post Office. This will take only as long as registered mail, five or six days to Colombo if you're lucky. Tell your bank to advise you where to cash this. The same Sri Lankan bank will sell you dollar or sterling travellers' cheques.

Caution. Beware of anyone offering plausible schemes for making you a large and quick profit. Sri Lanka's foreign trade is run by professionals who ship stuff by the container load. Anything else is illegal or a con.

TIPPING

Tipping (the word bakshish is rarely heard) is less prevalent in Sri Lanka than in most of Asia. It is very common for a 10% service charge to be added to the bill in all but the most basic hotels and restaurants. We are told that in most places this is distributed fairly to the staff. In the absence of a service charge leave 5% of the bill in cheap restaurants, and 10% in a smarter place. If the service has been excellent you can leave a little extra, no more than 5%, over the service charge. Where a service charge is made on your hotel bill tip only the porter who carries your baggage, Rs10/20 per major piece is enough. People who help you by opening buildings or showing you monuments should be given around Rs20. You can leave a similar amount in temples where there is no admission charge. Take no notice of Rs100 notes in offerings dishes or even bigger donations listed in books, they are bait for the gullible.

Taxi and three-wheeler drivers are not tipped, and drivers of private hire cars only if they have been especially helpful. Remember that they get a large commission on anything you buy, and adjust the tip.

WHAT TO TAKE

Baggage. What you take and how you take it depends on your style of travel. Doing things the comfortable way Sri Lanka is like any other civilised country, and you can pack accordingly.

Travellers on a tight budget need to take more with them. Upper sheets, towels, soap, and toilet paper are not provided in the cheapest hotels (the usual break is anything under Rs600 for a double room). Blankets are provided in even cheap hotels in the hills, and you do not need a sleeping bag.

Choosing a backpack, get one with detachable side pockets or none at all, the extra width is a real handicap in fighting your way on to crowded buses and trains. The alternative is a strong canvas or nylon bag with a shoulder strap, which has the merit of fitting more easily under a bus seat. Porters are very rarely available, even at major stations, so be prepared to carry everything yourself. Whatever you use, you will want a separate shoulder bag for your camera, lunch, guide book, and so on.

Most railway stations and a few major bus stands have left-luggage offices ('cloakrooms'). These are quite safe, but some will refuse baggage which is not locked.

Oddments. An unbreakable water bottle is useful, and a small torch and/or candles are essential.

Dress. For daytime wear lightweight cotton or cotton/polyester clothes are best. Trousers and a conventional shirt with button pockets are preferable to jeans and T-shirts, and more versatile. Longish shorts are acceptable for men. Except in the highest parts of the hills you will not need a pullover or jacket. If you do go to the hills unprepared the bazaar in Nuwara Eliya has good quality fleece jackets for £4.50/$7.50.

It is not acceptable for women to wear skimpy shorts or short skirts. A few very young Sri Lankan girls do wear them, but it is better to follow the vast majority who dress very modestly. A bra should always be worn, and a long sleeved blouse is better than a tight T-shirt.

Comfortable footwear is essential. Shoes must be removed in many places, so laces are a nuisance. Except in the hills few Westerners will want to wear anything other than sandals of some kind. Traditional leather sandals cost only £3/$4.50 a pair, and comfortable synthetic ones are the same price. Leather soles are less tiring on the feet than plastic ones.

You are required to remove your shoes before entering any temple or mosque. You may be permitted to keep your socks on or to use a clean pair. As long as the ground is dry there is no health risk in going barefoot. Shoe custodians at the entrance are tipped around Rs10 per pair. Don't worry if there is no custodian, shoes outside shrines seem to be sacrosanct. There are other requirements for visiting Buddhist temples. For men longish shorts are usually acceptable, and women should wear trousers or a skirt below the knees, otherwise sarongs will be available on loan. Shoulders should be covered for both sexes. Hats must be removed

A hat is very useful; it keeps your hair clean and the sun out of your eyes. The alternative is an umbrella; you won't look odd, many Sri Lankans use them. The clergy even have saffron ones colour-coordinated with their robes.

Sri Lanka is a major producer of men's and women's ready-made clothing for shops in the West. Production overruns, seconds, and rejects are unloaded on the local market very cheaply. Colombo is the best place for buying famous brands at knock-down prices; details on p87. Hippier stuff is on sale in Hikkaduwa and other beach resorts.

Sri Lankan women wear a wide variety of clothing. Both Sinhalese and Tamil women traditionally wear the sari in their own styles, the former wrapping theirs with a kind of frill around the waist. Many women of all religions and ethnic groups wear a blouse and calf-length skirt. Western style summer frocks are equally popular, and the Punjabi trouser suit is also seen. This has become a high fashion garment all over South Asia, the designs are stunning, and many western women take to this practical clothing. Saris are uncomfortable and score you no points at all.

India's ubiquitous dhobis do not extend to Sri Lanka and, except in major hotels, you will probably have to do your own washing.

Nudity. You can take the view that if Sri Lanka wants the money of foreign tourists it has to accept that some at least of them will want to sunbathe and swim topless. This is fair enough in Bentota, Beruwela, and Hikkaduwa where the package hotels are. It definitely does not apply in smaller places, and it is quite unreasonable to go to someone else's country and think you can behave without regard for their feelings.

Cameras. Sri Lanka is a photogenic country, and there are few difficulties over photography. Modern 35mm SLRs are lighter than they used to be, but for most purposes you will do just as well with a small 35mm or APS zoom. If you do opt for an SLR an 80-200mm zoom, or a 135mm telephoto, is essential for getting natural, unposed close-ups. Such shots have to be taken quickly, so autofocus is ideal.

Whenever possible fit a skylight 1A or a UV filter to each lens. Apart from cutting through haze they will protect the lens from dust and dirt. With an SLR you will find a polarizing filter very useful. Use a special brush to remove dust from lens and filter, and take lens tissues and cleaning fluid with you and use them regularly. Cleaning a lens or filter with your handkerchief will quickly ruin it.

Film, both 35mm and APS, is readily available, at prices comparable with the West. Before buying check the sell-by date, and the package for signs of tampering. Manufacturers advise you not to carry around exposed colour films for long in the tropics, though we have never had any problems. Fast processing is available in major towns, but of variable quality. Many of the best shots, in shops and narrow streets, are not well-lit, so 200ASA (24din) or even faster film is useful. Never pack your films in your baggage and insist on having your camera bag physically checked rather than x-rayed at airports.

Generally speaking, photography is permitted in holy places, the one major exception being Dambulla. In Cultural Triangle sites and most other places a photographic permit is included in the entry fee; in a few places a separate charge will be made. The one thing you definitely must not do is pose pictures of people with Buddha images. However ruined they may seem these are still holy places, so take care not to do anything else which may be thought disrespectful.

Communications

TELEPHONE

The telephone system within Sri Lanka is cheap and reasonably good. Overseas calls to and from major exchanges aren't too bad (there is direct dialling) but are chancy elsewhere. Trying to call reverse charge (collect) complicates matters greatly. Most larger post offices offer a telex service.

International calls from Sri Lanka. In most places you are likely to visit you will find IDD agencies where you can dial your call yourself. A stopwatch will be put where you can see it. Typical charges are Rs200 per minute (the charge to the line owner for the call is around Rs150) to Europe or North America, rather less to Australasia. Prices should be less by about 30% at off-peak times. Always check the price before making the call.

International codes:

Britain	00 44
USA	00 1
Canada	00 1
Australia	00 61
New Zealand	00 64
South Africa	00 27

Calling Sri Lanka from abroad. Most numbers in Sri Lanka can be dialled direct from abroad. The code for Sri Lanka is 96 preceded by the international access code of the country you are calling from.

Card phones. There are three card phone operators. Cheapest and hardest to find are Sri Lanka Telecoms, mostly in large post offices and railway stations. Metrocard and Lanka Pay booths are more expensive but well distributed. Cards are sold in many shops, look for the stickers.

Mobile phones. Several mobile phone companies operate in Sri Lanka, check with your supplier whether yours is compatible with their networks. Business people can hire on a short-term basis. Try Celltel (072 43333), Dialog GSM (077 330 073), or Mobitel (071 55777). The last named charges Rs120 per day (monthly terms).

Fax. Fax agencies operate all over Sri Lanka, usually the same places as IDD phones.

TELEGRAMS

Telegrams are a useful and inexpensive stand-by, especially if you cannot contact a remote place on the phone. They are fairly reliable, but you should always confirm in writing.

MAIL

The postal service in Sri Lanka is pretty good, at least for overseas mail to and from the main cities. Use aerograms when writing, they're inexpensive and most reliable. When sending anything with stamps on, have every single one franked in front of you. This is not insulting to postal staff, Sri Lankans do just the same. Letters posted in boxes tend not to arrive. British style red pillar boxes are used, a few still with the original royal cypher.

Poste Restante. Mail can be sent to you at any post office in Sri Lanka addressed thus:

J.D. LEAK
Poste Restante
GPO
Any Town
SRI LANKA

The name and address must be printed clearly and, to avoid confusion, use initials rather than given names or have the surname underlined, and leave out titles such as Mr. In Sri Lanka, as in other places, given names can come after the family name, so you can't blame clerks for misfiling. If mail you expect is not filed under your surname initial try that of your given name, or even all the mail they hold. It's not their alphabet, after all. Always take your passport as identity.

The Poste Restante in Colombo is at the General Post Office opposite the President's Palace in Fort, and is very efficient. Taxis and three-wheelers will drop you just around the corner as the street is closed to traffic. Letters are held for two months. You don't even have to go there; phone 01-326 203 to check whether they are holding anything for you. They will even forward mail to another post office (free of charge) if you phone 01-448 482. Take the passports of everyone for whom you are collecting mail.

MEDIA

Newspapers. Newspapers and magazines are published in English as well as Sinhalese and Tamil. The constitution promises freedom of the press, but censorship is used under the Anti-Terrorism Law (as it is for television and radio). The media as a whole carry very little foreign news. The papers are well worth reading, especially as they are fearless when it comes to denouncing government and police corruption. Some of the supplements in the weekend and Sunday papers carry excellent features.

English newspapers a couple of days old can be bought in the five star hotels and Vijitha Yapa and other good bookshops in Colombo.

Magazines. The magazine *Business Today* is useful for visiting business people. The English-speaking population of Sri Lanka is too small to support much in the way of women's and special interest magazines, but it is always worth checking the bookstalls. Like the newspapers these can give you a useful insight into the Sri Lankan way of life.

The Asian editions of *The Economist*, *Time*, and *Newsweek* are sold in Colombo and Kandy, harder to find elsewhere .

Radio. Sri Lanka Broadcasting Corporation is the government's voice. They broadcast regular news bulletins in English, and even the FTSE-100 index of the London Stock Exchange.

Yes FM (89.5 MHz) is a 24 hour English language station which has a good mix of music and news. Capital Radio (99.0 MHz) started out well but now does 24 hour pop music in all three national languages. TNL (90.0 MHz & 101.7 MHz) is another English language station with an eclectic range of programmes. New stations, including a western classical one, are on the way.

BBC World Service can be found on various short wave bands; try 11.96 MHz, 15.31 MHz, 15.56 MHz, or 17.79 MHz. For advice on frequencies contact the BBC Transmission Planning Unit in London (0171-257 2685).

Television. Terrestrial television is similarly controlled by the SLBC. The news in English is parochial and poorly presented; the occasional documentary is worth watching.

Satellite and cable have now arrived in a big way. Sky News (for what it's worth) is re-broadcast and accessible on most sets; BBC World Television is available on MTV, and the rest is all the usual sort of garbage.

Getting Around

Sri Lanka is a relatively small country with an efficient and cheap (if rarely very comfortable) transport system. When you want to make a move you simply catch a bus or train. There are none of the bureaucratic problems of India, and time spent travelling is a small proportion of your visit.

PLANNING

To plan or not to plan? It depends on a number of factors, notably the time at your disposal and your attitude towards being unable to do what you want when you want. In short if you have little time (or little patience) you need a fully planned itinerary with everything booked in advance.

This imposition of western standards, however, runs very much against the grain in a relaxed tropical country like Sri Lanka. You need to give yourself more time and the flexibility that goes with it. We describe all the main attractions of Sri Lanka accessible at the time of writing, but things change quickly. The east coast resorts may open up again, or you may hear from other travellers of a good cheap hotel started up in a previously unvisited place. Following up these leads is part of the fun of real travelling; getting in ahead of the travel writers is even more satisfying!

Maps. The best map for general use is Nelles *Sri Lanka* at a scale of 1:450,000.

Getting Around 51

Festivals. Before you go or as soon as you arrive find out from a tourist office whether any festivals are due (see p67). If necessary tailor your itinerary around them, the major ones are always worth seeing.

Stars. To help you in itinerary planning many sights have been graded with one, two, or three stars * to indicate what, in our opinion, is most worth seeing. A few places are awarded a ° suggesting that they are absolute duds. Others are not graded at all. These are mostly special interest items, and you will have to decide for yourself about these.

FLYING

There are at present no scheduled internal flights, no great disadvantage in so small a country.

If, however, money is no object air taxis and helicopters can make use of quite a number of airfields, most of them leftovers of the Second World War. Services, including helicopter charter, are run by John Keells Aviation and booked through Mackinnons Travels, 4 Leyden Bastion Road, Colombo 1 (Tel 01-329 887 Fax 01-447 603).

Sky Cabs (Tel 01-633 332) operate sightseeing flights from Ratmalana airport over the main resort beaches south of Colombo and around Adam's Peak.

RAILWAYS

Sri Lanka has a very useful though under-capitalised rail network of a little over 1400km. Approximately 400km of this comprises lines to the troubled areas of the north and east which are not at present in use. Work continues slowly on doubling single tracks and extending the line from Matara in the south. Given the awful state of the buses and the way they are driven, the railway is the best inexpensive way of getting around Sri Lanka.

All of the routes are very scenic. You see more than is possible from a bus, and the keen observer will learn more about Sri Lanka from a train window than any guided tour or museum. The easy pace of even the express trains matches rural life.

Sri Lanka Railways operates on the same 5'6" broad gauge as India. One narrow gauge line ran from Colombo to Ratnapura and beyond, but has been shortened and, for general use, converted to broad gauge (more details on p185).

Route planning. Planning is not the complicated matter it is in India with changes at God-forsaken junctions in the middle of a cold and sleepless night. Just as well, since the railways cannot even manage to print a timetable. This is not too great a problem as journeys are mostly short and in the daytime.

Classes. There are three basic classes, simply enough First, Second, and Third. **First class**, available on a limited number of trains comes in a variety of forms. The air-conditioned *AC observation car* is a dubious way of spending money as your chances are observing anything are slight. In eight of the 32 seats you can see nothing but the back of the seat in front. In the others you will find that either there is condensation in the double glazing or that the locals want the blinds down so they can sleep. The cool is pleasant, otherwise you are better off in second class.

The OFV or *Observation First Van* is a much better bet, as long as you don't mind having your back to the engine. It has panoramic windows at the end, the other windows open, and there are fans. The only snags are that seat numbering is random, so you can never be sure of getting a window seat, and the bouncy ride.

Sleepers are also operated on some night trains. These are moderately comfortable but, given the scenic nature of all the lines, of limited interest to the foreign visitor. In second and third classes there are **sleeperettes**, reclining seats where sleep is even less likely than in a proper berth.

Second class is reasonably spacious and comfortable. Socially this is the best class, especially on the Colombo-Kandy Intercities, where you will get into conversation with local commuters.

Third class is very basic. Whilst almost always full it seldom suffers the sort of overcrowding common on Indian trains.

Reservations. This is all much quicker and easier than in India. The catch is that reservations can only be made in the highest class on any given train (except the Colombo-Kandy Intercities), and then not on all trains. Always ask though; although not advertised it is, for instance, possible to reserve seats on certain trains on the Colombo-Matara line.

Tickets. Fares are very reasonable. To travel the 200km from Colombo Fort to Nanu Oya, the station for the hill resort of Nuwara Eliya, costs only Rs40 (£0.35/US$0.58) in third class, Rs110 in second class, or Rs180 in first class. Small extra charges are made for seat and berth reservations; these may be collected on the train. The Rs50 extra for a first class berth includes bed linen. No student discounts are given on any fares.

There has been talk for some years about introducing a rail pass of some kind, but this has yet to materialise.

Facilities. Some of the express trains have a buffet car which does hot and cold drinks, sandwiches, and lunch packets. These are usually good and very cheap. Alcohol is not allowed on the trains. When making a long journey always check whether there is a buffet car. Vendors often board the trains to sell drinks and food, but this cannot be relied upon. Thambili and green coconuts are sold at many stations and will be brought to your window. Anyone used to the station refreshment rooms in India will be disappointed by Sri Lankan ones which, when they exist, are generally dirty, uncomfortable, and serving poor food.

For the enthusiast. All regular services are diesel hauled. A number of **steam** locomotives, mostly of 1920s vintage, has been kept in working order to pull special trains. The Viceroy Special consists of four reconditioned coaches, and is run fairly regularly from Aluthgama or Colombo to Kandy and back. Accommodation is very limited, most runs being chartered to groups, and advance booking is essential; contact JF Tours and Travels, 189 New Bullers Road, Colombo 4 (Tel 01-587 996 Fax 01-580 507) or Railway Tourist Office, Fort Station, Colombo 1 (Tel 01-440 048). Other steam locomotives, notably a fine Beyer Garrett 2-6-2 + 2-6-2, are being renovated.

The only surviving **narrow gauge** (2ft 6in) line is the Kelani Valley Railway from Colombo Fort to Avissawella, the sections on from there to Ratnapura and Opanaike having been closed many years ago. For normal services this has in fact been converted to broad gauge, but a third rail allows narrow gauge operation. This is said to be the only line in the world with a Sentinel steam rail-car still working, details as for the Viceroy Special. Even if you can't get a ride on the Sentinel this is a most attractive run.

Signalling on the remoter lines is still done using Tyler's Patent Tablet machines, an electromechanical system which ensures that only one train at a time can occupy a single track line. The system may seem highly anachronistic, but is still considered good enough to cope with trains carrying nuclear waste on the Cumbria coastal line in England. Another idea borrowed from British railways is the Travelling Post Office, where the mail is sorted on the train; you can actually post your letters directly on to the train.

You may catch a glimpse of the Hitachi, called after its maker. This semi-streamlined diesel is used exclusively on charter.

BUS

Sri Lanka has a very comprehensive bus service, and if there is a road you can rely on someone running a bus along it.

Bus services are run by three groups. **CTB** (Ceylon Transport Board) is still government owned. Their buses are yellow and blue, and usually tolerably comfortable and well maintained. Most of the old CTB buses have been handed over to **Peoplised Transport Services** run by worker co-operatives, though still partly government owned. These are usually gungy red or bare aluminium buses and often still have the old CTB logo. **Private buses** run the whole range from comfortable air-conditioned intercity services to decrepit boneshakers even rougher and more crowded than the Peoplised services.

Most of these services, regardless of who they are run by, are uncomfortable and overcrowded. Conditions are made worse by poor road surfaces and too much traffic. Driving standards can be dangerously low, especially in the case of private buses. There are few video buses, but it is worth checking, the ear-splitting volume really puts the tin hat on an already uncomfortable and tiring journey. Music can be different; on an Indian bus you dread the sound system being in working order. On Sri Lankan buses sound systems are rare and, the popular music being what it is, usually quite soothing.

In theory at any rate reservations can be made on CTB services from the point of departure. Air-conditioned intercity buses can always be booked in advance, and this is necessary. Beware of seats at the front reserved for women and, if you are anywhere near the door, expect to be deprived of your seat by a Buddhist monk who has an absolute right to demand it.

For shorter journeys buses are generally faster than trains. Locals cost somewhere between the 2nd and 3rd class train fare. Air-conditioned buses are about twice as expensive, but still very cheap by western standards.

To sum up, the only buses really worth considering for long distance travel are the air-conditioned ones. The best rule is to take the train whenever possible and use the buses only when there is no alternative.

CAR HIRE

The most comfortable way of getting around Sri Lanka is a chauffeured hire car. The advantages over self-drive, which is very little cheaper, are that you have a built-in guide and interpreter and you don't have to worry about parking. Prices start at around Rs1600 per day plus Rs10 per kilometre. You will also have to pay a small amount for the driver's accommodation and subsistence. This will cover an air-conditioned small Japanese car, a Mercedes is five or six times as much. Full details from Mackinnons Travel Ltd, 4 Leyden Bastion MW, Colombo 1 (Tel 01-329 887 Fax 01-522 351) or Quickshaws, 3 Kalinga Place, Colombo 5 (Tel 01-583 133 Fax 01-587 613), and others. Check all the details very carefully.

Your hotel may offer to arrange car hire for you; always compare their price with booking it for yourself.

You may assume that chauffeured car hire is beyond your means. In fact, there is no real distinction, except a large saving in price, between it and using taxis on a long distance basis. See below.

SELF-DRIVE CAR HIRE

The main self-drive hire companies are Mackinnons (Avis concessionaire) and Quickshaws (Hertz) at the addresses quoted above. Charges start at around Rs1350 per day or Rs8000 per week plus Rs9 per kilometre. The weekly charge for unlimited mileage is around Rs12,500. A hefty deposit (Rs10,000-20,000) is levied, and the insurance excess can be even more than that. The minimum age varies but is usually more than 21, maximum is 65. You are not allowed to take hire cars into the National Parks or on dirt roads. Read the conditions of hire very carefully.

Smaller companies are considerably cheaper. We hired an air-conditioned Toyota Corolla from Selinico Tours, 12B St. Rita's Road, Ratmalana (Tel 01-716 171 Fax 01-732 188) for Rs1200 per day unlimited mileage. It had done 100,000km but was comfortable and reliable.

If you want to get an idea of what driving in Sri Lanka is like watch a round of the British Touring Car Championship on television, paying special attention to the in-car shots. Then imagine it with two way traffic, countless bicycles (mostly two-up) and suicidal pedestrians. This is not a silly analogy; the author did some racing in his younger days. The total concentration, confidence in handling a vehicle, and the ability to cope with a crisis every few seconds are just like racing. So are the techniques for preventing other drivers from boxing you in behind slow traffic and overtaking on the inside. Actually quite fun if you can cope, but never, ever get over-confident.

The upside of the lunatic driving is that everyone expects you to do something totally unpredictable and crazy at any moment, so when you do make a mistake they'll probably miss you anyway. However it may look, there is no malevolence in the driving, and accidents are comparatively rare. Drivers do seem to trust themselves and one another more than in India or Pakistan, where events are governed by karma or the will of Allah according to persuasion. Nor will you find a larger vehicle deliberately forcing you off the road, as happens in those countries. Turning right is the most dangerous manoeuvre. Following drivers simply do not expect you to be stationary in the middle of the road waiting for a gap in the traffic. The technique is to signal (perhaps) and lunge.

Conditions vary a lot around the country. The main roads from Colombo to Galle and Negombo are by far the worst; once you get past them driving actually becomes enjoyable. Road classification is no guide to condition or the speed you might average. You can bat along the B427 from Timbolketiya to Tanamalwila (on the way from Kataragama to Ratnapura) at an easy 80kph, yet when you join the A18, which you might expect to be a better road, you will be lucky to do 40kph because of the terrible surface and heavier traffic.

Diesel costs Rs13.40 per litre and petrol Rs50.20 per litre. A good reason for making sure your hire car is a diesel.

MOTORCYCLE HIRE

This option is quite fun, but strictly for experienced motorcyclists. Read the section above for traffic conditions. A 250cc road or trail bike costs between Rs400 and Rs600 per day. The deposit is Rs3000-4000. Start asking at Gold Wing, 346 Deans Road, Colombo 10 (Tel 01-685 750 Fax 01-698 787). There are several other hirers in Negombo and Hikkaduwa. Demand proof of proper insurance cover.

HITCHING

There is very little scope for hitching in Sri Lanka, and even in a country like this there are obvious dangers. Hitching is totally unsuitable for women, whether accompanied by a man or not.

LOCAL TRANSPORT

Apart from buses local transport usually takes the form of three-wheelers and taxis in various forms.

Three-wheelers are Indian scooter rickshaws, sometimes called tuk-tuks. These two passenger three-wheeler vehicles, based on scooter components, are common all over the island and the quickest way of covering short distances. They are all unmetered, and the average fare should be around Rs20 per kilometre. The drivers are often ready to undertake surprisingly long journeys; you have to offset the fun of immediate contact with your surroundings and the ability to stop at a moment's notice against the relative slowness and a very bumpy ride.

Taxis. Taxis in the western sense are found only in Colombo and Kandy. They are saloon cars with radio control, meters, and usually air conditioning. Fares are Rs26 per kilometre; you may be able to get a discount over long distances. They do have ranks, but it is more normal to phone for one (numbers quoted in Colombo and Kandy sections).

Beware of simply asking for a taxi at a major hotel; they will call you one of their pet tourist taxis. The car may be smarter and in better condition, but you will pay dearly for it.

In all the rest of the country taxis take the form of Japanese-built vans. These are never metered, rarely air conditioned, and comfortably seat six or seven people. The price per kilometre for the whole vehicle is Rs20-25, and you have an edge in bargaining if it runs on diesel, which is much cheaper than petrol. Thus the cost is hardly more than for a three-wheeler. These taxis often operate on a share basis, which reduces cost but can result in overloading and discomfort.

Fares. In unmetered taxis and rickshaws you should always settle the fare before getting in. Use the guide fares above and negotiate in a friendly fashion. You know you will pay a bit more than the locals, but the drivers are rarely unreasonable.

Bicycles. In the ancient cities of Anuradhapura and Polonnaruwa and some of the seaside resorts a bicycle is a good way of getting around. It's faster and less tiring than walking and, unlike a bus, you can stop whenever something catches your fancy.

Bikes can be hired from various sources; your hotel or a bicycle shop are the most likely places. Expect to pay anything from Rs75-150 per day. These bikes are rarely young, and it is a good idea to see if the brakes work before you leave the shop... Most come with a carrier which is useful for your camera bag, take a strap or elastic cord to secure it.

More serious cyclists will find Sri Lanka a bit of a mixture, some of the roads are delightful, others truly dreadful and dangerous with it. It is not impossible to buy good bikes in Sri Lanka. The alternative is to take your own; check with your airline beforehand. Read the section on self-drive car hire to get a better idea of road conditions. For long journeys you put the bike on top of the bus or in the luggage van of the train, the charge is about half the passenger fare.

GUIDED TOURS

Unlike many countries few guided tours are organised by the tourist authorities. Those that are run are for the benefit of package tourists and suffer from the usual problem of trying to pack too much into too short a time.

Accommodation

Sri Lanka offers a wide range of accommodation from international five star class hotels to family run guest houses. Generally speaking the standards are good, and you get what you pay for.

HOTELS AND GUEST HOUSES

There are luxury hotels in the cities and tourist places. Prices are in the order of $100-150 for a double room in Colombo, and $60-100 in Kandy and elsewhere. The large seaside resort hotels, which cater almost entirely for package tourists cost from $40-80 per night. Standards of service and food are generally very good.

The middle of the range is occupied by the government and municipal rest houses (see below) and some very good privately owned smaller hotels costing $20-40 per night. Away from the Cultural Triangle and major seaside resorts this will be the best accommodation available.

Then there comes the rather blurred distinction between the lower priced hotels and the guest houses. In some of the smaller places popular with backpackers, such as Haputale, you will find only guest houses, no hotels. The guest houses are simple but adequately comfortable and clean. They are run by hospitable families who can tell you a lot about their local area and their way of life. Prices are around $3-6/Rs250-450 for a double with bath, rather less with a shared bathroom; in busier places such as Nuwara Eliya or the seaside resorts expect to pay up to $8/Rs600 for the same thing. Meals in these guest houses (there is often no alternative place to eat) will set you back Rs100-200, for which you get some very good home cooking. In this price bracket you can expect hot water only up in the hills, and you will probably have to provide your own towel, soap, and toilet paper. Toilets are almost all western style, the 'hole in the floor' Asian variety being rare. Toilet paper is easily found in local shops. Fans and mosquito nets, according to location, should always be provided.

REST HOUSES

In the days before hotels were common, or much good, the central government and local authorities provided Rest Houses for the use of officials away from their base. Some of the Rest Houses were built in spectacular locations, and today all are open to everyone. They provide what, from their origins, you would expect: comfort rather than luxury, and good basic food. The staff are invariably charming and efficient. Most of the Rest Houses of use to foreign visitors are run by the Ceylon Hotels Corporation (CHC), 411 Galle Road, Colombo 4 (Tel 01-503 497 Fax 01-503 504), who take advance bookings for the chain. A double room usually costs in the $20-30 bracket, and a meal Rs200. They have bars serving beer, wine, and spirits.

OTHER ACCOMMODATION

Tea estate bungalows are sometimes available. Some of these are in beautiful quiet places and well managed. Expect to pay $36-50 per night for four or six people all inclusive. Try the Kelburne estate (Tel Colombo 01-575 644 Fax 01-575 408), Woodlands Network in Bandarawela (Tel 057-2735 Fax 057-2712), or the Ceylon Tourist Board in Colombo or your own country.

There are **National Park bungalows** in Yala West, Uda Walawe, and other parks. These are nicely located, and a great way to enjoy these beautiful places, but expensive for what they are. The basic accommodation costs $24 per person per day. On top of that there is $12 per person per day entry fee, plus $30 per day to cover the cost of the obligatory guide. And then you must provide your own transport, food, kerosene, and bedding. Bookings through Department of Wildlife Conservation, 18 Gregory's Road, Colombo 7 (Tel 01-694 241 Fax 01-698 556).

A few railway stations have **retiring rooms**. These are not as useful as in India where they are comfortable and invariably spotless bedrooms and dormitories. The only retiring rooms you might consider are those in the brand new station at Mihintale where the only alternative is the expensive (but very good) Rest House. Typical prices are $2 single and $4 double.

Very cheap **hostel** and **dormitory** accommodation is hard to find in Sri Lanka and often less than satisfactory. You just have to accept that this is a more expensive country than somewhere like India.

SPECIAL PLACES

Serious travellers tend to regard accommodation as incidental to getting to grips with a country. Most countries, however, have a few places to stay which are attractions in themselves. Sri Lanka has the following to offer:

Galle Face Hotel, Colombo. Colonial style at very reasonable prices.

Mount Lavinia Hotel, Colombo. Much the same but grander.
New Oriental Hotel, Galle. Totally unspoiled tropical colonial hotel.
The Dream House, Unawatuna. Tuscany in the tropics.
Taprobane Island, Weligama. Island house built by a French count.
Claughton, Mawella. The house of the renowned architect Geoffrey Bawa.
Rest House, Tissamaharama. Lakeside location.
Rest House, Polonnaruwa. The same; dive off the terrace or fish out of the dining room window.
Yala Safari Beach Hotel, Yala West National Park. Total seclusion and peace, plus wildlife and a good beach.
The Chalet Hotel, Kandy. Style and extraordinary murals.
The Hill Club, Nuwara Eliya. A Scottish sporting hotel.
The Tea Factory, Nuwara Eliya. Stylish converted tea factory with tremendous views.
Bandarawela Hotel, Bandarawela. Old tea planters' club.
The Rest House, Ella. The most spectacular view in Sri Lanka.

Do note that these are not claimed to be the best hotels in a given place or price bracket, just special in some way. Full details on prices and facilities are given in the relevant sections.

Seasons. The main season for visiting Colombo, the Cultural Triangle and the west coast beaches is December to March, outside this period you can expect substantial reductions in prices. In fact, with the tourist trade not doing very well, it is always worth haggling. Nuwara Eliya has its own season in April which is great social event, and quoted prices will multiply by a factor of three or four. The same applies in Kandy during the Perahera festival at the time of the July or August full moon.

PRICES AND TAXES

Hotels at the top of the range quote their prices in US dollars; you can actually pay in any hard currency or in Sri Lankan rupees.

Warning. In all but the cheapest places **Business Turnover Tax (BTT)** and a service charge can add 20% to the basic price of the room and food. Always check whether this is included in the price you are quoted.

Eating and Drinking

Sri Lankan food, in itself, is not very exciting. The staple is rice and curry; this usually means a mountain of rice with a small choice of meat and vegetable curries. The vegetables are good and varied, one particular delicacy is the flower of the banana palm. Interesting, but the novelty soon wears off. Luckily the Sri Lankans themselves have eclectic tastes and are very good cooks.

As befits one of the original and most important spice islands, the spicing of food is considered an art and can be surprisingly subtle. It can also be the exact opposite, though they tend to go easy on the chillies for Westerners; 'no chillies' is *miris nathuwa* in Sinhalese and *kāram vendām* in Tamil. Food hygiene is reasonably good, and tummy troubles are rare. Strangely, for a Buddhist country, vegetarian food is not popular.

RESTAURANTS

In Colombo, Kandy, and the seaside resorts you will find restaurants offering good Indian, Chinese, and western food. Western fast food is also available. Outside the main tourist areas there is a dearth of quality restaurants. The usual thing is to eat in your hotel or guest house. The food in the cheaper hotels can be very good, but is often comparatively expensive. You may find that you get a far better choice at a four-star hotel for little more money. In fact, whilst you are eating a rather ordinary rice and curry for Rs200 you could be having a very good buffet for Rs300 or, for that matter, rice and curry in a real cheapie for Rs40.

SRI LANKAN SPECIALITIES

Short eats are delicious little fried patties with a variety of fillings, mostly vegetable and fish. You are served a plateful and charged only for what you eat. **Hoppers** are crispy pancakes, a little like the Indian dosa, fried in a small wok. They come with many different fillings, the most popular being a fried egg. Similar fillings are found in the **rotty**; the name is obviously related to the roti of northern India, and one might expect a chapati. Actually it is an often doughy and rather indigestible bread cake. **String hoppers** are quite different from ordinary hoppers, being a rice vermicelli eaten mostly for breakfast with a light curry sauce.

Fish and shellfish. These are very popular along the coast. Most are good and fresh, but care should be taken. It is common practice to cook what is described on the menu as grilled or fried fish or shellfish with onions, spices, and so on. Apart from ruining the natural flavour, this means two things: you cannot find the bones in fish and, worse, it is hard to see or smell whether it is alright. Small prawns are usually frozen after cooking and can be defrosted quickly and safely. This is not true of jumbo prawns, lobster (actually crayfish) and crab which may have been frozen uncooked and then cooked whilst imperfectly defrosted. Do not order these things in a sauce, insist on them being plain grilled or boiled or fried with a little garlic. Look closely to see whether it is cooked all the way through or discoloured, sniff, and taste cautiously. Reject anything that you are remotely suspicious about. There are few things worse than shellfish poisoning. Prices may be tempting compared with home, but it is worth remembering that the best shellfish comes from cold water - and does not need to be mucked about in strong flavourings.

Desserts. A very popular dessert is curd and honey, the curd being excellent unpasteurised yoghurt and the 'honey' actually a tasty syrup made by boiling palm sap. If you keep on boiling it you get jaggery, an equally tasty coarse brown sugar. **Wattapatalam** is a sort of solid egg custard with coconut and cashews in it. See also 'Sweets' below.

Fruit is plentiful. There are many different **bananas** and plantains, and **papaya**, with a squeeze of lime juice, is popular at breakfast time. **Mangoes** from the north are good, as are **pineapples**. **Jak** is a large green spiky fruit which breaks up into segments looking a little like pineapple. Jak is also used in curry, when it assumes a totally different flavour. **Woodapples** make a very good jam which would also go well with a pork chop. Other fruits include **rambutan** (a bit like lychee), **custard apples**, **guavas**, and **mangosteens** (one of the best). Try whatever you see; even if you don't like it, it won't have cost you much. Fruit should be peeled or thoroughly soaked in strongly chlorinated or iodinised water. If you have the chance to cook for yourself you will find western vegetables ('English vegetables') in the main markets; these are grown up in the hills.

Most menus offer dahi, or curd which is fresh natural yoghurt. This is a good accompaniment to many dishes, including fresh fruit, and the bacteria in it will soothe a troubled tummy. It is also more effective than water for cooling you down after a very hot dish. A banana can also help.

Warning. In all but the cheapest places BTT (Business Turnover Tax) and a service charge can add 20% to the basic price of your meal. Check whether this is included in the menu prices.

SNACKS

Those used to the huge variety of snacks sold by the street vendors in India may be disappointed by Sri Lanka. The only real snacks with local character are short eats and hoppers. In all the larger towns you will find excellent bakery shops which do a wonderful range of cakes, pies, sandwiches, and so on.

Sweets. Sri Lankan sweets are closely related to the traditional Indian ones, and they are incredibly sweet. Rasa kavili (the Indian rasgulla) are little white balls made of milk and sugar soaked in syrup. Gulab jamun are the same, except that the balls are fried and soaked in rose-water syrup. Aluva (halwa) is a fudge, often with cashew nuts. Give them a try with your tea or coffee. Western style sweets and chocolate are found in the main towns.

Ice cream is mostly factory made and safe to eat.

DRINKING

Fluid intake is essential to health in a hot country like Sri Lanka. Neglect it and you rapidly start to feel the unpleasant effects of dehydration.

Soft drinks

Water. Tap water is safe to drink in places, but it is better not to risk it. Bottled water is readily available, usually costing Rs35-40 for 1.5 litres.

Tea and coffee. Not surprisingly, tea is a very popular drink and should be safe (water has to be boiled at least ten minutes to be totally safe). Unlike in India it is usually served with the sugar and milk (hot, unfortunately) separate. The equivalent of Indian chai, in which all the ingredients are boiled up together, is known as plain tea. This can come as a bit of a shock to refined tea drinkers, but is a great pick-me-up on a cold morning in the hills. The coffee is good on the rare occasions it is made strong enough.

Other drinks. Western brands of soft drinks are sold in most places. The local Elephant brand is equally good; best is their ginger beer, with plenty of real ginger in it. Vimto addicts will find Portello a very fair substitute.

Fresh coconuts are often on sale, and the juice of these is cool and refreshing. The best is the golden shelled thambili, or king coconut. When you have finished the juice have the vendor split the shell so you can scoop out the creamy white meat. Be wary of ice, freezing does not kill bugs.

Hard stuff

There are no hang-ups over alcohol in Sri Lanka, and you can have a drink pretty much where and when you feel like it. The one exception is Poya (full moon) days. Hotels usually have a way round this problem for residents.

Imported liquor is expensive compared with local drinks. A good range, from champagne downwards, can be found in the cities and major resorts. However nice an idea wine never seems to taste quite right in the tropics.

Beer. Sri Lanka has two breweries, and their products are available all over the country. Most commonly found is Lion, a very pleasant lager from the Lion Brewery in Nuwara Eliya, and much preferable to Three Coins brewed in Negombo by McCallums. Lion also brew their own stout and, under licence from Dublin, Guinness. Bottle shops charge around Rs65 a bottle, cheaper restaurants and bars upwards of Rs75. In better hotels expect to pay a minimum of Rs125.

Local drinks. The local country drink is Toddy, the fermented sap of the palm trees. A tube has to be inserted with some care into the soft growth at the top of the tree and a container fastened below. This is the job of the toddy tapper. Production is very organised, and a tapper will look after as many as a hundred trees. To save having to shin up and down each tree rope walkways are rigged to connect them. Traditionally earthenware pots are used to collect the sap, and the heat ferments it quite naturally into toddy at the top of the tree.

The local spirit is Arrack, distilled from toddy. Some of this is very palatable, either in a cocktail or simply with cola or ginger beer. The best known brand is Mendis, and the arrack comes in several grades. The best is pure coconut arrack (lesser grades are cut with neutral spirit) double distilled; generally, the more you pay the smoother. Rum is less good.

SMOKES AND PAAN

Sri Lanka grows quite a lot of tobacco for domestic consumption, and foreign cigarettes are available in the main towns. The home grown stuff is pretty rough. One of the most popular brands is Gold Leaf, which can come from either England or Sri Lanka. Look at the small print, the latter is hard on the throat (to say the least). Cigars, mostly local and from southern India, and pipe tobacco can be found.

Paan, the stuff that dyes pavements and stairwells red in India, is little used in Sri Lanka. Paan is crushed areca nut wrapped in betel leaf. The additional ingredients, which usually include lime paste, are a matter of choice, but the result is a very good and cooling digestif after a meal, and also mildly narcotic. Long term use plays havoc with the teeth, but once in a while does no harm. Mint or spearmint are probably the best bet for Westerners.

Exploring

MUSEUMS AND ART GALLERIES

Sri Lanka's various **museums** tend to be disappointing. They have some interesting collections, but information on them is very sketchy. National Museums are located in Colombo, Kandy, Ratnapura, and Galle. Galle also has a maritime museum, and there are archaeological museums at the main historic sites. Easily the best museum in Sri Lanka is the privately run Martin Wickramasinghe Museum of Folk Art and Culture at Koggala on the south coast.

The only non-commercial 'art gallery' is the National Art Gallery in Colombo, which is not wildly exciting. The best of historic Sri Lankan painting is murals in temples (refer to the index) and, most spectacularly, high up on the rock at Sigiriya.

The commercial galleries, mostly in Colombo, have some very good stuff, including the work of active local artists. You are welcome to browse, a hard sell is very rare.

THE GREAT OUTDOORS

Flora and fauna. Elevation and rainfall variations cause quite a variety of natural vegetation. The north-east has evergreen forests, largely of ebony and satinwood whilst the dry zones west and south of it are scrubby thorn. The east is a savanna grassland like the Deccan in India. In the winter season after the south-west monsoon the whole of Sri Lanka is decorated by trees with brilliant blooms every colour of the rainbow.

Two of the many kinds of palm trees in Sri Lanka are the palmyra, which dominates in the north, and the coconut palm of the south. The dark trunk and stiff foliage of the palmyra are said to symbolise the more serious Tamils, whilst the supple and feathery coconut palm represents the light-hearted Sinhalese.

Sri Lanka is best known for its unique sub-species of the **Asiatic Elephant**, which is fully described on p138 *Pinnewala*. Elephants are fairly readily seen in the wild in the national parks and elsewhere. The other really big game is the **Buffalo**, the same thing as the domesticated water buffalo. The only big cat in Sri Lanka is the spotted **Leopard** (or panther); this is a shy animal rarely seen unless you are prepared to spend a lot of time waiting quietly. Deer are much more common; **Chital** (the name means spotted and, like cheetah, comes from the same Sanskrit stem as chintz) are plentiful in the national parks. The much larger **Sambhar** prefer hilly ground with more cover. Other deer include the smaller and harder to see **Muntjac** and **Hog deer** imported from Bengal. The **Sloth bear** is occasionally seen. **Wild pig** do a lot of damage in the countryside. They are unpleasant and aggressive animals best given a wide berth.

Monkeys are common and include macacques and the **Purple-faced** and

Common Langurs. **Mugger** and **Estuarine crocodiles** may be seen in rivers and estuaries.

The **Common Mongoose** is frequently seen in villages and beside the road. They are famous as killers of snakes, but also eat rodents, birds, and their eggs. And everywhere are the lively little Striped Squirrels which, the Hindus will tell you, gained their stripes when Shiva stroked one. Large numbers of **Fruit bats** (flying foxes) roost in the trees of Vihara Mahadevi Park in central Colombo; at dusk you see them flapping slowly out to the countryside to feed.

The **Birdlife** is spectacular. Over three hundred species are resident, mostly similar to the birds of the Indian sub-continent, but with twenty-odd unique to Sri Lanka. The time most people visit Sri Lanka, from October to April, is when many birds from the north are wintering.

Handguide to Birds of the Indian Sub-Continent, by Martin Woodcock (Collins) is readily available in Britain. In Sri Lanka you can find *Guide to the Birds of Ceylon*, by G.M. Henry (Kandy, de Silva & Sons).

National Parks and nature reserves. For such a small country, and one with serious preoccupations, Sri Lanka has made huge efforts to preserve its countryside and wildlife. Unlike India these efforts are not prejudiced by virtually uncontrolled poaching. Some of the parks are at present inaccessible because of insurgency. Those that are open are detailed in the text (refer to National Parks in the index).

Most of these parks have basic accommodation in bungalows and at campsites; details from Wildlife Conservation Department, 18 Gregory's Road, Colombo 7 (Tel 01-694 241 Fax 01-698 556).

The Wildlife and Nature Protection Society, Chaitya Road, Fort, Colombo (Tel 01-325 248) organises trekking and bird watching tours.

RECREATION

Relaxing in Sri Lanka is not just lying on the beach. There are plenty of opportunities for spending your time in more active pursuits.

Sport and adventure

Scuba diving and snorkelling are reckoned to be nearly as good as the Maldives, and will cost you a great deal less. Hikkaduwa is ideal with its coral sanctuary and shoals of brightly coloured fish. Equipment can be hired and reasonably priced tuition is available.

The **surfing** is good at Hikkaduwa and better at Arugam Bay, though the latter is not always accessible. The open sea is rarely calm enough for **water skiing**, the lagoon at Bentota is the best place for this, **windsurfing**, and hiring wetbikes (see Aluthgama).

River angling in Sri Lanka presents a mixed picture. The once good trout fishing in the central highlands around Nuwara Eliya and Horton Plains is now defunct. Some rivers have mahseer, a superb fighting fish. These are not the giants found in India, as they average around 3lb, but 25 pounders are not unknown. Try the Mahaweli north of Kandy, the stretch near Katugastota Bridge is well known. You should take all your own tackle; unless you are after big mahseer you can have a lot of fun with just a telescopic spinning rod and cheap reel.

Sea angling. There is good beach casting off the west coast. At Mutwall, on the Kelani Ganga estuary near Colombo, 82lb trevali and 39lb barracuda have been caught. The outlet of Beira Lake at Galle Face is equally popular. You can beach fish in the southern part of Negombo Lagoon for barracuda, queen fish and estuary perch all year except monsoon time. Further afield, the Panadura estuary, Hikkaduwa, Matara, Tangalle, and Hambantota are all productive. The following should be able to provide information: Negombo Anglers Club; Ceylon Anglers Club, Chaitya Road, Fort, Colombo (opposite lighthouse), also has tackle for hire; Sport Fishing Club of Sri Lanka. Try Starling Travels (Pvt) Ltd, 32C Dickmans Road, Colombo 5 for boat hire.

Walking and trekking. There are good day walks around Haputale and Ella, and the guest houses have full information on these. It should be possible to string together longer walks through the tea plantations, but information is hard to come by. Ask Woodlands Network in Bandarawela who are trying to get things organised. The real problem is that no maps are available for security reasons. A very good little book, *Trekking in Sri Lanka*, details a number of walks, not all in the Hill Country. It has been out of print for a while, but copies are available.

Running. Contact Colombo Hash House Harriers on one of these numbers (all 01-): Kurt Zingg 697 821, Hilal Peries 581 675, Arthur Senanayake 910 480. The idea of running in this climate seems to be to have an excuse for drinking a lot of beer afterwards.

Golf. The game may well have been introduced by the Dutch long before the British arrived on the scene. There were once many clubs, but only two remain, the Royal Colombo and Nuwara Eliya.

Yachting. The Royal Colombo Yacht Club sails Dublin Waterwags in the Harbour (permit needed). Racing on Saturday at 1600. Commodore (Tel 635 993) or Secretary (Tel 580 413) for more details.

Ceylon Motor Yacht Club has dinghy racing on Sundays at Bolgoda Lake, Moratuwa, 22km south of Colombo. Good fishing here too.

Island Yacht Tours, 102/11 Templar Road, Mount Lavinia (Tel 01-737 483) have a 60ft German built yacht for three day cruises (eight passengers) from Galle or Beruwela.

Other ideas. Information on **white water rafting**, **canoeing**, and **mountain biking** from Tel 074-713 334, Fax 01-577 951, or e-mail: adventur@mail2.lanka.net.

Beaches

Sri Lanka has hundreds of miles of beautiful beaches. Care has to exercised as most have dangerous currents. Unawatuna is the safest; at others always observe warning flags. Off the beaten track never enter the water before seeking local advice. The best advice is never to go out of your depth, being a strong swimmer is not enough.

Swimming pools

The only pools you would want to use are those at the tourist hotels. All make some kind of charge to non-residents, ranging from the cost of a drink to Rs300.

Entertainment

Sri Lanka is a highly scenic country, and its towns and people a fascinating blend of the familiar and the exotic East. Keep your eyes open and make the most of it.

CINEMA AND THEATRE

Cinema. With a language spoken by only fourteen or so million people you would not expect Sri Lanka to have a prolific film industry. In fact a few films, some of high quality, are made each year. The cinemas show mainly Indian and western films of the more commercial kind. Higher quality western films are shown at the foreign cultural institutes.

Sri Lanka has been popular as a location for western film makers. Remember Indiana Jones jumping from a suspension bridge into a Himalayan torrent? Actually it was the Mahaveli river just outside Kandy, and the man who did the stunt will happily repeat it for you — at a price. It is better known that *The Bridge on the River Kwai* was filmed in Sri Lanka. The bridge was built at Kitulgala, and the loco was real, no messing around with models.

Theatre, in the western style, is quite popular in Colombo, and regular performances take place. Performances are frequently in English as well as Sinhalese. Contact the Lionel Wendt Theatre, 19 Guildford Crescent, Colombo 7 (Tel 695 794) and Tower Hall Theatre Foundation, 123 Wijerama MW, Colombo 7 (Tel 687 993) for details. Travelling companies from abroad are occasionally sponsored by the foreign cultural institutes (see p77).

MUSIC AND DANCE

Classical music. Sri Lanka has no tradition of refined classical music in the Indian or western sense. Music is used only as an accompaniment to worship or dancing. The mainstay of the music is a variety of drums and other percussion instruments, reed instruments being added only for devotional music. Western classical music performances are occasionally arranged by the western cultural institutes.

Popular music. Sri Lankan popular music is extraordinarily eclectic. In what the airlines call 'easy listening' you can detect traces of blues, big band, Hawaiian, and Latin American. The Portuguese had a strong influence on popular music, which accounts for Latin rhythms and the melancholy fado. An indirect product of the Portuguese presence is Caffrina, a blend of Latin and African. The name comes from the kaffirs, slaves and soldiers the Portuguese brought from Mozambique, and some of whom still form a distinct a community at Puttalam.

In Tamil areas you will be reminded that India has the largest film industry in the world, and that most of its output is lightweight stuff with plenty of songs and dances. The stars, and they really are very popular figures, do not sing themselves. That is the job of the 'playback singers' who are successful artists in their own right. The lyrics may be in Hindi, the main North Indian language, or Tamil, there is little to choose between them in shrillness.

Dance. The two main forms of dance are Kandyan and Low Country. Kandyan dance, performed by both men and women, is very athletic. The themes are both narrative and devotional, and the percussion music that accompanies the dance simply provides a rhythm for the dancer.

Low Country dancing divides into Kolam and Devil dancing, both making use of the masks you see on sale everywhere. Kolam dancing is really a form of folk theatre, and pure entertainment. The dances are narrative and look as far back as the fables about Buddha's birth and early years. It thus follows essentially traditional forms, but new characters (like the masks of colonial policemen seen in Colombo Museum) are introduced from time to time, so it can be quite topical

Devil dancing is a serious business of casting out the evil spirits that cause illness and other misfortunes. This is the domain of the most grotesque masks. Performing such dances for an audience is akin to sacrilege.

Performances are frequent, both in the major hotels and in public auditoria. The performances put on in tourist hotels are pretty sterile.

NIGHTLIFE

Sri Lanka is mostly a quiet, early to bed country. The major hotels in Colombo and the seaside resorts run discos and entertainment of various kinds. There are casinos in Colombo and Kandy.

SPECTATOR SPORT

Cricket is the number one spectator sport in Sri Lanka. After knocking on the door for many years the national team arrived in a big way when they beat Australia in the final of the 1996 World Cup. Their swashbuckling style provides the most entertaining cricket seen for many years.

Rugby has a keen following in Sri Lanka with a number of well-established teams in Colombo and Kandy. Despite the handicap of their generally slight build Sri Lanka sends teams to the Hong Kong Sevens and other tournaments. The first international in Ceylon was played as long ago as 1907 when the All Blacks' ship put into Colombo on the way to Europe. The required match fee of US$50 caused a lot of wrangling as the All-Ceylon team was supposed to be amateur. And the All Blacks won 33-6. Some things never change.

Football is popular but has yet to achieve much in the way of skill.

Horse racing was well established as a Sinhalese aristocratic sport certainly as early as the 13th century, and probably dates back to the time of the Aryan invasion. The British, of course, maintained the tradition, but in recent years the Buddhist authorities have persuaded the government to ban it. The course in Colombo has been taken over by the university and the grandstand converted into a faculty building. Racing of a sort still takes place on the rather ramshackle course at Nuwara Eliya during the April season.

You need not go without a punt however. In even small towns you will find a bookie's shop with, on the roof, a satellite dish nearly as big as the shop. This picks up British horse and greyhound races, followed by large numbers of enthusiastic punters. Which accounts for why the authors found the Wetherby racecard on a scrap of newspaper near the top of the holy hill at Mihintale.

Details of all these activities can be obtained from Ceylon Tourist Board offices.

FESTIVALS

Sri Lanka may well have more festivals and public holidays than any other country in the world. As elsewhere, the festivals mostly have a religious basis. Buddhism is well endowed with festivals and, Sri Lanka being a tolerant place, the festivals of all the other religions are observed as well. One suspects too that Sri Lankans need little excuse to celebrate and enjoy themselves.

There are two aspects to this from the visitor's point of view. Festivals are an essential part of the way of life, and observing and participating in them is an essential part of understanding the country, and great fun too. On the other hand many normal services come to a standstill far more often than the Westerner is used to. When planning anything in Sri Lanka look out for the red dates on the calendar.

Festivals in Sri Lanka are generally well mannered, but huge crowds can bring risks. Have fun but keep your wits about you and an eye on the exit.

Buddhist festivals

Poya is the full moon day every month and a public holiday. Everything shuts down and no alcohol is sold. The Poya days and the special events associated with them are:

January - *Durutu*. A major Perahera procession at the Kelaniya temple in northern Colombo to celebrate one of the supposed visits of Buddha.

February - *Navam*. A major Perahera from Colombo 7 to a temple in the Beira Lake area.

March - *Medin*.

April - *Bak*.

May - *Vesak*. Celebration of the birth, enlightenment, and death of Buddha. A festival of light with folk art and theatre.

June - *Poson*. Anniversary of the arrival of Buddhism in Sri Lanka. Major events at Anuradhapura and Mihintale.

July - *Esala*. The huge and spectacular procession in Kandy to honour the Tooth Relic. Similar events at Dondra and the Belanwila Rajah Mahavihara in southern Colombo.

August - *Nikini*.

September - *Binara*.

October - *Vap*.

November - *Il*.

December - *Unduwap*. Sangamitta brought the bo-tree cutting to Sri Lanka. Major celebrations at Anuradhapura and elsewhere.

Hindu festivals

Thai pongal (January 14) is a four day festival celebrating Indra the Vedic rain god, Surya the sun god, and the cow, all three seen as indispensable to the well-being of man. This is a Dravidian (i.e pure south Indian, not Aryan) harvest festival. The date coincides with the end of the north-east monsoon and the local harvest.

Pongal, if you really want to know, is the gerund of pongu meaning to boil over. Rice and milk are cooked in a new earthenware pot over a newly formed oven. When it boils over is known as pongal, and thought to be symbolic of bursting with joy.

Maha Shivaratri (February/March) is the wedding day of Shiva and Parvati.

Dussehra (September/October), also known as Durga Puja, honours Durga or Devi on the day that her husband Shiva slew a buffalo-headed demon. Of more relevance in Sri Lanka, it marks the day that Rama triumphed over Ravana.

Deepavali (October/November) is a four-day festival of light (the name means a line of lights), the most important in the Hindu calendar. Vishnu (or Krishna), who had killed a giant on this day, was greeted by his consort Lakshmi and other women bearing lamps. Fairy lights or, more traditionally, little earthenware oil lamps, line all the houses and temples. Deepavali, the Diwali of northern India, tends to be a quieter and more reflective affair than other Hindu festivals.

Muslim festivals

Bakr-Id commemorates Abraham's would-be sacrifice of Ishmael. The end of **Ramadan**, the month of fasting observed throughout the Muslim world, is marked in Sri Lanka by **Id-ul-Fitr**. This is a joyous occasion of feasting and new beginnings, gifts of rice being made to the poor. **Id-ul-Alha** falls in the month of Haj, the time of the pilgrimage to Mecca incumbent on all Muslims who can afford it. Special prayers are said in mosques, and sacrifices may be made. **Milad-un-Nabi** is Mohammed's birthday.

Christian Festivals

Good Friday is a public holiday. Passion plays take place at Hiniduma near Galle, Duwa and Borelessa near Negombo; the last is of 1930s origin and based on the Oberammergau play. A big procession to Mount Calvary at Maggona in the Kalutara district takes place. **Christmas Day** is similarly a public holiday.

Secular festivals

Major secular festivals are **National Day** (4 February), **May Day** (1 May), and **National Heroes' Day** (22 May). The Sinhalese and Tamil calendars coincide, and New Year's Eve and New Year's Day (13 & 14 April) are both holidays; these are lively occasions, especially in the country areas, and everyone tries to get home to their villages for them. It also marks the end of the Adam's Peak pilgrimage season which opens at the December full moon.

Many other festivals of a more local nature take place throughout the year, and some of these are mentioned in the text. These are often more spontaneous and enjoyable than the larger events.

Dates and details. The Ceylon Tourist Board produces a list each year giving the dates of the major festivals. Buddhist and Hindu festivals occur in the same period each year, the exact date depending on the phase of the moon. Muslim ones are based on a calendar of 354 days and in time take place in any season of the year. Festivities often spread over several days either side of the official date, and you can miss a lot arriving on the specified date.

Shopping

Opening hours. Shops generally open at 0830 or 0900 and close around 1900 Monday to Friday. Most close in mid-afternoon on Saturday, and some may close for lunch. Almost all the shops are shut on Sunday, but in many places they are replaced by lively street markets.

Shopping. Sri Lanka has a good range of handicrafts and souvenirs for a country of its size.

The **masks** used in different forms of dancing are unique to Sri Lanka. They are very colourful, especially appealing to youngsters, and start at very low prices. The ones finished in matt subdued colours are much closer to the original vegetable dyes than those done in modern gloss paint.

Sri Lanka is a major producer of **gem stones**. The main centre of the industry is Ratnapura, and there is information on the types of stones available in that section. The best advice, unless you are an expert, is to buy from Laksala or another reputable dealer. Many of the gems on offer elsewhere are fake or of low quality. It is, of course, extremely expensive to have loose stones mounted in the West, nor have you any chance of selling them at a profit. In recent years there has been considerable growth in the production of finished **jewellery**. This is very attractive and a much better buy. Except in fixed price shops (and even in some of them) you should be able to manage a discount of 20-25%, be suspicious if you are offered more.

Batik is a new thing in Sri Lanka. There are quite a lot of workshops in the Cultural Triangle area where you can watch the fascinating and very time-consuming process. The goods here tend to be expensive and inferior. Really artistic batiks are done by Upali Jayakody in Kandy and Fresco Batiks near Peradeniya. Another place is the village of Mahawewa, north of Negombo.

Cotton **textiles** are woven on traditional hand looms, see Manikdiwela (near Kandy). Many shops have attractive embroidery in bold designs ranging in size from cushion covers to bedspreads. Hikkaduwa specialises in more modern designs. Lace is made in Galle and Weligama.

Leather, **silver**, **brass**, and **lacquered boxes** are also good buys.

Take care over where you do your buying. Get an idea of prices in one of the government **Laksala** stores (taking care to avoid places with similar names); you should be able to buy for substantially less elsewhere. Be dubious of shops and workshops in the major seaside resort areas, where prices are highest.

Objects made of **turtle shell** (usually called tortoiseshell) and **coral** are protected in Sri Lanka and prohibited imports in most western countries, as is **ivory**. You will be in trouble if Customs at either end catch you with them. **Antiques**, defined as anything more than fifty years old, need an export licence.

Never go shopping with a hotelier, guide, courier, or taxi driver; do not buy where you are staying, and do not tell the shopkeeper the name of your hotel. That way he has no commission (anything up to 40%) to pay. Bargaining in Sri Lanka tends to be a friendly process, take your time and wear the man down.

Paying by credit card means that the card company will chase the vendor if necessary and, in Britain at least, they have to reimburse you if the goods do not arrive.

You may not find anything to buy in the local markets, but they are an important way of seeing how people live. Visit them whenever possible, especially the Pettah in Colombo.

Health and Hygiene

Sri Lanka is an unusually healthy place by Asian standards, and there seems to be a good understanding of food hygiene. Even staying and eating in the cheapest places few people have tummy troubles, never mind anything more serious. A few simple precautions will keep you out of trouble. If you have any particular worries read *Travellers' Health: How to Stay Healthy Abroad* by Richard Dawood (Oxford University Press).

NATURAL HAZARDS

Heat. The unaccustomed heat can easily lead to dehydration. Exhaustion, accompanied by thirst and sometimes nausea, are the result. The cure is simply to rest and drink copious amounts of water with rehydration salts. Dehydration is avoided by drinking enough in the first place. A good rule is that the body needs four litres of fluid a day at 20°C, five litres at 30°C, and six litres at 40°C. Coloured urine is an indication of insufficient fluid intake, though this does not work if you are using iodine as a water purifier. If things get serious, with body temperature apparently out of control, get into a cold shower or bath and seek medical advice.

Sun. There was a time when the children and soldiers of the Raj were punished for going out without a hat to protect them from sunstroke. Modern opinion is that sunstroke was caused not by the sun's rays but by dehydration. The real danger, only recently understood, is the damage the sun does to the skin, and the likelihood of skin cancer as a result. The air is clear in Sri Lanka, and proper precautions must be taken. Cover up. Sun screen creams are available in the main centres but rarely elsewhere.

Insects. Mosquito nets are usually provided in areas where mosquitoes are a real pest. Otherwise burn a mosquito coil under the bed (wrecks the throat but you sleep) or use one of the electric devices cheaply available in Sri Lanka. It is not much use taking your own net as there is rarely anything to hang it on.

In cheap or dirty lodgings beware of bed bugs. Little black spots on the bed frame or bedding are the warning. Apply a lighted match to the joints and wait for something like a squashed ladybird to emerge. If it does find somewhere else to stay.

Scorpions occur but are rare. It is always worth shaking out your clothes and shoes before putting them on.

Snakes. Unless you go traipsing around fields the only snake you are likely to see is a snake charmer's cobra. Many people in the country do die of snake bite every year, mostly during the monsoon when the snakes are washed out of their usual lairs.

DISEASES AND OTHER HEALTH HAZARDS

Inoculations. There are no official vaccination requirements for Sri Lanka unless you arrive from an area where **yellow fever** is endemic. Modern vaccines, however, are much more effective than in the past, and precautions are advisable.

Probably the worst thing you can get is one of the various forms of **Hepatitis.** Hepatitis A is the greatest risk, coming from impure water, dirty utensils, lack of hygiene, and joints shared with carriers. Apart from making your skin and eyes yellow, it is a debilitating disease which can cause permanent liver damage and recur over a period of years. The new Havrix vaccine is expensive but highly effective and lasts for ten years. The old gamma globulin vaccine, still available, was controversial. There is a suspicion that the protection, if it works at all, is short-lived and may well leave you more susceptible to the disease when it wears off.

Hepatitis B has much the same symptoms, but is contracted through sexual contact or contaminated blood products or needles. Immunisation is possible, but the course takes six months.

Western medicine has no real cure for hepatitis, the answer being immunisation against the A strain and avoidance of the risk of B. Sufferers have reported relief of the symptoms by using Ayurvedic medication. Ayurveda is the ancient Indian medical system based on natural ingredients.

Spending a lot of time in rural areas, especially around paddy fields and animals, there is a very slight risk of both **Japanese B Encephalitis** and **Meningococcal Meningitis.** Immunisation is simple and effective.

TABT protects against **typhoid, paratyphoid,** and, more usefully **tetanus.** **Polio** is a risk in Sri Lanka and, even if you have nothing else, a booster is a wise precaution.

Rabies is present in Sri Lanka. If you are bitten or even have a scratch licked by a dog, cat, monkey, or bat it is absolutely necessary to have a rabies shot. This is not as unpleasant as it used to be, and better than dying. There is no cure for rabies. The moral is simple, give all animals a very wide berth.

Malaria is a problem in Sri Lanka, especially in the Dry Zone, and it is essential to take precautions. Evidence of chloroquine-resistant mosquitoes exists, so make sure your doctor has the latest information. The current favourite is a combination of both daily (proguanil) and weekly (chloroquine) pills. Treatment must start well before you set out for Sri Lanka and continue for the specified period after leaving the country. This is fine for a short visit but, taken over a long period, this combination can leave many people feeling nauseous (and losing their hair). The weekly drug gives a reasonable degree of protection on its own, and some people accept the risk of taking just that. The nausea is avoided by taking it shortly before going to bed. A new drug which was supposed to deal with chloroquine-resistant mosquitoes, mefloquine or Lariam, has proved to have very unpleasant side effects on some people.

Basic precautions include covering up as dusk approaches. Loose fitting light coloured clothing is the most effective, bearing in mind that mosquitoes can bite through loosely woven fabrics. Apply insect repellent to exposed areas and burn a mosquito coil under the table. Sleep under a mosquito net if it is provided or burn a coil under the bed.

Gastric problems. Follow carefully the advice in the food and drink section, and you stand an excellent chance of having no health problems at all. It has to be admitted, however, that an attack of diarrhoea is not unknown in Sri Lanka. This can strike simply because the bacteria in your stomach and intestines which aid digestion are unused to the bacteria in the local food. There is nothing wrong with the food, it is just different.

For a simple attack of diarrhoea the first and most important thing is to go on a very strict diet. Fat in any form (including milk) is completely out, and so are fruit juices, fresh fruit and vegetables, cold drinks, and ice cream. All the things, in fact, which you might expect to soothe a troubled tum. Take two Lomotil every four hours and, if you can, stick to plain boiled rice and curd (sets like concrete), and drink hot black tea (sugar is okay). If this has not worked after three days at most, or if you are passing blood, go to a doctor and have tests done. Sri Lankan doctors are mostly very competent, they know the local bugs and how to deal with them.

The alternative is a bit naughty, because you are supposed to take antibiotics as a full course, but useful when you are on the move. Carry with you Flagyl or Oxy-tetracycline, which can be bought at a pharmacy without a prescription. Take one pill at the first sign of trouble, perhaps one more later, and hope for the best. I have found this method effective, and it has been mentioned in a book written by a doctor.

Severe diarrhoea, at its extreme in cholera, is a killer because of dehydration. If you are unable to keep down the necessary liquids it is worth knowing that a small amount of opium can save your life by stopping dehydration. It does not however, kill the bugs which are causing the trouble. This is strictly for emergencies.

AIDS. AIDS is a serious problem in Sri Lanka. It is largely associated with prostitution, both hetero and homosexual, in the tourist areas. Take all the usual precautions.

MEDICAL TREATMENT

As noted above Sri Lankan doctors are mostly well trained and understand their local bugs. Many have their own laboratories for doing tests.

Free medical care and hospitals are available but, away from the big cities, expect conditions to be extremely basic. Hotels and tourist offices are the best sources of information. You must have medical insurance to cover private treatment and repatriation, and expect to pay for drugs and treatment as you go along.

Dental care is extremely poor; in an emergency head for Colombo and get advice from your high commission or consulate.

Pharmacies. All but the smallest towns have well stocked pharmacies which provide sound advice on what to take. Your hotel or a doctor will advise which are open late or on Sundays. Most drugs are very cheap and sold without a prescription. If drugs appear not to work as quickly as they should try the same thing from a different source or an alternative; adulterated and counterfeit drugs are not unknown.

EVERYDAY HEALTH

Cuts, grazes, and insect bites can easily become infected by dirt and flies. Apply a mild antiseptic cream and keep the area scrupulously clean until the skin is completely healed.

Women's health. Imported tampons can be found in city supermarkets, and these are the safest bet. You will not find them in the smaller places, and local ones are not necessarily safe. If in doubt bring your own. Check with your doctor before having inoculations during pregnancy.

Toilets. Unlike India toilets are mostly western style rather than the hole in the floor variety. They are usually reasonably clean. Toilet paper, not always provided, is readily available in shops. Public toilets are uncommon. In desperation try a hotel, restaurant, or offices.

INSURANCE

It is absolutely essential that, before you leave home, you take out insurance to cover medical expenses, repatriation, and baggage and belongings. Arrange insurance when, though not necessarily where, you buy your air tickets or contact The Travel Insurance Club Ltd (see p41) for information on their packages. Cheap tickets are usually non-refundable, and the insurance should cover you against an emergency which prevents you travelling.

Crime and Safety

Sri Lanka is a safe country for the foreign visitor. Take simple precautions and you can reduce the risk of trouble almost to zero.

The black market. There is no black market to speak off in any commodity. Unofficial money changers are thus inevitably out to do you one way or another.

Crime against visitors. Little, if any, crime is aimed specifically at foreigners.

Take care at busy train and bus stations where the main target is hand baggage which is most likely to contain cameras, passports, and travellers' cheques. Beware, if your companion has gone for tea or whatever, of someone rushing up saying they need help. It's probably just a ruse to separate you from your baggage.

Far more of a risk is being swindled. It is very difficult when a personable young man professes friendship or an interest in what you are doing. Is he genuine, or is he out to cheat you? A common trick at the moment is for someone to approach you in the street saying that he works at the hotel where you are staying and just happened to recognise you. Bearing in mind how reserved well brought up Sri Lankans are this approach is unlikely to be altruistic. The best bet is to get rid of him as quickly as reasonable politeness permits. If you do get drawn into conversation watch for the slightest hint of any kind of financial transaction, including donations to orphanages and so on. You have a con-man on your hands. Paradoxically, older people find it easier to spot and brush off these pests than do the streetwise young.

Finally, do not hand over money to anybody until you are quite convinced that you have got what you are paying for.

How to avoid robbery. You've probably heard all sorts of horror stories about cunning oriental thieves, but theft is not really a major problem in Sri Lanka. Hardly a person who has been robbed has anyone but his or herself to blame. Mostly it is the result of stupidity or sheer carelessness. Wherever in the world you are, most thieves are opportunist rather than professionals; they are easily deterred, and if you make things at all hard for them they will go and pick on someone else.

Your most important belongings are your passport and travellers' cheques. There is only one place for these and that is next to your body. Money belts are useless outside clothing and very uncomfortable under it. The best thing is a purse hung round the neck and worn under the shirt. This should be unobtrusive and carry the valuables on the front of your body. Never use a belt pouch or bum bag.

Have a button-down pocket in your shirt or the front of your trousers in which to carry only the amount of cash (say Rs1000) you need for the day. It is bad security, not to mention unkind, to flash a large wad of notes in front of people who have to live on very little. Keep the rest of your cash in the purse or money belt.

Take a padlock and chain with you. They will secure your baggage on a bus or train, and the lock will close your hotel room more securely than the one supplied by the hotel. When you have to put your pack in the luggage compartment of a bus (don't if you can help it) take all your valuables into the bus with you. Standing on a bus or in a crowded place put your bag on the floor between your feet, that way no-one can delve into it or slice it open. The scrum to board a bus or train is a favourite place for pick-pockets.

Be very wary of letting anybody handle your watch or camera. Do not leave your camera or other valuables in a hotel room; if you don't want to take them with you, have them locked in the hotel safe and obtain a receipt. Check carefully when you get the things back, especially whether any travellers' cheques have gone from the back of the book, and even more so if they have kept you waiting till the last minute.

Violence. Reading the Sri Lankan newspapers you realize that there is quite a lot of violence in the country. Mostly it stems from political rivalry and turf wars. It is said that the price of having someone killed is as little as Rs5000 (£50). The risk of violence to foreigners is minute.

Police. Despite this the police do not have a very high profile in Sri Lanka. They are helpful to foreigners reporting theft, but the wheels of the law grind slowly.

In the event of any incident you must get the police to make a written record. In the case of theft you will need a copy of this for any insurance claim or to replace your passport or travellers' cheques. You will not get far with this process unless you can quote the serial numbers of your passport, travellers' cheques, camera, and so on. Sri Lankan police are not unused used to fraudulent reports of theft, and you can expect a certain amount of polite scepticism. In serious cases, a road traffic fatality or threat of arrest for instance, contact your embassy or high commission without delay. Do not expect them to be pleased to hear from you.

Drugs are illegal, it's as simple as that. They are, of course, readily available, but the police are really tough on possession and use, and you can expect no concessions because you are a foreigner. Nor should you assume that you can buy your way out of trouble.

Photography. Do not take photographs of anything, including public buildings with armed guards, bridges, or dams which may in any way be considered to be a potential terrorist target. You risk having your film and camera confiscated, and being locked up. Do not take photos of people posed with Buddha images, and ask before photographing monks.

Help and Information

Children. Apart from the obvious problems with food and dehydration children cope well with Sri Lanka. You will find that children open many social contacts — and get spoiled rotten. Western childcare products are stocked by supermarkets in the *main* towns.

Travellers with disabilities. Sri Lanka is not a good country for disabled travellers. People are friendly and helpful, but amenities are virtually non-existent. Blind or partially sighted travellers will find the streets difficult, and there is little or no provision for wheelchairs.

Electrical equipment. Supply is nominally 240volt 50Hz and pretty reliable. Power points in older properties are the old English round pin style. These are mostly 5amp three pin with earth or two pin without. Adaptors for the English three square pin plug are readily available in electrical shops and street markets and cost as little as Rs50. Square pin sockets are installed in some newer properties.

Youth and student concessions. Entry to certain sites, notably the Cultural

76 Practical Information

Triangle, is half-price with an International Student Card, a very worthwhile reduction.

Time. Time in Sri Lanka is nominally $5\frac{1}{2}$ hours ahead of GMT, as in India. In the winter, however, it is 6 hours ahead, as a form of daylight saving. Temple clocks are not altered from the usual $5\frac{1}{2}$ hours. In addition to this there is what the locals call 'Sri Lanka Time', an elastic concept running anything up to two hours behind the clock.

Weights and measures. The metric system is in universal use.

THE INTERNET

The *Explore Sri Lanka* magazine is at http://www.exploresrilanka.com. *Lanka Internet* provides information at http://www.lanka.net. The *Daily News* (newspaper) is at http://www.lanka.net/lakehouse. and the *Sunday Times* (of Sri Lanka) at http://www.is.lk/is.

The **Cyber Café**, 211 Union Place, Colombo 2 (Tel01-334 723) will fix you up with an e-mail address for your stay in Sri Lanka, and is available at http://www.cybercafe.ens.lk.

TOURIST INFORMATION

Sri Lanka has put a lot of effort into developing tourism, but the accent has always been on package tours. The independent traveller can find it hard to get the specific and detailed information he needs.

Tourist offices abroad. The Ceylon Tourist Board (they still use the old name) maintains tourist offices in major cities around the world, and these can provide most mainstream information.

Britain	22 Lower Regent Street, London SW1Y 4QD Tel 0171-930 2627 Fax 0171-930 9070
Ireland	59 Ranelagh Road, Dublin 6 Tel 65345 Fax 68043
USA	Tourist enquiries are handled by the Sri Lankan Embassy 2148 Wyoming Ave. NW, Washington DC 20008 Tel 202 483 4026 Fax 202 483 8017
Canada	1920-925 W Georgia Street, Vancouver V6C 312 Tel 662 7708 Fax 662 7769
Australia	39 Wintercorn Row, Werrington Downs, NSW 2747 Tel 4730 3194 Fax 4729 2327
India	D19 Defence Colony, New Delhi 110024 Tel 460 3124 Fax 460 3123
Thailand	5/105-6/105 Soi Rattanaprahm 2, Sukhumvit Soi 54/2, Bangkok 10250 Tel 332 9075 Fax 332 9076

Tourist offices in Sri Lanka. The head office of the Ceylon Tourist Board is at 78 Steuart Place, Galle Road, Colombo 3 (Tel 01-437 059 Fax 01-437 953);

access is from Galle Road between the Galle Face Hotel and the British High Commission. Other offices are at the airport, in Kandy, Negombo, and Bentota.

Tourist handouts tend to be a bit short on hard facts. The *Accommodation Guide* (Rs50) can be useful.

EMBASSIES, HIGH COMMISSIONS & CONSULATES IN SRI LANKA

Britain   British High Commission
190 Galle Road, Colombo 3
Tel 01-437 336

USA   Embassy of the United States of America
210 Galle Road, Colombo 3
Tel 01-448 007

Canada   High Commission of Canada
6 Gregory's Road, PO Box 1006, Colombo 7
Tel 01-695 841

Australia   High Commission of Australia
3 Cambridge Place, PO Box 742, Colombo 7
Tel 01-698 767

India   High Commission of India
36-38 Galle Road, Colombo 3
Tel 01-421 605
(Also an outpost in Kandy which can be a better place to renew an Indian visa)

Indonesia   Embassy of the Republic of Indonesia
1 Police Park Terrace, Colombo 5
Tel 01-580 113

Malaysia   High Commission of Malaysia
92 Kynsey Road, Colombo 7
Tel 01-686 090

Maldives   High Commission of the Republic of Maldives
25 Melbourne Avenue, Colombo 4
Tel 01-586 762

Myanmar (Burma)   Embassy of the Union of Myanmar
65 Ward Place, Colombo 7
Tel 01-696 672

Nepal   Royal Embassy of Nepal
153 Kynsey Road, Colombo 8
Tel 01-689 656

Thailand   Royal Thai Embassy
43 Dr CWW Kannangara MW, Colombo 7
Tel 01-697 406

Sri Lankan High Commissions and embassies abroad are listed on p42.

Colombo

Mask Dancers

Colombo, the capital of Sri Lanka, is the point of arrival for all visitors. This pleasant colonial city was a port and administrative centre for both the Portuguese and the Dutch, but achieved capital status only with the arrival of the British at the end of the 18th century. Even so it was only with the construction of the new harbour at the end of the 19th century that it overtook Galle as the country's main port and became one of the great entrepots of the East.

Colombo began life as the fishing village of Kalamba. Nearby were the religious centre of Kelaniya and the town of Kotte which was the capital of the Sinhalese lowland kingdom from the 14th century to 1565. Colombo's flat site is the delta of the Kelani Ganga river. This may have been Ptolemy's Headland of Zeus, so named because the nearby Kelaniya temple had a huge idol of Vibushana, a fore-runner of Vishnu. Fa Hsien, a Chinese Buddhist pilgrim, tells that he disembarked at Kua Lang Pou at the start of his fourth century visit. Ibn Battuta (1304-1377) states that a Muslim community had been established here for six centuries before his visit.

History

Colombo was still little more than a fishing village when the Portuguese arrived in 1501. They were soon kicked out by Muslims from Calicut, but were back by 1518 and had built their first fort. During much of the Portuguese presence Kotte, on the outskirts of modern Colombo, remained the seat of the king of the lowland kingdom, but this territory passed to Portugal in 1597. The Dutch captured Colombo in 1656 after a siege of seven months. Their influence can be seen in the well laid out and tree lined streets of Hulftsdoorp and also the canals which drained the delta and reclaimed much of the land.

Colombo fell into British hands in 1796, and the way this happened is instructive. The previous year the ruling party in Holland had allied itself to France which then occupied their country. The Stadholder, the hereditary ruler of the United Provinces, fled to England and was persuaded to instruct the Dutch colonies to submit to English occupation rather than risk a French takeover. The latter possibility greatly worried the British as it would have allowed the French to tie up with their ally Tipu Sultan in Mysore. It was a condition of the British occupation that as long as it were peaceful the territory would revert to Holland after hostilities ended. Most of the Dutch in Ceylon were in favour of this arrangement. A faction of the East India Company in Madras, however, managed to provoke a token resistance and used this as the excuse to hold on to Ceylon for good.

Nor was this the limit of British connivance. By 1795 the defence of Ceylon was mostly in the hands of Swiss and German mercenaries raised by the Swiss Count de Meuron, and under the command of his brother Pierre. The *Vereenigde Oost-Indische Compagnie* (the Dutch East India Company or VOC) was more or less bankrupt at the time and neglected to pay the Count for their services. He was suborned by Hugh Cleghorn, an academic of St. Andrews University, and one of Britain's most successful spies. The foreign troops marched out of Colombo, which had been holding out against the British, without firing a shot. The de Meuron brothers became generals in the British army before retiring to Switzerland, and their mercenaries fought on with the East India Company, many dying in the taking of Seringapatam from Tipu Sultan in 1799.

In the days of the British Empire Colombo had the nickname 'Charing Cross of the East', an indication of its position on the crossroads of eastern commerce and communications. Even these days, looking out to sea from Galle, the horizon is rarely free of shipping.

The population of somewhere between one and two million, depending on what you regard as Colombo, includes every ethnic and religious group in Sri Lanka.

Colombo is a pleasant city and, by Asian standards, quiet, relaxed, and organised. There is, however, less of interest for the foreign visitor than in most capital cities.

Fort

The Fort area of Colombo was the nucleus of the european city, fortified in turn by the Portuguese, Dutch, and British. As in Bombay (and many other cities around the world)

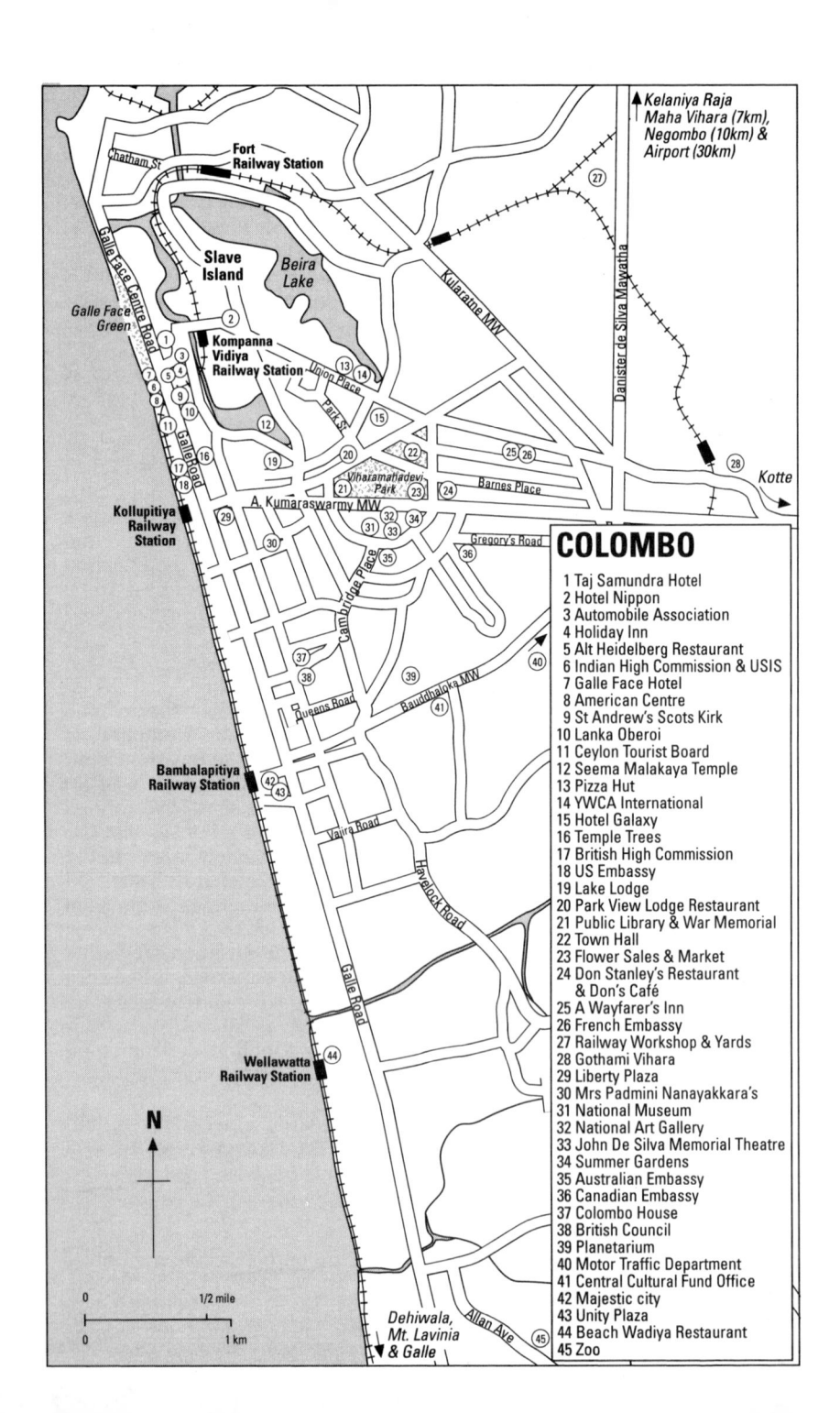

COLOMBO

1. Taj Samundra Hotel
2. Hotel Nippon
3. Automobile Association
4. Holiday Inn
5. Alt Heidelberg Restaurant
6. Indian High Commission & USIS
7. Galle Face Hotel
8. American Centre
9. St Andrew's Scots Kirk
10. Lanka Oberoi
11. Ceylon Tourist Board
12. Seema Malakaya Temple
13. Pizza Hut
14. YWCA International
15. Hotel Galaxy
16. Temple Trees
17. British High Commission
18. US Embassy
19. Lake Lodge
20. Park View Lodge Restaurant
21. Public Library & War Memorial
22. Town Hall
23. Flower Sales & Market
24. Don Stanley's Restaurant & Don's Café
25. A Wayfarer's Inn
26. French Embassy
27. Railway Workshop & Yards
28. Gothami Vihara
29. Liberty Plaza
30. Mrs Padmini Nanayakkara's
31. National Museum
32. National Art Gallery
33. John De Silva Memorial Theatre
34. Summer Gardens
35. Australian Embassy
36. Canadian Embassy
37. Colombo House
38. British Council
39. Planetarium
40. Motor Traffic Department
41. Central Cultural Fund Office
42. Majestic city
43. Unity Plaza
44. Beach Wadiya Restaurant
45. Zoo

increasing commercial activity in the second half of the 19th century saw the demolition of the walls. The boundaries of the walled city were Queen Street (now Janadipathi Mawatha), Chatham Street, named after William Pitt the Younger who was prime minister when Ceylon was seized, the harbour front, and the canal. Although new tower blocks are evident most of the fine old commercial buildings, notably the Chartered Bank, maintain the atmosphere of this historical area.

Fort was the main upmarket **shopping area** before the development of new centres along Galle Road. The two old department stores of Miller's and Cargill's on York Street are real throwbacks, and the arcades outside them shelter a lively street market. Laksala, the government emporium, is on the same street (see *Shopping* p87). Despite the heat this is a pleasant place to wander around.

The best traditional landmark in Fort is the **Clock Tower** which was built in 1857 and had the lighthouse added ten years later. The lighthouse has been supplanted by the new one on Marine Drive.

The **President's House** was built late in the 18th century by Van Angelbeek, the last Dutch governor, just in time for the British to take it over. It was known initially as King's House, changed to Queen's House when Victoria took the throne, and remained the residence of the British governor up to the time of independence in 1948. Its official title now is Janadhipathi Mandiraya, but the guards still wear the traditional red tunics and black trousers. The statue in front of the house is of Sir Edward Barnes (governor 1824-1831), the builder of the road from Colombo to Kandy. Appropriately enough all distances in Sri Lanka are measured from this point.

Facing President's House is the rather fine **General Post Office** which has a philatelic sales counter and stamp exhibition.

The **Grand Oriental Hotel**, known for a time as the Taprobane Hotel, overlooks the whole harbour area. The **splendid view*** from its Harbour Room restaurant-bar will cost you Rs48 for tea or Rs156 for a beer (both prices inclusive). Photography is banned.

Past the Grand Oriental the whole harbour and seaward side of Fort is a security area. You can visit the Church of St. Peter without trouble, but getting further depends on charm and luck. The **Garrison Church of St. Peter** is now the Mission to Seamen. The barn-like nave was converted from part of the old residence of the Dutch governors in 1804, and consecrated later in 1821. There are interesting monuments, but the church is poorly kept and rather depressing. The church plate was presented by George III.

In **Gordon Gardens**, next to the President's House, is one of the few reminders of Colombo as a fortified city. The Portuguese gate is dated 1518 and bears the arms of the king of Portugal. A padrao, a huge rock carved with a cross, coat of arms and the date 1501, is even earlier evidence of the Portuguese presence, a kind of 'De Silva was here'. The gardens were laid out in 1887 to mark the Golden Jubilee of Queen Victoria, and her statue still stands there.

The **Buddha Jayanthi Dagoba** was built in 1956 to mark the 2500th anniversary of Buddha's death. Raised above street level on arched pillars, it was paid for entirely by public donations.

Off Marine Drive are the **new lighthouse** and seawater Governor's Bath **swimming pool**.

COLOMBO FORT & THE PETTAH

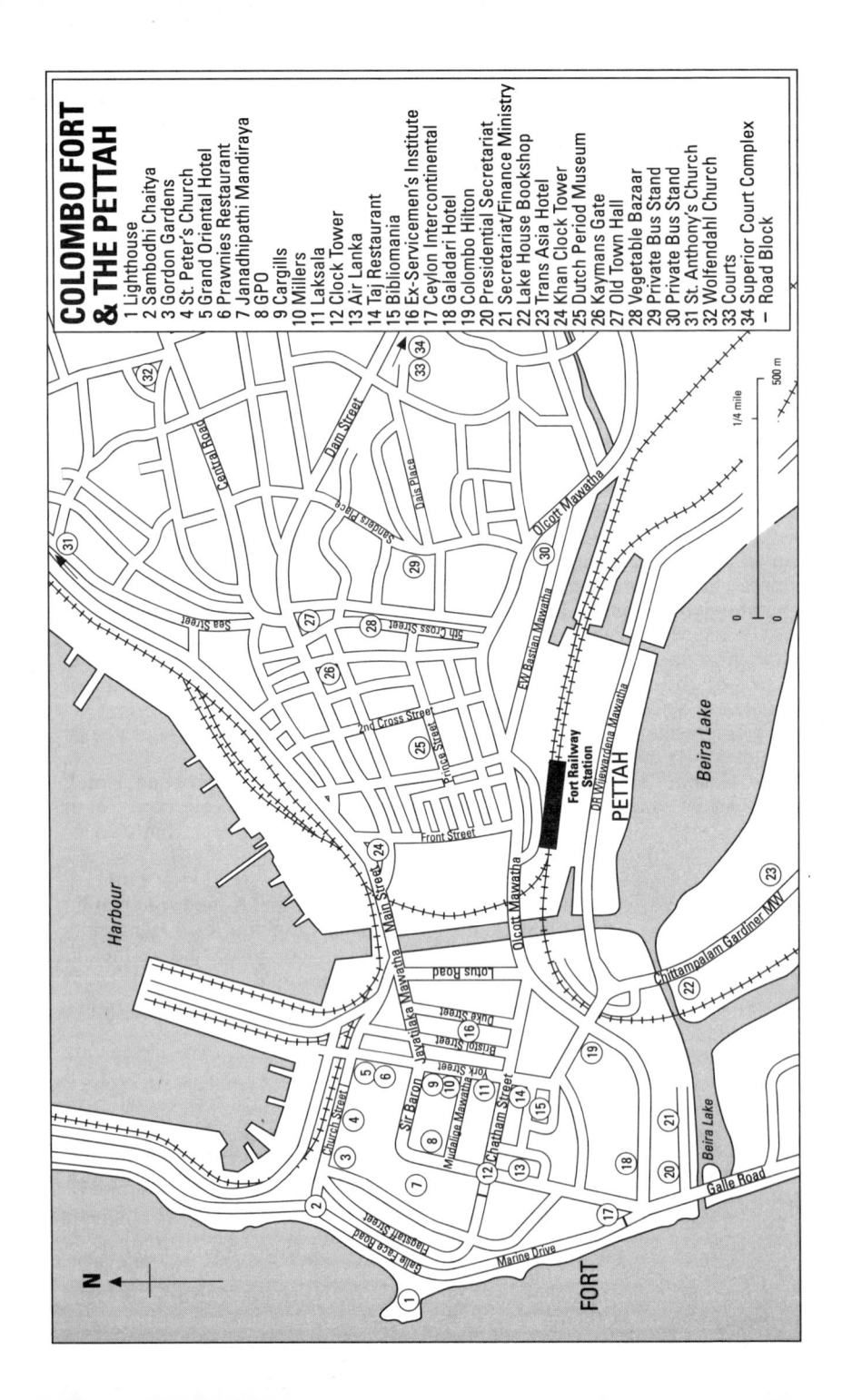

1. Lighthouse
2. Sambodhi Chaitya
3. Gordon Gardens
4. St. Peter's Church
5. Grand Oriental Hotel
6. Prawnies Restaurant
7. Janadhipathi Mandiraya
8. GPO
9. Cargills
10. Millers
11. Laksala
12. Clock Tower
13. Air Lanka
14. Taj Restaurant
15. Bibliomania
16. Ex-Servicemen's Institute
17. Ceylon Intercontinental
18. Galadari Hotel
19. Colombo Hilton
20. Presidential Secretariat
21. Secretariat/Finance Ministry
22. Lake House Bookshop
23. Trans Asia Hotel
24. Khan Clock Tower
25. Dutch Period Museum
26. Kaymans Gate
27. Old Town Hall
28. Vegetable Bazaar
29. Private Bus Stand
30. Private Bus Stand
31. St. Anthony's Church
32. Wolfendahl Church
33. Courts
34. Superior Court Complex
— Road Block

The Pettah

Pettah takes its name from the settlement which grew up outside the Fort, pettai being Tamil for village, though this was at first a Dutch area.

Outside Fort station (which is in Pettah rather than Fort) is a statue of Henry Steel Olcott, the American Buddhist evangelist. On the far side of the tracks from the main station buildings a narrow gauge Hunslet loco is on display.

Enter the Pettah by crossing from Fort station to Front Street, and then turn right into Prince Street. Here in Pettah you are conscious for the first time of being in the Far East in a way that you are not elsewhere in Colombo. This is a real oriental bazaar, no tourist tat, just everything you could think of from fish (dried) to chips (silicon). No-one will hassle you, so take your time and soak up the atmosphere. The only drawbacks are the heat and the shambolic traffic.

The **Dutch Period Museum**** on Prince Street (0900-1700, closed Friday) occupies the Old Post Office, a fine colonnaded Dutch building dated 1780. This was restored with help from The Netherlands in 1980. The displays are informative, and there is a good collection of period furniture. The most interesting thing is the building itself, and its garden, which give you some idea of what life was like in the tropics in the days before electricity and other mod cons.

Continuing up Prince's Street you come to a colourful vegetable bazaar on Fifth Cross Street where you turn left to the **Old Town Hall**. This was used until 1928 when the seat of local government moved to the new building facing Vihara Mahadevi Park. Adjoining this is a cast iron framed market hall which became a municipal museum in 1984. Exhibits include a steam roller, steam lorry, and sundry other steam engines and turbines. The original memorial from Galle Face Green is also here. Upstairs in the Town Hall waxworks in the council chamber re-enact a meeting of 1909.

Kayman's Gate° is a misnomer, as there never has been a gate here. Some say the structure is the belfry of the Portuguese church of Sao Francis in Kotte moved here by the Dutch, others that only the bell came from there. In Dutch kayman means just that, cayman, and probably refers to the crocodiles in the Fort moat.

From here you can visit the jewellery bazaar on Sea Street, the ayurvedic market on Gabo's Lane, and the fish market on St. John's Road. When you've had enough of this take a three-wheeler to Wolfendahl Church (see below).

The harbour and churches

Before the British takeover Galle had been the most important port in Ceylon. Better communications with Kandy saw the emphasis switch to Colombo, especially as Galle could not take larger steamers. This was also the incentive to improve Colombo harbour.

The breakwaters, which enclose a harbour of 2.5sq km, were built over a period of time. The longest, which connects with the Fort, is 1288m/1404yds long and was completed in 1885. The pilot station is at the end. The other two breakwaters were completed in the first decade of the 20th century. The port handles 3000 ships annually and is a major transhipment base. Outside the main harbour to the north is the fishing harbour where the population is mainly Catholic. The whole harbour area is closed, and the only way of seeing it is from the Grand Oriental Hotel (see above).

St. Anthony's Church, on the harbour front, attracts people of all religions. They come to pray, mainly on Tuesdays, to a statue of St. Anthony which is said to work miracles in solving family problems.

The **Wolfendahl Church*** was built by the Dutch governor in 1749. His name was not, as you might have suspected, Wolfendahl but Stein van Collenesse. So why call it Wolf Valley in a place as flat as a pancake and which has never had any wolves? Well, the Portuguese church it replaced was dedicated to the Virgin of Guadalupe. Guadalupe is a town in southern Spain whose name is a mixture of Arabic (the guada bit comes from wadi) and Spanish meaning, of course, valley of the wolves. Whether this shows a subtle Dutch sense of humour or plain unimaginativeness is open to conjecture.

The church is cavernous on a cruciform plan. As plain as you would expect of a Dutch Reformed Church, it is brightened by a few Dutch memorials painted on wood. The floor consists of finely carved tombstones. The graves of Dutch governors were moved here from Gordon Gardens in 1813.

The **Cathedral of Santa Lucia** was built between 1876 and 1910, its huge nave seating six thousand. The **Paramananda Purana Viharaya** nearby was built in 1806 and has murals of Buddha's life and the history of Buddhism in Sri Lanka. The **Supreme Court** buildings in Kandyan style were paid for by that champion of law and order China. The old neoclassical court buildings are nearby.

Galle Face and Slave Island

The brown stone neoclassical buildings at the north end of Galle Face Green were built for Ceylon's assembly during British rule. Later the seat of the independent parliament, it was relegated to the **Government Secretariat** when parliament moved to its new home in Kotte. Statues of heroes of the campaign for independence stand in front.

Galle Face Green was preserved as an open space in the same way as the maidans of Calcutta and Bombay. It has seen many different activities over the years including a parade ground for British troops and, before a new one was made south of Victoria Park, Colombo's race course. The man to thank for this space is Sir Henry Ward (Governor 1855-1860), and a memorial to him stands on the promenade. When the railway to the south was being built it was planned to run it down the coast the whole way. A public outcry saw it routed over Slave Island, joining the coast well south of Galle Face. The sea promenade is a popular place for an evening stroll, and the food and drink stalls make for a lively scene. Watch out for pickpockets.

The southern end of the Green is marked by the charming and historic **Galle Face Hotel***, its verandah a pleasant place for a cold beer and a snack. Some of Colombo's renowned kite flyers will probably be in action opposite the hotel. A short distance down Galle Road, on the opposite side is St. Andrew's Church, the **Scots Kirk**, built in 1842. A block further down is **Temple Trees**, the Prime minister's official residence, and marked by heavy security.

Beira Lake, the two parts of which cover 85ha, flows into the sea just south of the Secretariat. The name may come from the Portuguese *ribiera*, a beach or lake (and just like the French riviera), or the Arabic *bahira* a little sea. The lake played a part in the inland waterway system, being linked to the Kelani River by the San Sebastian Canal. The land between the two sheets of water was known as Slave Island because before abolition in 1845 slaves were kept there overnight. No need for guards, the lake was full of crocodiles. The Portuguese had introduced slaves from south-western Africa, and they were taken over by the Dutch who used them to build the Fort. The Dutch started to use the island, which they called Kaffir Veldt, to house the slaves after an insurrection in the 18th century.

The **Sri Shiva Subramania Swami Kovil** (Hindu) and the **Military Mosque** (Muslim) were built for soldiers of the British Indian Army which had an important base on the island. Standing out in the southern part of the lake is the **Seema Malakaya**, a Buddhist temple.

Modern Colombo

Vihara Mahadevi Park** (0600-1800 every day) (formerly **Victoria Park**) is named after the mother of Dutthagamani, king of Sri Lanka in the second century BC. This is beautifully kept and has a fine selection of flowering trees and plants. In the trees by the pond are many large bats and, on the banks of the pond, touch-me-not, a feathery little plant which curls up when touched.

In the corner by the Public Library a few elephants are kept and bathed twice a day. Preceding February full moon (and hence the *Perahera*, Colombo's main Buddhist procession and festival) the numbers can rise to 150. Some of these elephants walk down from Kandy, the journey taking them six days. Some of the old 2ft 6in gauge track from the Kelani Valley Railway has been installed in the park and trains are pulled by a Hunslet P1 diesel. The **Public Library** (0800-1845, closed Wednesday) offers a visitor's ticket for reading only at Rs2 per day.

The **New Town Hall** was opened in 1928, administration being transferred from the previous Town Hall on a cramped and noisy site in Pettah. The domed white neoclassical building would not look out of place in an American state capital.

The park occupies part of the site of the old Cinnamon Gardens. In the quiet streets around, still called Cinnamon Gardens, or more prosaically Colombo 7, are the fine houses where the big nobs hang out.

On the south side of the park is the **National Art Gallery** (open daily 0800-1700 except Poya days). This has a moderately interesting permanent display, and shows the annual exhibition in April. Behind it is the **John De Silva Theatre**, and alongside the **Mahaweli Centre** which houses the Royal Asiatic Society Library. The **Serendib Gallery** is a good commercial gallery.

Keen **gardeners** used to the Sunday pilgrimage to the local garden centre can check the corner of Ananda Coomaraswamy MW and Kannangara MW where a sale of exotic plants is often held on Sundays.

Curving to the south of the park is Albert Crescent. The **National Museum*** (Rs55; closed Friday, Saturday, and holidays; no photography) is housed in a fine building opened in 1877 by Sir William Gregory, whose statue stands in front, resplendent in court dress and muttonchop whiskers. He was governor of Ceylon 1872-77, and also built the lake in Nuwara Eliya. The entrance hall is dominated by a large granite Buddha from the Toluvila at Anuradhapura.

Nearby are fine bronzes brought from southern India including Shiva Nataraja, the cosmic dancer surrounded by flames. Reminders of Sri Lanka's position at the crossroads of eastern trade include Chinese export china (look for the VOC emblem of the Dutch East India Company) and coins dating back to the Roman era. The Romans in fact had a trading post near Pondicherry in South India. Pride of place goes to the gold throne of the last King of Kandy which spent 120 years in Windsor Castle before being returned here in the 1930s at the behest of King George V. The throne is inlaid with jewels and topped by large crystals. In the centre is a sun with a very Rajput looking face. Other regalia was returned during the brief reign of Edward VIII. The oddest exhibit is a German sea mine swept in the Second World War and neatly displayed on a table like an altar presumably because of its resemblance to a dagoba. On the stairs is a fine display of masks, the gruesome ones used in devil dancing to cast out the spirits causing illness. The jollier ones belong to kolam dancing, a form of entertainment, and include some of policemen showing how this art form was kept up to date.

The **Natural History Museum** (Rs35, closed Friday, Saturday, and holidays) is behind the National Museum, and this is the only access to it. This has its quota of stuffed animals and birds, but is of interest for the information on Sri Lanka's cash crops and the unpleasant bugs that attack them. A large model explains the working of the Mahaveli River hydro-power and irrigation scheme.

The **Lionel Wendt Art Centre** stages exhibitions of contemporary arts and crafts.

The **Gotami Vihara** Buddhist temple at Borella (2.5km from the Town Hall, take a three-wheeler) has murals on the life of Buddha done by George Keyt, a modern Sri Lankan artist of repute. You can usually see some of his work at the Serendib Gallery.

Further Afield

KELANIYA

This suburb, 18km from the centre, houses the most important Buddhist temple near Colombo. In pre-Buddhist times a great temple to Vibushana stood here, but Buddha himself is said to have visited, bathed in the Kelani River, and converted the local people.

The Rajah Maha Vihara (the Rajah in the name indicates that it was founded by a king) stands on the foundations of the temple destroyed under Portuguese rule. The temple has remarkable modern murals by Soliyas Mendis. The ancient dagoba was first built by King Yatalatissa in third century BC and is said to contain a jewelled throne of the Buddha. The Duruthu Perahera here at the time of the January full moon is second only to Kandy.

Sri Jayawardenepura-Kotte

The ancient capital of Kotte, which was almost completely destroyed by the Portuguese, has a new lease of life as the country's capital. The imposing new **Parliament Building** was designed by Geoffrey Bawa (brother of Bevis Bawa, see p102) and stands in an artificial lake. The name comes from J.R. Jayawardene, prime minister 1977-78, and president 1978-88 after he had altered the constitution to concentrate power in the president's hands.

The **Zoo** is at Dehiwala south of Colombo and, apparently, not bad. This is 9km from Fort; by public transport take a train to Dehiwala station or any bus down Galle Road to Hill Street, then bus 118 or a three-wheeler for the remaining kilometre.

Before it was engulfed by Colombo's southward expansion **Mount Lavinia** was a fashionable watering hole. Sir Edward Barnes (governor 1824-31) built one of his extravagant country houses here. Like his house in Nuwara Eliya this is now a rather splendid hotel, the Mount Lavinia. The beach and water are none too clean, but you can use the hotel pool for Rs200. The name is apparently a corruption of Lithiniya-kanda or Seagull Rock. This is 11km South from Fort.

Fort. The Laksala government emporium on York Street has just about everything that Sri Lanka produces at fixed prices. Cargills and Millers department stores, also on York Street, may reward a quick look, and the street markets are fun. Cigar smokers can investigate The Cigar Shop, Lobby Level, Colombo Hilton.

Pettah. The World Market is a lively little bazaar between Fort station and Fort itself, selling clothing, leather goods and so on. The markets in the Pettah are fascinating, but not really productive for souvenir shopping.

Down Galle Road. For anything other than souvenirs Galle Road has taken over from Fort as the shopping centre for trendy Colombo residents. Liberty Plaza on RS De Mel MW is an air-conditioned shopping complex ten minutes walk from Kollupitiya station. 2km further down Galle Road is the air-conditioned Majestic City, an immaculate large shopping centre with a supermarket, tea centre, and many shops selling export clothing, shoes, household goods, and so on. Stalls in the basement food mall sell meals of many different cuisines, and behind it is a Kentucky Fried Chicken. These places are a short walk straight uphill from Bambalapitiya railway station. This is roughly 4km from Fort; Rs100 by three-wheeler or Rs80 from Colombo 7.

Some fine porcelain is made in Sri Lanka with Japanese collaboration. Dankotuwa Porcelain, 283 Galle Road, Colombo 3, and Noritake at Lanka Ceramic Showroom, 696 Galle Road, Colombo 3.

Many shops sell export clothing at a fraction of the prices in the west. You will find Marks & Sparks at the London Shop, 252 Galle Road. Van Heusen is not far away, and the Natural Silk Centre is at 349 Galle Road.

The Oasis Company, 18 Station Road (just down from Majestic City) sells handloom fabrics, as does Barefoot at 704 Galle Road.

Colombo 7. Odel, 5 Alexandra Place, De Soysa (Lipton) Circus has a huge range of export clothing and a coffee shop with home-made cakes. This is their main shop, they also have a smaller branch in Majestic City. The other side of the Town Hall, on Dharmapala MW, Paradise Road has high quality household goods, antiques, and so on.

Bookshops. The very good Vijitha Yapa bookshop is in Unity Plaza, just opposite Majestic City on Galle Road. They sell British and American newspapers and magazines, and have another branch further up Galle Road. Lake House bookshop, 100 Chittampalam Gardiner MW is also good. The Cultural Triangle office at the Ministry of Cultural Affairs, 212 Bauddhaloka

MW, Colombo 7 sells cheap handbooks for many of the monuments (Rs40-150) and some well produced coffee table books on historical Sri Lankan paintings (around Rs3000). This road is closed for security reasons, if your car or rickshaw is denied entry the walk is only 100m or so.

Second-hand bookstalls on DJ Wijewardena MW at its junction with TB Jayah MW (near Maradana station). Try also Bibliomania, 32 Hospital Street in Fort.

Art galleries. Chamathkar, 35c Vijaya Kumaratunge MW, Colombo 5 displays and sells work by leading contemporary Sri Lankan artists. Serendib Gallery, 36 1/1 Rosmead Place, Colombo 7 has antiques, old and contemporary paintings, and specialises in old maps.

Gems and jewellery. Sri Lanka is a major producer of gemstones including rubies, sapphires and topaz, you can find more information in the section on Ratnapura (p183). Laksala is reliable. The Sri Lanka Gem and Jewellery Exchange is at 310 Galle Road. Other reputable firms are nearby, and the State Gem Corporation has a testing lab above the Gem Exchange. Beware of touts who try to take you to other places.

Entertainment

Colombo, and Sri Lanka as whole, is not really geared up for nightlife. The five star hotels in Colombo do have discos though these cater mainly for the affluent end of the local market, some actually have a members only rule. There are numerous casinos in Colombo, for example MGM Grand Club, 772 Galle Road, Colombo 4 (Tel 591 711), minimum stakes are Rs50 for roulette and Rs200 for blackjack; other places (which advertise in *Travel Lanka*) may have much higher stakes, check before going.

Tower Hall Theatre (Tel 687 993 for information) does a Sinhalese play the last Saturday of every month. Lionel Wendt Theatre (Tel 695 794) is another possibility. Live music at the Saxophone Jazz Club, 46B Galle Road, Colombo 3. Local cinemas show some western films, check in the newspapers.

British Council, 49 Alfred House Gardens, Colombo 3 (Tel 580 301); the American Center, 44 Galle Road, Colombo 3 (Tel 421 271); Alliance Française, 11 Barnes Place, Colombo 7 (Tel 694 162); and German Cultural Institute, 39 Gregorys Road, Colombo 7 (Tel 694 562) all have libraries with newspapers and periodicals and stage regular cultural events, details in *Travel Lanka*.

Practical Information

Ceylon Tourist Board, 78 Steuart Place, Colombo 3. Tel 01-437 059 Fax 01-437 953. This is actually on Galle Road opposite the Lanka Oberoi Hotel. Open Monday-Friday 0830-1615 Saturday 0830-1230. General information on the whole island.

Railway Tourist Office at Fort Station (Tel 01-435 838) is actually a commercial undertaking, but very helpful. They have information on trains, hotels, and especially the Viceroy Special steam trains.

Travel Lanka and *Explore Sri Lanka* are free publications for the visitor, the latter in particular having some excellent informative articles. Available from the tourist office and better hotels. *The Linc* is another free sheet aimed mainly at the expatriate community but also containing useful information.

Cultural Triangle Office, Ministry of Cultural Affairs, 212 Bauddhaloka MW, Colombo 7, (Tel 01-587 912) sells Cultural Triangle passes and very reasonable handbooks to the historic sites.

Arjuna's A-Z Street Guide costs Rs350 and covers Colombo, Kandy, Nuwara Eliya, Anuradhapura, and Polonnaruwa. The *Colombo Handbook*, also Rs350, is full of information of more use to the long-term visitor. Both from Vijitha Yapa bookshops listed above.

Arrival and Departure

Virtually all visitors to Sri Lanka arrive at Colombo International Airport, which is at Katunayake 30km north of the city centre.

Arriving at Colombo Airport

Friends can meet you at the airport only if they can show a letter from you confirming the arrangement.

Passport control is reasonably quick and will give you an on the spot **visa** for thirty days. **Duty free** goods can be bought after you pass through passport control. They are not cheap and of minimal interest to foreigners arriving in Sri Lanka.

After baggage reclaim **Customs** procedure is simple, foreigners usually being allowed simply to walk straight through the Green Channel. Outside customs a variety of banks will **change money** for you. In the same area you can book a fixed rate **taxi** for where you intend to stay. There is usually quite a queue here, but you may find someone going to your area so that the cost of the taxi can be shared.

Leaving this hall and turning sharp right you find the Ceylon Tourist Board (CTB) desk. They provide **tourist information**, will **book a hotel**, and arrange a fixed price **taxi**. Whilst this hotel may cost more than you plan to pay on the rest of your trip this is vastly preferable to traipsing around Colombo in the middle of the night trying to find somewhere a bit cheaper. Several major (i.e. expensive) hotels have desks which will make a room reservation for you and arrange transport. Always ask about the price of the latter, it is rarely complementary.

Transport into Colombo. Hardly in the budget travel league is the helicopter transfer to central Colombo. This can take twenty-six passengers and must be pre-booked. Nice to think about, especially when you have experienced the driving standards.

There is no airport bus service specifically for air passengers. Public buses pass by on the main road; turn left out of the terminal and walk 200m. A 187 will take you to the Bastian Mawatha bus-stand in Colombo for less than Rs10 and introduce you to the decidedly mixed pleasures of bus travel in Sri Lanka.

Trains are not a useful option, there being only two services a day from Airport Halt about 500m from the terminal building. Trains run more frequently along the main line, but the nearest station (IPZ1, short for Investment Promotional Zone One) is 2km/1mile from the terminal.

The best option is to book a taxi at one of the stalls mentioned above, the price into Colombo being around Rs900, well worth it for this long drive.

As in any other airport or public place keep a close eye on all your belongings. Theft is not unknown, and one is easily distracted when tired and flustered by the unfamiliar.

Leaving through Colombo Airport

For transport to the airport just reverse the above. If a friend gives you a lift you may well have to leave the vehicle in a car park some way from the terminal and take a shuttle bus the remaining distance.

Have Rs500 for the airport tax. Change any remaining rupees before you go through passport control; shops in the departure lounge are strictly hard currency only.

Trains and buses

The main railway station is Fort. The ticket windows are well organised and clearly labelled, and the queues orderly and fast moving. Refer to the regional sections for specific information on trains and reservations. There is a left-luggage office at the station. Some trains originate in Maradana, or pass through there, and, if you have no reservation, you have a much better chance of getting a seat there.

The main bus depots in Colombo are near Fort station. CTB buses operate from the north side of Olcott MW, private buses from Bastian MW. Both are a short walk from Fort station, and have information offices. Bus services are more frequent than the trains and often faster but, as a general rule, if there is a train to where you want to go, take that and not a bus.

Local transport

The most popular from of local transport is the scooter rickshaw, called here a three-wheeler or tuk-tuk. The drivers mostly have at least some English and know their way around well. All are unmetered, so agree a price before setting off. Fares are in the order of Rs80 from Fort station to Colombo 7 and pro rata, reckon about Rs20 per km. You will, of course, pay a bit more than the locals, but the bargaining is done with such good humour you can hardly complain.

Ordinary taxis are similarly unmetered. Radio cabs (GNTC Tel 688 688, Savoy Comfort 595 595, or Kangaroo 502 888) are a better bet, they have meters and the drivers use them, fare is Rs26 per km. Hotel taxis are far more expensive.

The buses are very crowded, route information in the *A-Z Street Guide* and, with three-wheeler prices so low, hardly worth considering.

Accommodation

(STD Code 01)

The modern five star hotels are in or near the Fort area and include:

Colombo Hilton, Lotus Road, Fort. Tel 544 644 Fax 544 657

Ceylon Intercontinental, 48 Janadipathi MW, Fort. Tel 421 221.

Galadari Hotel, 64 Lotus Road, Fort. Tel 544 544 Fax 449 875.

Trans-Asia Hotel, 115 Sir CA Gardiner MW, Colombo 2. Tel 544 200 Fax 449 184.

Taj Samudra Hotel, 25 Galle Face Centre Road, Colombo 3. Tel 446 622 Fax 446 348.

Holiday Inn, 30 Sir MM Markar MW, Colombo 3. Tel 422 001 Fax 447 977.

Lanka Oberoi, 77 Steuart Road (Galle Road), Colombo 3. Tel 437 437 Fax 449 280.

Prices are in the DWB A/C $100-150 bracket, and they have all the facilities you would expect.

Grand Oriental Hotel, York Street, Colombo 1. Tel 320 391, 448 734. Fax 447 640. SWB A/C $40/50 DWB A/C $50/60. Rest. Bar. Directly opposite the old passenger terminal (now the offices) of Colombo harbour. View of harbour from Harbour Room restaurant. Very good but lacks the space of the Galle Face or Mount Lavinia.

Galle Face Hotel, Galle Road. Tel 541 010 Fax 541 072. SWB/DWB A/C $35/55/65 Suites A/C $75-175. Breakfast $5, lunch or dinner $7, beer Rs165, Pimms Rs190. Real style. Built around a lawn overlooking the ocean. Swimming pool (Rs200 for non-residents). Great place for a drink and light lunch.

Hotel Nippon, 123 Kumarani Ratham Road, Colombo 2. Tel 431 887 Fax 332 603. DWB $17 DWB A/C $21. Rest. Bar. Attractive building with cast iron framing.

Hotel Galaxy, 388 Union Place, Colombo 2. Tel 699 320 or 696 372. SWB/DWB $35. Rest. Bar. Swimming pool on roof.

Lake Lodge, 20 Alvis Terrace, Colombo 3. Tel 326 443. SWB Rs706 DWB $12 (includes breakfast). Rest. Bar. Balcony with plants. Quiet. Apart from the rather grim places opposite the station the nearest lodge to Fort station.

YWCA, 393 Union Place, Colombo 2. Tel 324 181 or 324 694. SWB B&B $6 DWB B&B $13. Rest. Patisserie. Clean rooms (for men as well as women) in an old Dutch building. Good and very reasonable food. Open for arrivals 24hrs. Will arrange transport to and from airport.

Mrs Delini Peiris, 62/2 Park Street, Colombo 2. Tel 328 350. SWB $5 DWB $6. No meals. Only two rooms, so phone in advance.

Wayfarers Inn, 77 Rosmead Place, Colombo 7. Tel 693 936 Fax 686 288. SWB/DWB $13/15 SWB/DWB A/C $19. Rest. Bar. Breakfast Rs150, dinner Rs250. Good quiet place to relax with large bosky garden and menagerie. The owner's wife is a music teacher, so on Saturdays you get strains of Rachmaninov and Mozart. Ever so slightly ramshackle but highly recommended.

Mrs Padmini Nanayakkara, 20 Chelsea Gardens, Colombo 3. Tel 573 095. SWB $10 DWB $13 (incl. breakfast). Just one lovely room in a nice house, so phone first.

Colombo House, 26 Charles Place, Colombo 3. Tel 574 900 Fax 574 901. SWB $14 DWB $17 (+$5 A/C). Rest. Bar. Large rooms in an old house.

At Mount Lavinia

Mount Lavinia Hotel, Mount Lavinia, Colombo. Tel 715 221 Fax 738 228. SWB $40 DWB $50 SWB A/C $80/100 DWB A/C $90/110 Suite A/C $125-300. Rest. Bar. The non-A/C rooms are the original ones and have more character. The Mount Lavinia has a style all of its own with the doormen dressed like colonial policemen in white pith helmets. Right by the sea and probably the quietest of the major hotels (and the furthest from any likely trouble). Swimming pool (Rs200 for non-residents). Prices in the half dozen restaurants are quite reasonable.

Numerous other hotels and restaurants at all prices in the Mount Lavinia area.

Eating and Drinking

Fort area:

Harbour Room, Grand Oriental Hotel, York Street, Colombo 1. Tel 320 391. SL/Chi/Cont. Mod/Exp. Quiet cool bar-restaurant with tremendous view of busy commercial harbour. Beer Rs156, tea Rs48. Pasta dishes Rs150, other main courses up to Rs240, lobster Rs840. Buffet lunch Rs250 (all prices inclusive). If you want the view at lunchtime you have to eat; buffet is good, avoid the snacks. Buffet with live music Friday evenings. A great place to relax.

Seafish, 15 Sir CA Gardiner MW, Colombo 2. Tel 431 826. Mod/Exp. Seafood. Main courses around Rs200-250, also good salads.

Prawnies, York Street (50m from GOH). Cheap/Mod. Seafood. You want prawns, they got'em. Prawn sandwich Rs60, prawns with dip and fries Rs180.

Taj, 99 Chatham Street. Cheap. Rice and curry, short eats, and cold drinks.

Many other inexpensive restaurants on Chatham and Hospital Streets. The cheapest place for a beer (men only) is the *Sri Lanka Ex-Servicemen's Institute*, 29 Bristol Street; *British India*, 13 Mudalige MW, is slightly more salubrious. At the other end of the scale there is the *Echelon Pub* in the Hilton.

Colombo 7 area:

Don Stanley's, 69 Alexandra Place. Tel 686 486. Exp. Good Western food nicely served. Main courses Rs300-500.

Don's Cafe, upstairs from Don Stanley's. Mod. A/C inside, or you can sit out on the balcony. Interesting range of good food including burgers, bacon spare ribs (mostly just under Rs200), and a Mongolian barbecue. Fun place, but the music is sometimes very loud.

Pizza Hut, 323 Union Place. Mod. Good pizzas from Rs375 up, excellent salad bar.

Summer Garden, Ananda Coomaraswamy MW, Colombo 7. Cheap/Mod. SL/Cont. Tables set in an attractive garden beside a cricket ground. Interesting menu includes bangers and mash, or just have a quiet, cold beer.

Park View Lodge, 70 Park Street (near Town Hall). Tel 326 255. A/C. Mod. Chinese. Large portions of good food.

There is a good cheap rice and curry place on Kannangara MW opposite the mosque behind the Town Hall.

Galle Road and around:

Alt Heidelberg, Galle Road (opposite Galle Face Hotel), Colombo 3. Mod/Exp. Main courses Rs300-400. German food and beer.

Majestic City. The food mall in the basement has self-service stalls selling good food of many different cuisines, reckon about Rs100 for a main meal, fine when the A/C is working. Kentucky Fried Chicken is just behind Majestic City. For a real cheapie, short eats or rice and curry, try the Gulf Cafe a little down the street towards the sea.

Cricket Club Cafe, 34 Queens Road, Colombo 3. Tel 501 384. Mod/Exp western food. Decor of cricket memorabilia. Bradman Bar has real pub atmosphere. Excellent place.

Beach Wadiya, 2 Station Avenue, Wellawatta. Tel 074-514 477. Mod/Exp.

Excellent seafood right on the beach. Note that Beach Wadiya is adjacent to Wellawatta railway station, not Bambalapitiya.

Other places include *88 Chinese Seafood Restaurant*, 98/1 Havelock Road, Colombo 5. Tel 593 017. Mod/Exp; *Kebabish*, 526 Galle Road, Colombo 3. Tel 574 479. Pakistani; *Santa-Fe Mexican*, 46B Galle Road, Colombo 3; and, for a drink *Regency Pub*, 324 Galle Road, Colombo 6.

West Coast Beaches

Stilt fishermen

The west and south coasts of Sri Lanka boast a succession of some of the finest beaches in the world. There is something for everybody here, from the brash and busy resorts of Negombo and Hikkaduwa through hippy hang-outs to total peace and seclusion. Take your pick.

One word of caution: strong tides, currents, and undertows are common all along this coast. This is not just a feature of the monsoon period, as some people may tell you, it is a problem all year. Even people who regard themselves as strong swimmers are advised not to go out of their depth. There are no lifeguards, and people drown every year. The best season on these beaches is from November to April. After that the monsoon means rough seas and cloudy skies. If you are in Sri Lanka at that time, and few visitors are, the east coast offers calm seas and good weather.

NORTH OF COLOMBO

The only developed beach resort north of Colombo is Negombo. This is, however, an interesting area historically, having been part of the coastal strip colonised first by the Portuguese and then the Dutch. The Portuguese influence remains obvious in the great number of Catholic churches and the high proportion of Christians. The coast north of Negombo could be an interesting place to explore. For a long time the area was unsafe because of insurgency and it has always been off the beaten track.

NEGOMBO

The original name was Migamuwa, which the Portuguese corrupted to Nigombo. The Dutch took it in 1644, and it became one of their main bases, especially as a centre for the cinnamon trade. Negombo fell into British hands, along with the rest of Ceylon, in 1796.

Negombo was the first beach resort to be developed in Sri Lanka, and some might say it is showing its age. In fact, it seems to be fashionable to run it down. Actually the authors find it preferable to Hikkaduwa, though that may be damning by faint praise; at least it hasn't got a main road down the centre of it.

Around town

The Dutch built a **fort** to replace the earlier Portuguese one on the headland commanding the entrance to the lagoon. The British demolished most of this, building a prison in its place. The prison is still in use, and the only reminder of the fort today is a gateway dated 1678 which now has a clock tower on top of it. Across the green from here is an old Dutch building, now the New Rest House. Very little else that is old survives, though there are a few attractive buildings at the southern end of Main Street.

Negombo has been sometimes called Little Rome because of the number of churches. **St. Mary's Church** was started in 1874 but took nearly fifty years to build, being completed in 1924. The **Sri Muthu Mari Amman** Hindu temple, by way of contrast, has a typical South Indian brightly coloured gopuram.

If the Portuguese legacy to Sri Lanka is churches, the Dutch trademark is equally characteristic, canals. When the Dutch supplanted the Portuguese transport in Ceylon relied on pack animals. In the days before railways and efficient road transport canal barges were the most effective way of moving goods, especially bulky ones. The Dutch accordingly set about building a system of inland waterways, mainly by linking up rivers and lagoons. The canals had secondary uses for drainage and land reclamation, especially in the flat area outside Colombo Fort where the city needed to expand.

The **Dutch Canal** (the British called it the Hamilton Canal) runs from

Colombo through the formidable Muturajavala Swamp to Negombo Lagoon. It then runs through the town in an artificial cut, north to Chilaw and Puttalam, and then across the lagoon to Kalpitiya to reach the anchorage in Dutch Bay. The main goods carried were cinnamon, rice, copra, and salt from Puttalam. The canal is no longer used for its original purpose, but the broad section south of Negombo (see Arrival and Departure below) is still busy with fishing boats and boatyards. The entrance from the lagoon to the canal north can be seen from St. Joseph's Road but it is pretty insalubrious at this point. North of town the towpaths are said to provide pleasant walking and cycling. Some of the big hotels run boat trips on the canals.

This was not the only canal the Dutch built. There are actually 280km/ 175miles of canals between Kalpitiya in the north and Galle to the south, with an unbroken link between Kalpitiya and Bentota. Batticaloa had a system 90km long, and there were shorter links around Galle and Matara.

The **lagoon** is the largest fishing harbour in Sri Lanka. The inshore fishing is still done by traditional sailing boats which have a surprising turn of speed. You can watch the boats return to the lagoon from the road bridge or the little promontory past the jail. There is a fish market over the bridge, and another takes place at 1700 near the fort.

Duwa Island is a fishing and boatbuilding community over the causeway from Negombo town. The villagers perform a Passion play every year like that at Oberammergau.

Negombo Beach

Compared with those south of Colombo the beach is a disappointment, being narrow at the southern end (where the budget hotels are) and none too clean. It does get better as you go further north, though this is not saying much. There is a reef 3km off beach with coral starting at the 10m level. Swimming is dangerous in the May to October monsoon period.

Deep sea fishing trips are run by the Halcyon Beach Hotel, and **Scuba diving** through the Blue Oceanic Hotel. Serendib Watersport Paradise offers **paragliding**, **water skiing**, and **windsurfing**. Most of the main hotels have **discos**, and there is also the Club Tropicana on Porutota Road.

Because it is so near the airport Negombo is a popular place for travellers to spend their last day or two in Sri Lanka. When you can get a taxi to the airport from somewhere really nice like Unawatuna for Rs2000 there seems little point.

Shopping. Negombo is not a good place for last minute shopping. There are stalls and shops near the tourist hotels, but the quality is dubious and because the shopkeepers are used to taking easy money off tourists you have to bargain really hard.

Festivals. Easter as noted above and also a big fishermen's festival at St. Mary's Church in July.

Information. Ceylon Tourist Board office at 12/6 Ethukala, Lewis Place (behind Tourist Police post). 0900-1700 Monday to Saturday.

Arrival and departure. Negombo is 1hr from Colombo (train or bus). As an alternative to driving (or taking a taxi) all the way up the main road, which is awful, cross either bridge over the Kelani Ganga, and after 2km turn left towards Hekitta. Continue to the canal and turn right. Follow the canal (this an attractive and quiet drive), turning left over a bridge 200m before the road turns away from the canal. Go right at the next T-junction and follow your nose, the sea always on your left.

Getting to the airport: taxis around Rs400, three wheelers Rs250.

Local transport. Hotels list agreed taxi rates, three wheelers should be cheaper. Bicycle hire around Rs75 per day. Motor cycle hire from Gold Wing Motors, 546 Colombo Road (Tel 2895) and others for around Rs400 per day.

Accommodation

(STD Code 031).

Browns Beach Hotel, 175 Lewis Place. Tel 714 441 Fax 433 755. SWB A/C $54 ($24) DWB A/C $65 ($30). Rest (3). Bars. Swimming pool, tennis court, squash courts, watersports, night club.

Royal Oceanic Hotel, Ethukala. Tel 22377 Fax 38384. SWB A/C $50 ($45) DWB $55 ($50). Two swimming pools (open to non-residents). Scuba diving.

Golden Beach Hotel, 161 Lewis Place. Tel 22318 Fax 38285. SWB/DWB A/C $40 B&B $45. Rest (2). Bar. Swimming pool.

Golden Star Beach Hotel, 163 Lewis Place. Tel 33564 Fax 38266. SWB $30 DWB $35 (+$5 A/C). Rest. Bar. Breakfast $4, Lunch or dinner $7.

Golden Star Beach Hotel, 163 Lewis Place. Tel 33564 Fax 38266. SWB $30 ($20) DWB $35 ($25) (+$5 A/C). Breakfast $4, lunch or dinner $7.

Icebear Beach Hotel, 103/2 Lewis Place. Tel/Fax 33862. DR $18 ($13) DWB $22 ($14). Rest. Bar. An old villa with a nice garden, but seems expensive.

Hotel Sunset Beach, 5 Carron Place. Tel 22350 Fax 38384. SWB $20 DWB $25. Rest. Bar. Breakfast Rs50-120, main courses Rs150-425, beer Rs110. Swimming pool. Rooms have private balconies and lovely furniture. Recommended.

Catamaran Beach Hotel, 209 Lewis Place. Tel 22206 Fax 38026. DWB $20 ($16). Rest. Bar. Breakfast $5, lunch or dinner $7. Swimming pool and watersports. A friendly place.

De-phani Guest House, 189/15 Lewis Place. Tel 28225. DWB $9 ($8 incl.). Rest. Bar. Probably the nicest rooms you will find in this price bracket. Quiet. Small garden. The restaurant may just have been having an off day when we tried it.

Oasis Beach Resort, Porutota Road. Tel 38238 Fax 38002. SWB $10 SWB A/C $11 DWB $13 DWB $17. Rest. Bar. Swimming pool. Clean but not quite finished off.

Starbeach Guest House, 83/3 Lewis Place. Tel 22606 Fax 38266. SWB $4/5 DWB $5/8 (+$3 A/C). Rest. Bar. Breakfast Rs100, lunch Rs200, dinner Rs225. Rooms have balconies overlooking the sea, and there is a garden.

Beach View Tourist Guest House, Ethukala. Tel 22706. SWB $6 DWB $7. Rest. Breakfast Rs100. Very good value at the top end of the beach.

Rainbow Guest House, Carron Place. Tel 22082. SWB $5 DWB $6. Breakfast (only) Rs88.

Ocean View Guest House, 104 Lewis Place. Tel 38689. DWB $5 Rest. Breakfast Rs75. On inland side of road.

NEGOMBO TOWN & BEACH

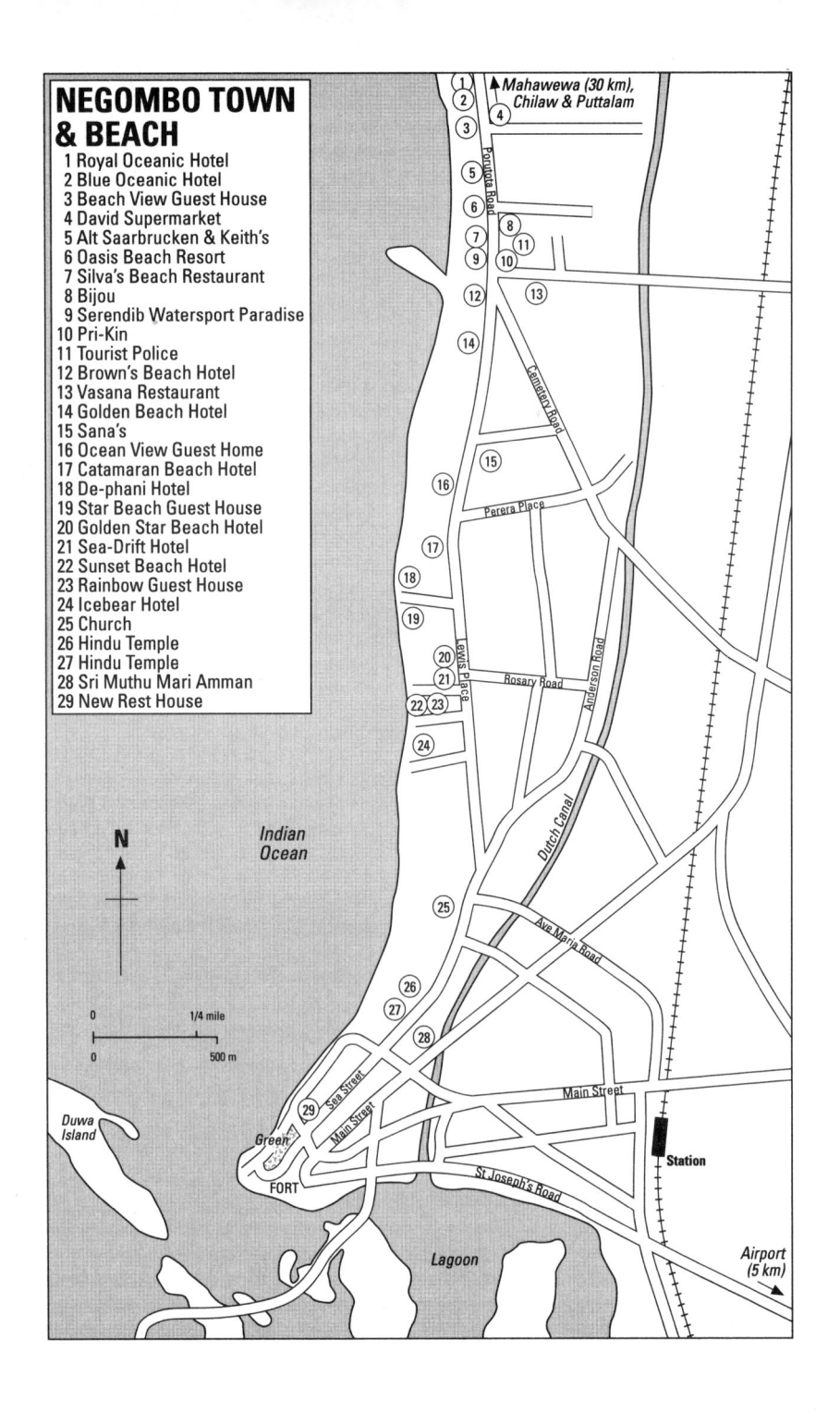

1. Royal Oceanic Hotel
2. Blue Oceanic Hotel
3. Beach View Guest House
4. David Supermarket
5. Alt Saarbrucken & Keith's
6. Oasis Beach Resort
7. Silva's Beach Restaurant
8. Bijou
9. Serendib Watersport Paradise
10. Pri-Kin
11. Tourist Police
12. Brown's Beach Hotel
13. Vasana Restaurant
14. Golden Beach Hotel
15. Sana's
16. Ocean View Guest Home
17. Catamaran Beach Hotel
18. De-phani Hotel
19. Star Beach Guest House
20. Golden Star Beach Hotel
21. Sea-Drift Hotel
22. Sunset Beach Hotel
23. Rainbow Guest House
24. Icebear Hotel
25. Church
26. Hindu Temple
27. Hindu Temple
28. Sri Muthu Mari Amman
29. New Rest House

Sea Drift, 2 Carron Place. Tel 22601. DWB $4 with fan and net. Breakfast (only) Rs60. Clean and pleasant.

New Rest House. Old Dutch building but at the wrong end of town. Beach nearby messed up by fishing boats.

Eating and Drinking

A huge choice. *Vasana* does good Chinese and Sri Lankan food. *Pri-Kin* is even better for Chinese. *Silva's Beach Restaurant*, 5 Porutota Road, has good seafood. *Keith's* does good English cafe food. There are several expensive German/Swiss restaurants, including *Alt Saarbrucken, Rudi's Bar*, and *Bijou*. *Sana's*, Lewis Place, has what looks like a Morris 8 in the entrance.

NORTH FROM NEGOMBO

Mahawewa, 30km north of Negombo, is noted for its batiks. The rearing horse outside the Taniwelle Devale in **Madampe** recalls an old legend. A traveller failed to offer the customary alms at the shrine here and was thrown by his horse. Badly hurt, he promised that if he recovered he would set up a rearing horse statue to remind others not to make the same mistake. He recovered.

Chilaw is at the head of a large lagoon, now extensively used for prawn farming. Whilst satisfying the insatiable demand for prawns in the West and boosting the local economy the effluent and waste food do the ecology no good at all. A short distance inland on the road to Wariyapola is the **Munneswaram Temple**, a popular place of pilgrimage. It is one of the isvarams, the five most important Shiva shrines in Sri Lanka, where a fire walking ceremony takes place in August. The road continues another 30km or so to **Panduvas Nuwara** the site of the capital of the prince who later became the great king Parakramabahu I (12th century).

Arrival and departure. Chilaw is 95km from Colombo, 55km from Negombo by train or bus.

Accommodation. The *Rest House* (Tel 032-2299) on the beach, 5 mins walk from station, is reasonable.

Chilaw, and the Deduru Oya river just to the north, mark the transition from the Wet Zone to the Dry; note the change in vegetation.

Unlike most of this coastal area, which has a high proportion of Christians, **Udappawa** is a Hindu village. Their major festival in July or August involves fire walking. The village is on the coast off the main road.

Puttalam is a fishing town on the shores of the second largest lagoon in Sri Lanka, second only to Jaffna's. The lagoon is used for extensive shellfish farming, and the evaporation pans share with Hambantota Sri Lanka's supply of salt.

Arrival and departure. Puttalam is 132km north of Colombo and, for passenger traffic, the end of the railway line. Bus to Anuradhapura ($2\frac{1}{2}$ hrs.).

The spit of land which encloses Puttalam Lagoon and, to the north, Dutch Bay is interesting. The Church of St. Anne in **Talawila** is the focus of a popular festival which culminates on 26 July every year. This is a huge event which attracts devotees of all Sri Lanka's different religions.

Kalpitiya has a small Dutch Fort still in good condition and an 18th century church, this was a thatched gabled Dutch building renovated by the British in 1840.

Arrival and departure. Talawila is 25km from Puttalam by road, and Kalpitiya a further 16km north. A ferry may run from Kalpitiya to Karaitivu enabling a round trip, though transport from Karaitivu could be problematic.

Accommodation. Rest House (Tel 032-65299) in Puttalam.

Eating and Drinking. Lake View Restaurant at 139 Colombo Road, Kalpitiya.

Wilpattu National Park and Game Sanctuary

On the coast north of Puttalam and bounded by the Kala Oya and Madaragam Aru rivers Sri Lanka's largest reserve covers more than 1000sq km. It is noted for leopard, a sub-species of sloth bear unique to Sri Lanka, deer, and birdlife.

The park has been closed for years because of the security position. Should it reopen the alternatives are to stay in the park, for which you need your own transport, or to stay at Kala Oya (the entrance is near here) and take government organised tours from there.

In the park, near the village of Pomparripu, is an archaeological site where funeral urns from the 4th century BC were found; these are very similar to sites in south India. The people apparently worshipped a god called Madaragam who evolved into Murugan. Like Shiva one of his symbols was the trident.

Arrival and departure. Bus to Kala Oya 30km north-east of Puttalam on the Puttalam to Anuradhapura road.

Accommodation. Basic *bungalows* in the park, reservations through Wildlife Conservation Department, 8/18 Gregory's Road, Colombo 7 (Tel 01-698 086 Fax 01-698 556). *Wilpattu Hotel* (Tel 29752) at Kala Oya sounds good.

SOUTH OF COLOMBO: COLOMBO TO HIKKADUWA

The road from Colombo to Galle is one of the busiest on the island, and the standard of driving is appalling. Unless there is something below of great interest to you take the train straight through. Do not use the buses; the drivers are paid only Rs50 for the 115km/72miles from Colombo to Galle, and the only way they can make a living is by driving like lunatics to do as many trips in a day as they can. So they are overtired as well. If you are driving be very, very careful.

RATMALANA

The **railway workshops** here harbour a Beyer Garratt 2-6-2 + 2-6-2 locomotive undergoing restoration. The **Sri Lankan Air Force Museum** is at Ratmalana airport, visit by prior arrangement only.

KALUTARA

Kalutara stands at the mouth of the Kalu Ganga (Black River), and that is what the name means.

The traditional trade in Kalutara is making rope and mats from coir, the rough stuff from coconuts, and also reed baskets and mats.

The Portuguese demolished the original **Gangatilaka Vihara** temple and built a fort on the site. After Dutch use it was converted into a house by a British official. The huge new dagoba is hollow inside with murals. Beside the road is a shrine which passers-by throw coins into in the hope of a safe journey. Very necessary given the standard of driving.

Kalutara is famous for mangosteens (one of the tropical fruit for which Sri Lanka is famous), and another exotic species in the area is the hog-deer which the Dutch brought in from Bengal. Inland is Sri Lanka's main rubber growing area. Graphite is mined nearby, and these two commodities are important exports.

At Katukurunda (a little inland) is a motor racing circuit, once a Second World War airfield. They even race three-wheelers!

The beach is nothing to write home about, and most people go straight through on the way south.

Arrival and departure. Kalutara is 43km south of Colombo. By train use Kalutara South station, or bus.

Accommodation. Several package tour hotels; the *Garden Beach Hotel* in Kalutara North (Tel 034-22380), in the $10 bracket, is an alternative.

BERUWELA

The Muslims established their first foothold in Sri Lanka here in around 760AD. The **Kechimalai Mosque,** with its graceful minarets, and the 1000 year old tomb of the Muslim saint Sheikh Ashareth overlook the harbour. This is a popular pilgrimage place at the end of Ramadan. Muslim gem traders still live in the China Fort area on the landward side of the main road.

An Anglican church has a brightly coloured statue of St. George which looks uncommonly like Buddha and a bit apologetic about killing the dragon!

Beruwela is package tour country catering mainly for German groups.

Arrival and departure. 58km south of Colombo (train or bus).

Accommodation. The Barberyn Reef Hotel is notable for its ayurvedic (herbal medicine) treatments, highly fashionable in Germany, hence highly expensive. Its advertising, even in Sri Lanka, is in German.

ALUTHGAMA

Aluthgama means new village, and this is a popular weekend escape from Colombo. Good oysters are caught locally, whether you would want to risk eating them au nature is another matter.

Aluthgama and Bentota are either side of the Bentota River and lagoon, which provides sheltered water for **watersports**, even in the monsoon. Fun Surf Water Sports Centre (next to Terrena Lodge Tel 071-65029) hire windsurfers for Rs300 per hour (lagoon) or Rs400 (sea), tuition available. Water skiing costs from Rs300, and a jet ski is Rs1000 for 15mins. The river is navigable for at least 20km, and a small boat (up to five people) costs Rs500 per hour; you can visit the Galapota Vihara (12th century) 5km upstream, though little remains, and various other places.

Brief** (open 0800-1700 every day, Rs125) is the house and gardens of Bevis Bawa who died a few years ago. Bawa was a fascinating man, a 6'7" Burgher of Portuguese, Sinhalese, Scottish, and Muslim extraction, a socialite and dilettante in the better sense of both words. Over a period of forty years he developed a barren family property into a delightful house and gardens, actually a series of small gardens which grew according to his mood. The gardens, despite the tropical vegetation, have a very English landscape garden feel. The house, its furniture, art collection, and photographs provide a perfect insight into a leisured life in the tropics in the early part of this century. The young man who shows you round the house will explain much more. This is, for reasons you may infer, a wasting asset to be seen sooner rather than later.

Arrival and departure. Aluthgama is the travel centre for Beruwela to the north and Bentota to the south as express trains stop here rather than in those places. The Viceroy Special steam train sometimes runs from here up to Kandy.

For Brief (7km/4miles inland) go south through Aluthgama, fork left at the fish market and follow the B157 through Dargha Town with its white mosque, turn left at a yellow 'Brief' sign, continue to the next village, and go right downhill at another yellow sign.

Accommodation (STD Code 034). Most accommodation is expensive resort hotels. A notable exception is *Terrena Lodge*, River Avenue (turning just at north end of bridge). Tel/Fax 75001. SWB $15 DWB $17 (incl. breakfast and tax). Rest. Bar. Starters Rs105 up, main courses around Rs200, beer Rs138 incl. Most attractive Austrian-owned place with riverside garden. Free transport by boat to the beach. A far better place to break your journey than Hikkaduwa.

BENTOTA

The Sri Lankan government has designated Bentota as its National Holiday Resort, and it is the country's main tourist trap. There are many resort hotels along its beaches.

There are several **turtle hatcheries** along this coast, of which the Sea Turtles Project (Tel 034-75850) is a good example. Both turtles and their eggs have traditionally formed part of the diet of local people, and it's not so long ago that many good restaurants in the West had turtle soup on the menu. Now development, pollution, and disturbance mean that turtles are threatened in most of their natural habitats.

Local fishermen are paid Rs3 for every egg that they bring in to discourage them from eating them or selling them in the market, a practice which is illegal but hard to stop. The eggs are re-buried in sand pens where there may be as many as 16,000 at any one time. When they hatch the baby turtles are transferred to tanks where they are kept for three days before release. They are released at night to reduce the risk from predators, mongooses and monitor lizards, as well as birds, will take the young turtles. They have to be released on the beach, rather than out at sea which would be safer, so that they know where to return to lay their eggs ten years later. Even so the survival rate is very low, and it is ten years before a female turtle matures and returns to lay her eggs. Assuming that young turtles are ready to be returned to the wild you can release some yourself in return for a contribution to the project's funds

The hatchery keeps a couple of rare albino turtles (one in a half-million), and also a large turtle which lost a flipper in a fisherman's net, none of which would survive in the wild. The Project runs schemes with local schools to educate the children and, hopefully, to discourage their parents from taking eggs. There is simple accommodation locally for anyone wanting to do research which is welcomed.

Arrival and departure. Train from Colombo via Aluthgama (1½-2hrs) or bus.

Accommodation (STD Code 034).

The *Bentota Beach Hotel* is built on the site of the old Portuguese fort and follows its star plan. Bentota was for a time the frontier between Portuguese and Dutch territory.

Susantha Guest House, Resort Road (off road signed Police Station or a short walk from the station). Tel/Fax 75324. SWB $8 DWB $9 ($11 with hot water) DWB A/C $18 Suite A/C $19. Rest. Bar. Comfortable quiet place a short distance from the beach.

Goldi Guest House, as for Susantha Lodge, or walk south down tracks from station. Tel 75415. DWB $9 DWB A/C $11. Rest. Bar. Breakfast Rs150, other meals reasonable. Beach view.

Eating and Drinking.

Aida Restaurant, Main Road (over Aida's Gem and Jewellery Store). Mod/Exp. SL/Western. Great location overlooking river. Interesting menu. Strong afternoon coffee and an insipid schwartzwaldekirschtorte (Black Forest gateau!) for Rs120. Sit and watch the lorries and buses wedging themselves into the bridge. Also six very good rooms DWB $14.

INDURUWA

There is a good quiet beach here and a turtle hatchery.

Arrival and departure. 5km south of Bentota.

Accommodation (STD Code 034)

Asha Dream Cottage, Main Road (½ km south of station). Tel 75906. DWB B&B $18. Rest. Bar. Rice and six curries Rs200. Spotless. Nice garden runs down to the safe beach.

Long Beach Cottage, Main Road (200m north of station). Tel 75773. DWB $6. Rest. Rice and curry Rs180. Clean simple accommodation on the beach.

The beach at **Kosgoda** (3km south of Induruwa on the main road) is said to be the best place in Sri Lanka for turtle viewing. The turtle hatchery was endowed by Hasselblad, makers of very expensive cameras; nice to know where some of the money goes.

The **Ahungalla Animal Park** (8km south of Kosgoda) has closed, and there are no plans for reopening.

Numerous **antique shops** stand along the Colombo-Galle road. They have mainly rather indifferent china and repro furniture. **Batiks and handwoven** cotton are on offer. Always beware of prices in main road places in tourist areas.

AMBALANGODA

Ambalangoda is the most congested of a number of little towns down this coast. Driving through is bad enough, set foot in the town centre and you will question your sanity.

Ambalangoda is famous for its mask carvers. Several skilled carvers work on the quieter north side of the town, and this is the place to look for authentic but expensive masks. The **Ariyapala Mask Museum** is here. Puppets, some of them very large, are also made.

Arrival and departure. Bus or train from Colombo.

Accommodation. You would have to be mad to stay here. *Sena's Lake View House* is said to be quiet. The *Rest House* overlooks the sea and has a rock swimming pool.

A couple of **moonstone mines** are signposted off the main road. The one at Mitiyagoda is 15km/10miles inland, turn off the main road at Kahawa.

HIKKADUWA

Hikkaduwa was the original hippy hang-out in Sri Lanka. Times change, hotels get built, and the seekers of peace and quiet at minimal cost move on. Hikkaduwa today is at the cheap end of most travel agents' brochures, and it reflects in the clientele.

Beaches

The narrow strip of land between the beach and the busy main road is an unbroken chain of hotels and restaurants for a good 3km. From north to south the beaches are **Hikkaduwa** itself which has most of the resort hotels. **Wewala** is much the same, whilst **Narigama** is the place for surfing. As you get into **Thiranagama** the beach broadens considerably. There is more greenery, fishing boats are pulled up, and this is generally quieter and more pleasant. Right at the southern end is **Patuwata**.

The **Coral Sanctuary** is at the north end of Hikkaduwa Beach. Much of the coral around Sri Lanka's coasts has been destroyed, dredged out to be burned to make cement. This process is now illegal, but still often observed along the coast. The sanctuary, protected by a reef, preserves at least a small area.

Watersports

Scuba diving is popular, and there are several schools and agencies. Two of the best are Poseidon Diving Station (Galle Road, Tel 09-77294) and International Diving School (Coral Sands Hotel, Tel/Fax 09-57436). The proprietor of the latter was trained by Richard Larn. Poseidon do a Discover Scuba course for $35, a single dive for Rs900 or Rs700 if you have your own equipment; five dives at that rate and you get one free, ten and you get two free. A one day wreck safari with two dives is Rs2000. IDS prices are very similar. Both do PADI courses at standardised rates: open water $320, advanced open water $220, rescue $370, all inclusive of certificate. Divemaster and assistant instructor by arrangement. At Poseidon you can reduce costs by doing the courses over a longer period and helping out.

The diving season is mid-November to the end of April. There are several accessible wrecks in the area, mostly in 30-40m of water. They include the 'Earl of Shaftesbury', an iron-hulled clipper, and more recent steamships.

Snorkelling is good. In the coral sanctuary consider the swell before swimming over the reef, you could find yourself painfully grounded. And watch out for the glass-bottom boats, a driver at the back of a bow-up boat cannot be relied on to see you, even if he is looking where he's going. Aqua Marine Sports, 9 Hikkaduwa Road, hire quality snorkel masks and fins for Rs350 per day. You can buy Italian equipment there quite reasonably (masks Rs1900 up and fins Rs1600 up). Other places may be cheaper, check the quality. **Spear fishing** is totally forbidden. Poseidon will hire you an **underwater camera**.

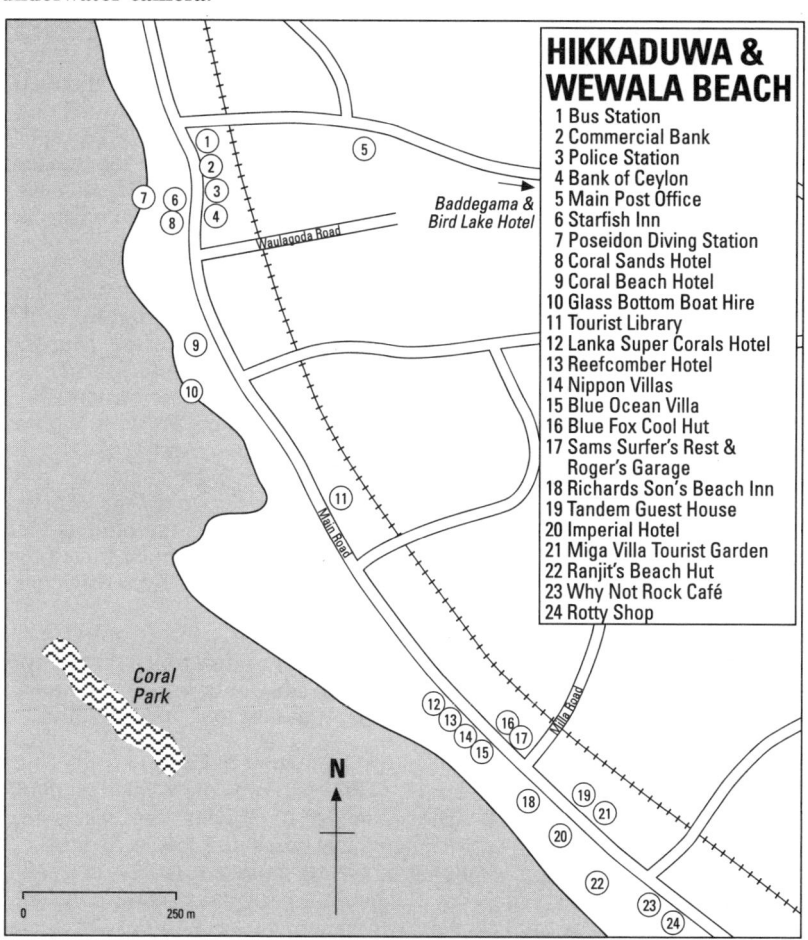

HIKKADUWA & WEWALA BEACH

1 Bus Station
2 Commercial Bank
3 Police Station
4 Bank of Ceylon
5 Main Post Office
6 Starfish Inn
7 Poseidon Diving Station
8 Coral Sands Hotel
9 Coral Beach Hotel
10 Glass Bottom Boat Hire
11 Tourist Library
12 Lanka Super Corals Hotel
13 Reefcomber Hotel
14 Nippon Villas
15 Blue Ocean Villa
16 Blue Fox Cool Hut
17 Sams Surfer's Rest & Roger's Garage
18 Richards Son's Beach Inn
19 Tandem Guest House
20 Imperial Hotel
21 Miga Villa Tourist Garden
22 Ranjit's Beach Hut
23 Why Not Rock Café
24 Rotty Shop

There is good reliable **surf** on Narigama beach. Surfboards cost around Rs100 per hour to hire, a boogie board Rs75, longer periods by negotiation. There is talk of making **windsurfers** available.

Caution. The currents all down this coast are treacherous, and there is no-one to help if you get into trouble. Do not be fooled by the calm spell before a series of big waves. Even strong swimmers should stay well within their depth. Drownings are far from infrequent.

Other ideas

Deep-sea fishing off Hikkaduwa for yellowfin and bluefin tuna, marlin and sailfish is exciting, and large barracuda can also be caught. Trips are arranged by both Poseidon and International Diving School. Poseidon will take four to eight people at Rs1000 per head for 4-5 hours and provide four rods. International Diving School does 4 hours trolling for marlin and tuna (two rods) for $60.

Poseidon Diving Station has a small and interesting **museum** of artefacts salvaged from local wrecks.

Glass-bottomed boats do tours of the coral sanctuary at Rs250 for about 20 minutes. This is moderately interesting, but the coral and marine life are unlikely to impress people who have seen other reefs. The boats lack proper canopies, and reflection in the glass panel reduces visibility and makes photography impossible. There are too many of these boats and they damage the coral by both impact and pollution. They are also a serious danger to snorkellers in the area.

Further Afield

The Hikkaduwa Ganga river broadens out like a **lake** 2km inland. This is good for bird-watching, and you can explore the lake by boat (Rs350 per hour). See Hotel Bird Lake below for accommodation and more details.

Backtracking 3km north and going inland 2km you find the **Telwatte Vihara** (or Totagama Rajamahavihara). The present temple dates from 1805 though this has been a holy place for much longer. Among the makara-toranas is a Cupid figure complete with sugar cane bow and flower-tipped arrows. Murals near the ceiling depict the six heavens. This temple is dedicated uniquely to Anangaya who is a form of Kama, the god of love, and thus much visited by lovers. This dedication seems a little odd since in Buddhism Kama signifies sexual desire, a major obstacle on the path to enlightenment.

Whether you enjoy Hikkaduwa depends on what you want. It is certainly the place for surfers and the young who want a lively, noisy time. These days a high proportion of visitors are Germans who socialise only with one another. Anyone seeking peace and interesting company should look further south.

Practical Information

The real problem with Hikkaduwa is that the Colombo-Galle road runs the whole length of it. The standard of driving on this road, especially of the buses and lorries, is lunatic. Walking or cycling along the road is not only unpleasant but dangerous. Whatever hoteliers may say, noisy traffic runs all night, and if you want to sleep seek a room as far as possible from the road. At least on the sea side the sound of the waves masks traffic noise.

The Bank of Ceylon will keep passports and other valuables for around Rs500 per week, a good idea given that a certain amount of thieving goes on.

Shopping. You could do all your souvenir shopping in Hikkaduwa; everything is available here including some local items like nice patchwork bedspreads. The snag is that all the shops are on the main road.

Local transport. You can hire push-bikes for Rs75 a day. Several places hire motorbikes, reckon on Rs400 a day for Honda CB250 or 250R trailbike, reducing to Rs350 a day over a week, 125s are a little cheaper. Ask about insurance and what happens if you have a breakdown.

Arrival and departure. 98km south of Colombo by train from Colombo Maradana station (2hrs). Many buses run on this road, but are best avoided. A taxi from Colombo to Unawatuna costs around Rs2000 and would allow a quick look at whatever took your fancy along the way.

Accommodation

(STD Code 09)
This is a small selection of what is available and generally does not include hotels or guest houses on the landward side sandwiched between the road and the railway line.

Hotel Reefcomber. Tel/Fax 77374. SWB A/C $50 DWB A/C $55. Rest. Bar. Swimming pool and garden. All rooms have balconies.

Hotel Lanka Supercorals. Tel 77387 Fax 77897. SWB $20 DWB $31. Rest. Bar. Swimming pool and garden.

Coral Sands Hotel, 326 Galle Road. Tel 77436 Fax 77513. SWB $21 B&B DWB $32 B&B A/C +$5. Rest. Bar. Starters Rs70-150, main courses Rs150 up, beer Rs110. Swimming pool.

Blue Ocean Villa, 420 Galle Road, Wewala. Tel 77566. DWB $21 ($17) (includes breakfast). Rest. Bar. Restaurant has good murals.

Villa Paradiso Guest House, Galle Road. Tel 77147. DWB $210 (includes breakfast and small sitting room). Rest. Bar. Main courses Rs110-390. Nice garden.

Nippon Villa, 412D Galle Road, Wewala. Tel/Fax 77429. DWB $17 ($11) (includes breakfast). Rest. Bar. Interesting menu. Well furnished rooms with batiks on the walls. Recommended.

Tandem Guest House, 465 Galle Road, Wewala. Tel/Fax 77103. DWB $10 ($8). Breakfast only.

Hotel Bird Lake, Baddegama Road (2km from Hikkaduwa). Tel 77018. SWB/DWB $8. Rest. Bar. Breakfast Rs110, rice and curry Rs110, main courses Rs150-400. Balconies overlooking the lake and nature reserve. Spice and orchid gardens. Totally quiet compared with Hikkaduwa itself, but misses the sea breezes.

Miga Villa Tourist Garden, Wewala. Tel/Fax 77092. DWB $5-8. Apartment with kitchen and sitting room $10. Rest. Bar. Breakfast Rs85, rice and curry Rs150-200. Nice garden.

Hotel Imperial, 500 Galle Road, Wewala. Tel 074-333 109. DWB $8. Rest. Bar. Breakfast Rs150, main courses Rs225-350, some Chinese food. You can hire a motorbike for Rs500 per day.

Poseidon Diving Station, Galle Road. Tel 77294. SWB $6 ($8 B&B) DWB $8

($11 B&B) all incl. Rest. Bar. Occasional beach grills. A lively social place for divers and others.

Richards Sons Beach Inn, 414 Galle Road. DWB $7. Breakfast (only) Rs80. Reasonably quiet.

Starfish Inn, 322 Galle Road. $5. Breakfast only (Rs90). Garden overlooking the fishing and glass-bottom boat anchorage, which makes it a bit noisy at weekends.

Coral Beach Hotel, 338 Galle Road. Tel 77137. Rest (Mama's). DWB $5.

Dewasiri Guest House, 472 Galle Road. Tel 077-901 195. DWB $5. Rest. Bar. Breakfast Rs150.

Eating and Drinking.
There is a large selection of restaurants, the following stand out for one reason or another.

Mama's, Coral Beach Hotel. Huge choice of food from simple inexpensive dishes up to set menus (Rs400-800) and a seafood platter for Rs1400. The first beach restaurant in Hikkaduwa, what were you doing in 1972?

Blue Fox. Excellent seafood and a relaxed atmosphere, take a table away from the road. Probably the best reasonably priced place in Hikkaduwa.

Sam's (or Roger's Garage), near the Blue Fox, rarely looks busy but shows a different film every night.

Ranjit's Beach Hut, *Why Not Rock Cafe*, and *Rotty Stop*, all close together where Wewala joins Narigama Beach are cheap lively late-night places.

DODANDUWA

The **Sailabimb Aramaya** temple has 19th century murals depicting the life of Buddha. A monastery on an island in the lagoon acts as a Buddhist seminary. The **Turtle Research Centre** is based at Kumarakanda.

Arrival and departure. On the main road just south of Hikkaduwa.

Accommodation. The *Lake Rest* a little inland at Dodandugoda sounds idyllic.

GALLE

Galle was perhaps the Tarshish of the Bible. The account of Solomon receiving 'gold and silver, ivory and apes and peacocks' sums up Sri Lanka's image as an island of riches and plenty.

History

Known to Ptolemy as Odoka, the port of Galle was used for centuries by Muslim traders who called it Qali. The local name Galla means rock, but the Portuguese misinterpreted it as galo which to them meant cock, an emblem they used on the buildings.

The Portuguese set up in Galle in 1507, and 1545 saw a visit from Francis Xavier on his way to the Far East. After an altercation with Rajasimha I the Portuguese had to recapture Galle in 1587. By 1640 the Portuguese lacked the manpower to hold on to their far flung empire, and the Dutch under Admiral Wilhelm Coster took Galle. They handed it to the king of Kandy, with whom they had an alliance, but were back permanently in 1656. The marriage treaty of Catherine of Braganza (the Infanta of Portugal) with Charles II of England in 1661, which gave Bombay to the British, also promised Galle should the Portuguese recapture it. They did not, and the British had to wait until 1796 when, despite the impressive fortifications, Galle surrendered with scarcely a shot fired. Catherine, incidentally, introduced the habit of tea drinking to the English court, an event to have a large and lasting impact on Sri Lanka.

Galle is the most historically interesting town in Sri Lanka. There is very little traffic inside, especially on the roads by the walls, and it is pleasant to explore on foot. Despite its long Dutch associations Galle actually has the sleepy, relaxed feel of the little outpost of Diu, the smallest of the Portuguese territories in India.

The walls and bastions

The fortifications of the town evolved over a long period. Their genesis was the small Portuguese fort of Santa Cruz built, on a site now occupied by the Zwart Bastion, soon after they arrived in 1507. The growing danger from the Dutch in the 17th century led the Portuguese to fortify the whole town by building defences across the 300m wide isthmus connecting it to the mainland. This consisted of three bastions linked by a wall; these bastions (with their Dutch successors) were Santo Antonio (Star), Conceiçaõ (Moon), and Saõ Jago (Sun). They relied on the sea for defence on the other three sides. When the Dutch occupied Galle permanently in 1656 they turned it into one of the main strongholds of their eastern empire. They increased the height of the walls across the isthmus and built new bastions. Right around the rest of the headland they constructed walls and a series of salients so that their guns could cover the harbour and other approaches.

It must be remembered that the seaward defences are not at all as the Dutch built them. Their old cannons, firing through V-shaped embrasures were replaced in the 19th century by fewer but larger guns on traversing carriages. You can see the semi-circular iron tracks for these in several places. Then in the 20th century modern emplacements were built on the bastions. Some of these were done in a hurry in response to the Japanese threat in 1942 and were of dubious strength.

A tour of the walls*** is the highlight of a visit to Galle. Until late in the 19th century the only access to the town was the road past the Sun Bastion, where there was a defensive outwork, to what is now called the **Old Gate**. This approach could be swept by fire from both the Sun and Zwart Bastions.

On the outside of the Old Gate are the British royal arms of the time. The gatehouse houses the **National Maritime Museum** (0900-1700, closed Friday and Saturday, Rs55), This is in fact more a marine museum than a maritime one as it majors on sealife, though without providing any useful information. The same can be said of the ship models: a modern and rather basic one of a Dutch ship and a display of local vessels. At least you can see the source of the word catamaran; it comes from the Tamil *kattu* (to bind) and *maram* (tree).

On the inner face of the gate are the arms of the VOC, the Vereenigde Oost-Indische Compagnie, or Dutch East Indies Company. Above is the cock emblem inherited from the Portuguese. The long building inside this section of the wall was a provisions store for the fort. Turn left after passing through the gate and follow the road round a little green past the District Court in the old

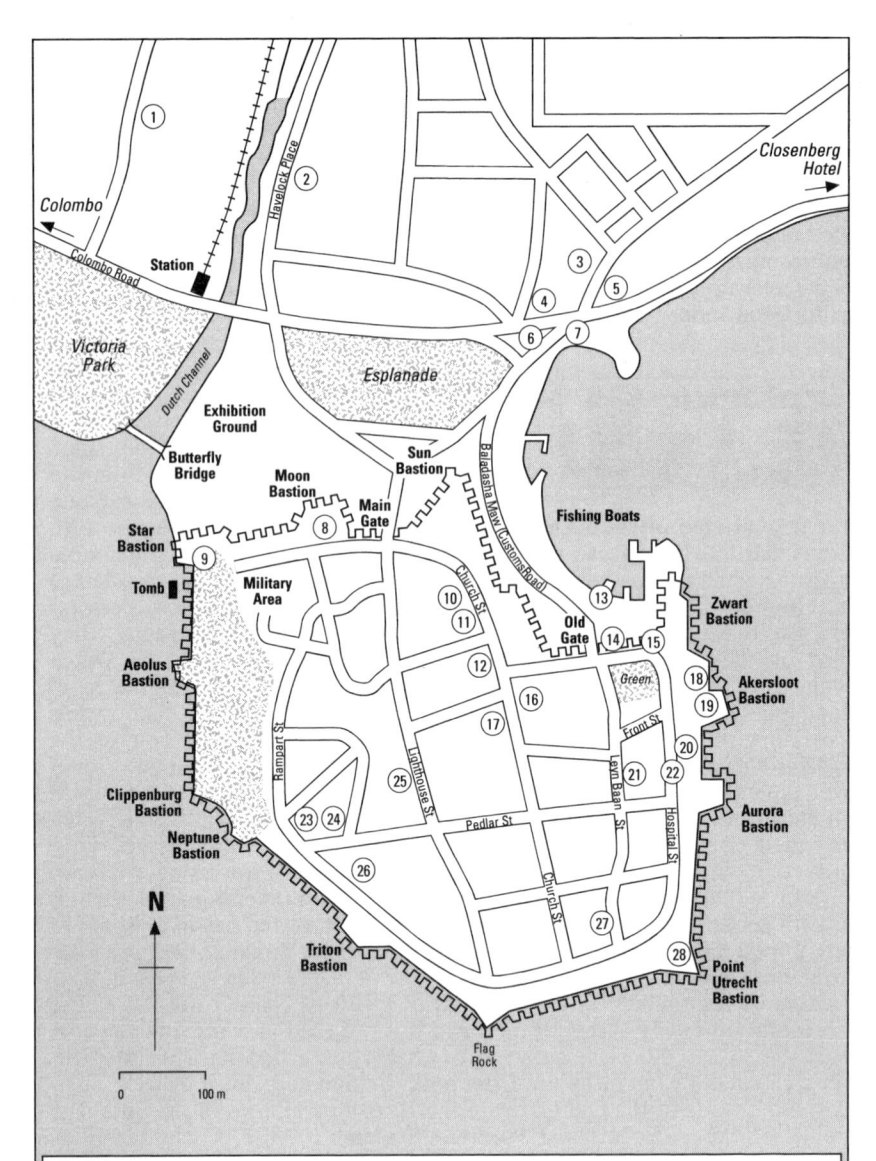

GALLE

1. St Mary's Cathedral
2. Chinese Globe Restaurant
3. Post Office
4. Police Station
5. Statue
6. War Memorial
7. Laksala
8. Clock Tower
9. Magazine
10. Museum
11. New Oriental Hotel
12. Groote Kerk
13. Fish Market
14. National Maritime Museum
15. Food Store
16. Walker & Sons
    (Old Dutch Govt House)
17. All Saint's Church
18. Old Hospital
19. Magazine
20. Kachcheri
21. Historical Museum
22. Mansion
23. RK Kodikara's Hotel
24. Weltreveden Hotel
25. Old Dutch House Hotel
26. Ramparts Hotel
27. Mosque
28. Lighthouse

hospital building and a squat white-painted magazine. You cannot walk along the walls of the Zwart Bastion. The **Akersloot Bastion** is named after birthplace of Admiral Coster, who captured Galle for the Dutch.

Further down Hospital Street is the Pilots' House, which was provided for retired pilots who were not allowed to leave Galle for fear that they would reveal the notoriously difficult entrance to the harbour. From here there is access to the walls on the left.

Opposite Aurora Bastion you can make a detour down Pedler Street, then right into Leyn Barn (Ropewalk) Street to visit the **Historical Mansion Museum*** (open every day). This is actually a commercial operation but worth visiting anyway. The house was totally derelict before careful restoration (photos of it beforehand are on display), and parts have been left unplastered to show the construction, largely of coral rock. The front is an antique shop with some interesting stock, and there are also gem and jewellery showrooms. The major part, however, is a slightly jumbled but interesting domestic display. An old woman may well be handworking lace.

Returning to the walls, walk down to the **lighthouse** on Point Utrecht Bastion. This is a modern concrete structure 18m high built in 1938. The keeper sometimes shows visitors round. If he doesn't find you first try knocking on the door of Lihiniya Trades opposite. On the landward side of the lighthouse is an old magazine with an immensely thick masonry roof to protect it from plunging shellfire. On the bastion itself is the 20th century base for a coastal defence gun, and its underground magazine.

This corner of town is the Arab Quarter, and the white building which looks like a Portuguese church is actually a **mosque**. When the muezzin calls, white-clad youngsters stroll out of the nearby madrasa for their prayers.

Flag Rock was a signal station for ships entering and leaving the harbour. The upper part of the bastion was completely reshaped in the 20th century. There is pleasant shade under the trees here, and the Snack Bar does cold drinks and a good egg sandwich for only Rs10.

The **Neptune Bastion** and the section of wall along to the Clippenberg Bastion are probably nearest to original condition. You can see how the **Clippenberg Bastion** has been filled in to form the base of a modern emplacement. The north-western corner of town is a military area. At the time of writing it was possible to follow the walls up to the **Sun Bastion** where there is a large magazine. In times of tension this may be closed, in which case you can gain access to the landward defences by the **clock tower**. Looking back from the Sun Bastion you can see the spray-swept tomb of a Muslim saint. Because they had no further use after the British had taken Galle these three landward bastions and their batteries have not been too much butchered. Looking down from the upper part of the Moon Bastion the foundations of two cell blocks show through the parched grass.

In the old town

Descend from the walls now and head up Church Street. The **National Museum°** (0900-1700, closed Sunday & Monday, Rs35) is a waste of time. Instead of concentrating on the interesting history of Galle there are bits and pieces from all over the place, none of them adequately described.

The fine building that now houses the **New Oriental Hotel*** started life in 1684 as the Dutch headquarters. After a variety of uses, including a British barracks, it became a hotel in 1865. Claimed to be the oldest hotel in Sri Lanka, it has been in the hands of the same Burgher family since 1902. The hotel has a good collection of historic prints of Galle, well worth a look for the price of a pot of tea (Rs120).

The Dutch **Groote Kerk*** in Church Street is the oldest Protestant church in Sri Lanka. It was built in 1754 on the site of a Capuchin monastery by the wife of the Commandeur (governor) Casparus de Jong to mark the birth of a son. Her memorial is in the floor just on the left as you enter. There are many more finely carved gravestones with the traditional hourglass and skull and crossbones *memento mori*. Wooden memorials on the walls follow the same themes. Going by other memorials the Dutch Reformed churches were run by the Methodists after the Dutch eclipse. Note the suspended wooden pulpit and its canopy.

On the corner of Queen Street opposite a cock emblem and the date Anno 1683 mark the old **Dutch Government House**, later known as Queen's House. This is now the offices of Walker & Co, a trading company which, on request, will probably give you a quick look.

The Anglican **All Saints Church***, consecrated in 1871, is more attractive inside than out. Its woodwork and stained glass make it like a little piece of England transplanted to the tropics. The church bell in the left side aisle took a convoluted route from one of the Liberty merchant ships mass-produced in America during the Second World War to Galle.

Under the grid pattern of streets the Dutch constructed a system of sewers which were flushed by the sea. Leave the Fort by the Main Gate, opened up by the British in 1873.

The new town

Exploring the new town is less rewarding, and a lot busier and noisier. The **Kerkhopf** Dutch cemetery, which dates from 1786, has *memento mori* emblazoned on its gates. Water monitors, large lizards which locals may tell you are crocodiles, can be seen by the noisome canal on Havelock Place. The disgusting stink should discourage anyone from exploring here. **St. Mary's Cathedral** is of little interest. The division of Main and Sea Streets on the way to Unawatuna is marked by an **equestrian statue**.

At the far end of the harbour from town is Watering Point, so called as ships used to replenish their supplies from the springs here. The rock above the springs, Rhumassala Kanda, is a chunk of the Himalayas dumped here by Hanuman.

Shopping. Galle is notable for lace and embroidery. Charming saleswomen will pounce on you near the lighthouse.

Arrival and departure. Bus or train (2½hrs.) from Colombo, the train is safer and vastly preferable.

Accommodation

(STD Code 09).

New Oriental Hotel, 10 Church Street, Fort. Tel/Fax 34591. DWB $35 Suite $50. Rest. Bar. Totally unspoiled colonial hotel. Vast rooms with acres of polished wood and all original furnishings. Billiards room. Small swimming pool. Highly recommended.

Closenburg Hotel, off Matara Road near new docks (3km from town). Tel 32241 Fax 34248. SWB $20 DWB $30. Rest. Bar. House built on the foundations of an old Dutch fort by a P&O captain. Fine views, though not improved by land reclamation for the new harbour. Most attractive place, and reasonable for the quality.

Rampart Hotel, 31 Rampart Street. Tel 074-380 103. DWB $17. Rest. Bar (beer Rs150). Very pleasant combination of old and new buildings in a quiet location. Good views, jewellery showroom.

Old Dutch House, 46 Lighthouse Street, Fort. Tel 22370 Fax 32045. SWB $5 DWB $7. Rest. Dutch 17th century house with original furniture and old prints. The rooms are all named after Dutch governors.

Hotel Weltrevreden, 104 Pedlar Street, Fort. Tel 22650. DWB $7. Rest. Bar. Quiet garden, just like staying in a family home, which it is.

Mr RK Kodikara, Beatrice House, 29 Rampart Street, Fort. Tel 22351. SWB/DWB $5. Rest. Simple rooms in a friendly household.

Eating and Drinking.
Best to eat where you are staying. *Queen's Court Restaurant & Bar*, near the Old Gate, does good rice and curry for around Rs80. *Chinese Globe Restaurant* on Havelock Place is said to be good, but looks less than inviting. *Closenberg Hotel* and its terrace bar have good views across the bay.

The South

High Buddha at Wewurukannala

Past Galle everything quietens down and the pace of life slackens. Even the buses travel at a slightly saner speed. Now, safe from package land, the independent traveller can start to discover the real laid-back Serendib, quiet and beautiful beaches, temples, and Sri Lanka's holiest town, Kataragama. Take your time, like the locals, and enjoy it.

UNAWATUNA

Looking for a quiet inexpensive beach resort, Unawatuna is the first place to try on the way down from Colombo. The beach is an attractive curve backed

UNAWATUNA

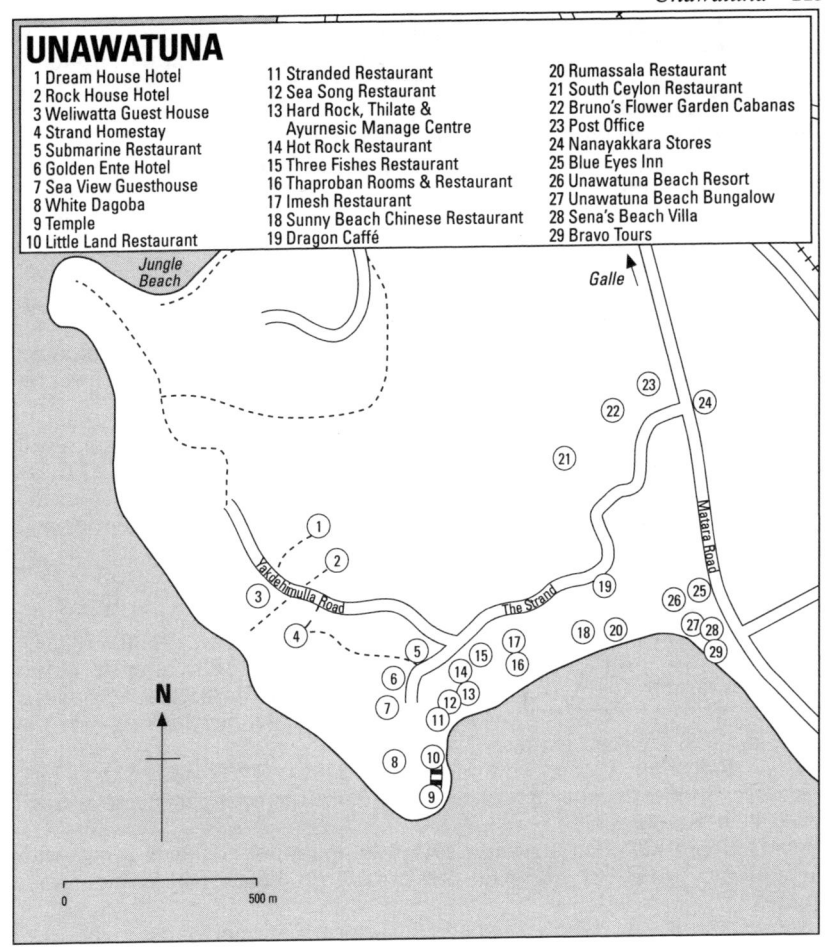

1 Dream House Hotel
2 Rock House Hotel
3 Weliwatta Guest House
4 Strand Homestay
5 Submarine Restaurant
6 Golden Ente Hotel
7 Sea View Guesthouse
8 White Dagoba
9 Temple
10 Little Land Restaurant
11 Stranded Restaurant
12 Sea Song Restaurant
13 Hard Rock, Thilate & Ayurnesic Manage Centre
14 Hot Rock Restaurant
15 Three Fishes Restaurant
16 Thaproban Rooms & Restaurant
17 Imesh Restaurant
18 Sunny Beach Chinese Restaurant
19 Dragon Caffé
20 Rumassala Restaurant
21 South Ceylon Restaurant
22 Bruno's Flower Garden Cabanas
23 Post Office
24 Nanayakkara Stores
25 Blue Eyes Inn
26 Unawatuna Beach Resort
27 Unawatuna Beach Bungalow
28 Sena's Beach Villa
29 Bravo Tours

by palm trees. Closer to the sea are madulla trees, one of the few broad-leaved trees that thrive on sand and salt water. The western end of the beach is marked by a Buddhist temple and, above that, a white dagoba. There is a wide range of places to stay and good inexpensive restaurants right on the beach.

Much of the **beach** is rather narrow and shelves quite steeply, but because of the reefs a short distance offshore it is sheltered and safe. Even when waves are breaking high over the rocks by the temple it is calm on the beach. The beach close to the temple is very shallow and ideal for children and weak swimmers, one of few places in Sri Lanka that is. The nicest bit of beach is from the Sea Song to the Hot Rock restaurants where trees grow right down to the tideline and provide natural shade. Moving along, the beach between Eagle Restaurant and Samson's Chai Shop is a bit of a tip, and then gets more pleasant again.

Some way away (an hour's walk or Rs100 each way in a three-wheeler) is what the locals call **Jungle Beach** which is very secluded. You need to take

116 *The South*

food and drink with you, nothing is provided there. You can get a boat trip round to Jungle Beach from Submarine Restaurant (see below), including snorkelling, for Rs1500, and the same people do evening barbecues there for Rs1000 all inclusive.

Snorkelling along the reef is popular, and several places hire outfits, the Thilak Restaurant, for example, at Rs50 per hour. Turtles are often seen here. The Submarine Restaurant and Diving Station (Tel 074-380 358) does one-day fun **diving courses** for Rs3500 and more serious UDI courses. Scuba hire is Rs1300 per dive, or Rs5000 for five, after which you qualify for one free. They also run a **glass-bottomed boat** at Rs1000 per hour. The Thilak Restaurant will do a two-hour **fishing** trip around the reefs and rocks by outrigger canoe for up to three people for Rs1000.

Walking up to the dagoba you have a **view*** of Galle from the lighthouse and white mosque in the south up to All Saints Church and the clock tower on the old walls. Great place to watch the sunset, too.

Arrival and departure. Any bus from Galle (¼hr at most) towards Matara will drop you at the Yaddehimulla Road junction just past the post office. There are always three-wheelers here. The alternative is a three-wheeler from the station or bus-stand in Galle for around Rs200. Several travel agencies and hotels run air-conditioned taxis to the airport for around Rs2000.

Accommodation (STD Code 09)

Unawatuna Beach Resort. Tel/Fax 32247. DWB H/B $35. Rest. Bar. Lunch buffet Rs250, dinner buffet Rs325, or a la carte. Some rooms have balconies looking over the beach and sea. Pleasant garden.

Beach Bungalow, Parangiyawatha. Tel/Fax 24327. DWB B&B $12-13 incl. Rest. Bar. Spotless rooms in a pleasant garden. Interesting menu at average prices, beer Rs100.

Sena's Beach Villa, Parangiwatta. DWB $6. Plain but adequate rooms with fan and net. Meals at Mermaid Restaurant on beach where the owner cooks.

Strand Homestay (take path behind *Golden Ente* and cross right footbridge). Tel 24358. DWB $10-12. Suite $21. Rest (*Stranded* on the beach). Spacious rooms in old house. All have private verandas and most fridges.

The Dream House, Yaddhehimulla Road. Tel 078-68513 Fax 078-68310. DWB $17 (a snip). Rest (non-residents welcome). Bar. Traditional house beautifully renovated by an Italian couple who are in residence from October to May. Truly authentic Italian food. One of the outstanding places to stay in Sri Lanka.

South Ceylon Lodging, Yaddehimulla Road. DR $2 with fan. Rest (veg.). Breakfast Rs30-75, stuffed peppers Rs100. Rooms a little dark, but who's complaining at this price?

Thaproban Rooms, Yaddehimulla Road. Tel 077-901 559 Fax 074-380 019. DWB $21. Rest (said to be very good). Bar. Interesting menu. Brand new building.

Three Fishes, Yaddehimulla Road. Tel 32241. SWB $11 ($8) DWB $17 ($14) (both include breakfast). Rest. Bar. Colonial style house on the beach. Old style bedrooms with four-poster beds.

Zimmer Rest, Valledewala Road. Tel 074-380 366 Fax 22747. DR $3 with net and fan. Rest. Bar. Breakfast Rs75, free tea, and you can cook for yourself in the kitchen. Colonial house.

Seaview Guest House, Devala Road. Tel/Fax 23649. DWB $10-14. Rest. Bar. A pleasant place, but they will probably try to force H/B or F/B terms on you.

Bruno's Flower Garden Cabanas, Welladevala Road. Tel 077-900 134 Fax 53387. DWB $10 incl ($7 incl). Rest. Bar. Main courses Rs100-270. Spotlessly clean cabanas each with its own verandah and little garden full of bougainevillea. One of the very best guest houses in Sri Lanka, even if not on the beach.

Golden Ente, Devala Road. DWB $8. No meals. Nine spacious (but rather sparse) rooms with sea-view balconies for the upper six.

Colonial Holiday Inn, Yaddehimulla Road. Tel 58043 (reservations only). DWB $5 ($3). Breakfast Rs65.

The *Blue Eyes Inn* is new and looks nice, just for Sinatra fans? Also a smart new hotel (as yet unnamed) next to Colonial Holiday Inn, around $28 The *Bay Guest House* and its *L'Escale Italian Restaurant* on Yaddehimulla Road are said to be good.

There are several more places along the main road which we have not covered because they are noisy.

Eating and drinking

Thilak Restaurant & Cabanas. Tel 074-380 356. SL/Western. Very good seafood, had a butterfish cooked to perfection. Also has four basic cabanas on the beach at DR Rs300.

Close to the Thilak are the **Hot Rock**, **Hard Rock**, and **Seasong**, all OK. and much of a muchness. *Sonya's Health Food Restaurant* is just that, the **Sunny Beach Chinese Restaurant** is good, the **South Ceylon Restaurant** does a wide variety of vegetarian food and, for a bit of a splurge, the Italian food at **The Dream House** (imported olive oil and all) takes a lot of beating.

Several places put on a disco now and then, and the Unawatuna Beach Resort sometimes has live entertainment. Both are advertised locally.

UNAWATUNA TO WELIGAMA

The coast eastwards from Unawatuna comprises 23km of attractive beaches. The problem is that the main road is close to them almost all the way. This is less busy than the Colombo to Galle road, but it is still hard to find peace or seclusion.

KOGGALA

The Sri Lanka Air Force airfield at Koggala is a legacy of the Second World War, and Koggala Lake, a little inland, was an RAF base for flying boats. The Japanese fleet which attacked Ceylon was spotted by a Catalina flying boat from here. The **lake** (which is signposted from the main road) has good birdlife but, lacking 4WD, you will have to explore on foot in extreme temperature and humidity.

The **Martin Wickramasinghe Museum of Folk Art & Culture**** (open daily 0900-1700, Rs15) is probably the best and most informative museum in Sri

Lanka. There is a lot of interesting stuff on the local way of life well arranged and explained. Note the section on games and pastimes; things long popular in the west have their counterparts here. If a private trust can organise a place like this, why can't the government? Or is that a silly question?

Arrival and departure. Frequent bus services between Galle and Matara. Koggala has a railway station, check that the train stops there.

KATALUWA

The **Kataluwa Purvarama Rajamaha Viharaya**** temple was extensively restored and repainted in the 19th century, and has some of the most interesting frescoes in Sri Lanka.

The entrance to the temple is dated 1886. Over the right entrance to the shrine is a painting of Queen Victoria supported by lion and unicorn. In the same position over the other door is Purva Rane. Between the two doors are male and female forms of a peacock deity. In the shrine is a large reclining Buddha, flanked by a seated one in meditation mudra and a standing one in teaching mudra. Facing the reclining Buddha are Kataragama and the dark figure of Vishnu. The paintings on this wall and the corresponding outer wall are in Kandyan style, bold uncomplicated figures on a red ground.

The ambulatory around the shrine is completely covered by frescoes in different styles. Going clockwise, as you should, note the european influence both artistically and in the background details. As you approach the front wall again note the group of Portuguese figures and, near them another image of Victoria, again with lions and unicorns. The painting in this area displays the intricacy one finds in Indian Mughal painting. The bottom row the whole way round depicts purgatory and the many unpleasant consequences of wrong-doing. The frescoes are not in perfect condition, but justify careful study and the effort of getting there.

Arrival and departure. Bus (or train) to Kataluwa, which is on the main road. The temple is signposted, and a three-wheeler usually waits at the junction, from where it is 3.5km. In your own transport turn off left just before the 133km marker, go left at the first T-junction and right at the second.

Ahangama is the best place to see the famous **stilt fishermen** at work, depending on the tides. They perch on stakes well out from the shore and fish with rod and line. The beach at **Midigama** is said to have good surf at times, but the area behind it makes Hikkaduwa look very attractive.

Accommodation. There are hotels and guest houses of all sorts along this road. All are close to the road and suffer traffic noise, and the surroundings tend to be pretty bleak.

WELIGAMA

Weligama means sandy village, and that sums it up. The bay is sheltered and was used as a port in ancient times. In the bay, close to the Rest House, is **Taprobane Island**, the house on it built by a French count and once home to the writer Paul Bowles. The **beach** is too close to the town and main road to be either clean or peaceful.

Weligama has a famous **rock figure** 4m high which is usually reckoned to be

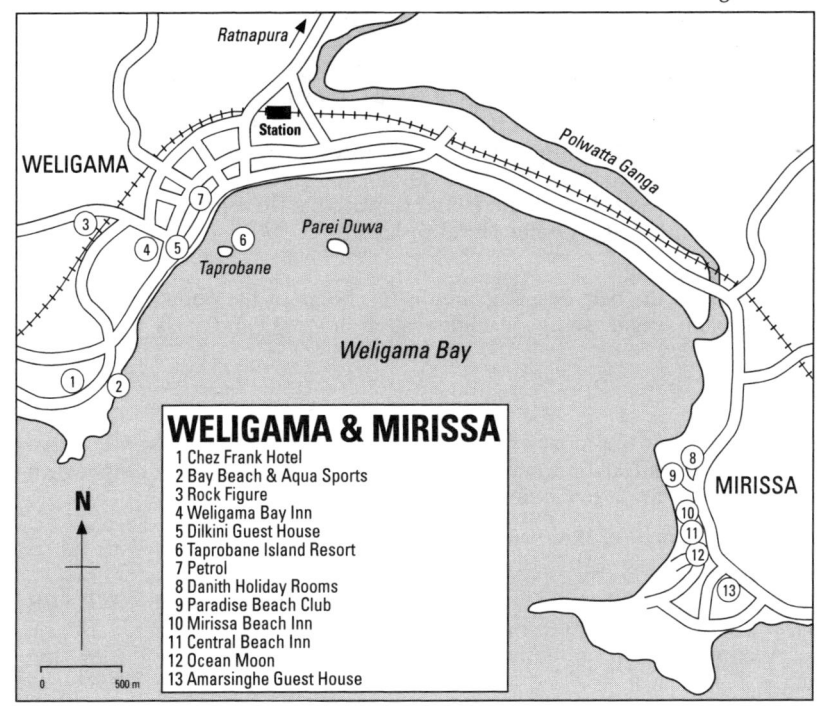

WELIGAMA & MIRISSA
1 Chez Frank Hotel
2 Bay Beach & Aqua Sports
3 Rock Figure
4 Weligama Bay Inn
5 Dilkini Guest House
6 Taprobane Island Resort
7 Petrol
8 Danith Holiday Rooms
9 Paradise Beach Club
10 Mirissa Beach Inn
11 Central Beach Inn
12 Ocean Moon
13 Amarsinghe Guest House

of Avelokiteshwara (vigilant master), one of the maitreyas or Buddhas to come. An alternative explanation is Samantabhadra, which would suggest the presence of Tantric Buddhism in Sri Lanka. The evidence for this is that the crown has four (five with the implied one at the back) images of the Dhyani Buddha making this an Adi-Buddha, lord of the five Buddhas who control the four quarters and the centre of the cosmos. There are more fanciful interpretations too: local legend makes the statue 2000 years old (much more likely eighth or ninth century) and of Kusta Rajah or the leper king, for no good reason. Others refer to it as Agbo or Agrabohi, the nephew of King Mahatissa who brought coconuts to Sri Lanka. Stylistically this figure is similar to those at Buduruvegala (see p180).

Shopping. Weligama is notable for its handmade **lacework and embroidery**.

Arrival and departure. Bus or train from Galle (1hr) or Colombo ($3\frac{1}{2}$hrs).

For the rock figure take a three-wheeler from the bus-stand or station. In your own transport turn off the sea road to Weligama Town (just past the filling station coming from Galle), and left at the bus-stand down the old main road, continue to the level crossing.

Accommodation (STD Code 041).

Weligama Bay Inn (CHC), New By-Pass Road. Tel 50299. SWB $12 DWB $13. Rest. Bar. Usual CHC menu, three course meals for $7. Rooms have balconies with views to Taprobane Island and the fishing harbour.

Dilkini Tourist Inn (opposite Weligama Bay Inn). Tel 50281. DWB $90. Rest. Bar. Attractive garden.

Chez Frank, 158 Kapparatota Road (near Bay Beach Hotel and signposted off New By-Pass Road on Galle side of town). Tel 50584. DWB A/C $19 ($15) DWB $13 ($10). Rest (very good, average prices). Bar. The accommodation is in bungalows in a nice garden. Quiet and highly recommended. 500m from a clean, quiet beach.

The idyllic house on Taprobane Island is available for rent; if you think you can afford it contact the Chalet Hotel in Kandy.

Eating and Drinking.

Chez Frank is the best bet. This area is the home of the popular dessert of curd and palm sugar syrup (usually called honey), and it is at its best locally.

MIRISSA

Mirissa has one of the most attractive beaches in Sri Lanka, a gentle curve with a forested hill at one end and a rocky islet at the other, both worth exploring. There are a few quiet places to stay.

Arrival and departure. 4km south of Weligama (bus).

Accomodation (STD Code 041)

Paradise Beach Club, 140 Gunasiri Mahime MW. Tel/Fax 50380. SWB H/B $18 DWB H/B $24; out of season DWB B&B $13. Rest (good, average prices). Bar. Accommodation in detached bungalows. Good place right on the beach.

Mirissa Beach Inn, Galle Road. Tel 50410 Fax 50115. DWB $9/11 incl. Rest. Bar. An old house with fretwork round the eaves for which this area is notable. Will collect you from the airport for Rs2800.

Central Beach Inn, Galle Road. Tel 072-612 170. DWB $5 ($5) also a cabana $8 ($6). Rest. Bar. Rice and curry Rs95. Don't be put off by the dilapidated building in front.

Danith Holiday Rooms, Gunasiri Mahime MW. Tel 071-72229 Fax 50115. DR $2/3 DWB $5. Rest. Bar. Main courses from Rs100, rice and curry Rs125.

Ocean Moon, Galle Road. Tel 50959. SWB $4 DWB $5 also a DWB $8 very close to the beach. Rest. Bar. Clean and comfortable rooms with net and fan. Rice and curry Rs120, grilled fish with chips and salad Rs190, beer Rs90. All prices incl.

Amarasinghe Guest House. Tel 51204. DWB $3-5. Rest. Bar. Breakfast Rs70, rice and curry Rs125. Run by the same family as the Amarasinghe Guest House in Haputale, and equally relaxed and happy. In a quiet wooded area the landward side of the main road. When first arriving take a three-wheeler from the road junction, it is not the 60m the sign says. Later you can use the short cut to get to the beach.

Eating and Drinking. One beach restaurant near the Paradise Beach Club, probably closed when things are quiet.

Polhena (3km from Matara on the Mirissa side) has a coral reef and various places to stay. Much of the beach is given over to the smelly processing of coconut husks into coir. The beach also gets crowded with local people at weekends and Poya days. It is hard to see why anyone would choose to stay here when Mirissa is so close and so much nicer.

MATARA

The name comes from Mahatara or Great Harbour. The Portuguese used Matara at various times, but it was left to the Dutch to establish a permanent presence. Their hold on the coast allowed them to control the supply of salt to the hinterland, and this was the cause of the Salt War. Kirti Sri swept down from Kandy, took the fort and held it for six years until 1766. In retaliation the Dutch sacked Kandy in 1765 and Kirti Sri had to withdraw. The war, however, crippled the Dutch financially and was one of the causes of the English walkover twenty years later and, indirectly of course, of the ultimate demise of the kingdom of Kandy.

Exploring

The Dutch built two forts in Matara. The gate of the **Star Fort** (more properly Redoute van Eck) has the VOC emblem and the coat of arms of Baron van Eck and the date 1703. On either side are slots for the drawbridge chains. Until they complete the new bridge you have to walk the plank over the moat. Inside the gate are the names of the two engineers who built the fort. The Archaeological Department has recently restored the interior of the fort nicely. In the barrack rooms surrounding the little lawn and well are two old drawings of the fort and a model of it.

The rest of the space is occupied by a **Museum of Ancient Paintings** (closed Thursday). This is well arranged and, for a change, there are lots of informative captions. The catch is that they are all in Sinhalese only. Southern Sri Lanka is the heart of Sinhala nationalism, and the unwillingness to make concessions to any other culture is obvious.

The Star Fort covered the river crossing to the other, much larger, **fort** which was formed by building a wall across the peninsula the other side of the Nilwala Ganga river. This fort has some old military buildings and a Dutch Reformed Church by the parade ground, but little of real interest.

In the new town is the **Sri Madura drum factory**. The drums here are the real thing, made for temples and drumming schools, not the usual tourist rubbish. All the work is done by hand and, considering the quality, prices are very reasonable, ranging from Rs600 up to Rs3500. Tablas are Rs4000-6000 depending on quality. The people, all related to one another, are happy to explain the various processes. That black disc on the drumskin is many thin layers of a secret formulation; application and tuning takes a skilled person four hours. The factory is tucked away behind a traditional building with the sign People's Dispensary; the old cobbler on the corner will show you the way, anyone else who does will be after a commission.

Matara was the birth place of Sir Henry Lawrence (1806) who died commanding the defence of Lucknow during the Indian Mutiny of 1857.

Arrival and departure. Train from Galle or Colombo (4hrs) or bus from Galle. Matara is at present the rail terminus, but an extension to Katagarama is under construction.

MATARA

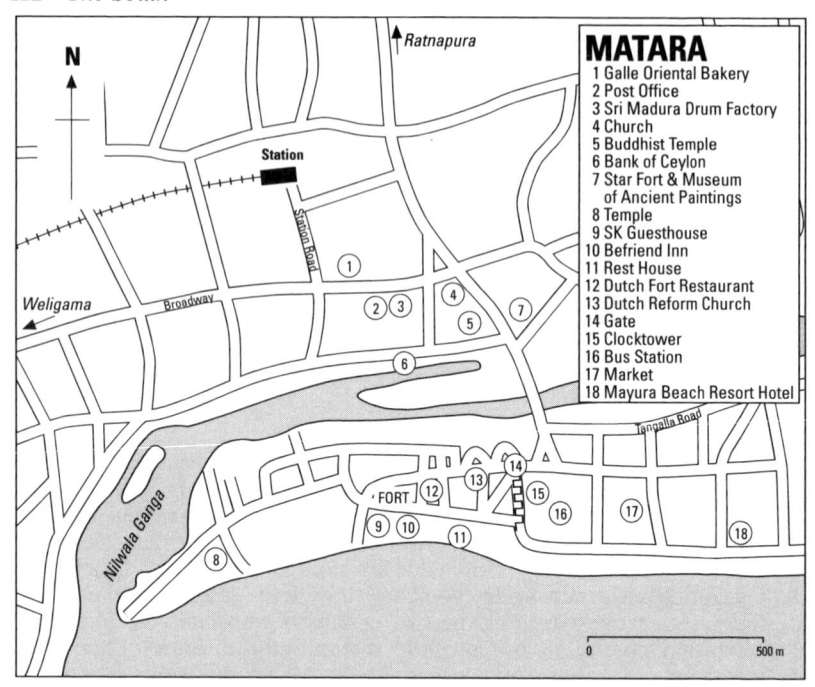

1 Galle Oriental Bakery
2 Post Office
3 Sri Madura Drum Factory
4 Church
5 Buddhist Temple
6 Bank of Ceylon
7 Star Fort & Museum of Ancient Paintings
8 Temple
9 SK Guesthouse
10 Befriend Inn
11 Rest House
12 Dutch Fort Restaurant
13 Dutch Reform Church
14 Gate
15 Clocktower
16 Bus Station
17 Market
18 Mayura Beach Resort Hotel

Festivals. Until very recently the traditional form of local transport was by bullock cart. These are mainly seen now racing at the time of the Sinhalese New Year. A pair of good bullocks has a surprising turn of speed.

Accommodation (STD Code 041).

Rest House, Fort (100m from bus-stand). Tel 22299. DWB $8. Rest. Bar. Starter plus rice and curry Rs225. Good location by the beach.

If the Rest House is full, or for something slightly cheaper, try *SK Guest House* or *Befriend Inn* a short walk away.

Eating and Drinking. Apart from the *Rest House* the best bet is the *Galle Oriental Bakery & Restaurant* on the main road in from Galle.

MATARA TO TANGALLA

The **Weherehena Temple*** (near Matara) is one of two along this coast boasting huge Buddha statues. The original temple is 250 years old and underground, like the 600m of passages which have many of the 20,000 murals to be seen here. A small collection of Buddha figures from other countries is in the entrance. The main attraction however is the Buddha figure 39m/128ft high seated in the meditation mudra. The statue was started in 1900 and took fifteen years to build. For a long time it stood in solitary splendour, then, in the 1980s an ugly concrete structure was built behind it, and finally Japanese Buddhists paid for the fibreglass canopy. Why can't they leave anything alone? The bo-tree in front of the statue is 600 years old and an offshoot of the

Anuradhapura one. You can climb the structure more for the view than anything else. The turning to the temple is signposted about 1km out of Matara. You can ignore the dusty car park and drive down to the temple forecourt. There is no entry fee, a donation of Rs100 is expected. If you only have the time or inclination for just one giant Buddha statue save it for the larger and more pleasing one at Wewurukannala.

Moving on towards Tangalla, from the main road you see the attractive buildings of **Ruhuana University**.

DONDRA HEAD

Dondra Head (6km from Matara) is the southernmost point of Sri Lanka. Like Kanya Kumari in India this is a very holy place; the alternative name of Devinuwara means City of the Gods. Kataragama landed here, and this is where Rama was reunited with Sita. A huge Krishna temple stood here until destroyed by the Portuguese in 1587. The Maha Vishnu Devala (seventh century) was a magnificent building with a gilt copper roof. Like other great coastal temples it was an important landmark and must have been familiar to sailors from all over the orient. Rama and Krishna are of course both avatars of Vishnu. A small shrine on Gal Ge Hill is the only reminder, and an important festival and procession takes place here at the same time as Kandy Perahera.

The **lighthouse*** is well worth seeing. It was built in 1889 of masonry, octagonal outside and circular within. You can climb the spiral stairs through the immaculate interior to the platform around the light, great views, for Rs50. The light has been modernised, so instead of one huge bulb and mirrors and lenses there are banks of small quartz halogen units. A tiny beach at the foot of the lighthouse is the place for a holy paddle. To reach the lighthouse take a bus to Dondra (or Devinuwara) village. Turn towards towards the sea at the clock tower and go straight past the new standing Buddha figure for 400m, then turn left.

Dinawar is now just a fishing village. It used to be a busy port and this was where Ibn Battuta landed.

DIKWELLA

Dikwella is a beach resort with a range of hotels, useful as a base for visiting the places described below.

WEWURUKANNALA TEMPLE

Just inland from Dikwella is the **Wewurukannala Vihara***** with its giant 50m/164ft high Buddha, the largest in Sri Lanka. Entry costs Rs25, and a camera Rs50. The earliest temple on this site is 350 years old and of no great interest. Its 19th century (2443 of the Buddhist era) successor is a very different matter. The facade of this could equally belong to a baroque church or a mosque. Have a look at the mock heraldry above the two entrance arches; in each case a shield with a crown above is supported by two lions rampant. There are quarterings on the right one including what appears to be an angel with a harp, and on the left is an elephant carrying a dagoba shaped relic casket. Beyond those, like bookends, are unicorns.

The ambulatory around the shrine has a series of kneeling figures paying homage to Buddha and representing his 550 former incarnations. Around that is a series of figures in tableaux, some of which have a very Victorian look to them. At the back are murals which include holy places in Sri Lanka including Adam's Peak and this temple. In the shrine is a large reclining Buddha; to the left is a seated one in earth-witness mudra and, facing that two standing ones, one with a begging bowl. The muted colours of the murals, the subdued light, coloured glass, and high painted ceiling are all reminiscent of a cathedral. Notice the angels in the spandrels of one of the ceiling rosettes and the group of three monks who look for all the world like Christian saints. A most pleasing building, so don't let any guide hustle you around it.

The huge statue outside is covered in ceramic tiles and has a brightly coloured spiral sirispata on its head instead of the usual flame shaped one. This somehow has a more benevolent feel than the statue at the Weherehena Temple. It too, unfortunately, has an ugly building behind (you can climb it if you wish), but at least it is invisible from the front.

MULKIRIGALA

Further inland is Mulkirigala. The Portuguese and Dutch both thought of this hill, for no very good reason, as the tomb of Adam. It had, in fact, been a holy place even before the coming of Buddhism, and there is evidence of old fertility cults. The monastery was founded in the second century BC, one of the very first in Sri Lanka.

The **Cave Temples**** (open 0600-1800, entry Rs100), on different levels, follow the usual pattern and are linked by steps. Harder to find are the rock cells of the monks.

The first terrace has two temples with reclining Buddhas, nice ceiling painting in the first, and a dagoba. Note the dripstone carved into the rock above the temples to prevent water running in. The temple on the second level is very similar.

There are three temples on the third level, all with reclining Buddhas. That on the left has standing figures at the head end in the fearless mudra and nicely painted ceiling. At the feet of the Buddha in the centre temple is a white marble Buddha in witness mudra with his fingers touching the earth, the topknot typical of the statue's Burmese origin. In the last temple tableaux of sorrowful followers stand at the Buddha's head and feet. Facing that are murals of the funeral procession and cremation at Kushinagar. On the ceiling is a florid painting of Nirvana. This is a very pleasing cave temple.

Above here the steps get steeper, you can even take a different route to the summit by using the old rock-cut steps. At the top are a couple of bo-trees, a dagoba, and good views, mainly to the south. The red and white mast is at Tangalle.

Arrival and departure. 22km north of Dikwella, bus via Beliatta, where you may need to change, and on towards Wiraketiya. 16km north of Tangalla, bus as above or direct to Wiraketiya, then change or take a three-wheeler for the 3km to Mulkirigala. Buses will drop you at the junction 1km from the hill, three-wheelers wait there. Driving, from Wewurukannala Vihara return to the B101, continue to Beliatta, go straight on at the clock tower, and after 3km look out for a sign to the right.

MAWELLA

At Mawella (6km from Dikwella towards Tangalla, and well off the main road) is an ocean **blowhole**, said to be the second largest of only six in the world. Longer lists on a postcard, please. During the south-east monsoon, and especially in June, the waves force water into a cleft in the rocks 20m high. From there it can spurt upwards like a geyser for 18m. The noise it makes has given rise to the nickname *Hoom-manaya*. This is really not worth visiting outside the monsoon time, and the surroundings are tawdry.

Arrival and departure. Frequent buses along the Matara-Tangalla road.

Accommodation
Dikwella Village Resort. Tel 041-55271 or 01-698 346 (Colombo) Fax 041-55410 or 01-685 555 (Colombo). SWB $45 DWB $55 B&B. Rest (2). Bar. Beautifully done resort with good beaches on both sides. Windsurfing and PADI diving courses for $60.

Just over the road is the much less expensive *Michael Inn & Restaurant*. In between these two in quality and price is the *Dikwella Beach Resort* (Tel 041-55326). There are one or two other restaurants and places to stay.

The following places are on the road from Dikwella to Tangalle in that order. The first three are probably only practicable if you have your own transport.

Manahara Beach Cottages and Cabanas, Mahawela Road, Moraketiyara (200m past 189km marker, turn right at gates). Tel 071-24960. DWB H/B $20 incl. Rest. Bar. Very quiet and adequately comfortable. Peaceful beach said to be safe from strong currents.

Sunrise Beach Cabanas, Moraketiyara. DWB $17 F/B. Rest. Bar. A little basic for the money, but if you're after peace...

No name. A new development down the same lane and more or less next door to the above.

Palm Paradise Cabanas, Goyambokka (just before 194km marker). Tel/Fax 40338 or (Colombo) 01-685 107. DWB H/B $24 incl. Rest. Bar. Attractive cabanas built on stilts, but can feel damp and salty. Good food and service. Very pleasant but overdue for some maintenance. Fronts directly onto a small secluded beach.

Goyambokka Guest House, Goyambokka (as above). Tel 40838 Fax 40401. DWB $12.

Calm Garden Cabanas, Goyambokka. (as above). Tel 40523. DWB $12 ($7 out of season). Rest. Bar. Rice and curry Rs200. Just two peaceful cabanas 5 minutes walk from the beach.

Claughton must also be mentioned. This was the house of Bevis Bawa's (see p000) architect brother Geoffrey. By all accounts most attractive, it stands in 2ha/5acres of landscaped grounds overlooking the sea. Renting the whole house (one double, two twin rooms) costs $1500 per week full board. This sounds a lot until you think of it as $36 per person per day for luxury, personal service, and the privacy you never find in a hotel. Food and service are said to be excellent. Phone Colombo 01-509 134 for reservations.

TANGALLA

Tangalla is spelled in various ways; pronunciation usually comes out as Tengol. Tangalla used to be the seaside town for tea planters and others wanting a change from the hills. A pleasant enough little town, its beaches have little to commend them to travellers. Working from the north, Medaketiya Beach suffers from strong currents and is wide open. The part in front of the Shanika Beach Inn and Lanka German Guest House is inhabited by cows and in the state you would expect. South of the Gayana Guest House buildings between the road and the sea provide some privacy. Although a few westerners stay here the accommodation on this beach is geared to Sri Lankan visitors. The beach north of the Tangalla Bay Hotel is reasonably sheltered though overlooked by the main road. By far the best bet is the beach in front of the Palm Paradise Cabanas, and the smaller one just to the north, which are private enough for skinny-dipping. Interesting rock pools, too, with strange little fish which live and feed above the waterline.

Arrival and departure. 195km from Colombo. Frequent buses from Matara (1hr)

Accommodation (STD Code 047).

Tangalle Bay Hotel. Tel/Fax 40346. SWB $21 DWB $24 (+ $4 A/C). Rest. Bar. Starters Rs100, main courses Rs200-350, four course dinner Rs400, beer Rs110. A modernist building rather nondescript outside but well kept and fun inside. Large nicely furnished rooms with private balconies and sea views. Terrace and swimming pool above the rocks. Good beaches on both sides.

Rest House. Tel 40299. SWB $8 DWB $12. Rest. Bar. Main courses Rs250-275. The core of the building is Dutch, dated 1774 by the foundation stone in the steps. Accommodation is mostly in a modern concrete block. Land reclamation for the fishing harbour has spoiled the outlook, and it is expensive for what it is.

Touristen Gasthaus, 13 Pallikkudawa Road. Tel/Fax 40370. DWB $8/10. Rest. Bar. Spotless.

Namal Garden Beach Hotel, Medaketiya Road. Tel 40352. DWB $5 (downstairs) $8 (upstairs) B&B + $2. Rest. Bar. Nice view from upstairs rooms, and that's about it.

Gayana Guest House, 96 Medaketiya Beach. Tel/Fax 40447. DWB $5-8. Rest. Bar.

Anila Beach Inn & Restaurant, Medaketiya Beach. Tel 40447. DWB $5/6. Rest. Bar.

Santana Guest House, 55 Parakrama Road. Tel 40419. DR $2 DWB $4/5 with nets and fan. Rest. Bar. The restaurant is on stilts over the creek, and a footbridge leads to the beach. Quiet, a pleasant place to stay.

Shanika Beach Inn, 69 Medaketiya Beach. DWB $5 ($3). Rest. Bar. Breakfast Rs85, rice and curry Rs140, also a la carte and barbecues.

Samans Travellers Nest, 75 Wijaya Road. Tel 40464. DWB $3/4. Rest. Bar. Motorbike hire Rs400 per day, push-bikes Rs100.

Palm Beach, Medaketiya Beach. DWB $3. Breakfast (only) Rs95.

A couple of places north of Shanika Beach Inn were inaccessible at the time of our visit as the road was up. Women travelling alone should beware the *Green Jewel*.

Eating and Drinking. A number of good restaurants, apart from the hotels. *Chanika's*, near the Tangalle Bay hotel gets very good reports.

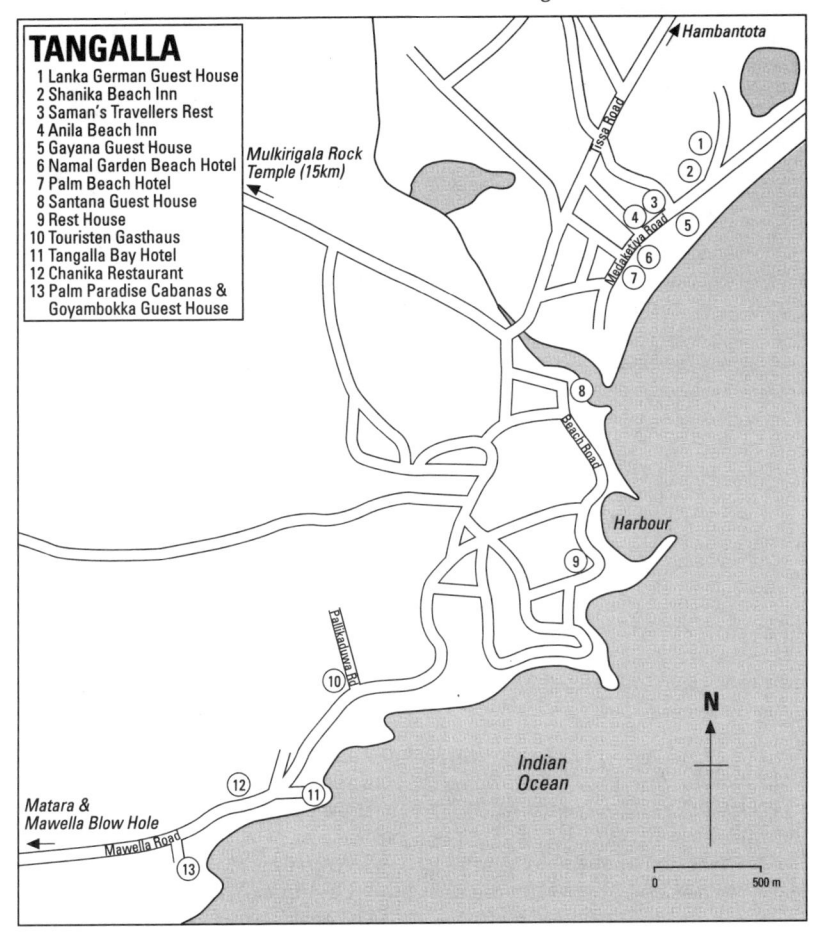

TANGALLA
1 Lanka German Guest House
2 Shanika Beach Inn
3 Saman's Travellers Rest
4 Anila Beach Inn
5 Gayana Guest House
6 Namal Garden Beach Hotel
7 Palm Beach Hotel
8 Santana Guest House
9 Rest House
10 Touristen Gasthaus
11 Tangalla Bay Hotel
12 Chanika Restaurant
13 Palm Paradise Cabanas & Goyambokka Guest House

TANGALLA TO TISSAMAHARAMA

As you leave Tangalla you encounter a completely different landscape of lagoons and marshes. This is part of the Dry Zone, unaffected by the south-westerly monsoon. Rice is still grown in large quantities, but is entirely dependent on major irrigation works. These fell into disrepair during the population drift to the more easily farmed Wet Zone, and were restored only after eight hundred years of neglect.

In **Nonagama** is a little puzzle, a statue of a woman in what appears to be Dutch costume though the inscription is in Sinhalese.

HAMBANTOTA

The name means port of sampans, a kind of boat brought here by Malay seafarers who subsequently founded their own Muslim community in this area.

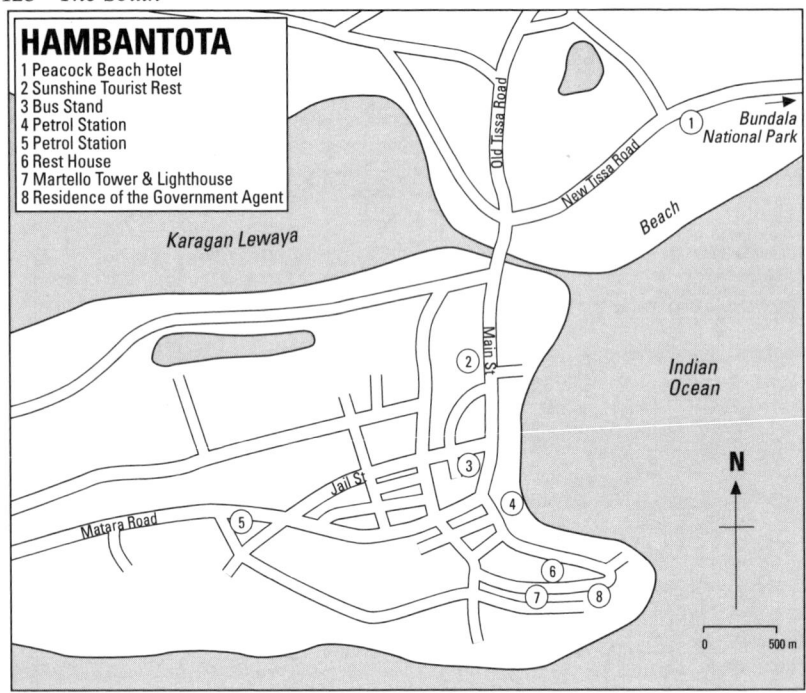

HAMBANTOTA
1 Peacock Beach Hotel
2 Sunshine Tourist Rest
3 Bus Stand
4 Petrol Station
5 Petrol Station
6 Rest House
7 Martello Tower & Lighthouse
8 Residence of the Government Agent

Today it is more noted for its extensive salt pans, producing nearly half of Sri Lanka's needs. The method is the oldest known; let sea-water into shallow pans, and wait for it to evaporate. Before modern roads the salt was carried up to the Hill Country and Kandy by pack bulls.

The town is not of surpassing interest. The government enclave behind the Rest House has one or two buildings of note. On the way up the hill from the clock tower and the little harbour you pass the **residence of the Government Agent**, once home to Leonard Woolf. After a short but distinguished career in the Ceylon Civil Service he married Virginia and settled down to a literary life in Bloomsbury. Ceylon had made a deep impression on him, and one result was his novel *The Village in the Jungle*. This masterpiece is almost forgotten in Britain but still in print in Sri Lanka. Colette thought it the most depressing book she had ever read.

Further up, opposite the entrance to the Rest House, something very like a **Martello tower** stands next to the black and white zig-zagged **lighthouse**. Hambantota's beaches are no attraction, though that in front of the Peacock Beach Hotel is kept clean. Most people visit only to use Hambantota as a base for the Bundala National Park.

Arrival and departure. Bus from Colombo (6hrs), Tangalla (1¼hrs) or Matara (2¼hrs) and into Hill Country.

Accommodation (STD Code 047)
  Peacock Beach Hotel (3km from town centre). Tel 20365 Fax 20377. SWB/

DWB $43 Suite $120 (super). Rest. Bar (Lion beer Rs150). Set lunch Rs400 incl. Swimming pool. Top class.
  Rest House. SWB $7 DWB $12. Rest. Bar. Huge, high-ceilinged bedrooms. Splendid location but not a lot else going for it.
  Sunshine Tourist Rest, 47 Main Street (100m from bus-stand). Tel 20129. DR $5 DWB $6. Breakfast Rs85. Clean and convenient, but not very quiet.

BUNDALA NATIONAL PARK

This is one of the smaller national parks, covering around 65sq km. It is nothing like as well known as Yala National Park, and consequently much quieter and less visited. Before achieving National Park status it was designated a bird sanctuary, and that remains its main distinction. Over the winter season the lagoons and lakes attract thousands and thousands of migratory birds, most notably flamingoes, pelicans, and painted storks. There are also large flocks of water fowl. Crocodiles are common, and there is the occasional elephant.

The usual way to visit the park is on an organised safari from Hambantota. This is simplest if only because no-one in the wardens' office speaks English. The Peacock Beach Hotel charges Rs1800 for jeep hire plus Rs315 per person, plus Rs120 service charge, plus Rs60 for the driver. You will find cheaper (around Rs1200 for the jeep plus all the other charges), but they are the most reliable.

Arrival and departure. The park entrance is on the Weligatta to Bundala road and, even without entering the park, this road gives you good views of the lagoons and bird life. Although shown as a pecked line on maps the road from Bundala on to Kirinda in fact presents no problems for 2WD vehicles.

KIRINDA

Kirinda was the port for Tissamaharama in the days when it was a capital city. Kirinda may have been Ptolemy's Headland of Dionysus. The Greeks had had contact with Shiva through their holding the province of Gandhara (in present day Afghanistan) and equated his elemental force with that of Dionysus.

These days Kirinda is a dead and alive sort of place, the only point of note a Buddhist temple and dagoba among huge boulders.

The really intrepid military enthusiast may hunt down **Fort Brownrigg** near Palutupana, built out in the jungle in 1813 by the British. Sir Robert Brownrigg, Bart, was governor of Ceylon at the time and laid the foundation stone himself.

Arrival and departure. 10km south of Tissa by bus. The road from Bundala village is no problem for 2WD vehicles and this is an interesting drive right off the beaten track, mainly paddy fields and very sparsely populated compared with the wet zone.

Accommodation. *Kirinda Beach Resort* may be alright inside, there's certainly nowhere else to stay, but access is through a rubbish tip and it looks out over a filthy lagoon.

TISSAMAHARAMA

Then known as Mahagama, Tissamaharama (Tissa for short) was the main town of Ruhuna principality, a state often independent of whoever was running the north of the island. It was also a traditional fall-back capital of Sri Lanka. King Tissa took refuge here, and Dutthagamani (who was born here) made it his base before leaving to retake Anuradhapura from the Tamils in the second century AD. Neglect of the irrigation system made this an arid and poor area (and one plagued by malaria) until restoration work in the 19th century.

Exploring

There are few visible reminders of Tissa's former glory, and most visitors simply use it as a base for birdwatching on the three large tanks nearby or for visiting the Yala West National Park.

For the **birdwatcher** both the Tissawewa and Wirawila Tank (the latter a bird sanctuary) are rewarding. The obvious thing is to hire a bicycle the evening before and make an early morning tour of the triangle Deberawewa-Wirawila-Pannagammuwa. The main road actually runs on a causeway right through the Wirawila Tank. From Pannagammuwa on the way back you can cycle along the top of the bund.

The few archaeological remains are mostly on the way out of town towards Deberawewa. First is the large restored **dagoba** of the Yattala Wehera, the

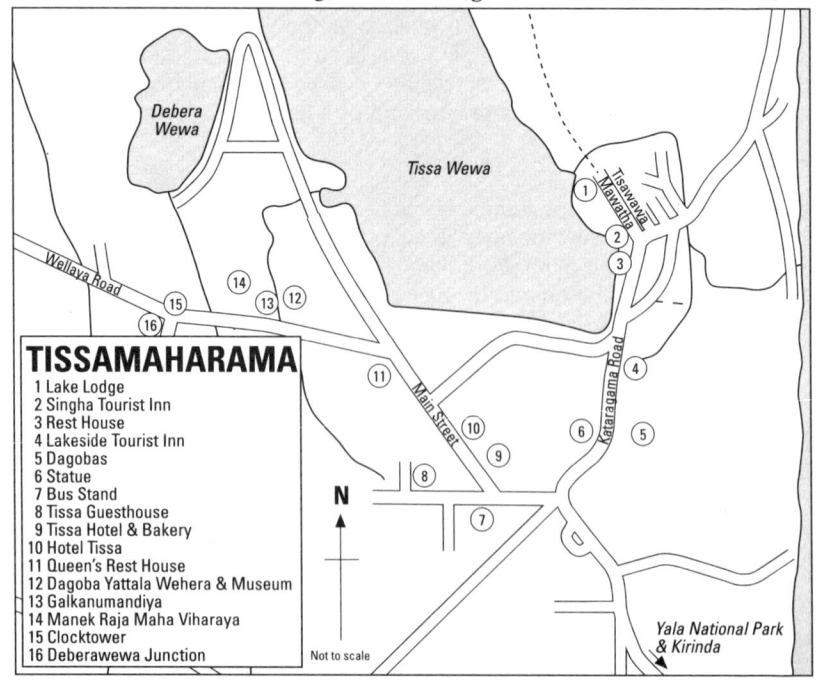

TISSAMAHARAMA
1 Lake Lodge
2 Singha Tourist Inn
3 Rest House
4 Lakeside Tourist Inn
5 Dagobas
6 Statue
7 Bus Stand
8 Tissa Guesthouse
9 Tissa Hotel & Bakery
10 Hotel Tissa
11 Queen's Rest House
12 Dagoba Yattala Wehera & Museum
13 Galkanumandiya
14 Manek Raja Maha Viharaya
15 Clocktower
16 Deberawewa Junction

main monastery. This is surrounded by an elephant wall and a moat full of water lilies. Four gatehouses at the cardinal points lead to flower altars, and there are various other small buildings in the compound. Excavation and restoration was continuing at the time of our visit. The little **museum** adjacent has bits and pieces of terracotta tiles and pipes and, outside, a large ornate urinal stone.

The **Galkanumandiya** is usually known as the King's Palace but is more likely, given its small size, to have been a monastic building. All that remains is a thicket of pillars notched at the top for wooden beams. It was most probably a multi-storey structure like the Brazen Palace in Anuradhapura. The **Manek Raja Maha Viharaya** is more notable for its fine bo-tree than its buildings.

On the road out towards Kataragama is a large **dagoba**, over-restored early in the 20th century. Despite this it seems to be in danger of collapse and is wrapped up in steel tensioning cables and scaffolding. Facing the dagoba is a modern statue of Queen Vihara Maha Devi (mother of Dutthagamani), and behind it an unrestored brick dagoba.

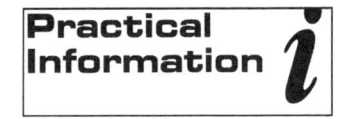

Practical Information

Arrival and departure.
Bus from Colombo (A/C 6hrs) or Hambantota (1hr). Heading for the Hill Country you will almost certainly need to change in Wellawaya.

Accommodation (STD Code 047)

Rest House (CHC), Tissawewa MW. Tel 37299. DWB $27.50 A/C + $6. Rest. Bar. Swimming pool. Comfortable and immaculately kept. Spectacular location right on the tank, well worth saving for.

Lake Side Tourist Inn, Tissawewa MW. Tel 37216. DWB $8-10 DWB A/C $15. Rest. Bar. Breakfast Rs100-160, rice and curry Rs160, main courses up to Rs350. Clean and with lots of flowers.

Singha Tourist Inn, Tissawewa MW. Tel 37090 Fax 37080. DWB $8 DWB A/C $17. Rest. Bar. Breakfast Rs90, rice and curry Rs180. On the lakeside.

Queens Rest House, 196 Kachcheriyagama. Tel 37264. DWB $8. Rest. Bar.

Hotel Tissa (opposite bus-stand). Tel 37104. DWB $7-10. Rest. Bar. Convenient and well kept.

Tissa Guest House (near bus-stand). DR $5 DWB $6. Rest. Pleasant place to stay, reasonably quiet down a side road.

There is also accommodation in Deberawewa and even further out (the Tissa Inn is one of the best-known). This is handy for the Wirawila Tank if you are a birdwatcher, but otherwise rather inconvenient, so make sure touts do not drag you out there. Despite its name the *Tissa Hotel and Bakery* does not have accommodation.

YALA WEST NATIONAL PARK

This **National Park**** was formerly known as the Ruhuna National Park, and is still sometimes referred to as that. Covering 1260sq km (of which only a small part is open to the public) the park has very varied scenery ranging from dry scrub to dense jungle. Near the coast are lagoons. Elephants are present in numbers and best seen near water sources in the dry January to May period.

Other big game includes wild buffalo, crocodiles, bear, and the more elusive leopard. Well over 100 species of birds including both resident and migratory water birds can be seen, mainly around the many tanks. Wepandeniya Leopard Rock is reputed to be the most likely place to see leopard.

The park is open from mid-October to July 0630-1800. Entry permits must be obtained from the park office at Palatupana and is limited to vehicles, no exploring on foot. All visitors must be accompanied by a park official. Costs are $12 per head entry fee plus Rs90-120 for the vehicle plus $6 service charge. Jeeps can be hired from the park office at Rs1500 for three hours.

Most visitors make a safari from Tissamaharama. In fact you will be bombarded with offers from the moment you step off the bus. Expect to pay around Rs1200 for a four or five seat Land Rover, plus the other charges listed above. The best times to visit are at dawn and dusk; for a dawn trip you need warm clothing. In theory only thirty vehicles are allowed into the park at a time, but it can still seem very crowded and noisy.

You may well be approached (Ella seems to be the most likely place) by 'guides' who offer to take you to parts of the park not officially open. This can sound very attractive: camping rough, seeing animals unused to man, and so on. It is of course illegal. The guides probably have little understanding of wildlife, so it is easy to get into a dangerous situation, especially with wild elephants and buffalo. There is also the risk of running into Tamil insurgents.

Arrival and departure. The park office is 10km from Kirinda; 2WD vehicles can manage this and the extra 3km to the park entrance and Yala Safari Beach Hotel only in the dry. No buses. In places on this red dirt road you could feel you were in the vastness of Africa rather than a crowded little island.

Accommodation (STD Code 047).

Yala Safari Beach Hotel, Amaduwa (near main gate). Tel/Fax 20471 or (Colombo) Tel 01-345 700 Fax 01-345 729. SWB/DWB A/C $60. Rest. Bar. Attractive place overlooking both the sea and a lagoon with crocodiles and interesting bird life.

Brown's Safari Beach Motel (close to Safari Beach). Tel (Colombo) 01-326 767. This was closed (supposedly for renovation) and semi-derelict when we called. Shame, as it was a cheaper alternative to the above.

Bungalows in the park: Patanangala on the coast and Heenwewa overlooking a tank can both be booked through Department of Wildlife Conservation, 82 Rajamalwatta Road, Battaramulla, near Kotte (Tel 433 012) up to three months in advance. Other bungalows are being renovated. There are cooks at the bungalows, but you must take your own food. Also a couple of campsites on the Manik Ganga river.

KATARAGAMA

Kataragama is one of the holiest places in Sri Lanka, ranking with Adam's Peak and the Temple of the Tooth Relic in Kandy. Primarily a Hindu place of worship, there are also Buddhist and Muslim shrines, and even Sri Lankan Christians visit here on the principle that a pilgrimage is a pilgrimage.

Skanda is the ruling deity of Kataragama as, indeed, he is for all the south of the island. It is hard to unravel all the various deities in their different forms, but here at least Skanda and Kataragama are the same thing. Elsewhere, of course, Kataragama is seen as a god in his own right. He is the most popular god in southern Sri Lanka, perhaps pre-Vedic and certainly pre-Buddhist. He is personified as a warlike forest-dwelling character said to have arrived by sea.

The sacred area

Access to the **holy area**** is by a footbridge over the Menik Ganga, the Ruby River. The river is sacred, and beneath the footbridge are ghats, steps up the bank, so pilgrims can bathe (and the locals do their washing) even when the river is high. Save your spare toast from breakfast and drop it from the bridge to attract shoals of fish.

Kataragama is a special place for the Muslims as well as Hindus and Buddhists. Directly ahead as you cross the footbridge is a compound of **Muslim shrines**. Near the entrance is the tomb of a saint who came from Tashkent in Khirgizistan in the 19th century. Going by the length of tomb he must have been what is known as a 'nine yard saint'. The tomb, beside a small mosque, is completely covered by vines. A larger mosque stands behind with its tank for ritual ablutions and also the tomb of an Indian saint. A tree in the centre of the compound is festooned with green flags, just like a bo-tree.

Moving on one passes a Kali temple, and then comes to the **Satara Mahadevalaya** which is dedicated to Vishnu, Kataragama, and Vibhushana. Holy talismans, which will solve all your problems, are sold here.

The **Archaeological Museum** (closed Tuesday) is to the right of the entrance to the Maha Devale, and is of absolutely minimal interest. Restoration is supposed to be taking place; it certainly needs it, most of the rooms are infested by bats and stink of their urine.

The major temples are all in a large white-walled compound. The wrought iron gates are decorated with peacocks. Facing the gate in the centre of the compound are three temples. The **Maha Devale**, the holiest, is on the right. Not surprisingly this is dedicated to Skanda. It is a surprisingly plain building both inside and out. There is not even an image in the shrine; a lance (vel) represents the god of war, but this is accessible only to the priests and kept well out of sight.

Alongside is a **Ganesh temple**; he is popular as the protector of small enterprises, and is often asked to intercede on the worshipper's behalf with the less approachable and all-powerful Shiva. Another **temple** to the left has Buddha in front with Vishnu and Skanda behind. Bo-trees stand behind these three temples, and behind the old one is a yellow **temple of Pattini**. The grey painted canopy is the place the elephants are dressed for Perahera. The interiors of these temples are not very interesting, and the only times you can see them are the *pujas* at 0430, 1030, and 1830, except on Saturday when the early morning one is missed out. Buddhists may also pay their respects at the Hindu shrines on the way to their dagoba, and the most serious pilgrims then head for two simple shrines near the top of Wedahitikanda or Kataragama's Peak (423m/1387ft).

Behind this Hindu compound a long, straight, tree-lined avenue leads to the Buddhist **Kiri Vihara** (White monastery). You have do this walk barefoot and, so, better early in the day. The female flower sellers will sing out their wares but, in truth, the dagoba is of minimal interest. The small **museum** has photos of the dagoba before its heavy-handed restoration and, most interesting, the various relics that were found inside it. Walking clockwise around the dagoba you see first a statue of King Mahasena who built the original dagoba and then a lamp which always burns.

The sacred area is not startlingly interesting on an ordinary day, but it is very pleasant, lots of trees, birds singing, and quiet.

Devotions and festivals

Ten thousand people converge on Kataragama every weekend, and many more than that on Poya and festival days. The atmosphere may be at its liveliest, but many foreigners would regard this as a good time to be elsewhere. The biggest festival of all is the Perahera at the time of the July or August full moon. This is when fire-walking is most likely to be seen.

Pilgrims come to Kataragama to do penance. Shiva, Skanda, and Kataragama are not easy-going deities, and their forbidding characters prompt some strange forms of self-abasement. Few people walk the whole way from their homes these days, but some will crawl from the entrance to the shrines. At a major festival you are likely to see sights which take a westerner with his sanitised faith (if he has any at all) straight back to the Middle Ages. One is really not prepared for men swinging on hooks piercing their skin, or the casual way others put hefty skewers through their cheeks and tongues. In the Muslim area the self-flagellation can be even more extreme. At other times you may see ascetics, many of whom base themselves here, going off into a trance. More light-hearted is the Kavadi folk dance, typically athletic and done with hoops held aloft.

Practical Information

Arrival and departure. Bus from Tissa (15km). On the outskirts of Kataragama, beside the Tissa road, is a large lily-covered tank popular with water birds.

Accommodation (STD Code 047)

Chamila Rest, 85 Tissa Road. Tel 35217/35294. DWB $9. Rest. Bar. Breakfast Rs60-90, lunch or dinner Rs75-110.

Robinson Rest, Tissa Road. Tel 35175. DWB $7 DWB A/C $13. Rest. Bar. Breakfast Rs98, rice and curry from Rs125. Snooker table, beer Rs100.

Jayasinghe Holiday Resort, 32A Detagamuwa (close to the two above, about 1.5 km from bus-stand on the road back towards Tissa). Tel 35146. DWB $9 DWB A/C $15. Rest. Bar. Breakfast Rs125, rice and curry Rs95-160. Clean rooms. Small swimming pool.

Rest House, (walk towards temple area from bus-stand, bear left, 300m). Tel 35227. DWB $6. Rest (veg. only). Basic.

New Rest House (near above). DWB $6. Rest. Breakfast Rs75, rice and curry with fish Rs110. Clean, and pleasant little garden.

Bank of Ceylon Rest House (opposite Bank of Ceylon, from the bus-stand backtrack 150m towards Tissa). Tel 35229 or (Colombo) 01-544 315. DWB $5. Rest. Breakfast Rs30, rice and curry Rs30. Large clean rooms, a good place.

A little further on from the Bank of Ceylon Rest House are the *Dushan Rest House* and *Sunshine Rest House*.

A couple of small and rather basic looking places are opposite the bus-stand. All the accommodation in Kataragama is geared to the pilgrimage trade and, whilst mostly clean, is decidedly lacking in frills.

On from Kataragama

The options on public transport are to return to the coast or to head north towards the Hill Country. From Hambantota on the coast you should be able to get a direct bus to Ratnapura (see p183). This road passes through Timbolketiya for the Uda Walawe National Park.

Direct buses may run from Kataragama to Wellawaya (see p179), otherwise change in Buttala. Near Wellawaya are the Buduruvagala Buddhist statues (see p180). From Wellawaya there are frequent buses to Ella (p175) and less frequently to Haputale (p171), both on the Hill Country railway line.

UDA WALAWE NATIONAL PARK

This park was created as a home for animals displaced by the huge Uda Walawe Reservoir. The 308sq km are mostly grassland. Elephants are common and best seen during the May to September dry season. Wild buffalo are often seen, and deer are plentiful. Uda Walawe is comparatively little visited (public transport and accommodation are problematic), but certainly worth a visit if you have your own transport.

The Safari Village charges Rs1200 for a half day safari or Rs2000 for a full day, and you also have to pay $12 per head entry fee, plus Rs100 for the vehicle, plus a 10% service charge. Independent Land Rover operators hang around the park entrance. Many roads in the park, including those leading to two bungalows, are safe for 2WD in the dry.

The entrance to the park is on the B427 (the Timbolketiya-Tanamalwila road) just over 11km from Timbolketiya, and there are always Land Rovers hanging around for safaris. This road, the B427, is a useful short cut on the way from the south-east back to Colombo and one of the most pleasant in Sri Lanka, being mostly broad, straight and traffic-free. It is bordered by the electric fence of the National Park, and when you reach the large Uda Walawe Reservoir there are good views of the hills.

Arrival and departure. See above if you have your own transport. This is not an easy destination on public transport. Occasional buses run along the Tanamalwila-Timbolketiya road, but it is probably better to use the Ambalantota-Ratnapura road, taking a three-wheeler from Timbolketiya.

Accommodation

Walawa Safari Village, R.B. Canal Road, Uda Walawe (2.5km from Timbolketiya on B427). Tel 047-33201 or (Colombo) 01-591 728 Fax (Colombo) 01-591 223. SWB H/B $28 DWB H/B $38. Rest. Nicely done. Small garden and absolutely quiet except for birdsong.

The two *Bungalows* in the park can be booked through Department of Wildlife Conservation, 82 Rajamalwatta Road, Battaramulla, near Kotte (Tel 433 012) up to three months in advance. There are cooks at the bungalows (which are far from cheap), but you must take your own food.

There are, apparently, no cheaper options.

The Hill Country

Pinnewala Elephant Orphanage

Roughly one-fifth of Sri Lanka is land above 300m/1000ft. It is surprising, especially so close to the equator, how this affects the climate. Kandy, at 490m/1520ft, is a world apart from Colombo's sticky humid heat. Further south and higher the climate becomes even more pleasant, and decidedly cool at night in winter. This is lush countryside and manicured tea gardens rather than rugged mountains, but beautiful all the same.

The railway line from Colombo to Kandy and on towards Badulla is one of the most scenic in the world. The lolloping gait of the trains past Kandy, limited by tight curves and indifferent track to 16kph/10mph, is the perfect way to see this delightful area.

COLOMBO TO KANDY

Unless you have your own vehicle the train is preferable to the road. Seats (observation car and second class) on the Intercity Expresses can be booked in advance, and the best views are from the right-hand side of the train.

The road is interesting, and narrow and winding in places. As a matter of defence policy the Kings of Kandy did nothing to improve access to their domain. In 1815 there was no road, just footpaths following a much more circuitous route. This facilitated the ambushing of invaders and, if they did get through to Kandy, cutting their supply lines. As soon as they had assumed government of all Ceylon the British set about building a proper road. Conditions were appalling, and malaria took a heavy toll of both British engineers and their labourers.

Between Maradana and Dematagoda stations are **locomotive sheds** and workshops. Most of Sri Lanka Railways' surviving steam locos are kept here. The easiest means of access is on foot from Maradana station. This is, needless to say, not officially encouraged, but nobody seems to mind.

Ragama Junction is one of the earliest railway stations in Sri Lanka. This is where the line to Negombo and Puttalam branches off. During the Boer war the British had a prisoner of war camp here, the buildings later being used as a hospital.

HENERATHGODA BOTANIC GARDENS

These gardens (open 0730-1700; Rs50) were the site of the first rubber plantation in Ceylon. Seeds of para rubber trees had been acquired in dubious circumstances from Brazil and germinated at Kew Gardens in London before being planted out here in 1876. Some of the original trees are still here. Experiments were carried out with other sources of rubber, and ipecacuanha, a medicinal tree, also of South American origin, was grown here. The 15ha/36 acre gardens were opened in 1876. Despite the distance from the coast the gardens are only 10-15m above sea level.

Arrival and departure. The gardens are 32km from Colombo. Train to Gampaha (an unusual statue of a group of volleyball players stands outside the station) on Colombo-Kandy line or bus. Buses and scooter rickshaws run from the station (other side of the tracks from the main buildings).

Eating and Drinking. Snack bar at gardens.

PASYALA

Cashew nuts are an important crop in Sri Lanka. The nut grows on the outside of a fruit that looks very like a small pimento. Processing involves roasting and peeling the nuts. Pasyala is a centre of the business to such an extent that it has become known as Cadjugama, or Cashew City. Nuts are sold from roadside stalls.

Arrival and departure. Pasyala is 48km from Colombo on the main road to Kandy.

ALAWWA

Betel leaves, the green leaves used for wrapping areca nut, lime, and other ingredients to make paan, are auctioned early on Tuesday and Friday mornings near the bus station.

Arrival and departure. Alawwa is 54km from Colombo by train or road.

Accommodation. *Rest House* at Ambepussa, a short bus ride away. An old and attractive establishment. Ambepussa has its own station, but only the slowest trains stop there.

DEDIGAMA

This is the birthplace of King Parakramabahu I, the man who built most of Polonnaruwa. The Kotavehara dagoba built by him in the 12th century has ten or more relic chambers. The museum (closed Tuesday) nearby has a lamp in which an elephant piddles extra oil into the burner as required.

Arrival and departure. Dedigama is 5km south of Nelundeniya where you have to turn off the main A1 road from Colombo to Kandy.

The railway track is double as far as Polgahawela Junction (only 75m/246ft altitude despite being a good 70km/43 miles from Colombo). From Rambukkana (95m/313ft) the real ascent to the hills starts, the line climbing at 1:45 for the next 19km/12miles to Kadugannawa at 518m/1700ft. In steam days banker locomotives used to help the heavier trains up the incline.

PINNEWALA ELEPHANT ORPHANAGE

The animal most associated with Sri Lanka is of course the elephant. The indigenous wild stock (elephas maximus maximus) is a sub-species of the Asian elephant (elephas maximus) unique to Sri Lanka. The Asian elephant as a whole is now regarded as an endangered species in the wild.

The Asian elephant is generally smaller than the African; a fully grown male may weigh six tonnes compared with the eight tonnes of an African tusker. Like other Asian elephants it is distinguished visually from its African cousins by smaller ears and eyes. Unlike the African elephants, only the males have tusks. Despite a record pair 2.7m/9ft long these are generally smaller, and only about 10% of males actually have tusks. This has protected the species from the poaching all too prevalent in Africa, but numbers have still fallen from 12,000 at the start of the 20th century to around 2,500 now. Scarcely controlled shooting early in the century, one man alone is said to have killed 1400, did a lot of damage, and latterly the demands of a growing population for land has destroyed the wild elephants' habitat. The elephant's gestation period is 22 months, and weight at birth is around 82kg/180lb. A grown elephant eats a good 200kg/440lb of vegetation daily, so as the average lifespan is up to 70 years, a family group needs a large territory.

Historically Asian elephants have been far more used by man than their African counterparts. Hannibal's elephants were Asian ones, not African. The elephant remained a common sight on the battlefield long after the introduction of gunpowder, and elephants can still move timber in places inaccessible to tractors. Elephants can only be trained fully when they are twenty years old, so there is always a need for fresh stock from the wild, which does not help conservation. The corollary is that a young captive elephant has to be fed for twenty years before he starts to pay his way.

Whilst usually placid elephants can be upset by explosions, and this has led to a lot of accidents during the civil war. There is also a strong suspicion that the Tamil Tigers have slaughtered elephants near their hideouts and bases. Male elephants come into season (must or masth) every year, marked by secretion from a gland in the head,and this makes them very hard to handle. They can well run amok at this time, and an angry elephant can do an awful lot of damage.

The **Pinnewala Elephant Orphanage***** is a government-sponsored refuge for abandoned and orphaned wild elephants. Before the civil war intensified only eight elephants were kept here. Fighting has led to family groups being split up, and to some elephants being driven onto farmland where they are shot by villagers. Others animals have been injured by gunfire or landmines, so the total has now risen to fifty or more. This has introduced problems of crowding as elephants are by no means always friendly to one another.

The Rs100 entrance fee is good value as you can watch all of the fifty or so elephants living here, at places near Kandy you pay more to see only four or five. The ticket office is on the main road, and you walk down to the bathing place on an attractive stretch of the Ma Oya river. You can watch in comfort from the Pinnelanda Restaurant for the price of an expensive cold drink or there are shady places on the bank. Bathing times are 1000-1200 and 1400-1600.

Feeding takes place in the main compound behind the ticket office, and you need to be there on time to see the tiniest elephants, who get fed first, glugging down their bottles of milk. Feeding times are 0915, 1315, and 1700.

Two pleasant places to stay have opened recently and, when the tourists have gone, this is a quiet and relaxing place. There are spice gardens around the orphanage; interesting if you will not see one elsewhere, but an expensive place to buy spices.

Information. Two of the best books on working elephants (albeit set in Burma) are *Elephant Bill* and *Bandoola* by J.H. Williams, the famous Elephant Bill. These books are easily found in second-hand bookshops.

Practical Information

Arrival and departure. Kegalle, the nearest town to the orphanage, is 77km from Colombo and on the main road from Colombo to Kandy. Train to Rambukkana station from Kandy (1¼hrs.) or Colombo (1¾hrs.) then a three-wheeler from outside the station (3km, Rs80 return) or walk 200m into the village to find a bus towards Kegalle. The 0645 train from Kandy gets you to Pinnewala in time for the 0915 feeding and the start of bath time; you can get the 1200 back to Kandy or the 1115 or 1347 on to Colombo. The 1000 from Kandy lets you see the tail-end of the early bathing and the 1315 feeding; get the 1420 back to Kandy or the 1654 on to Colombo. Travelling by bus between Colombo and Kandy change in Kegalle.

Accommodation (STD Code 035)

Elephant View Hotel, Elephant Bath Road, Pinnewala. Tel 65292/3 Fax 0094-35 65283. SWB A/C $15 DWB A/C $17 (chance of 10% discount if you arrive without a tout or driver). Rest (good). Bar. Professional and originally appointed smaller hotel. Mini-bars and TV in rooms. Rice and curry Rs125, fish and prawn dishes Rs200, snacks Rs100, beer Rs125.

Green Land Guest House, Elephant Bath Road, Pinnewala. Tel 65668. DR $3 DWB $8 (latter includes breakfast). Rice and curry Rs100. Only three rooms so phone in advance. Quiet comfortable house with nice garden.

Eating and Drinking.
Pinnelanda Restaurant, river bank. Mod/Exp. Rice and curry Rs200, sandwiches Rs100. Nicely done. Most people would feel the location justified the prices.

Pinnewala Restaurant (CHC), in orphanage behind ticket office. Mod. Curry and rice Rs200, snacks Rs100.

BALANA

Balana means lookout in Sinhalese because, as in several other places, the kingdom of Kandy maintained scouts here.

The train artist Upali Jayaweera, whose colourful pictures you see in several stations along this line, is based here.

Arrival and departure. On Colombo-Kandy railway line.

MAWANELLA

The hill of Utawankanda (430m/1410ft) to the north was the hideout of a 19th century outlaw called Saradiel. He acquired something of a Robin Hood reputation because he once returned twice the amount of money he had stolen from an old man who was travelling to pay his daughter's dowry. Otherwise he was just a highway robber and murderer. He was eventually captured and hanged.

Mawanella is surrounded by spice gardens.

Arrival and departure. On the main road from Colombo (88km) to Kandy (27km).

KADUGANNAWA

A short distance out of Kadugannawa on the Colombo side the road passes through a tunnel in a rock outcrop. An old legend had it that Kandy would never be taken until this massif was pierced. Admittedly the tunnel was made well after Kandy had fallen, but it could be said that the prophecy was fulfilled. This is visible fleetingly from the train. The train itself burrows through some huge rocks at this point and, if you are leaning out of the door you will see more overhanging the track.

To the south is the prominent square shape of Bible Rock (it supposedly resembles an open book), known to the Dutch as the Coffin, and more properly Batalagala (798m/2617ft). North is Belungala (775m/2542ft) known as Scout Hill because a watch was kept from there for invaders of Kandy.

The **Captain Dawson memorial**, a 38m/125ft high brick replica of the Duke of York's Column (in London), commemorates the army engineer who built the first proper road over the hills to Kandy.

Arrival and departure. On the road and railway from Colombo (100km) to Kandy (15km).

KANDY

Kandy owes its name to a historical misunderstanding. The Sinhalese always knew it as Maha Nuwara, the Great City. In the chaos caused by the Portuguese invasion the local governor Vikrama Vira declared his independence and took the title Kande Rajah, or King of the Mountain. The Portuguese misinterpreted this as King of Kandy, and the city has been called that ever since.

Kandy's importance is out of proportion to its size. It maintained its independence despite 250 years of Portuguese and Dutch harassment. During British rule it was a symbol of Sinhalese independence, and it remains the main religious centre on the island. The Perahera festival is one of the great religious events of the world.

Having a pleasant climate, pretty lake, and good shops and restaurants Kandy is much more like the better Indian hill stations such as Naini Tal and Kodaikanal than is Nuwara Eliya. In addition to its many historical sites it is a charming place just to wander around; it deserves more time than most visitors give it.

History

The kings of Gampola (p160) had built palaces and temples here, establishing the idea of an independent hill kingdom, but the history of Kandy as a city starts with Jayavira in 1542. Initially relations with the Portuguese were friendly, not least because they ganged up on the king of Sitavaka who was the focus of resistance to the Portuguese. The attitudes of the Portuguese, particularly their priests, soon made them unpopular, and when Rajasimha I reconverted to Hinduism and started to persecute the Buddhists there was a popular rebellion which threw out both.

In 1592 Vimala Dharma Suriya I founded a new dynasty committed to upholding the Dharma and Buddhist ideals. This it continued to do for two hundred years. The city was taken by both the Portuguese (1594, 1611, 1629 and 1638) and Dutch (1765) on occasions, but each time the Sinhalese burnt the city and retreated to the forests. From there they waged a successful guerilla campaign against the invaders' supply lines forcing them to retire.

The British took Ceylon from the Dutch in 1795 and, after a disastrous few years in the hands of the East India Company, made it a crown colony. The new governor, Frederick North, was soon involved in intrigues with the King's prime minister; these centered on the fact that whilst the king was a Malabari from Kerala in India the prime minister was Sinhalese. These efforts culminated in a small British garrison in Kandy being massacred in 1803. After this Kandy was left alone for a time, but then the British became alarmed by the excesses of King Sri Vikrama Rajasimha. Having disposed of his previous prime minister he fell out with the new one who fled leaving behind his family. The king slaughtered them; the children were beheaded and their mother forced to smash up their heads in a rice mortar before she and her sister were drowned in Bogambara tank. Apart from this cruelty the extravagance of Sri Vikrama Rajasimha strained the loyalty of his nobles. They were required to provide funds and manpower for his building projects, with very unpleasant consequences in lieu. They were so fed up that when the crunch came with the British they just stood aside.

Citadel & Fair
Havens Hotels

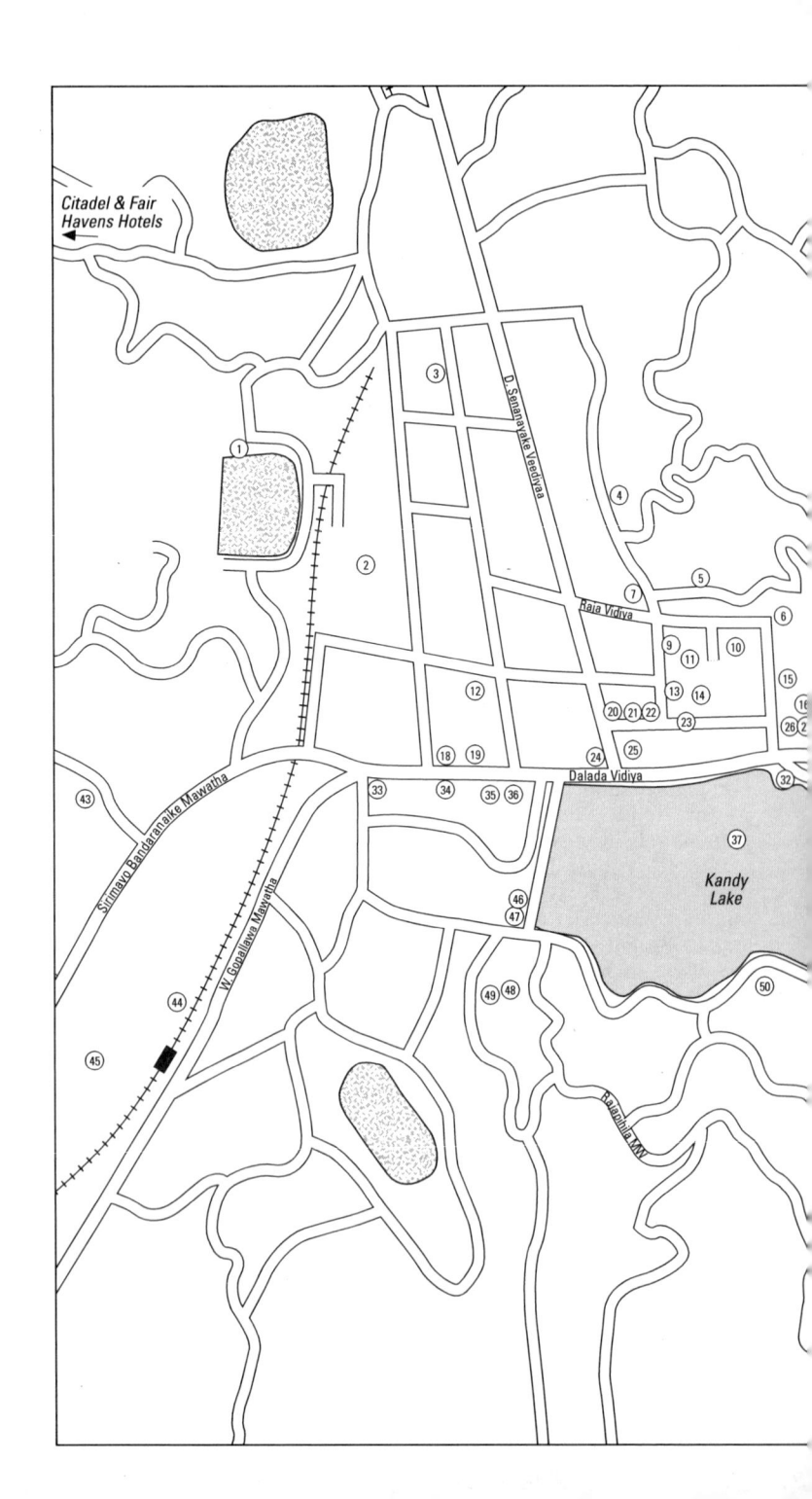

Kandy Lake

Raja Vidiya

Dalada Vidiya

D. Senanayake Veediya

Srimavo Bandaranaike Mawatha

W. Gopallawa Mawatha

Rajapihilla Mw

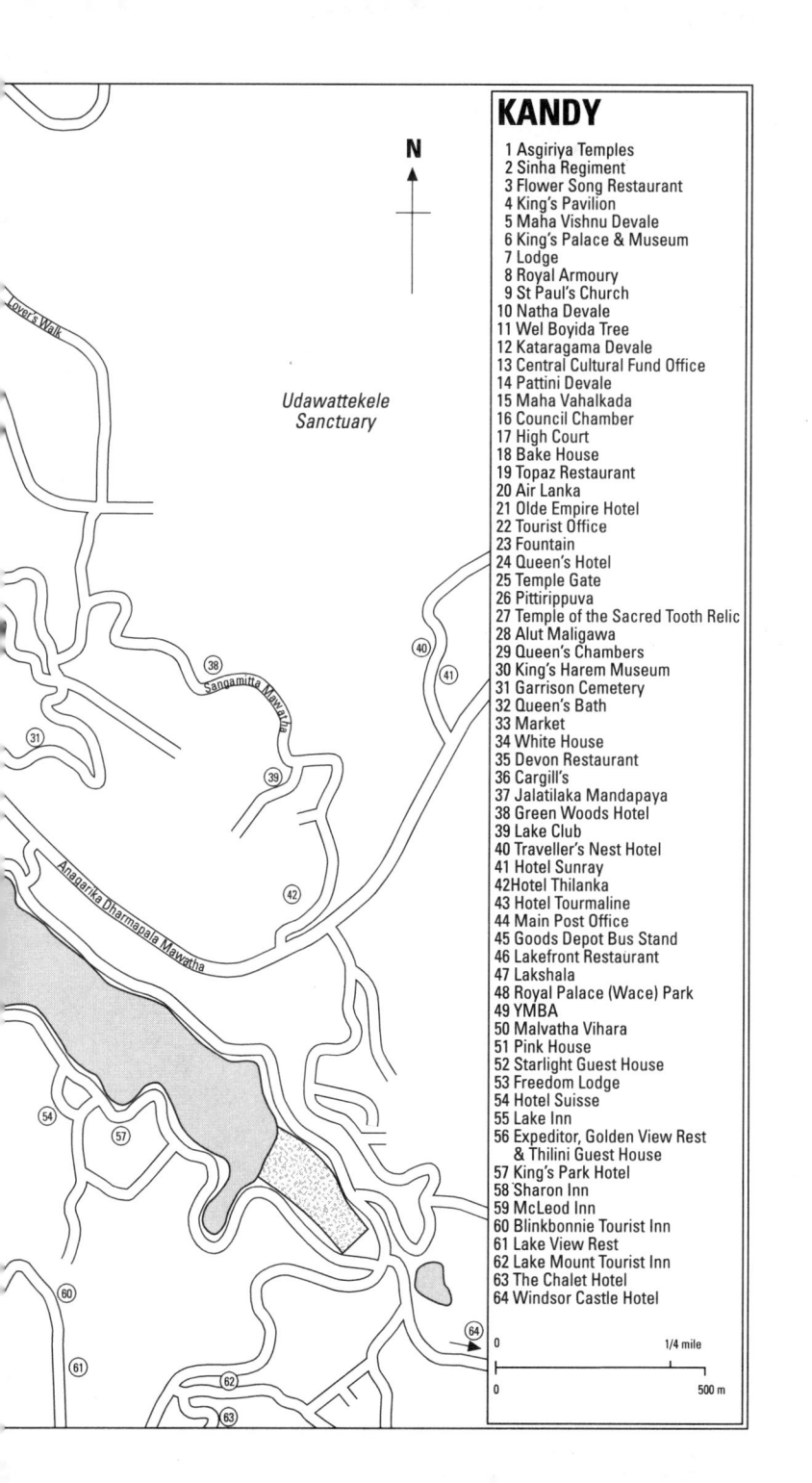

KANDY

1. Asgiriya Temples
2. Sinha Regiment
3. Flower Song Restaurant
4. King's Pavilion
5. Maha Vishnu Devale
6. King's Palace & Museum
7. Lodge
8. Royal Armoury
9. St Paul's Church
10. Natha Devale
11. Wel Boyida Tree
12. Kataragama Devale
13. Central Cultural Fund Office
14. Pattini Devale
15. Maha Vahalkada
16. Council Chamber
17. High Court
18. Bake House
19. Topaz Restaurant
20. Air Lanka
21. Olde Empire Hotel
22. Tourist Office
23. Fountain
24. Queen's Hotel
25. Temple Gate
26. Pittirippuva
27. Temple of the Sacred Tooth Relic
28. Alut Maligawa
29. Queen's Chambers
30. King's Harem Museum
31. Garrison Cemetery
32. Queen's Bath
33. Market
34. White House
35. Devon Restaurant
36. Cargill's
37. Jalatilaka Mandapaya
38. Green Woods Hotel
39. Lake Club
40. Traveller's Nest Hotel
41. Hotel Sunray
42. Hotel Thilanka
43. Hotel Tourmaline
44. Main Post Office
45. Goods Depot Bus Stand
46. Lakefront Restaurant
47. Lakshala
48. Royal Palace (Wace) Park
49. YMBA
50. Malvatha Vihara
51. Pink House
52. Starlight Guest House
53. Freedom Lodge
54. Hotel Suisse
55. Lake Inn
56. Expeditor, Golden View Rest & Thilini Guest House
57. King's Park Hotel
58. Sharon Inn
59. McLeod Inn
60. Blinkbonnie Tourist Inn
61. Lake View Rest
62. Lake Mount Tourist Inn
63. The Chalet Hotel
64. Windsor Castle Hotel

Udawattekele Sanctuary

0 — 1/4 mile
0 — 500 m

The final straw came in 1815 when the king captured a group of merchants who were British subjects and had visited Kandy to trade. He accused them of spying and sent them back to Colombo with various severed parts of their anatomy hung round their necks. This was the clear excuse the British needed, and they despatched an army. The king acted in the manner of a true tyrant, beheading or impaling the messengers who brought news of the rapidly advancing British, then panicked and fled his capital. He was captured and exiled to Vellore (in the Indian state of Tamil Nadu) where he lived in some style at British expense until his death in 1832.

Planning and architecture

It is not clear when the grid pattern was laid out. Robert Knox wrote in the 1660s that it existed by that time. Ancient Indian writings on architecture regard a grid plan as auspicious, and the kings of Kandy may have drawn on them for inspiration. The main axes are east-west; the streets crossing these are not truly north-south, and mostly they converge slightly. Despite preserving the street plan the town looked nothing like it does today. Before 1807 the area of the lake was occupied by paddy fields. In the town, instead of shops and offices, there were the houses and compounds of the nobles and court officials. These houses were not very grand, mostly single storeyed and constructed of timber and mud on a stone base. Contemporary accounts make Kandy sound more like a small country town than a capital city. The fact that it still feels like that is half its charm.

Kandyan architecture is of elegant simplicity. There is none of the grandeur of Anuradhapura or Polonnaruwa. The basic form is a timber frame on a stone base with mud wattle and daub walls and a tiled roof. Much of the woodwork is finely carved. This is the architecture of a rural community at ease with its surroundings. When the Kandyans came to use stone, as in the Shrine of the Tooth Relic, the same structural pattern was followed as for a wooden building.

Temple of the Tooth Relic

The **Temple of the Tooth Relic***** is one of the most important Buddhist shrines in the world. Its quiet and attractive buildings have a light-hearted feel that welcome all visitors.

When the Buddha died and was cremated at Kushinagar (in Bihar, North India) in 543BC the remains were divided and sent to various holy places. Before this, however, and apparently unofficially, one of his teeth was plucked from the fire. It became a much revered relic, but by the third century AD Buddhism was declining in India in the face of a revived and aggressive Hinduism. The tooth found refuge for a time in Orissa, one of the last strongholds of Buddhism in India, but the danger grew. Eventually it was brought to Sri Lanka early in the fourth century AD, hidden in the hair of an Orissan princess, and received with great ceremony.

The tooth may have started as a religious relic but, over time it came to be regarded as a symbol of sovereignty. Thus the Sinhalese kings always housed it in the capital of the time, and it has had the same ups and downs as they have. The Cholas captured it in 1283 and took it off to India, to be redeemed by King Parakramabahu III some years later. The Portuguese claimed to have seized it in Jaffna early in the 16th century and taken it to Goa where it was burnt with some ceremony; the Sinhalese contend that that was just a replica.

The tooth came to Kandy in 1592, and a temple was built for it next to the already existing palace. That temple, and others that followed, were destroyed during the various sackings of Kandy.

The entrance to the temple compound is the **arched gate** opposite the Queen's Hotel. An elephant usually waits in the temple approach for photographs (at the cost of a Rs20 tip) and more ceremonial purposes. We watched a man leave the temple with a baby no more than a month old; when he reached the elephant he carried the baby three times under the elephant's belly and then touched it to its mouth. Stalls nearby sell puja offerings.

Approaching the temple observe the octagonal **Pittirippuva** which was added by the last king of Kandy Sri Vikrama Rajasimha. This was not actually part of the temple. The name implies that it was a lookout or viewpoint; in fact the king could use the upper part to address the people, and the lower part as a quiet retreat. This lower level, now a library of sacred books, was used as barracks after the British captured Kandy. The two white walls which contain the moat are also noteworthy. The outer is the **Diyareli Bemma** (wave-swept wall) and the inner the **Walakulu Bemma** (cloud drift wall), the idea being to produce an effect of lightness and movement. Recesses in both are for oil lamps. The main entrance is through the **Maha Vahalkada** (Great Gate), built over the moat and now lacking its doors. This was the main gate to the palace as well as the temple. A moonstone is at the foot of the steps, which are supported by elephants, and reliefs of elephants are on either side. In the moat (*Diya Agala*: simply water moat) are tortoises and fish.

The gateway to the Tooth Shrine is finely carved stone. Doratupalas (doorkeepers) stand either side; above are relief *makara-toranas* (mythical monsters), and at top centre a dragon to ward off evil. More doratupalas appear on the painted wooden doors, and figures blowing conch shells to signal the start of prayers and call for purity and prosperity. Above is a half woman half peacock figure, a little flight of fancy. On the walls of the *Ambarawa* or tunnel leading to the shrine are pilgrims carrying puja offerings, just as they do today. Entering the **Hewisi Mandapaya** (drummers' courtyard) is a large glass chandelier which would look more at home in a mosque, and a large brass lantern of Chinese or Tibetan origin. The shrine still works on the old Sri Lanka time $5\frac{1}{2}$ hours ahead of GMT, and all the clocks (one above the tunnel) are therefore half-an-hour ahead of your watch. Check on this when visiting the shrine for a specific ceremony.

The two-storeyed **shrine** is the work of Narendra Simha (1707-1739). The lower level is of stone construction, following the Kandyan wooden style, with a colonnade around, the brackets and undersides of the eaves gaily painted. The most frequent motifs on the painted medallions, some unfinished, are the sun, moon, and rabbit. In the west we speak of the man in the moon, in Sri Lanka they see the rabbit in the full moon. The structure above this level is of wood and, around the actual shrine still of wattle and daub.

The interior of the lower level is in two parts, the first being the Digge (long house). Behind is the Maha Arumadala (great treasure store) for the gifts of former kings and dignitaries. Steps for monks officiating in ceremonies lead to the upper shrine.

Lesser mortals take stairs up to the **Pirit Mandape** (Recitation Hall). On the stairs the sandalwood Buddha comes from Japan. The central doorway of the tooth shrine is framed in silver with a sun above. The door itself is perforated brass. Either side are paintings of doratupalas bearing bowls of lotuses with grotesque figures above. Outside those are brass panels with, at the top, the sun and moon. Below them are two geese, their necks entwined (a popular motif at weddings) and, below two parrots, a large panel with a dagoba and other auspicious symbols. Outside that dwarves hold up vases of flowers. The shrine behind consists of three rooms. The first is the **Handunkumana** (Sandalwood Shed) where you may glimpse four large elephants' tusks. It is in this perfumed room that the rare showings of the tooth itself take place. Then comes a small antechamber, and finally the **Vedahitina Maligawa**, the Shrine of Abode.

The tooth itself, which you are most unlikely to see, is mounted on a gold wire rising from a lotus. This at the centre of seven concentric gold dagoba-shaped reliquaries. The three central doors are opened for puja three times a day, at 0600, 1000, and 1900. The service commences with music outside the lower shrine ten minutes beforehand. Then a small procession of priests and white-garbed attendants with huge shoulder pads unlocks the silver doors and enters. Some time later, having used the internal stairs, they reveal the reliquary in its brightly painted inner chamber, and worshippers (and tourists) file past. At the evening puja there are, in fact, more tourists than worshippers. Early morning is best.

Leaving the Pirit Mandape at puja times go down the narrow staircase (not the main one) to see the lower level of the Pittirippuva library and its collection of ola palm leaf books. Beside this is a small shrine with a bronze Buddha image from Burma. Up a few steps is another shrine with a collection of Buddha figures. The main figure is gold plate on bronze, and the others and the miniature dagobas come from different Buddhist countries. The reliquary casket holds a rock crystal Buddha, and there is also a green jade one. Elephant tusks arch over them. This shrine and its wall paintings were damaged in the bomb attack referred to below, and restoration will take time.

Behind the shrine of the tooth is the **Alut Maligawa** (New Relic Chamber), completed in 1956 to commemorate the 2,500th Buddha Jayanti (the festival that celebrates Buddha's birth, enlightenment, and death). A moonstone leads to steps supported by dwarves, on either side are Hindu-looking figures shaded by five-hooded cobras. The collection of images gives an interesting opportunity to compare national variations on a formalised style. The main image, from Thailand, is gilded and surmounted by flames representing enlightenment. Of the ancillary images to the left the white one with black hair is from Korea, the smaller gold one with pointed topknot from Thailand, and the white marble one from China. To the right a gold one with black hair comes from Taiwan, and the white marble one with large halo and hands together in teaching mudra from India. A series of twenty-one paintings tells the story of the tooth from the birth of Buddha up to the present day. The Buddha figures below are a gift from Thailand to mark the fiftieth anniversary of Sri Lanka's independence. Above the columns are elephants, the capitals being makaras leading into a lotus. This is a very attractive building despite its modernity. Outside, beside the steps is a triple bell tower.

Parts of the temple, notably the front of the upper level, the Pittirippuva, and the roofs were damaged in a bomb attack carried out by the Tamil Tigers in January 1998. Places of worship had previously been regarded as sacrosanct, and the attack seemed to be a response to increasingly successful military pressure by the Sri Lankan army. The attack had the incidental effect of ruining arrangements for Sri Lanka's fiftieth anniversary of independence to be held in Kandy.

The Royal Palace

The Temple of the Tooth Relic was the core of a large palace enclave, only fragments of which remain today.

The **Queen's Bath** is a two-storeyed building, the lower part filled by the lake like a very grand boathouse. The British altered this, enclosing the ground floor and adding the upper storey, to make a library. It has recently been restored to something like its original form.

The island in the lake once held the **Jalatilaka Mandapaya**, a pleasure resort for the king and the royal harem. The British saw it as a safe place to store gunpowder, and little remains today. A drawing of the building made in 1849 can be seen in the museum.

The **King's Harem** houses the **National Museum** (0900-1700, closed Friday. Entry Rs55 plus Rs135 for a camera). Not wildly interesting and in need of more informative captioning, it has a useful display on ola palm leaf books and some truly grotesque masks. In the garden is the bronze statue of Sir Henry Ward (governor 1855-1860).

The **Queen's Palace**, a traditional building round a central pool, has recently been rescued from misuse and is receiving some restoration. The white **High Court** is a British colonial job dating from 1887. The **Armoury** is now occupied by a District Court.

Most imposing of all these rather sorry remains is the **Audience Hall****. The foundation stone is dated 1784, but there is controversy over when it was finished. It is said to have been still incomplete in 1815, but this may be due to its having been set on fire at the time of the British attack of 1803. The fire was put out by British soldiers and the building later restored. This is a place of poignant memories, as it was here that the Kandyan chiefs met to hand over power to the British; they thought they were just getting rid of a hated king. The lower section is an extension made in 1875 for the visit of the then Prince of Wales (later Edward VII). The wooden columns for this were taken from the King's Harem, which is why they are more ornate than the others. The Audience Hall has been used for meetings of the Sri Lanka Supreme Court. It has been heavily restored recently.

The **King's Palace** was perhaps built by Vimala Dharma Surya I (1591-1604). The private apartments have been destroyed, only the public parts of the palace remaining. In the early days of British rule the governor used this as a residence, and it now houses the Archaeological Museum (0800-1600, closed Tuesday). Access is from the Maha Vishnu Devale.

The four devales and the palace precincts

Opposite the Tourist Office is a rather fine cast iron **fountain** made by the Sun Foundry in Glasgow. It was erected in 1875 by the coffee planters of Ceylon to commemorate the visit of the then Prince of Wales. It now provides a source of water for the elephants which perform in the temple approach. Drinking often causes them to have a pee and, in the case of a male, this is an interesting spectacle.

Up towards the church is the neoclassical **Central Cultural Fund Office**. Cultural Triangle passes can be bought here.

The **Pattini Devale** is directly behind the Central Cultural Fund office. Pattini is a Hindu goddess of chastity and health. Better known now in Sri Lanka than India, she is of Dravidian origin and very popular with country folk. Knox mentions this devale in his account of Ceylon, so we know that it is at least 300 years old. Entry to the temple is through a vahalkada gateway. The structure of the main temple is traditional mud on a stone base. A woman officiates in one of the side shrines, blessing packets of food and coconuts brought as offerings. The brass deepmal, or light tower, here is similar to those seen in southern India and surmounted by a cock, an emblem of Sri Lanka. As you leave you can reflect on the harmony of this Hindu shrine, the Buddhist bo-tree, and St Paul's Church.

The **Natha Devale**, built by the kings of Gampola in the 14th century is the oldest building in Kandy. Natha is a deity who, in Sri Lankan terms, ranks above Vishnu and provides political influence, significant so close to the palace. He is also reckoned to be a boddhisatva, a Buddha to come, and so a popular figure. A new king was required to worship here and to announce the name in which he would reign. In front of you on entry is a dagoba and the foundations for another. The Natha Devale is over to the right. The sikhara over the shrine is obviously Dravidian, probably borrowed from the style of Vijayanagar (Hampi) in southern India. Recent reconstruction has taken place. Another, brightly painted, shrine faces the entrance. Beside that the bo-tree has grown from a cutting of the very holy one at Anuradhapura.

The **Wel Bodhiya*** is a sacred bo-tree. The stepped enclosure has several shrines and altars for offerings of flowers. The tree itself is decked in multi-coloured flags. It is usual in many Buddhist shrines to walk around clockwise; here no-one seems to worry.

St Paul's Church* is very Victorian-tropical in style, light and airy. Some of the memorials are interesting, with a sprinkling of Dutch and Portuguese names. A major in Her Majesty's Ceylon Rifle Regiment avoided the usual perils of the tropics only to be struck by lightning at Haputale Pass. Someone drowned at Trincomalee, another man was 'cut off by disease incidental to the climate at the early age of twenty-eight years' — a description that would apply to tens of thousands of Englishmen (and women), mostly in less pleasant places than this. A British officer was killed at Silistria on the banks of the Danube in 1854 fighting on the side of the Turks against the Russians, and his brother officer died at Alma serving in His Majesty's 95th Regiment, the inscriptions flanked by two soldiers with reversed arms. Two civilian brothers, one of whom was killed by the Japanese the other died in internment. The banners and colours of the Ceylon Planters Rifle Corps and Ceylon Mounted Infantry were taken to the National Army Museum in London in 1967. Lt-Col Thomas Fletcher survived the battles of Vimiera and Corunna fighting his way through the Peninsula and Walcheren, then the fighting in Kandy in 1815 and 1818, only to die in Malta on the way home after thirty-five years military and civil service.

A neoclassical **lodge** stands at the foot of the lane up to the King's Pavilion (see below).

The **Maha Vishnu Devale** stands on a terrace overlooking the palace and

Temple of the Tooth Relic. Vishnu was known to the Buddhists as Upulvan, the protector of Buddhism, not surprising as Vishnu's ninth avatar, or incarnation on earth, was as Buddha. The doratupalas are men blowing conch shells. The image here is said first to have graced a temple at Dondra, the southernmost point of Sri Lanka. At the time of the Portuguese incursions it was taken first to Alutnuwara and then brought here. Behind and to the left is a shrine of Upulvan. During processions all the elephants stop here to pay homage to their master Vishnu as lord of elephants.

Away in the town is the **Kataragama Devale**, the newest and most pleasing of the four with its shady courtyards. To the left of the main Kataragama shrine is a Buddha one, and behind that are two others with seated Buddhas and a bo-tree. To the right are several shrines to Hindu deities, notably Ganesh.

The presence and popularity of these devales, Hindu temples in a devoutly Buddhist country, takes some explaining. Hinduism has a peculiar all-embracing nature, and in India the admission of Hindu images to Buddhist temples heralded the end of Buddhism by its reabsorbtion into the Hindu mainstream. Today at least part of the troubles in Punjab stems from the fear of Sikhs that precisely the same thing will happen to their religion. Yet here the Hindu deities are revered, especially Vishnu as a protector of Buddhism, but only as servants of the Buddha. In Sri Lanka Buddhism has had the strength to purify itself from time to time and emerge stronger than ever. Sometimes the process has been aided by holy men from Thailand or Burma, on other occasions monks have gone from Sri Lanka to those countries to help them preserve the faith.

The lake

One of Kandy's greatest assets, the **lake** is artificial, conceived and built by the last king Sri Vikrama Rajasimha. Completed in 1807 the lake was built by the process of *rajakariya*, whereby the populace provided free labour. The system was unpopular at the best of times, the more so in the case of the lake as it served no useful function for irrigation or anything else. Several people who protested ended up being impaled on the work site *pour encourager les autres*. Rajasimha called his lake the Kiri Muhuda, or Milk Sea. The walk and parapet around the lake are the work of the British. Opposite the temple gate a milestone on the bund informs you not only that it is 72miles to Colombo but precisely 2miles and 46ft around the lake. Motor boats provide a quick tour of the lake.

Old maps show a lower lake, the Bogambara Tank, about one-third the size of the Kiri Muhuda, below the bund.

The **Malvathu Vihara** monastery is on the south side of the lake marked by the monks' bathhouse on the lake side of the road. The meeting hall is a colonnaded building on an ancient stone base. Close by is an octagonal building matching that at the Temple of the Tooth Relic across the lake. The museum is a modern building very well done in traditional style. This place is not geared to tourism, and unless you arrive at puja time the temples will be locked.

Around town

The **King's Pavilion** was built by Sir Edward Barnes (governor 1824-1831). Barnes was extravagant where his own comfort was concerned. He built equally palatial houses at Mount Lavinia and Nuwara Eliya which are both now hotels. The expenditure got him into trouble with the Colonial Office, but the governors managed to hang on to the King's Pavilion, and this is today the up-country house of the president (not open to the public).

The **Sinha Regiment** has a collection of interest to military buffs at the barracks of the Second Battalion on Yatinuwara Vidiya. Because of the present security position it is necessary to arrange in writing in advance to see this. In the grounds of the officers' mess next door a mounted rifleman brandishes his Lee-Metford. A fine statue, unfortunately painted green.

The **Asgiriya Temples** date from the 18th century. With the Asgiriya Vihara this is the headquarters of the Siyam Nikaya sect and, generally speaking controls Buddhists living in the north of the island. The monks here participate in the running of the Temple of the Tooth Relic with their counterparts from the Malvathu Monastery. The smaller shrine, the Parana Viharaya or Old Temple, dated 1766, has murals of many different figures paying homage to Buddha and ornate ceilings. The larger shrine, the Alut Viharaya or New Temple, has unusual tapering square pillars, painted doors, and a large reclining Buddha inside. The temple was built by the son of the chief minister, and his portrait is to the right of the door as you enter; on the other side is Sri Vikrama Rajasimha, the last King of Kandy. Round the back the large rock from which the Buddha figure is carved is incorporated in the wall, and on it are two large stone inscriptions in Pali telling the history of the building in 1801 and its later restoration. A separate shrine in the monks' house has the 18th century ivory-inlaid ebony throne and various other memorabilia of Sri Vikrama Rajasimha. There are interesting buildings in the Asgiriya Vihara grounds, but little or no provision is made for visitors.

The main **post office** is of interest because it was built as the Grand Hotel. It soon went bust confirming the old belief that this locality, once the rajas' place of execution, is ill-omened.

The **Garrison Cemetery**, just off Rajasinghe Mawatha past the National Museum, is undergoing some restoration after years of neglect. Even for enthusiasts of such places there is not a lot to see. A separate **War Cemetery** is signposted off Sirima Bandaranaike MW (the road from Kandy to Peradeniya). The **Riverside Elephant Park**, just past the War Cemetery, will charge you Rs150 to see elephants being bathed, something you can see for free elsewhere. The railings of the Hatton National Bank are decorated with lions, roses, thistles, and shamrocks.

About 4km from the town centre a few elephants are bathed near Katugastota bridge.

Walks

You can walk around the **lake**, pleasantly shady, as long as you can put up with the traffic noise and fumes. The north side past the Temple of the Tooth Relic is closed to traffic and much quieter.

Steps opposite Laksala (the government handicrafts shop), carved with traditional motifs, lead up to the **Royal Palace Park*** (otherwise Wace Park). This has many fine mature trees and shady places for young lovers, if the local example is anything to go by. No colonial park is complete without a captured enemy gun, in this case a Japanese howitzer guarded by kittenish lions. Very pleasant, but views of the lake are elusive.

Udawattekele Sanctuary*, which means Higher Garden Forest, (open 0800-1730, Rs60) was a royal reserve. Two of the walks, Lady Horton's and Lady Gordon's are named after the wives of British governors, and it is best to stick to these main routes. Birdlife is plentiful and varied. At the top of the sanctuary are pools and a small Buddhist hermitage. This is not a good place for women to walk on their own.

There are also good views from Frederick E De Silva Mawatha, which used to be called Gregory's Road, on the south side of the lake.

Entertainment

Kandyan music is mainly a matter of drums with a little help from a twin-reed woodwind instrument. The drummers achieve intricate rhythms, and a surprising volume, from a variety of instruments, and sometimes two notes from each end of the drum.

Dancing, traditionally an all-male affair, is vigorous and lively. This is seen at its best in one of the religious processions such as the Kandy or Colombo Perahera.

It has to be borne in mind that real folk dances are performed on rare and special occasions, and usually in an open air village atmosphere. Done every night in a hall, and in front of an alien audience they quickly lose their spontaneity and charm. These days, unfortunately, no package holiday is complete without a folk dance performance, and the dancers soon get stale, sometimes to the point where you feel they are not taking things seriously.

There are at present three places in Kandy where you can see local music and dance. Currently the most popular is the Kandy Lake Club on Sangamitta MW. Other performances take place at the Kandyan Art Association on the lakeside and in the Red Cross building next door. The Queen's Hotel will presumably resume when it reopens after bomb damage. Most hotels and guest houses have tickets priced at Rs150.

There is a School of Kandyan Dance at Gunnepana village, and Amunugama village is home to drummers.

At the Kandy Garden Club (Tel 222 675) you can play tennis and billiards.

Festivals

Kandy's main festival is the **Esala Perahera***** which takes place over the ten days leading up to full moon in July or August. The origins of this date back to when the Tooth Relic arrived in Sri Lanka in the fourth century AD, and the ceremony has remained substantially unchanged since Knox described it late in the 17th century. The main action occurs on the final four nights. This is a tremendous show with, on the last night, a replica of the tooth relic taken in procession. The climax is a parade of sixty or more elephants brilliantly decked out, and the largest and most brilliant carrying the tooth relic in an ornate howdah. Preceding them are literally thousands of drummers, musicians, dancers, stilt walkers, whip crackers, and so on. Some of the men carry fire pots, others swing them round their heads. Book accommodation early, expect to pay far more than listed below, and reserve seats either through your hotel or the tourist office. For video makers part of the route between the Tooth Temple and the Queen's Hotel is floodlit.

Shopping

The government-run **Laksala** has an outpost selling good stuff at fair prices, though the selection is smaller than in Colombo. Always check prices here before looking elsewhere, and remember that shopping with a guide, taxi driver, or anyone else means a 40% commission going on your bill, whatever they may say. The **Kandyan Arts and Crafts Association**, which was founded in 1880, has a wider stock than Laksala, at perhaps slightly higher prices.

The **shopping centre** for Kandy's population is the grid of streets northwest of the lake, and it really is worth exploring here. There are many jewellery and 'antique' shops. On a domestic level Colombo Street has fruit and vegetables, household goods, and many kinds of dried fish. Little arcades have a multiplicity of small textile shops and it is here that you can get a feel for how people really live. The **market** behind the war memorial has fabrics in every colour of the rainbow and ready-mades. Because tour groups call here asking prices tend to be higher than in the centre of town, so hard bargaining is called for. The **Municipal Market** nearby has more of the same plus fruit and veg, and the whole street down to the railway station is a lively bazaar.

Srimavo Bandaranaike MW (the road out to Peradeniya) has many smart shops, especially for jewellery, gems, and batik.

Practical Information

Information. Ceylon Tourist Board information office (Tel 08-222 661) round the corner from the Olde Empire Hotel. *Kandy* by Anuradha Seneviratna, Rs125 from the Central Cultural Fund, 212 Bauddhaloka MW, Colombo 7. **British Council Library** at 178 DS Senanayake Vidiya. The **Buddhist Publication Society** on Sangaraja MW has a wide range of books on Buddhist subjects.

Arrival and departure
There is no airport at Kandy, but Air Lanka has an office (Tel 08-232 494) in the building next to the Olde Empire Hotel.
Colombo. Six **trains** daily (discounting the Night Mail) run from Colombo Fort to Kandy. The two Intercities at 0655 and 1535 are the best bet as all seats (1st observation car and 2nd, no 3rd) can be reserved in advance, tickets from window 17 at Colombo Fort; these trains take 2½hrs, the others 3¼hrs. In the Podi Menike (0555) seats can be reserved in the 1st observation car only, 2nd and 3rd are unreserved, but 2nd usually has seats if you are quick. The same applies to the Udarate Menike (0945) but this does not actually run to Kandy, you have to get a bus or three-wheeler from Peradeniya Junction. The other three trains, No19 at 1015, No23 at 1245, and No39 at 1715 have only 2nd and 3rd and are unreserved.

From Kandy to Colombo the Intercities leave at 0630 and 1500, the Podi Menike at 1705, No24 at 1000, and No20 at 1530. Same conditions as above.

Frequent **buses**, private and CTB, air-con and otherwise, connect the two cities. As elsewhere in Asia the train is always better than the bus.
Colombo Airport. One direct bus daily (Rs28) from the Goods Shed Busstand, leaves at 1700 and takes 3hrs. About Rs2000 by **taxi**.

Hill Country. The Podi Menike passes through Kandy at 0906 on its way to Hatton (for Adam's Peak), Nanu Oya (for Nuwara Eliya), Haputale, Ella, and Badulla; book well in advance if possible, only four seats are allocated to Kandy.

To the Cultural Triangle. Trains run only as far as Matale and, whilst they provide a good view of the Hunas Falls, are not very helpful. **Buses** for Dambulla and Sigiriya (No 49), and all the other places in the Cultural Triangle, leave from the Goods Shed bus-stand frequently; these include an A/C express to Anuradhapura. A **taxi** to Dambulla will cost around Rs1200 one way making as many stops on the way as you wish, add another Rs300 for Sigiriya.

To and from the coast. Train No39 leaves Matara daily at 1255 and runs through all the south and west coast resorts and Colombo reaching Kandy at 2025. No65 leaves Matara on Saturday only at 0700 and arrives in Kandy at 1402. Train No40 leaves Kandy at 0500 reaching Matara at 1215. No66 leaves Kandy at 1310 on Sunday only and reaches Matara at 1945. These trains are 2nd and 3rd only, no reservations. By **bus** you must change in Colombo.

Getting around. Three-wheelers are the best bet. Allow Rs40 from station or centre to Sharon Inn area, Rs70 to Green Woods, or Rs80 out as far as Blue Haven. Radio cabs are operated by Savoy Comfort (Tel 233 322).

Accommodation

(STD Code 08)

Mahaveli Reach Hotel, 35 PBA Weerakoon MW. Tel 232 062 Fax 232 068. SWB/DWB A/C $100. Rest. Bar. Set lunch or dinner Rs450, a la carte starters Rs90-190 main courses Rs210-490, buffet Rs684 incl. Rooms have balconies overlooking either Mahaveli river or courtyards with plants and flowers. A first class modern hotel.

Citadel, 124 Srimath Kuda Ratwate MW. Tel 226 173 Fax 232 085. SWB $59 DWB $71 (+$10 A/C, +$20 deluxe). Rest. Bar. Breakfast RS345, lunch Rs500, dinner Rs700, buffet Rs550 incl. Good modern place used mainly by tour groups. Swimming pool, boat trips, bicycle hire, etc.

Hotel Topaz and *Hotel Tourmaline*, Anniwatte. Tel 224 150 Fax 232 073. SWB/DWB A/C $70. Rest. Bars. Breakfast Rs340, lunch Rs580, dinner Rs600, beer Rs183. Well kept modern places, but a long way out, best if you have your own transport. Splendid views. Swimming pool, tennis, etc.

Hotel Suisse, 30 Sangaraja MW. Tel 222 637 Fax 232 083. SWB A/C $45 DWB A/C $50 (+$10 for deluxe rooms, +$15 for suite), also FB and HB terms. Rest. Bar. Breakfast Rs340, set lunch Rs550, set dinner Rs550, buffet dinner Rs590 incl. Nice old hotel with views of the lake. Colonial style rooms, beer garden, billiards room, swimming pool (non-residents Rs75). Charming place, especially the bar.

King's Park Hotel, 34 Sangaraja MW. Tel/Fax 223 620. SWB/DWB A/C $45. Rest. Bar (rooftop). Set dinner Rs360 incl, a la carte main courses Rs175-350, beer Rs100. Good, stylish modern hotel. Bedrooms in Indian style and dining room has Mackintosh style chairs.

Queen's Hotel, Dalada Vidya. Tel 323 290 Fax 232 079. Closed at the time of our visit due to bomb damage. A traditional place which should be even better after restoration.

The Chalet Hotel, 70 Frederick De Silva MW. Tel/Fax 234 571. SWB $22 DWB $30 Suite $45. Rest. Bar. Breakfast $350, set meals Rs360 up (very interesting menu), beer Rs175. One of the most extraordinary hotels in the world, never mind Sri Lanka. The walls, inside and out, are covered with murals, a delight to flower children of the sixties. Comfortable slightly beat-up furnishings and family photos, altogether more like being in the home of an eccentric friend than a hotel. Best views of the lake. Swimming pool. If you can't afford to stay call in for a beer and sandwiches (allow Rs450 for two).

Hotel Thilanka, 3 Sangamitta MW. Tel 232 429 Fax 225 497. SWB $16 DWB $26 (extra for A/C). Rest (SL/W/Chi). Bar. Breakfast Rs250, lunch Rs375incl, a la carte starters Rs120-180, main courses225-275, rice and curry Rs200, beer Rs121. Nice quiet hotel with lake views, rooms have balconies. Swimming pool (non-residents Rs121).

Windsor Castle Hotel, 40/2 Ampitiya Road. Tel 224 386. SWB $7-10 DWB $14. Rest. Bar. Breakfast Rs125, rice and curry Rs175. Former Planters' Club. Being renovated when seen, looks very promising.

Fair Havens, 47 Sir Kuda Ratwatte MW, Kandy (6km from centre). Tel 223 555. DWB $11. Rest. Bar. Large high-ceilinged rooms in a quiet house overlooking the Mahaveli Ganga river and elephant bathing place at Katugastota. Interesting menu; rice and curry Rs100, western dishes Rs200, beer Rs90.

Hotel Sunray, 117/8 Anagarika Dharmapala MW. Tel/Fax 222 207. DWB $10. Rest. Bar. Breakfast Rs150, rice and curry Rs180-225. Modern place with lots of plants about, Sri Lankan style restaurant.

Sharon Inn, 59 Saranankara Road. Tel/Fax 094-8-225 665. DWB $7-12. Rest. Bar. Breakfast Rs125, buffet dinner Rs200. No BTT, just service charge. One of the best budget hotels in Sri Lanka, nicely furnished and absolutely immaculate. Very good food, open to non-residents (must book in advance). Adding more rooms and an open-air restaurant on top (great views). Laundry service, international calls, etc. The owners do not pay touts, so expect the usual rubbish from three-wheeler drivers about it being closed and so on.

Lake Inn, 43 Saranankara Road. Tel 222 208. SWB $7 incl DWB $10 incl. Rest. Breakfast Rs100, main courses Rs100-140. The restaurant walls are covered with rush matting with Sri Lankan paintings on them.

Lake View Rest, 71A Rajapihilla MW. Tel 232 034 Fax 948-232 203. SWB $7 DWB $8-11. Rest. Breakfast Rs100, rice and curry Rs150-175. Good food and views across the hills, but expensive for what it is.

Lake Mount Tourist Inn, 195A Rajapihilla MW. Tel/Fax 233 204. SWB $4 DWB $7-11. Rest. Breakfast Rs90-140, rice and curry Rs100-130. Spotless bedrooms in Japanese style. Will pick you up from station.

McLeod Inn, 65A Rajapihilla MW. Tel 222 832. SWB $8 DWB $9. Rest. Breakfast Rs125, rice and curry Rs175-250. Views of the lake.

Blue Haven Guest House, 30/2 Poorna Lane. Tel 232 453 Fax 232 343. DWB $8. Rest. Bar. Breakfast Rs150, main courses Rs200. Spotless modern rooms with nets and balconies, good food, and a quiet location. Will collect you from the station, the Tourist Guide office at Colombo Fort station will arrange this for you.

Golden View Rest House, 46 Saranankara Road. Tel 224 978. SWB $4 DWB $8. Rest. Breakfast Rs125, rice and curry Rs150. The top bedroom has a good view. Massage and herbal bath Rs1300.

Blinkbonnie Tourist Inn, 69 Rajapihilla MW. Tel 222 007. SWB $7 DWB $8 (includes breakfast). Rest. Rice and curry Rs200. OK, free transport into city.
Freedom Lodge, 30 Saranankara Road. Tel 223 506 or 074-471 589. SWB $7 DWB $8. Rest. Breakfast Rs125, main courses Rs200. Nice and clean.
Starlight Guest House, 15A Saranankara Road. DWB $7. Rest. Breakfast Rs150, rice and curry Rs200. Hot water and nets.
Travellers Nest, 117/4 Anagarika Dharmapala MW. Tel 222 633. SWB $3 DWB $7 (+$1.50 for hot water). Rest. Breakfast Rs150, rice and curry Rs150. Clean and good.
Mrs Clement Dissanayake, 18 First Lane, Dharmaraja MW. Tel 225 468 or 072-220 462. SR $3 DR $5 SWB $5 DWB $6. Rest. Breakfast Rs100, rice and curry Rs200. Clean rooms, and travellers say the food is good. Does not pay commission.
Green Woods, 34A Sangamitta MW. Tel/Fax 070-800 674. DWB $5. Rest. Bar. Breakfast Rs (different every day), rice and curry Rs. Lovely quiet location facing the jungle of Udawattakelle Sanctuary. Kusum's home cooking may well be the best you will have in Sri Lanka.
Expeditor, 58A Saranankara Road. Tel 0094-070-800 611 Fax 0094-70-800 611. DWB $5 (+$1.50 for hot water). Rest. Breakfast Rs125, rice and curry Rs150-200 including dessert. Nice rooms with fans and nets. Organise trekking tours.
Thilini Guest House, 60 Saranankara Road. Tel 224 975. DWB $4. Rest. Breakfast Rs125, rice and curry Rs150. Pleasant, clean guest house.
Olde Empire Hotel, 21 Temple Street. Tel 224 284. SR $4 incl DR $5 incl. Rest. Bar. Rice and curry Rs45. Pleasant colonial type place with simple rooms and lots of polished wood. Upstairs balcony to watch the world go by.
Pink House, 15 Saranankara Road. DR $3. Rest. Breakfast Rs120, rice and curry Rs200. A friendly family and good cheap accommodation.
The YMBA is truly awful.

Eating and Drinking

Kandy is one of the few places in the Hill Country which has a good selection of restaurants, and where you might be tempted to eat out from your guest house or hotel.
Flower Song Chinese Restaurant, Kotugodalle Vidiya, is an expensive but good Chinese restaurant; the *Queen's Hotel* also has a Chinese restaurant. *Topaz Restaurant*, Dalada Vidiya, is said to be good. *Paiva's Moghul Restaurant*, Yatinuvara Vidiya, has moderately priced North Indian food. *Lake Front*, next to Laksala, does simple moderately priced Chinese and western food. *White House*, Dalada Vidiya, (closed in the evening) does good lunches and excellent ice cream. *Bake House*, Dalada Vidiya, has a huge choice of food at reasonable prices. *Sam's Fast Food* looks interesting. *Devon Restaurant*, Dalada Vidiya, is very reasonable for Sri Lankan and western food. *Olde Empire Hotel*, 21 Temple Street, does good cheap rice and curry and is pleasant for just a drink. *Pub Royale*, Queens Hotel, is a real Edwardian pub, (Lion beer Rs96 incl), good and very cheap snacks from the *Pastry Shop* next door, an excellent establishment.
Cargill's Food City and the various bakeries provide everything for an

156 *The Hill Country*

interesting picnic, and the *Pastry Shop* in the Queens Hotel does excellent packed lunches for Rs70.

Excursions

Kandy is an excellent base for exploring the attractive and interesting countryside around.

Peradeniya Botanic Gardens

These **gardens**** (0800-1800, Rs150 or Rs75 for students) have been developed over the last century and a half on the site of a royal garden. The 59ha/150 acre gardens contain a complete flora of Sri Lanka and many other tropical and temperate plants and trees as well. You could easily spend all day in this beautiful place; with less time consult the map at the entrance and pick the bits that most interest you.

For a quick look (1½hrs) walk straight ahead from the entrance to the Great Circle which has trees planted by visiting politicians, British royalty, a Tsar of Russia, and some real heroes, the Apollo 12 astronauts. Continue down the Palm Avenue, noting on the left the large congregations of fruit bats (or flying foxes). Just past there are two fig trees with intertwined branches, any youngster's dream of a climbing tree. When you reach the Mahaveli Ganga river (the activities of the sand and gravel men are interesting) turn right and follow it before detouring into the flower gardens, orchid house, and plant house. The path back to the entrance is through a scented grove of cinnamon, nutmeg, and clove trees. If you have been lucky enough not to see a scorpion up to now one of the keepers will probably oblige. Cars are (unfortunately) allowed in for Rs65 or your push bike for Rs10.

As an historical aside, Peradeniya Palace was the headquarters of South-East Asia Command in the Second World War. This was commanded by Lord Louis Mountbatten who had visited this place earlier, in 1922, when accompanying his kinsman the Prince of Wales (later Edward VIII and Duke of Windsor) on one of his world tours. They stayed in a building, known then as King's House, sited in the centre of the Great Circle, and Mountbatten was unimpressed by the standard of accommodation. This, like all the other buildings in the gardens, and a large number of temporary huts, became part of the headquarters. Special commando operations, for instance, were planned in what is now the superintendent's office. Mountbatten's organisation was a stylish but incredibly extravagant affair keeping 10,000 men and women from more active duty. He even had an airstrip built 30km/19miles north of Kandy which was unusable most of the time because of weather conditions.

Information. Map just inside the entrance.

Arrival and departure. Taxi (Rs500) or three-wheeler (Rs400) return including a reasonable wait. Bus from Torrington Street or clock tower.

Eating and Drinking. Cold drinks and refreshments both outside and in the park. A very pleasant place for a picnic. The *Rest House*, only a short distance from the entrance, is more expensive but good and comfortable (and has beer).

The older buildings of **Peradeniya University**, by Sir Patrick Abercrombie, in traditional style, are said to be attractive.

KANDY EXCURSIONS

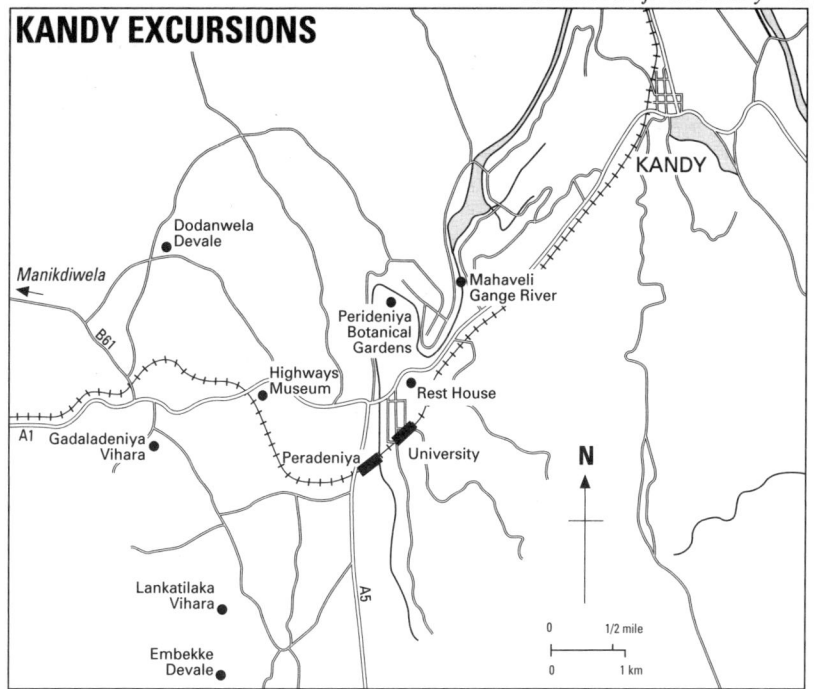

[Map of Kandy excursions area showing locations including Kandy, Mahaveli Gange River, Peradeniya Botanical Gardens, Highways Museum, Rest House, University, Peradeniya, Dodanwela Devale, Manikdiwela, Gadaladeniya Vihara, Lankatilaka Vihara, and Embekke Devale, with roads A1, A5, and B61 marked.]

Historic temples

The **Gadaladeniya Viharaya** stands on a hill south of the Kandy-Colombo road and about 15km from Kandy. An inscription tells how it was built in the 14th century to the design of a monk who had previously studied at Amaravati in Andhra Pradesh. At the entrance is a group of five dagobas. Rather faded murals decorate the four shrines, and more on one of the porches suggest that the whole exterior was once plastered and painted.

The corner pillars of the porch of the main shrine are said to have been carved by a master mason (left) and his pupil (right). On the left carved medallions depict dancers and drummers; these are absent on the right pillar but, on the outer face, is a Shiva Nataraja (the Cosmic Dancer) and above Krishna with his flute. Looking up in the porch you can see the huge slabs of stone forming the roof, and in the shrine the corbelling method of overlapping layers of stone which was popular before the adoption of arches and vaulting. The wooden doors are as old as the building and decorated with paintings. The makaras are composed of seven different animals, and a rather severe plastered and gilded Buddha sits in the meditation position.

The **Lankatilaka Viharaya****, gleaming white on its hilltop, and surrounded by intense greens, is one of the most imposing temples in Sri Lanka. The name means Glory of Lanka Temple or, more literally, Lanka's tilak, a tilak being the beauty spot Hindu women wear on their foreheads. The approach from the lower car park (there are two) is by steps cut in the solid rock. This temple was built in the same year as the Gadaladeniya, but by the chief minister rather than the king. The architect was a south Indian, and some aspects of the design relate to temples at Pagan in Burma. The main structure dates from the 14th century, whilst the roofs, possibly showing Keralan influence, are as late as the 19th century. Old records say that the shrine was originally four storeys high and had a stupa over the Buddha shrine; only the ground floor and part of the first survive.

This is a most unusual building both in its design and in that, for a devale, Buddha takes pride of place. Approaching from the steps you find a moonstone cut from the rock at the foot of the temple steps and then enter a Buddha image house. Two guardian figures with raised swords stand either side of the painted doors. Inside the large seated Buddha is flanked by standing ones in the abhaya-mudra. The murals, dating from the 17th century, show many different characters, mostly kings but including Hanuman and the demon king Mara, paying homage to Buddha. Some of the floral painting has a Mughal look.

Now walk clockwise round the outside of the temple, passing a huge rock inscription, and you find a traditional devale. From the drumming hall you enter a vaulted brick ambulatory around the Buddha shrine. Contrary perhaps to appearances this is said all to have been built at the same time. The ambulatory may, however, have been an afterthought. The five images were obviously planned for the outer walls of the Buddha shrine, and it seems a late decision was made to give them more protection from the elements. Note the moulded bricks and the thickness of the walls. In a niche opposite the entrance are Vishnu and Lakshmi. Going clockwise you find first Saman and then Kataragama on his peacock. Round the other way are Upulvan and a very pot-bellied Ganesh. And that is an odd thing, because Ganesh is not one of the traditional guardians of Buddhism and has no real place here. Kataragama has to face east, like the Buddha but, because of the entrance to the Buddha shrine, he cannot be in the centre. Hence the introduction of his brother Ganesh for balance.

The **Embekke Devale** was built in 1371 by King Vikramabahu III, and is dedicated to Kataragama. The most notable feature is the drumming hall in front of the shrine. The wooden pillars have a large variety of carvings, mostly traditional, and including wrestlers, a double-headed eagle, dancers, a lion attacking an elephant, and a mounted Portuguese soldier. Carving extends to the lotus pendentives and elements of the roof structure.

The original pillars are thought to have come from a previous king's audience hall at Gampola (see p160). The temple had to be heavily restored in 1948, mainly because of the depredations of white ants, and most of the timber and carving date from that time. Puja times are 0600, 1130, and 1900. The shrine will be closed at other times, and the door covered with a hanging showing Kataragama on his peacock.

Down the hill towards the Kandy-Nuwara Eliya road is the Embekke Ambalama (worth seeing only if you are coming that way). The stone pillars are the remains of a pilgrim's resting place, slightly earlier than the Devale.

Metalworkers (mainly brass) abound in the villages around these temples. Most is sheet metal work, but castings are still made by the lost wax process.

Arrival and departure. Gadaladeniya temple is about 1km from kilometre post 105 (from Colombo) on the Kandy-Colombo main road. Lankatilaka temple is 1½km from there, and the Embekke devale a further 3km. Buses run on all these roads, and also from Kandy and Peradeniya to Embekke. The roads are too hilly to consider cycling. You may find paths to walk through the fields, but that will be very hot. A three-wheeler to Peradeniya Gardens and around the three devales will cost around Rs800-1000.

North of the Kandy-Colombo road is the **Dodanwela Devale**. The legend behind this is interesting as King Rajasimha II (1635-1687) was on his way to fight the Portuguese when the pole of his palanquin broke here. In a placatory gesture he promised, if he won, to give his gold crown and sword to the temple. He duly defeated the Portuguese at Danture and kept his promise. Unfortunately the temple gave the crown to Kandy Museum for safekeeping, and it was stolen from there. That is about the end of interest in this temple, though some of the figures outside would hardly look out of place on the more florid sort of altar piece.

Arrival and departure. Take the B61 out of Pillimattalau, turn right over railway track, and then left at the first T-junction.

Shopping

A **handloom weaving** school and workshop was established in the village of Manikdiwela in the 1950s by Edith Ludowyk. Saris, bedsheets, tablecloths, and so on are produced, and the prices almost make you feel guilty.

Arrival and departure. Take the B61 out of Pillimattalau, go straight on to the 9km marker, and turn sharp left.

A short distance closer to Kandy is the **Highways Museum**. This has a collection of four preserved, but not working, English steamrollers. In the small museum building are antique surveying instruments and a model of a steam dredging barge. Visible from the museum is a stone arched bridge built in 1826 by Captain Brown for the original road to Kandy; there is also a replica of the wooden bridge at Bogoda (see p179) put together without metal fastenings. There are said to be more steam engines at Kegalle.

Arrival and departure. At the 107km marker on the Colombo-Kandy road.

Further Afield

Kandy towards the East Coast. Few travellers venture this way while Batticaloa is out of bounds, but the area is not without interest for the intrepid.

Taking the A26 for 4km from Kandy, and then the B413 you skirt the south side of the huge Victoria Reservoir formed by damming the Mahaveli River. The **Victoria Dam** and its information centre are unlikely to be open for security reasons.

Hanguranketa (27km/17miles) was used as a fall-back capital for brief periods. Raja Sinha II fled here during a popular revolt in Kandy in 1644. In the following century Kirti Sri was driven out of Kandy by the Dutch during the Salt War (1765). Little of interest remains as the town was taken twice by the British (1803 and 1817) and almost completely destroyed. The **Potgul Maliga Vihara** is a library with a fine collection of traditional palm leaf books. The dagoba is unusual in that the murals are where they can be seen instead of sealed out of sight in the relic chamber.

160　*The Hill Country*

Facing the vihara is a **Vishnu devale** which may still have the hangings donated by Raja Sinha II to commemorate his victories over the Portuguese. As elsewhere off the tourist track these places are open only at puja time. The Rest House here is not recommended.

The **Kirundu Oya Falls** 189m/649ft high are along a rough narrow road from near Rikilligaskada (5km from Hanguranketa). Going on from here the **Maturata valley** is said to be very beautiful.

Taking the A26 road down the north side of the Mahaveli river leads through cacao plantations (established in 1830) to Teldeniya. Roads run from near Teldeniya and Uragala through Corbett's Gap to Rangala and Bambrella in the **Knuckles Range** (1862m/6107ft). The highest point on the main road is at **Hunnasgiriya** and gives a splendid view. A track goes from here to the fort at **Medamahanuwara** which was the site of Vikrama Rajasimha's last stand against the British in 1815. The main road now goes through a twisty and hairy descent of over 600m/2000ft to the plains. From Hasalaka (a good bungalow here) at the bottom a road leads to the **Ratna Ela Falls** (110m).

A small limestone cave with stalactites and stalagmites is near Sitakotuwa Vihara, a short walk from the village of Gurulupota. In the **Rantambe Gorge** the Mahaveli Ganga is funnelled boisterously through a narrow canyon.

Mahiyangana (or Alutnuwara, the New Town) is 75km from Kandy. It was formerly known as Mahanaga or Royal Cobra, and has been a holy place for a very long time. There is a legend that Buddha came here to preach a short time after his enlightenment. His audience was not humans but yakshas, forest deities who represent the forces of nature. He left a lock of his hair, and this was enshrined in a dagoba later enlarged by Dutthagamani in around 100BC. Despite there being no evidence that Buddha ever visited Sri Lanka this has made Mahiyangana a popular place of pilgrimage.

The Maha Vishnu Devale once enshrined a 14th century sandalwood image of Vishnu from Dondra, the very holy temple at Sri Lanka's southernmost point. This is now in the Vishnu Devale in Kandy. The new deity causes trances and hysteria in women. A festival takes place in Esala month. The Rest House is nicely situated by the river (but swimming is dangerous).

A new road makes it possible to link these two excursions into a round trip, but always check on the security position first, roads can be closed at short notice. These trips are really not worthwhile on public transport.

KANDY TO ADAM'S PEAK AND NUWARA ELIYA BY RAIL

Gampola was the capital of Sri Lanka from 1344-1408 when it was known as Gangasiripura, but little remains of its past glory. The Mahaweli River is prone to bursting its banks, and the flood levels are marked on the station buildings. The buildings disappeared under water completely in 1947, necessitating an additional pole marker.

Arrival and departure. Train or bus from Kandy (21km) or Colombo.

Hatton is the nearest railway station for the shorter approach to Adam's Peak. The town is a centre of the tea industry, but otherwise of little interest for the visitor.

Arrival and departure. Train from Kandy, Colombo, or Nanu Oya (the station for Nuwara Eliya), also buses but the train is preferable.

Accommodation. Try the *Ajantha Guest House* (Tel 0512-337) which is within walking distance of the station. An expensive alternative is *Brown's Upper Glencairn Guest House* (Tel 0512-348), 3km south of Hatton, advance booking essential. The house has character and is set in tea estates.

Bogawantalawa is a short detour from Norwood, between Hatton and Maskeliya. In St Mary's Churchyard lies Julia Margaret Cameron, one of the great pioneers of photography. Apparently good walking and a pleasant Rest House.

Maskeliya, at 1280m/4198ft, is on the road from Hatton to Dalhousie. There is simple accommodation, and its relative quietness may recommend it as a base for Adam's Peak. The problem is getting from Maskeliya to Dalhousie in the middle of the night. Outside the pilgrimage season you may need to change buses here.

ADAM'S PEAK

Adam's Peak (2243m/7362ft) is sacred to the people of four faiths and has the alternative names of Sri Padai and Saman or Samanta Kanda. Sri Padai means sacred footprint, and the Buddhists will tell you that there is indeed a footprint of the Buddha on the summit, though he never visited Sri Lanka himself. Saman or Samanta was the supreme god of the indigenous people and became assimilated into Hinduism.

The Muslims believe that it was Adam who formed the footprint when he fell from the Garden of Eden, the other print being in the Kaaba in Mecca. Adam has a special place in Muslim belief as he was not only the first man but also the first prophet.

The legend that Adam was buried here made it not only a place of pilgrimage for Muslims but also visiting Christians. They have yet another theory, holding that it is the footprint of Thomas the Apostle who was martyred in Madras. Marco Polo was here in 1294, and so fifty years later was a shipwrecked Florentine monk. At much the same time Ibn Battuta, that inveterate Moroccan traveller, remarked on the chain handrails already in place. Even the Portuguese poet Camoens mentioned it in the Lusiad.

Feminists are advised to think carefully about doing this pilgrimage. Apparently reaching the summit guarantees the very considerable boon of guaranteed rebirth as a man.

Dalhousie and the ascent

Dalhousie is really just an overgrown bazaar with restaurants and limited accommodation at the foot of the short climb up Adam's Peak.

From the bus-stand you walk down through the bazaar, over a footbridge, and up again to the beginning of the path. This path was opened just before the Second World War and lit by electricity from the beginning. The path starts off gently enough, and the first landmark is the **Japanese Peace Stupa**. Beyond this the path steepens gradually, and at night the string of lights seems to climb up to the stars. As you near the top it gets steeper and steeper, and eventually you are almost hauling yourself up on the handrails. There are refreshments most of the way up at regular intervals, but not on the summit. One is torn between having tea before settling down to wait for the sunrise and the knowledge that there is nowhere for a pee.

The holy footprint

Having reached the summit pilgrims visit the two shrines and then wait for the sunrise. The footprint is a rather vague outline 170cm by 80cm. The use of a footprint to represent a divinity was in common use in India during the first millennium BC, and the device is probably most often seen in Jain temples. In the early days of Buddhism this and devices such as an empty throne were used rather than a representational image. These days the imprint is mostly covered by a white cloth to catch the offerings of pilgrims. The simple wooden shelter which sufficed for most of history has been replaced by an ugly stone structure painted silver.

This holy site passed into the hands of the Hindus in 1582 when Rajasimha I converted to Hinduism. Its use as a shrine of Bhairava, a horrific form of Shiva, lasted until 1763 when Kirti Sri Rajasimha, who restored Buddhism to its leading place in Sri Lanka, returned it to the monks. A smaller temple recalls this Hindu interlude.

From the other side of the summit you see the lights of the two paths leading up from Ratnapura and, as it starts to get light, lightning flickering through the clouds to the West. As the sun rises Sri Lanka starts to reveal itself. A little later, as the sun climbs higher, the mountain casts its shadow on the clouds below. A shadow rapidly swallowed by the mountain itself. In full daylight the views are stunning in the December to April period, encompassing the lighthouses at Colombo, Galle, Dondra Head and Trincomalee.

The beauty makes one reluctant to set off down again, as does the feeling that it will be even harder on the knees than going up. And do make sure you get the right exit from the summit. You don't want to set off for Ratnapura; it has been done.

The catch

Now for the bad news. Do not come to Adam's Peak expecting too much of a spiritual or even an aesthetic experience. Dalhousie bazaar is like Blackpool on a bad day, complete with silly hats and incessant loud music. This noise extends all the way up the hill. A thick trail of rubbish also follows the route, much of which is very rough. Worst of all, the trees which might have provided some shade for the descent, have been cut down. A pilgrimage should have beautiful flowering trees and aromatic herbs and spices by the way. All you get at Adam's Peak is dirt. At the top are ugly concrete buildings and more mess. You can see an equally good sunrise just ambling out of your guest house in Haputale or Ella, and panoramic views are not exactly at a premium in Sri Lanka.

The behaviour of some visitors, notably groups of young men, can leave a lot to be desired. Take advice on when the Peak is likely to be relatively quiet, especially avoiding festivals, weekends, Poya days, and the days between Poya and the nearest weekend.

It is a very odd thing that in India, a universally dirty country where very little is maintained properly, the pilgrimages are mostly kept clean and in good repair. Yet in Sri Lanka, which very rarely feels like a Third World country, the most important pilgrimage should be in such an awful state.

Adam's Peak seems to be one of those things that have been enjoyable in the past but have changed character with growing population, ease of transport, surplus spending power and leisure time. Because the authors had such mixed impressions they polled a sample of other foreign visitors. They divided 50:50 into those who thought it was one of the highpoints of their visit to Sri Lanka, and those who thought it was a complete waste of time and effort. So it's up to you.

Arrival and departure. Bus 925 from Goods Shed bus-stand in Kandy via Hatton. Train to Hatton, then bus 33km (2hrs). Walk (7km/4miles and a climb of 975m/3200ft) from Dalhousie, this takes 2-5hrs depending on your state of fitness. Alternatively, there is the much longer walk (27km/7hrs) from Ratnapura.

Accommodation
Green House, at foot of path up hill. No phone. $10 for two including vegetarian breakfast and dinner. Basic, but a nice place to stay, and a gargantuan Sri Lankan breakfast awaits when you totter back.

St Andrews Lodge, on the left before you enter the bazaar, is the most comfortable place to stay, but the price can fluctuate from $11 to $17 or even more.

Past Hatton, on the way up to **Talawakele**, you get good views of the Devon and St Clair Falls from the railway. The road from here up to Agrapatana is spectacular. Looking out from the train you can also see how the line doubles back on itself to gain height.

Kandy to Nuwara Eliya by road

The road passes through Gampola (see p160). After Pussellawa tea gardens start to dominate the landscape. There is a fine 100m high waterfall at Ramboda, and a bit further views over heavily wooded country to the Kothmale Reservoir. The huge corrugated iron Labookellie Tea Factory (15km from Nuwara Eliya) is surrounded by its plantations. The factory is open to visitors 0900-1700. The road is much faster then taking the train and, if you are short of time, you could use a taxi and visit Peradeniya Gardens, and the Lankatilaka and Embekke temples on the way.

NUWARA ELIYA

Nuwara Eliya, surrounded by the highest mountains in Sri Lanka, was founded as a hill station by the British in around 1830. The main promoter was Sir Samuel Baker, an extraordinary man who, in his spare time, went on freelance expeditions up the Nile trying to stop slave trading. The 1900m/6232ft altitude raises it well above the steamy heat of the coast and Kandy, and gives a fresh atmosphere. It was formerly an estate of the king of Kandy, and the name means Plain of the City, i.e. of Kandy. Part of the British process of making themselves feel at home was the introduction of European fruit, vegetables, and flowers. To this day 'English vegetables' are sent down to the lower levels.

Publicity suggests that Nuwara Eliya is still a hill station and social centre for tea planters. In reality it is a busy commercial centre for the surrounding area. The bazaar is lively and pleasant though physically unattractive, most of the old buildings having been destroyed in anti-Tamil rioting in 1983.

Exploring

Hill stations are traditionally a place for both relaxation and exercise. **Mount Pedro**, or more properly Pidurutalagala, at 2530m/8820ft Sri Lanka's highest point, used to be a popular climb. It is now, almost inevitably, defiled by a television antenna. A more recent addition is a radar station, and since this is heavily guarded you are allowed to make the ascent only with police permission.

The alternative is **Single Tree Mountain**. Walk out of town on the Badulla Road as far as the Clifton Inn and take the rough road with the Keerthi Learners sign. The road leads up through tea gardens bordered with elder to the communications tower, and from here you can see to the south and east as far as Adam's Peak. You can see the road up from Nanu Oya and also pick out the course of the old narrow gauge mountain railway. The views on the way up are all of the town. Across it are the depressing signs of deforestation for yet more smallholdings to grow vegetables.

Victoria Park, in the centre of town, is pleasant for a stroll. The flower beds are at their best during the April-May season and again in Autumn.

The Hill Club has four clay **tennis courts** which cost Rs120 per person per hour, balls are Rs400, and racquet hire is Rs30. **Horse racing** takes place during the April season, but the racecourse is very run down.

The **Golf Club** was founded in 1889 and has one of the most attractive and best kept courses in Asia. The club house is equally good and has all the facilities you would expect including a bar, dining room, library, and badminton court. There is also some accommodation. Non-playing temporary membership at Rs250 entitles you to use all the facilities. Green fees are Rs1200 on weekdays and Rs1485 at weekends and public holidays; seven days costs Rs6800. Up to three hours practice costs Rs715. Clubs (Rs300) and shoes (Rs100) can be hired by the day, and there is a strict dress code. A caddie is obligatory and costs Rs175 per round. Further details from The Secretary, Tel/Fax 052-2835. Naval buffs will be intrigued by a couple of photos in the office.

Nuwara Eliya was a popular place for **angling**. Streams were stocked with rainbow trout and the lake with brownies. The position at the moment is that the Wildlife Department has banned all angling.

Other attractions

One would expect **Holy Trinity Church** to have some interesting memorials inside, but it is kept locked.

On the way out of town to the south part of the **racecourse** is used for burning the town's rubbish. Beyond that is a huge area of poly-tunnels for growing carnations. **Gregory Lake** is named after Sir William Gregory (governor 1872-77), who was responsible for its creation. Unfortunately the noisy polluted Badulla Road runs down one side of it. The northern third of the lake is completely choked with water hyacinth and other weed. The area

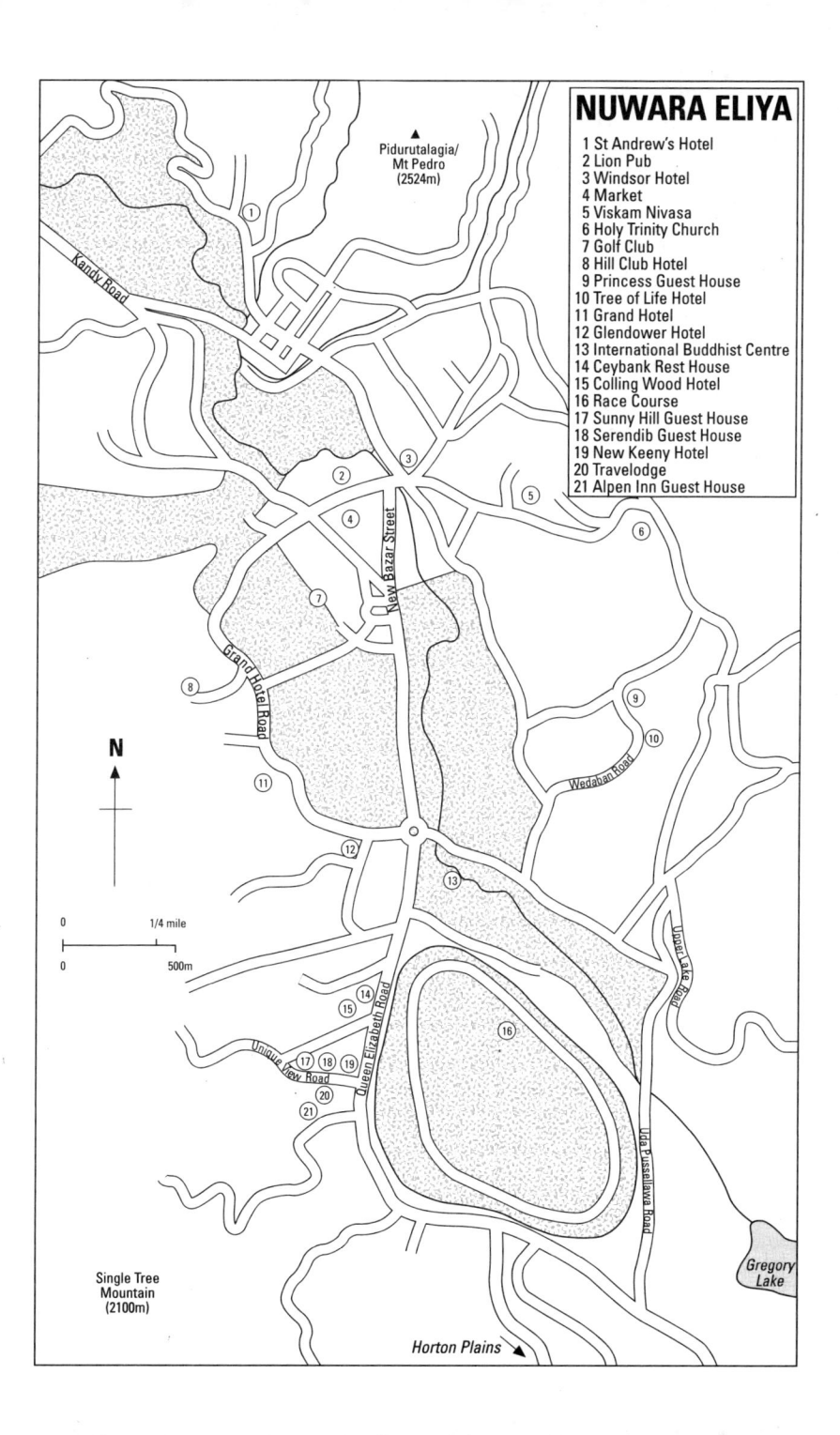

NUWARA ELIYA

1. St Andrew's Hotel
2. Lion Pub
3. Windsor Hotel
4. Market
5. Viskam Nivasa
6. Holy Trinity Church
7. Golf Club
8. Hill Club Hotel
9. Princess Guest House
10. Tree of Life Hotel
11. Grand Hotel
12. Glendower Hotel
13. International Buddhist Centre
14. Ceybank Rest House
15. Colling Wood Hotel
16. Race Course
17. Sunny Hill Guest House
18. Serendib Guest House
19. New Keeny Hotel
20. Travelodge
21. Alpen Inn Guest House

around the lake is cleared of trees, and you can forget about any ideas of pleasant walks. Canoes and pedaloes can be hired from the Chalet du Lake (sic), not cheap and rather pointless.

A site in the middle of Nuwara Eliya has been earmarked for a **tea centre and museum**.

Your view of Nuwara Eliya is likely to be conditioned by your spending power. Staying at the Hill Club or one of the nice old hotels is great fun, and you can enjoy the refreshing climate whilst using their facilities or playing golf. Budget travellers and those looking for good walking and the best views will do a lot better at Haputale or Ella.

Shopping. Viskam Nivasa is a handicrafts shop run by Laksala, the government agency, some nice stuff at fixed prices. Those who omitted to bring warm clothing can buy fleece jackets in the bazaar. Well known brand names, complete with English price tickets showing £40, carry an asking price of Rs450 (£4.50). These may be seconds or rejects so have a good look first.

Information. A consortium of local hotels is funding an information centre in Victoria Park.

Arrival and departure. Bus from Kandy (3hrs). Train from Kandy to Nanu Oya station (9km) then bus. Between 1910 and 1940 a narrow gauge line connected Nanu Oya and Nuwara Eliya but, like many other amenity lines it did not long survive competition from buses. Also trains direct to Colombo (6hrs).

Accommodation

(STD Code 052)

The Hill Club, Grand Hotel Road. Tel 2663/3192. Fax 2654. SWB $20 DWB $30-45 Suite $55/75. Rest. Bars. Breakfast $5, lunch $8, dinner $10, the latter two set five-course meals. Drinks reasonable, local spirits Rs90, draught beer Rs100, wine from Rs1000, champagne Rs3000. Great fun and totally relaxing. Everyone calls this English, actually it's more like the better sort of Scottish sporting hotel. Beautifully kept gardens and four clay tennis courts.

Grand Hotel, Grand Hotel Road. Tel 2882 Fax 2265. SWB $60 DWB $66. Rest. Bar. Breakfast Rs244, lunch Rs366, buffet dinner Rs427 (all incl) or a la carte Thai food. Startlingly reminiscent of an English seaside hotel. Nice gardens for afternoon tea and cake.

St Andrews Hotel, 10 St Andrews Drive. Tel 2445 Fax 009452-3153. SWB/DWB $60 (+$10 at peak times). Rest. Bar. Stylish and comfortably old-fashioned hotel. Wood panelled bar with church pews. Garden with view to the hills, a nice place for afternoon tea. Breakfast $4, set lunch $6, set dinner $8, buffet dinner Rs480. A la carte main courses around Rs300. By contrast with the Hill Club this looks more English than Scottish.

Windsor Hotel, PO Box 01 (town centre). Tel 3217 Fax 2889. SWB/DWB $35. Rest. Bar. Breakfast Rs175, main courses Rs200, buffet dinner Rs400incl. Modern hotel very well appointed with spacious rooms and garden on first floor. Excellent food.

Hotel Tree of Life, Wedderburn Road. Tel 3684. Fax 3127. SWB $27 DWB $35 SWB F/B $44 DWB F/B $69. Rest (very good). Bar. An unspoiled period bungalow complete with the family photos. Fine gardens and a quiet location. Operated as an ayurvedic clinic. Ayurvedic diet available under medical supervision, but non-vegetarian food (even a BLT sandwich!) and beer also obtainable at average rates. A full (1½hours) treatment of ayurvedic massage, steam bath, and herbal bath costs Rs1746. Highly recommended.

Ceybank Rest, Badulla Road. Tel 3053. SWB $14 DWB $17 Suite $19. Rest. Bar. Comfortable but has a slightly spartan feel. Rice and curry Rs150, other main courses Rs100-200.

Glendower Hotel, 5 Grand Hotel Road. Tel 2501 Fax 2749. DWB $18 incl. Rest. Bar. Nicely renovated and well managed smaller hotel. Nice garden. Excellent Chinese restaurant open to non-residents (main courses Rs120-250, whole Peking duck Rs700). Cosy bar, for which the owner (who is mad on Scotland) picks up bits and pieces at car boot sales in England! Billiards room.

Chalet du Lake (sic), Badulla Road. DWB $14 DWB H/B $20. Rest (reasonably priced). No bar. Nicely appointed wooden chalets overlooking the lake.

Princess Guest House, Wedderburn Road. Tel 2462. DWB $9. Breakfast Rs150, dinner Rs300. An old bungalow in a quiet location.

Colling Wood Inn, 112 Badulla Road. Tel 3550. DWB $8 Rest. Bar. Old planter's house with polished wood floors, new bathrooms with hot water, and fireplaces (a fire costs Rs150) in most rooms. Breakfast Rs125, dinner Rs200. A good place to stay, but the food is disappointing.

Travelodge, Badulla Road. Tel 2233. DWB $8. Rest. Bar. Breakfast Rs85, rice and curry Rs175.

Serendib Guest House, 15 Unique View Road. Tel 2077. DWB $7. Rest. Bar. This and the Sunny Hill are a little quieter than places on Badulla Road.

Sunny Hill Guest House, 18 Unique View Road. Tel 2300 Fax 3700. DWB $7-10 Rest. Bar. Rooms have balconies looking out to One Tree Hill.

Alpen Inn Guest House, 4 Haddon Hill Road. Tel 3009. DWB $7. All bedrooms have fireplaces. Garden and home-grown vegetables. Breakfast Rs125, main courses around Rs200.

New Keenly Hotel, 122 Badulla Road. Tel 3168. DWB $6. Breakfast Rs100, rice and curry Rs150.

In April and possibly in August and early September expect a $8 room to cost anything up to $43, if you can find one. Best to phone in advance at these times.

15km from Nuwara Eliya:

The Tea Factory, Kandapola. Tel 3600 (or 074-714 441 for reservations) Fax 2026. SWB $35 DWB $45 (Suites +$15/$30). Rest. Bar. Breakfast Rs310, lunch Rs450, dinner Rs500. Something completely different. Superb conversion of a traditional tea factory maintaining all the old structure and much of the machinery as well. Good location and very comfortable.

Eating and Drinking

Nuwara Eliya is home to the *Lion Brewery*, one of only two in Sri Lanka. The brewery itself is on the outskirts of town, and you need permission from head office in Colombo to visit. The *Lion Pub*, next to the Bank of Ceylon in the town centre, is fun; a real social pub atmosphere rather than just a drinking shop. Inside is probably not really for women, but the terrace is pleasant. Cheapest beer in Sri Lanka and good cheap snacks.

The bars at the Hill Club and Glendower are fun and reasonably priced (as long as you drink the local stuff). The Hill Club has a strict dress code in the evening.

Grand Hotel Pastry Shop. Sit outside for reasonable snacks, ice creams, and cold drinks.
Windsor Hotel Terrace. Pleasant place for coffee and cake or a beer.
Cheap basic restaurants in the town centre.

Excursions

The **Sita Amman Kovil** (or Sita Eliya Temple), 1km before the Hakgala Botanical Gardens, is one of the places where Sita is said to have been held prisoner by Ravana.

The **Hakgala Botanical Gardens**** (10km away) are named for the hill above, which is said to look like a jawbone. The gardens cover 27ha/67acres at an altitude of around 1670m/5478ft. This was once a cinchona plantation for the production of quinine, the first effective anti-malarial drug and, more pertinently these days, the essential ingredient in tonic water. Temperate plants are still acclimatised here.

There is something here for everyone. The keen gardener will enjoy the rose and formal gardens (at their best in April and May) and would kill for the Curator's Bungalow. As you climb higher it becomes more jungly with pine trees, birds, butterflies, and views, everything in fact that you expect of a pukka hill resort but don't get at Nuwara Eliya itself. Allow three or four hours to see everything, even bring a picnic and spend all day. The booming 'hoo-hoo-hoo' calls come from the bear monkey which grows to 1.2m/4ft tall. Entrance is Rs150 (Rs75 for students), money well spent.

Arrival and departure. On the bus route from Nuwara Eliya to Badulla. You could take a taxi out here (Rs150) and chance a bus back, they look not too bad. This is too good a place to rush by keeping a taxi waiting.

Accommodation
Humbugs Inn & Restaurant (150m downhill from the entrance to the gardens). Tel 052-2709/3308. DWB $9. Rest. Bar. Only four rooms, all with balconies, and two sharing a sitting room. Better view than anywhere in Nuwara Eliya. Strawberries and cream. A great place to stay.

Nuwara Eliya to Badulla by rail

Istripura Caverns is a series of deep and interconnected chambers which sound suitable for caving and cave diving. The name means City of Women and comes from an old story about a giant who kept his harem in the caves. Access is from Welimada on the Nuwara Eliya-Badulla road.

Pattipola is the highest railway station in Sri Lanka at 1891m, though the highest point on the track (1897m/6222ft) is 1km further on. The scenery all along this line is stunning.

HORTON PLAINS

Horton Plains is a small part (32sq km/12sq miles) of the Peak Wilderness Sanctuary dominated by the mountains Totapola (2360m/7741ft) and Kirigalpota (2177m/7857ft). This is a most attractive area of sub-tropical forest and open grassland very like an English heath.

The usual public transport approach to the Plains is by train to Ohiya station. To **walk up from Ohiya station** follow the rail tracks for 800m or so towards Kandy and turn left into the jungle just after crossing a stream and before the tunnel. The path is reasonably clear all the way up but rough, and in places you need to push through vegetation. You need proper shoes or boots, and it would be unpleasant and difficult after rain. This is a climb of about 600m/2000ft, and you emerge from the jungle onto quite English looking heathland. From here there is good fast walking, though the path weaves around quite a bit; as long as you are heading generally south-west you are OK. Where the path meets the tarmac road turn right for Farr Inn. The alternative walk up the tarmac road from the station takes at least 4hours.

Now comes decision time. Are you prepared to cough up $12 ($6 with a student card) for the view from **World's End**, a view not much different from the free one at Ella Gap? The answer depends on time. After 10 or 11am the view is frequently obscured by cloud forming over the rising ground. Arriving after this time or with less than the 3½hours needed for the circular walk you will do better missing out World's End and just having a stroll on the Plains.

The walk to World's End and Baker Falls

It is an hour's walk, mostly through woods, to **World's End**. Here the land falls away sheer at your feet for over 300m/1000ft and almost as steeply for another 1000m/3300ft. World's End is marked by a large slab of rock (with a bench mark if you look closely) on the edge of the cliff. You can walk up along the cliff from here to the blasted trees for an even better view, but do not follow this path any further, it just leads downhill to one of the villages. Backtrack to the stone and take the clear path through open country. After pleasant walking through very English country (even peat bogs!) you come to the **Baker Falls**. These are named after Sir Samuel Baker, the Nile explorer who virtually created Nuwara Eliya. The pool is safe for swimming, but rocks make diving dangerous; a young Sinhalese did this while we were there and did not come up again. The path continues back to the entry gate. Both above and below the falls you have the galling sight of the few trout the locals have not poached rising to fly in beautiful pools. Yet angling is banned because this is a National Park. Allow 3½hours to do this walk in comfort.

Around the Plains

If you decide not to pay the $12 the trackers will suggest other walks on the large part of the Plains where access is free.

Wildlife on the Plains is rather disappointing. There are large herds of sambhar (sometimes referred to as elk), though these come into the open only in the evening, often very close to Farr Inn. The manager at Farr Inn, Mr V.P. Premasiri, can show you a photo of a leopard taken near Anderson Lodge by an Australian. Bird life is confined mainly to the woodland; on the heath there are a few LBJs (little brown jobs to the uninitiated) and the very occasional crested serpent eagle. The latter presumably feeds on the wide variety of lizards. There seem to be no rabbits or other small mammals to support other large raptors. The woods also harbour bear monkeys and purple faced leaf monkeys.

Horton Plains suffers a severe attitude problem on the part of Sri Lankan visitors who seem to have no understanding of how to treat a wilderness area. Nor has it occurred to the managers to devise different walking routes or to prepare even sketch maps or notes on the flora and fauna. Recently 200ha/

HORTON PLAINS

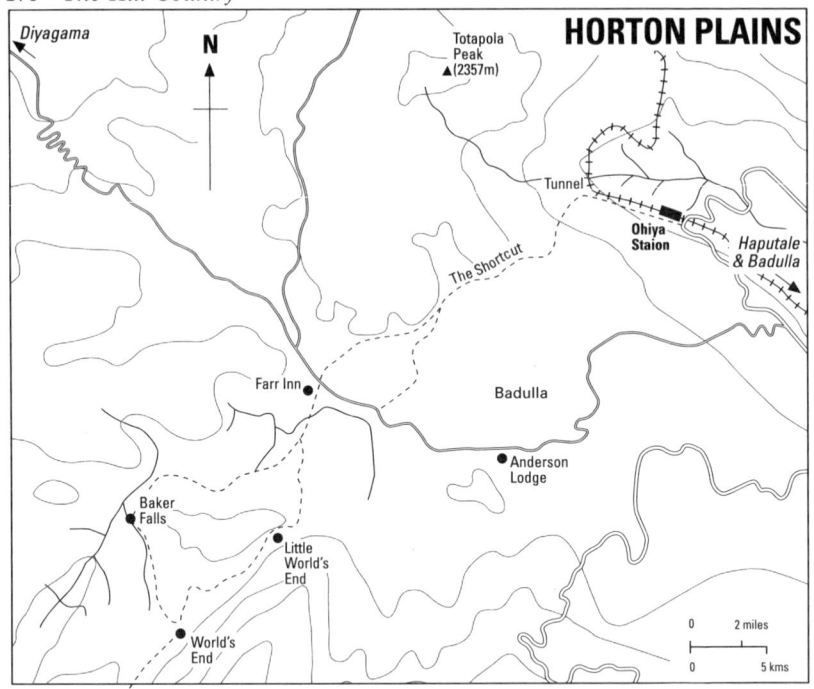

500 acres was burned out by a young visitor just for the fun of it. Weekends, with groups of local youths getting noisily sloshed, are to be avoided. A big commendation, though, to the school groups who keep the litter under control.

Practical Information

The trackers at the National Park office are knowledgeable and helpful.

Arrival and departure. Most people visit Horton Plains on a day trip. **From Haputale**, catching the 0755 train you arrive at Ohiya station about 0845, have a 3hr (at least) walk to Farr Inn, and must allow 1½ (pushing it) or 2hrs to return to Ohiya by the short cut (three hours down the road, but you can often cadge a lift, ask around at Farr Inn) for the train at 1630. This allows only a quick there-and-back to World's End, not the round trip. It is much better to get together a group to share a taxi (Rs800-1200 one way) to Farr Inn so that you arrive much earlier than by train, and you have a downhill walk to return to the station.

From Nuwara Eliya you really need to take a taxi (Rs1200-1500), as the only early train goes through Nanu Oya at 0253. You can return to Nanu Oya on the Night Mail which runs through Ohiya at around 2030. This is much better than being hustled around on a taxi day trip. In wet weather you will most probably find that only 4WD vehicles will attempt the roads from either Haputale or Nuwara Eliya.

An alternative, if not a very useful one, is the 11km/7miles **walk from Belihul Oya** (better down than up) on the Ratnapura-Haputale-Badulla road.

Accommodation

Farr Inn Rest House (CHC). Tel Colombo 323 501 (more than 24hrs in advance) or 070-522 029 (less than 24hrs). DWB $24 3WB $30 Dorm $5. Rest. Bar. Breakfast Rs200, lunch Rs400, dinner Rs550. Beer Rs125incl. Rooms plain but comfortable. Hot water in the evening. A quiet and romantic place to stay. Farr Inn is not *that* expensive and a thoroughly worthwhile place for a little splurge. You have the opportunity to see wildlife in the evening, and can get to World's End very early in the morning.

Anderson's Lodge, on road up from Ohiya station, 2½km before Farr Inn. Reservations through Department of Wildlife Conservation, you must take your own food (you could eat at Farr Inn) and sleeping bags.

Eating and Drinking. Meals, snacks, tea, and beer in the pleasant garden of the *Rest House*. The *Cafeteria* attached to the Rest House is expensive, much cheaper is the little stall round the back of the National Park office.

HAPUTALE

Haputale is a small market town built on a ridge with views down on both sides. When it is misty one side it is usually clear the other. The views are most striking at dawn, and on a clear day you can see Hambantota lighthouse 75km/47miles to the south. Later in the morning in the winter season the views to the south are often obscured by cloud. The weather here is very changeable, cloud and rain are common but it is worth waiting for it to clear. Haputale is a friendly and inexpensive place, an ideal base for the budget traveller to explore the surrounding area.

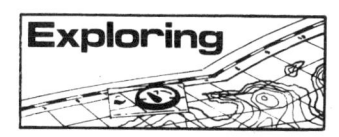

Walks and an English country house

Adisham is a Benedictine house usually referred to as a monastery; to be pedantic it is a novitiate. Walk out of town on Temple Road, through the Glennanore tea estate, and fork left uphill. You then enter the Tangamalai Wildlife Sanctuary, there is a cold drinks stall here. Adisham itself is a very 1930s English house though what appears to be a slate roof is in fact wooden shingles. Two rooms are open to visitors, the sitting room and library, and these are a perfectly preserved specimen of interior design of that time. One can understand how the outlook is conducive to the contemplative life.

From Adisham two interesting **walks** are possible, both starting on the path to the left of the gate. The simpler option (better when there is mist to the south) is to follow the path until it joins the railway line. From there you can walk back to Haputale along the line or continue to Idalgashinna station, spectacularly located on a ridge with views down both sides, and catch a train back.

Otherwise, follow the path through the first pine and eucalyptus plantation and then some dense jungle. When you reach another pine and eucalyptus

HAPATULE

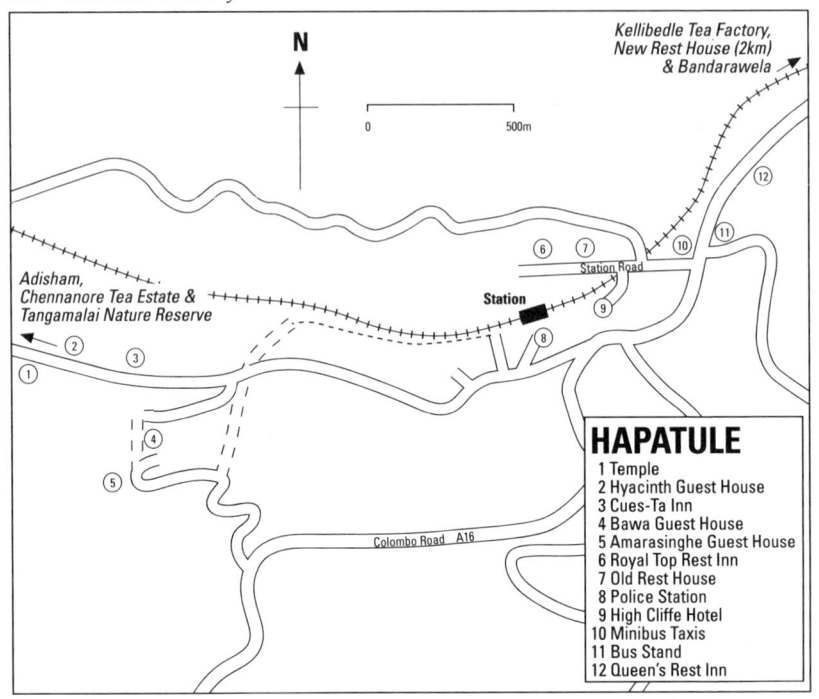

1 Temple
2 Hyacinth Guest House
3 Cues-Ta Inn
4 Bawa Guest House
5 Amarasinghe Guest House
6 Royal Top Rest Inn
7 Old Rest House
8 Police Station
9 High Cliffe Hotel
10 Minibus Taxis
11 Bus Stand
12 Queen's Rest Inn

plantation stay on the path until it reaches a small patch of jungle and turns slightly downhill. Turn uphill (there is no actual path) keeping the jungle hard on your left until you strike a track which leads to the summit. At the summit you come to a tea garden, and you need to go straight down to the plantation path. This is an organic garden, so the weeds are not cleared from around the tea bushes, making this something of a scramble. Watch out for leeches. When you meet the path simply turn left. The path eventually joins an unmade road leading back to Temple Road. This walk is obviously best in clear weather (spectacular views), but the hill walker used to English conditions will enjoy it at any time.

Visiting a tea factory

The first tea bushes in Ceylon were brought from China in 1824. However coffee was still king, and it was 1867 before the Scot James Taylor planted the first commercial tea garden at Loolecondera. It was another five years before the first 10kg were shipped to London. Today Sri Lanka produces 9% of the world's tea, remarkable for so small an island. Current production is around 250 million kg annually, and tea still accounts for 25% of Sri Lanka's export earnings.

The **Kelliebedde Tea Factory** is only 1km out of town on the Badulla road. This factory, typical in size, processes the output of a 486ha/1200 acre estate, which indicates why there are so many of them. The process starts at the top of the factory where the green leaves are put in trays and dried air blown through for eleven hours to reduce the moisture content. The leaves are dropped down to the curling machines where they spend 20 minutes. The result, which looks a bit like wet grass cuttings, goes through the tearing machines, like a butchers mincer, the pressure generating quite a bit of heat. After sifting the tea is raked into shallow piles to oxidise and develop its flavour. It is then dried at 200°F. Stalks are removed by static electricity and the tea is then sifted into the various grades.

This factory produces 5 tonnes of finished tea a day. Picking and processing goes on all year, but is seasonal in that in the dry season output drops to half the wet season level but the quality is higher. The workers are paid the same Rs101 per day as the pluckers, and the lack of guards and safety devices on the machines is pretty frightening. Tea factories are very dusty places (another health hazard for the workers) and you will leave needing a shower. They prefer you to visit before 1200, and the tour costs Rs100, beware of paying more.

Practical Information

Most of the guest houses have books detailing walks and so on.

Arrival and departure. Train from Nanu Oya, the station for Nuwara Eliya (1¾hrs), Kandy (6¼hrs), Colombo (7½hrs), Ella (1hr), or Badulla (2hrs). Note that in addition to the expresses goods trains which have passenger carriages run on this line in the middle of the day.

Direct bus from Nuwara Eliya and Colombo. Frequent buses to Bandarawela where you change for Ella, Badulla, or Wellawaya.

Accomodation (STD Code 057)

Queens Rest Inn, 68 Badulla Road. Tel 8206. DWB $10 (incl breakfast). Rest. Bar. Rice and curry Rs150, interesting menu. Clean and pleasant. Convenient location but not the quietest place in Haputale.

Vegetable Garden Hotel, contact through Highcliffe on Station Road. DWB $8. Rest. Bar. In process of conversion when seen. Good views down to the plains.

Bawa Guest House. Tel 8260. DR $3 DWB $5. Rest. Breakfast Rs95, rice and curry Rs115. A very hospitable Muslim family. Kate Adie stayed here.

Cues-ta Inn, Temple Road. Tel 8097. DWB $5. Rest. Bar. New place with great views, comfortable sitting room, bedrooms have balconies. Breakfast Rs150, rice and curry Rs175. Book exchange, taxi service (Rs13 per km).

Royal Top Rest Inn, Station Road. Tel 8178. DR $4 DWB $5. Rest. Bar. Breakfast Rs140, rice and curry Rs140. New place with good views.

Old Rest House, 6 Station Road. Tel 3206. DWB $5. Rest. Bar. Hot water. Breakfast Rs100, rice and curry Rs75, beer Rs75. A bit scruffy.

Highcliffe, Station Road. Tel 8096. DWB $5. Rest. Bar. Hot water. Breakfast Rs110, curry Rs90-160. Dingy.

Amarasinghe Guest House. Tel 8175. DR $3 DWB $4. Rest. Bar. Nice clean rooms and a flower filled garden. Mrs A is a very good cook, and the whole family make you very welcome. And the beer's only Rs75. Mr A is usually at the station if he has vacancies and will pick you up by arrangement. A very good place to stay.

Hyacinth Guest House (Mrs Q Daniels), Temple Road. Tel 8283. SR $2 DR $2/3 Dorm $1.50. Rest. Breakfast Rs75, rice and curry Rs100. Basic rooms. Lovely hostess, the Queen of Scrabble, who is always laughing.

The *New Rest House* is about 2km out of town on the Badulla Road.

Further Afield

Diyatalawa

Around the turn of the century there was a prisoner of war camp here for Boers. Diyatalawa was later used by the Royal Navy as a rest home for sailors. The Sri Lankan military still has strong presence here.

From the Haputale-Bandarawela road (and fleetingly from the railway line as the train enters the station from Haputale) you can see the outline of a running fox on a hill over Diyatalawa. Underneath is '1913 - HMS Fox'. This was done by mutineers from HMS Fox who had to carry the white stones up there. It is still known as Fox Hill.

BANDARAWELA

Bandarawela at 1230m/4034ft is said to have the most equable climate in Sri Lanka. Temperate fruit, such as pears and strawberries, are grown locally. This is another place, like Nuwara Eliya, which was a hill station and social centre for planters. It is now a busy market town and useful for shopping when you stay in Haputale or Ella. Pleasant enough, it has little to offer the traveller.

Suwa Madhu Suwasetha is an **ayurvedic treatment centre** which provides massages and other treatments. Massage, herbal steam bath, and so on costs Rs1500. We mention this place, which we do not necessarily endorse, in view of the growing popularity of alternative medicine. If you want to set up your own ayurvedic centre they will supply the equipment and materials. The centre is on the Badulla Road 2.5km from the centre of town.

The **Dowa Temple** is 4.5km from Bandarawela on the way to Badulla. On either side of the entrance are old murals with a Tibetan tantric look. The ceiling of the entrance hall has the signs of the zodiac, and below that are scenes from Buddha's life and some gruesome stuff. The main chamber is partly cave, partly structural with many images of Buddha. Brass doors with suns lead into a further cave with two reclining Buddhas and murals of Hindu deities. Note the moonstone tiles. In a gallery beside the river are murals including one of Buddha's birth with him standing on the seventh lotus. In renunciation of the world he cuts off his hair and casts off his fine clothes, followed by enlightenment and death. In the next room are the temptation by Mara's daughters, the committing of the Buddhist canon to writing at Aluvihara, the arrival of the bo-tree in Sri Lanka, and the meeting between Mahinda and King Tissa (see p233 Mihintale), with the deer making good its escape.

On a rock face above the temple is a Buddha figure partly cut from the rock and partly built up with brick rubble and plaster. Unfinished it is thought to be a Maitreya.

Information. Woodlands Network, 30/6 Esplanade Road. Tel/Fax 057 22735. Sarojinie Ellawela and six other women train guides for the local area and provide local information on walks and so on. Harry Haas, who is associated with them, is a fund of knowledge on many subjects.

Arrival and departure. 10km north of Haputale. Train or bus from Haputale, Ella, etc.

Turn left out of the station, left through a subway, and right to the clocktower. Past Cargills foodstore the main road swings left in front of a mosque; follow it for most of the accommodation, or bear right for Woodlands Network and a short cut to the main bus-stand (the best place to ensure a seat).

Accommodation (STD Code 057).
Bandarawela Hotel, 14 Welimada Road. Tel 22501 Fax 22834. SWB/DWB $33. Rest. Bar. Main courses Rs100-175, spirits Rs80 up, beer Rs140. Once a clubhouse and built round flowery courtyards. Bedrooms with high cast iron beds like grannie's (but new mattresses!). Immaculately kept. Good food. Worth calling in for a snack and beer on the lawn, the club sandwich (Rs120) is the best anywhere, and the burger (Rs100) is slices of filet mignon in little buns, delicious.

Ventnor Guest House, 23 Welimada Road. Tel 22511. DWB $11. Rest. Bar. Breakfast Rs130, curry and rice Rs200, main courses Rs200. A clean and pleasant place. *Caps* next door is similar.

Queens Hotel, Badulla Road, Bindunuwewa (2½km from town centre). Tel/Fax 22927. SWB $8 DWB $9. Rest (average prices). Bar. Modern place, very well kept. Over the road from the Suwa Madhu Suwasetha ayurvedic centre. Has its own ayurvedic massage room, Rs1100 for massage and steam bath.

Hill Side Holiday Inn, 34/10 Welimada Road. Tel 22201. DWB $5-8. Rest. Bar. Breakfast Rs70, rice and curry Rs115. Some rooms have balconies and overlook the local recreation ground.

Mountview Guest House, 35/2 Welimada Road. Tel 22561. DWB $5. Rest. Breakfast Rs75, rice and curry Rs90. A bit dingy.

Woodlands Farm and Leisure Resort, Marlodge Lane (about 2km, all steeply uphill from the station). Tel 22426. DR 5 or you can rent the whole bungalow, which sleeps eight, for $100 a week. Meals can be provided (rice and curry Rs100) or you can cook for yourself. Quiet and peaceful. The owner is developing a small organic farm and plans to improve the house which is a bit basic at present.

ELLA

Many people would say that the **view through Ella Gap***** is the best in Sri Lanka. The Gap is a deep valley which frames a view reaching as far as Yala National Park and, on a really clear day, the lighthouse at Hambantota. Not so far away is a crag looking like a medieval castle. The road down the valley was constructed only in 1969. Because there was no easy transport the area was never overrun by tea gardens. What you see is an authentic pre-plantation Sri Lankan landscape of forest, paddy terraces, and vegetable patches.

Ella itself is a small quiet village at 1100m/3600ft. It has a good range of accommodation, and little shops provide for basic needs. Like Haputale it is an ideal base for the budget traveller to explore this part of the Hill Country.

Visible from the Rest House is the **Rawana Ella Rock Temple**. With its mushroom shaped rock above, this looks like a fairy-tale elf house. Walk (or catch any bus) downhill from the Rest House to the bridge over the stream from the small waterfall, and take the track to the right. A pleasant shady stroll through paddy fields will bring you to a small Buddhist monastery. A monk will show you the rest of the way and unlock the temple. King Valagambha

ELLA

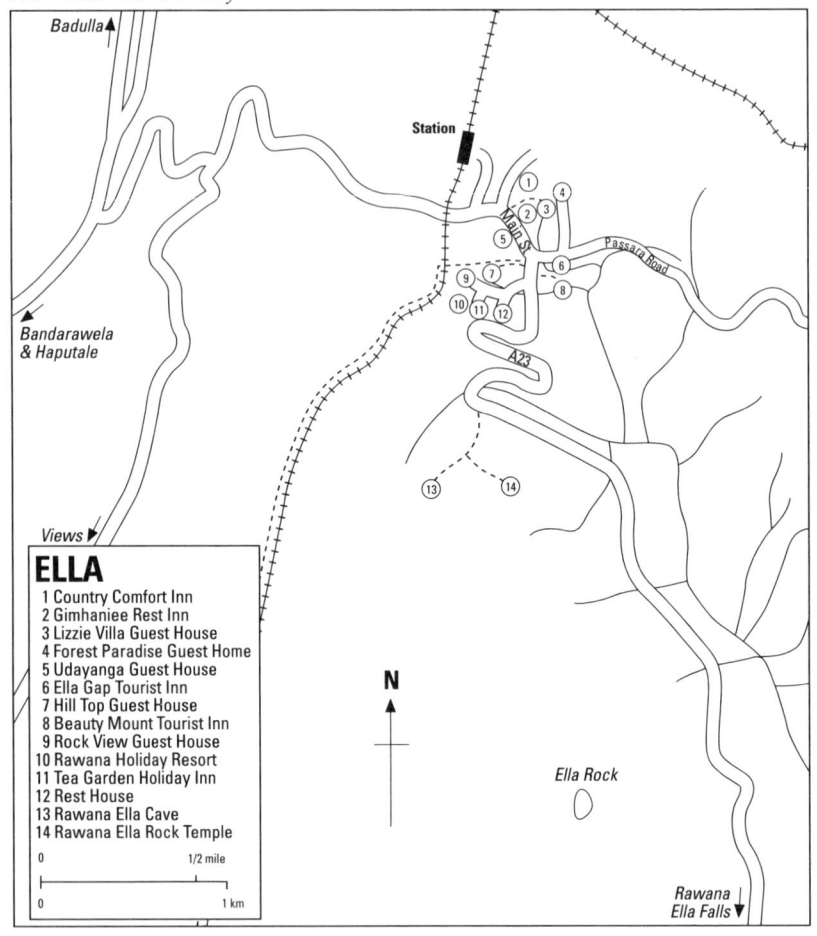

Map legend:
1 Country Comfort Inn
2 Gimhaniee Rest Inn
3 Lizzie Villa Guest House
4 Forest Paradise Guest Home
5 Udayanga Guest House
6 Ella Gap Tourist Inn
7 Hill Top Guest House
8 Beauty Mount Tourist Inn
9 Rock View Guest House
10 Rawana Holiday Resort
11 Tea Garden Holiday Inn
12 Rest House
13 Rawana Ella Cave
14 Rawana Ella Rock Temple

Bahu (103 and 89-77BC) took shelter here after being defeated by his brother in a succession dispute. After collecting a new army and sorting out his brother he built this temple in gratitude. The temple disappeared in jungle for many years and was rediscovered only in 1952.

Returning along the same track, just over the crest of the hill, a rough path leads off to the left steeply uphill to the **Rawana Ella Cave°**. This is one of a number of places where Ravana is said to have held Sita captive. The cave was excavated some years ago, and remains of a cannibal local species of homo sapiens, dating back to perhaps 8000BC, were found. Today there is nothing to see, even the view is obscured by trees. The path is on dangerously loose ground (walking shoes or boots are essential) and there are snakes about. Except for the most dedicated Ramayana follower or enthusiast of esoteric neolithic habitats this is a Grade 1 triple-starred waste of time and effort. There is apparently, though, scope for cave divers.

The **Rawana Ella Falls*** are 6.5km further on down the valley and not visible from Ella. Despite the obligatory graffiti on the rocks these are an attractive, rugged set of falls. The young and fit can scramble some way up the rocks, and there is a very rough path to the right of the falls. Again any bus will drop you there and take you back to Ella (Rs4.50 each way).

Practical Information

Arrival and departure. Train from Colombo (10hrs), Kandy (7hrs), Nanu Oya for Nuwara Eliya (2½hrs), Haputale (1hr) or Badulla (1hr). Ella station has its original small canopy under the rather ugly new one; note the train layouts painted on the inside of the valance. Be prepared for the view from the left of the train as it heads out of the station towards Haputale. Buses from Tissamaharama (via Wellawaya), Badulla, and Haputale (change in Bandarawela).

Accommodation (STD Code 057).
Rest House (CHC), Main Street. Tel 22636. SWB/DWB $23. Rest. Bar. Standard Rest House menu. One of the best views of any hotel in the world. Have a pot of tea or a beer and relax and enjoy it in comfort.
Country Comfort Inn, Police Station Road. Tel 23132. DWB HB $28. Rest. Bar. A good place but they insist you take half board terms.
Ella Gap Tourist Inn. Tel 22628. DWB $12. Rest. Breakfast Rs125, Main courses Rs250. Good but expensive.
Forest Paradise Guest Home. Tel 23507. DR $5 DWB $9 (latter includes breakfast). Rest. Very quiet location, but only three rooms. Bob Marley was poular in Sri Lanka, and this is one of several places decorated with his posters.
Hill Top Guest House. Tel 30080. SWB $5 DWB $9. Rest. Bar. Breakfast Rs100, main courses Rs125-175. Good views and well kept.
Tea Garden Holiday Inn. Tel 22915. DWB $9. Rest. Bar. Breakfast Rs125, main course Rs200. Great views. Rock View, Rawana, and Tea Garden are all in the same ownership and are good and clean. They may try to insist that you eat in which is unacceptable when there are good cheaper restaurants in the village.
Lizzie Villa Guest House, off main street. Tel 23243. DR $3 DWB $7/8. Rest. Bar. Lovely garden growing spices and fruit trees. You can eat as much fruit as you like, and Mrs Rodrigo will show you how to prepare Sri Lankan food.
Rock View Guest House. Tel 22661. DWB $5/7. Rest. Bar. Breakfast Rs140, main course Rs225.
Rawana Holiday Resort. Tel 22661. DWB $7. Rest. Bar. Breakfast Rs140, main course Rs225.
Gimhaniee Rest Inn, Main Street. Tel 22127. DWB $6. Nice restaurant and good food. Breakfast Rs100, main courses Rs200.
Udayanga Guest House, Main Street. Tel 23308. DWB $5. Rest. Breakfast Rs80-125, main courses Rs90-225. A popular place.
Beauty Mount Tourist Inn, main street. SWB $3 DWB $5. Rest. Breakfast Rs75, rice and nine curries Rs225, also ordinary rice and curry Rs50. Very good views, good value, and a charming owner.

All the accommodation is within walking distance of the station or the bus stop.

178 *The Hill Country*

Eating and Drinking
Ella Village Restaurant, main street. Cheap/Mod. SL/Chi/Western. Main courses Rs80-125. Run by the son from Lizzie's.
Indra Hotel, main street. Cheap. SL. Curry and rice Rs50. Good food and a friendly Alsatian.

On to the end of the line

The **Demodera Loop** is a must for rail enthusiasts. The line from Badulla is climbing steeply here, and to gain 30m/100ft in the shortest possible distance it runs around a hill in a complete loop. The line actually runs under Demodera station in a tunnel. The Night Mail from Badulla sometimes crosses the Udarata Menike from Colombo here (depending on whether or not it is on time) which would make a good photo. You would need to be up one of the hills which begs the question how you are going to get home afterwards.
Arrival and departure. Railway station on the Bandarawela-Badulla line.

BADULLA

Badulla is the end of the railway line; at 730m/2394ft it is well on the way down to the lowlands. The town was once a lively centre for planters. A pleasant enough place, most visitors just change from bus to train on the way from the south coast to the hills.

Mutiyangana Vihara Buddhist temple is said to have been founded by Devanampiya Tissa, the first convert to Buddhism in Sri Lanka, though the present buildings are of no great age. It is one of the sixteen holiest Buddhist places in Sri Lanka. Neither this nor the Kataragama Devale is very interesting.

An old book says that in the garrison burial ground a grave dated 1817 has been lifted up by a bo-tree. To find the garrison burial ground, first find a three-wheeler driver (or anyone else) who knows where it is.

Arrival and departure. Bus from Nuwara Eliya (2hrs). End of the railway line from Kandy and Colombo. Trains from Ella, Bandarawela, Haputale, and Nanu Oya.

Accommodation (STD Code 055).
Dunhinda Falls Inn, Bandaranayake MW. Tel 23028 Fax 094-1-23028. SWB/DWB $15. Rest. Bar. Nice and clean, and soft beds. Rice and curry Rs85, other prices average. Beer Rs130.
Rest House, adjoining bus-stand. Tel 2299. SWB $5 DWB $8. Well maintained and clean. Built round a small garden with a bougainvillaea arbour. Reasonably priced food, beer Rs85.
Eagle Nest, Lower Street. Tel 2841. SWB $3 DWB $6. Plain rooms with fan and nets, worth the money. Rice and veg curry Rs60, with chicken or beef Rs100, breakfast Rs125, beer Rs60.
New Tourist Inn, on road to Dunhinda Falls. Moderate prices. Garden overlooking stream.

For places on Dunhinda Falls Road take a three-wheeler. Going straight ahead from the station, over the bridge, and up to the roundabout are several dubious lodges. Cross the roundabout into Lower Street, and take second or third left for bus-stand.

Excursions

In an attractive pastoral valley is the **Bogoda bridge and cave temple**. The monastery, at a higher level, is an attractive unspoiled traditional building. Steps lead down to the ancient wooden bridge over the Galanda Oya stream. As built there were no metal fastenings in the bridge which, with its tiled roof, has rather a Swiss look. The bridge is said to date from the Dambadeniya period, making it 700 years old. The path from the bridge leads up to the village.

The cave temple has some painting which would not look out of place on an English canal narrow boat or the more florid kind of china. Sections of the narrative painting on the back wall has a very European medieval look complete with the Buddha enthroned in a Gothic building. Belying this is a placid Buddha figure with two fearsomely fanged elephants and sundry other monsters above. The temple is not really very interesting; you come here for the setting.

Arrival and departure. Bus from Badulla to Heli Ola (6km), and take the B100 road out of Heli Ola for 8.5km, buses will take you this far, the temple is signposted and a further 2.7km. This would be a pleasant and fairly shady walk, but all uphill on the way back. The alternative is to get off the bus at Katewala (6.5km from Heli Ola) and take a three wheeler.

Accommodation You can stay for free (on the floor) in the hall behind the bo-tree. There are no facilities, but the woman in the little shop will boil water for you.

Dunhinda Falls** (Smoking Water). The main falls are 60m/200ft high in a tight wooded valley and much better than many of the higher ones. The falls you see from the beginning of the path are the lower falls, impressive themselves but inaccessible. A viewing platform at the main falls gives a good view, and a large family of friendly monkeys waits to snaffle any food left unguarded. You can walk down to the pool, but the rocks are very slippery. The falls are at their best in November and December, but well worth seeing at other times. Rainbows form in the clouds of mist rising from the cascade, and house martins hurtle around.

Arrival and departure. Bus (No 314) or three-wheeler for the 6km from Badulla; do not try cycling. The path to the falls (½hour walk and very sweaty coming back) is very rough and would be dangerous in flip-flops, sloppy sandals, or anything with leather soles. There are many drinks stalls on the way.

Namunkula (Nine Peaks) 2036m/6679ft is 10km south-east of Badulla. Walk up through Spring Valley tea estate.

Further Afield

WELLAWAYA

Wellawaya is a crossroads town on the way from the Hill Country to the south coast. It is on the plains and hot and sticky. There are several interesting places to visit nearby.

Arrival and departure. On road from Badulla to Tissamaharama 39km from

Badulla or only 23km from Ella which is on the railway line. The bus-stand is 200m south of the central crossroads.

Accommodation (STD Code 055).
Saranga Holiday Inn, 37 Old Ella Road. Tel 74891. DWB A/C $10 DWB $8. Rest. Bar. Breakfast Rs100, rice and curry Rs150. Nice and clean.
Rest Inn, next to Saranga. Tel 74907. DR $2 DWB $4. Clean enough. For both these places head north from the crossroads in the centre of town.
New Rest House, New Ella Road. Tel 74899. Rest. Very sparse and not too clean. Continue from the previous two until you reach the main road.

Huge monolithic statues

In a jungle glade stand the **Buduruvagala Buddhist statues*****. These are Mahayana monuments and, because of this the monks who wrote the mainstream Therevada history ignored them, so there are conflicting opinions on what they represent.

The seven huge figures, probably 10th century, are carved in low relief into a vertical rock face which bears a passing resemblance to a kneeling elephant. The central figure (and the largest on the island at $15\frac{1}{2}$m/51ft) is of the Buddha, his right hand in the fearless posture. The robe was moulded from plaster, and traces of colour are visible. To the left of the statue a hole has been cut in the shape of an oil lamp flame. The rock is stained by oil which is said to seep through the rock; keen olfactory organs may detect the smell of mustard oil.

The Buddha is flanked by two groups of three figures. To the left, as you view them, the central figure is Avelokitesvara who is a defender of the downtrodden.

This is the only figure to retain much of its plaster coating, and there are traces of red paint on the halo. Avelokitesvara is accompanied by the protective goddess Tara and prince Sudhanakumara who is an example to young people, though this latter attribution is open to doubt. Both are in the thrice-bent posture.

In the centre of the right group is Maitreya, the Buddha to come, sculpted in more detail than the others. He wears an elaborate headdress, and the robes are well represented. You can just make out the lotuses on the shoulders which identify this as Maitreya. To the right is Vajrapani, a Tantric Boddhisatva. Sculpted above his right hand is a dorje, the Tibetan Tantric emblem of the thunderbolt. To the left is a figure representing compassion. This is finished above the waist, but not below, and both hands are missing. Above the statues are sockets for shelters. The figures are best photographed before mid-day. Because of the low relief carving these are not the most spectacular Buddha figures in Sri Lanka, but they are certainly in the prettiest and quietest location.

The feathery ground plant along the path to the statues is touch-me-not; if you do touch it it curls up and plays dead.

Buduruvagala is a living place of worship. A senior monk, the Rev Obbegoda Dhammatilaka, runs a **meditation centre** here which can provide simple accommodation. His little **museum**, well worth seeing, has a fine collection of illustrations of Therevada holy places.

The **tank**, which was restored in 1976 at the instigation of the Rev Obbegoda Dhammatilaka, attracts birds and wildlife and looks promising for fishing.

Arrival and departure. Travel 5km south of Wellawaya on the Tissa road (frequent buses) to a clutch of shops, then an unmade road of 6km. At present this road is suitable for 2WD vehicles only in the dry. This would be an interesting, if sticky, walk or cycle ride.

Eating and drinking. Stalls at the main road. Take a picnic and lots of water, and don't forget the insect repellent.

Wild elephants

Handapanagala Wewa has a herd of 125 wild elephants, apparently fairly easy to see, and free compared with Yala where you can spend a lot of money and see nothing. The trouble is that nothing is organised. A couple told the authors how they had been taken there by two young men claiming to know what they were doing. They went out in a boat, and the two 'guides' panicked when elephants came too close. The couple felt lucky to have escaped unscathed. Think carefully and take sensible advice.

For the intrepid here is a quick seminar on elephant behaviour. When disturbed in the wild an elephant will give you a very clear sequence of warnings. Ear flapping and pawing at the ground are the first indications of unhappiness. The brave (or foolhardy) are next treated to trumpeting followed by a much louder roar. If you haven't taken the hint by now watch for him to put the tip of his trunk out of harm's way in his mouth. This means he is really narked and out to do you a severe mischief.

Arrival and departure. The tank is about 15km from Wellawaya, you need to take a taxi or three-wheeler.

More statues

At **Maligawila** stands a recently restored 11m/36ft high Buddha figure. Unlike those at Budurvagala this is carved in the round, one of the largest of its kind. Another statue, this time of Avelokiteshwara, stands nearby.

Arrival and departure. Bus to Buttala and possibly on to Okkampitiya or Dambegoda, otherwise taxi or three-wheeler. The main road continues to Monaragala which, when it is safe to visit there, is on the way to Pottuvil and Arugam Bay.

Accommodation. Either Wellawaya or Monaragala, a *Rest House* and cheaper hotels at the latter.

WELLAWAYA TO HAPUTALE OR RATNAPURA

The lowlands around Wellawaya are a sugarcane growing area, and you will catch the distinctive whiff of boiling cane juice as you pass the small factories. On the road from Wellawaya to Ratnapura after 6km is a group of shops; a yellow sign (in Sinhalese only) points left to the **Bat Cave**. This cave, 3km from the main road down a track unsuitable for vehicles, is full of horseshoe bats.

Continuing towards Ratnapura on the left is a cacao plantation, and to the right rubber trees. The road is narrow and twisty for an A-road but initially through gentler and more pastoral country.

The **Diyaluma Falls** are the highest unbroken waterfall in Sri Lanka at 171m/560ft and attractive in a weedy, feathery sort of way despite the obligatory graffiti on the rocks. You can reach the top, and a pool suitable for swimming, by heading down the road towards Wellawaya for about ¾km. Turn sharp left up a rough jeepable track which leads to some houses and, beyond them, a small rubber factory. Go through the factory compound and up to some more houses, following the path through these. The path becomes steeper and eventually comes out above the pools above the falls. Allow 1½hrs to walk up. The alternative is to walk up the Poonagala road from Koslanda to the 4km marker, backtrack slightly, and a path on the right leads to a pool above the falls.

Arrival and departure. On the road from Wellawaya to Ratnapura. For Haputale change at Koslanda. Buses and other traffic are infrequent on this road. There is a walking route from Bandarawela, information from the Woodlands Network.

Accommodation. A new hotel is being built facing the falls.

Belihul Oya is one of the access points for Horton Plains, though it's a tough walk up. 12km towards Haputale are the **Bambarakanda Falls**, 241m/790ft high, of which the lowest part is an unbroken 141m/461ft, the highest in Sri Lanka. These are unimpressive during the dry season.

Arrival and departure. On road between Ratnapura and Badulla or 35km from Haputale. Walk down from Horton Plains.

Accommodation (STD Code 045). The *Rest House* (Tel 045-7200), around DWB $22, is beautifully located by the river. Also less expensive places.

Kurugala Caves. Hituwalena Cave is the venue of a Muslim pilgrimage every year. A Muslim holy man meditated here for twelve years, and the cave is the start of an underground passage said to go all the way to Mecca. For experienced cavers only. There are palm prints of unknown age in the entrance. Access is by a footpath from the village of Taniantenna. Across the ravine is a Buddhist cave temple, the Budugala.

Arrival and departure. 24km/15miles from Balangoda on the Haputale-Ratnapura road. Definitely one for people with their own transport.

Accommodation. There is an attractive Circuit Bungalow at Uggalkaltota, 3km from the caves, make a reservation first.

SINHARAJA BIOSPHERE RESERVE

The Sinharaja (Lion King) Reserve is one of UNESCO's World Heritage Sites. The name comes from the belief that this was the last stronghold of the Asiatic lion now extinct in Sri Lanka.

This is the most important reserve in the Wet Zone, a remaining fragment of Sri Lanka's rain forest. It covers around 190sq km/73sq miles and ranges in height from 200m to 1300m. The average rainfall is 250cm, a year and even in the dry season you can expect a heavy shower in the afternoon. Rainfall is heaviest during the two monsoons. Most of Sri Lanka's unique species, of both animals and plants, are found here, and there are many rare birds.

The great advantage of Sinharaja is that you are allowed to walk instead of being stuck in a noisy jeep with a lunatic driver. Three trails run from the Forest Department Camp at Kudawa: Waturawa Trail 4.7km, Moulawella Trail

7.5km, and Sinhagala Trail 14km. The last takes all day and is easily the best. The one downside of all the wildlife is leeches, millions of them.

Information. Guide map from the Forest Department Camp. The best person to contact is Palitha Ratnayake on 041-73368.

Arrival and departure. Bus (30km) from Ratnapura or Colombo (120km via Matugama) to Weddegala.

Accommodation. Basic dormitory accommodation at the Forest Department Camp at Kudawa. Reservations through Conservator of Forests, Rajamalwatta Road, Battaramula, Colombo Tel 566 626. The only alternative is to stay in Ratnapura and travel up on a day trip.

RATNAPURA

The name is Sanskrit (*ratna* = gem + *pura* = town) and well describes Ratnapura's place in history and commerce. Sri Lanka has been a producer of gem stones from time immemorial. They are in fact found in other parts of the island too, but Ratnapura is the main centre for both polishing and marketing.

The **gem mining** process is extremely basic, consisting of just shallow pits from which the illan (the gem-bearing gravel) and, hopefully, the raw stones are extracted. Sifting and selection are done by hand; many gems are found, but only a few are good enough to be worth anything. Flaws are common, and most stones lack the intensity and purity of colour that make them attractive. The process is labour intensive, even the pumping out of water is still done by hand in some places.

The most valuable **gem stones** found in Sri Lanka are the corundums, which include the sapphire and the ruby. The popular belief that rubies are red and sapphires blue is misleading. In fact in Sri Lanka rubies tend to be pink, and it is not inaccurate to call them pink sapphires. Sapphires range from blue to a stone as clear as a diamond. Aquamarine, a very attractive stone, is, like emerald, a member of the beryl group.

The best of the semi-precious stones are moonstones and tiger's eyes. Moonstone is a variety of felspar; these are mined near the coast (see p104). Tiger's eye is a chrysoberyl, usually yellowy-brown, with a three-dimensional effect; alexandrite is another member of this group. Garnets are very common and often referred to as a poor man's (or should it be poor woman's?) ruby, they range from red through to brown. Spinels are pretty and mostly used in a setting with other stones.

Diamonds, topaz, red rubies, and emerald are not found in Sri Lanka. Anyone offering these is most likely trying to pass off something else. In fact for the non-expert gems are a very tricky game. Experts spend years learning about gems; if you want to buy do so from a reputable retail outlet.

There are numerous so-called Gem Museums in the town. Many of these are simply sales outlets. The **Ratnapura Gem Bureau and Museum*** (about 1½km from the town centre on the road to Haputale) is also a commercial undertaking. It has, however, some very good displays on gem mining, the production of synthetic stones, and specimens of stones from all over the world, not just Sri Lanka. Adjoining the museum is a showroom with some pretty mouth-watering stock. Unlike most places in Ratnapura they sell fully finished jewellery, not just polished and raw stones. There is no hard sell, and everything is priced, though this should not inhibit you from bargaining.

Ratnapura **National Museum** (near the bus-stand, closed Friday & Saturday) is a lot less interesting, having the usual collection of old bones and broken pottery.

The **Kaluga Ellas Falls** are only 2km from the town centre, and there is river swimming here. Snack bars make this a pleasant place to relax, but it is not recommended at weekends.

The **Pompakelle Urban Forest Park** on Reservoir Road aims to provide a feel of the rain forest in a convenient location.

A huge **Buddha statue**, a replica of that at Aukana (see p218) towers above the town.

Ratnapura is the base for many pilgrims setting out to climb Adam's Peak (see p161). This 25km route (the first 11km can be done by bus or three-wheeler) is much longer than that from Dalhousie. There are good views of Adam's Peak from various points around town, notably the old fort. In fact the surroundings are very beautiful altogether. One word of caution, though: Ratnapura has one of the highest rainfalls in Sri Lanka. This makes it brilliantly green but also very humid and sticky.

| Practical Information | **Arrival and departure.** Bus from Colombo (3hrs), Haputale (3hrs), Avissawella, and Galle, a twisty and spectacular road. The main bus-stand is by the clock tower. |

Accommodation (STD Code 045).

Rest House, Rest House Road. Tel 2299. DWB $17. Rest (good). Bar. Large, airy, and rather basic rooms. Good views, and quiet until 0430 when loudspeakers at the huge hilltop Buddha start to play grossly over-amplified prayers, this goes on for 50 minutes. One gets used to the Hindus and Muslims doing this kind of thing; Buddhists usually seem too self-contained (and self-confident) to need to follow suit.

Hotel Kalavati Holiday & Health Resort, Polhengoda Village, Outer Circular Road, (1½km from bus-stand). Tel 2465. SWB $10/12 DWB $11/13 (+ $5 A/C) Dorm $3. Rest (very reasonable, veg/non-veg). Bar. Most attractive place to stay, decorated with antiques and located in a quiet garden and coconut grove. Better value than the Rest House, but less convenient. Alternative therapies.

Nilani Lodge, 21 Dharmapala MW. Tel 22170. DWB $9 DWB A/C $21. Rest. Breakfast Rs60-175.

Travellers Halt, 30 Outer Circular Road. Tel 23092. DWB $7. Rest. Breakfast Rs125, rice and curry with chicken grill Rs250.

Darshana Inn, 68/5 Rest House Road. Tel 22674. DWB $6. Rest. Bar (large stock of cold beer). Rooms a little dark, but very reasonable.

The *Ratna Gems Halt* at 153/5 Outer Circular Road is said to be good, some of the rooms overlook the paddy fields.

RATNAPURA

1 Hotel Kalivati Holiday & Health Resort
2 Ratna Gems Halt
3 Traveller's Halt
4 Buddha
5 Rest House
6 Darshana Inn
7 Ratnapura Gem Bureau & Museum
8 Clocktower

Further Afield

The **Maha Saman Devale** is a Hindu temple, but who it is dedicated to is a matter of argument. Saman or Samanta was probably a pre-Buddhist god and is usually regarded today as an aspect of Shiva, though some say he is related to Laxman, Rama's brother and one of the heroes of the Ramayana. The Buddhists, for their part, associate him with Samantabhadra, a Maitreya or Buddha to come. The argument causes no conflict, and the temple is a popular place of pilgrimage for both religions.

At the entrance is a bo-tree with oil lamps just as at a Buddhist temple. There is no need to leave your shoes at the outer gate, though the female shoe custodians after a tip will tell you you should. To the right of the main steps in a recess is a piece of sculpture in low relief. This is variously described as a Portuguese soldier freeing a Sinhalese prince and a Portuguese knight in armour trampling on a Sinhalese. It may be uncharitable, but the second looks more plausible. This sculpture is the only point of real interest here.

Inside the high wall of the temple compound the present temple is architecturally similar to those of Kerala. Nearby is a 16th century Portuguese church on the foundations of another temple.

Arrival and departure. 4km from Ratnapura on the Panadura road (A8).

Ratnapura to Avissawella and Colombo

The road from Ratnapura to Avissawella is wide and in good condition. In early 1998 a new telecoms link was being installed by New Zealand engineers in a trench along the road. This trench encouraged moonlight gem mining which in places actually undermined the road surface, to the fury of the Public Works Department and the expense of Sri Lanka Telecoms.

Avissawella is the terminus of the **Kelani Valley Railway**. This was a narrow gauge (2ft 6inches) light railway which ran from Colombo Fort to Ratnapura and a further 25km to Opanayake near Balangoda. Unfortunately the line was not economically viable, and only the Colombo-Avissawella section survives. This has recently been converted to broad gauge, though with an extra rail allowing narrow gauge trains still to run. This is to the advantage of rail enthusiasts who can enjoy the unique experience of riding in a Sentinel steam railcar. A Hunslet 4-6-4 tank loco is preserved in working order at Nugegoda. See p52 for details of steam train operations.

Over the river from Avissawella is the site of yet another former capital city. **Sitavaka** takes its name from Sita of the Ramayana legend. Although an important place in the 16th century it has been fought over so often that nothing much is left except the base of a temple of Bhairava (Shiva in his horrific form) and that was never finished anyway.

Arrival and departure. Train (infrequent) from Colombo Fort. Bus from Ratnapura and Kandy.

From **Hanwella** travellers with their own transport may choose to take the B1 which follows the Kelani River through **Kaduwela** into Colombo rather than the main A4. This is slightly less busy, but really makes sense only if you intend make detours to explore the river. Until recently the river was a busy trade route, the paddas, boats with matting roofs, working their way up to Hanwella and beyond. There are few bridges over the river, and several ferries, signposted from the main road, still operate. There is abundant birdlife on the river. The Rest House at Kaduwella (16km/10miles from Colombo) has a veranda right on the river; that at Hanwella (34km/21miles from Colombo), built on the foundations of a Portuguese fort, also has good river views. The Prince of Wales planted a jackfruit tree here.

The alternative is the Kelani Valley Railway, which makes its way into Colombo beside the links of the **Royal Colombo Golf Club**.

Another option is to travel from **Avissawella into the hills**. The A7 runs east and north from Avissawella to **Karawanella** where it joins the attractive valley of the Maskeliya Oya river. Just north of Karawanella is **Ruwanwella** where the Rest House is built on the base of a Dutch fort. The road crosses the **Ginigathena Pass** (spectacular views) and continues to **Kitulgala**, where the Rest House was used as a location for 'The Bridge on the River Kwai'. Thousands of Stone Age implements were found in a large cave nearby. The road continues to Carolina Falls and Hatton, where you can change on to a train for Kandy or Nuwara Eliya. With your own transport you can explore some of the quiet country roads.

The Ancient Capitals

Image House at Medirigiriya

The remains of many former capitals stand in Sri Lanka. This is mainly a result of the fractured nature of Sri Lanka's history, the whole island rarely having been under the undisputed control of one king. Another factor was the particularly eastern problem of struggles over succession, power rarely passing peacefully from father to elder son.

The other determining factor was geography. It will be seen from the list below that until 1293 all the capitals were in the Dry Zone, the northern and eastern three-quarters of the country. These cities and the economies which supported the extravagances of their kings and monks were dependent on the extensive irrigation works which had evolved over more than a thousand years. The maintenance of these works in turn depended on peace and prosperity. The wars of the 11th to 13th centuries put paid to all this, and the fall of Polonnaruwa marked the end of the attempts to keep up this hydraulic civilisation. After that the capital and the bulk of the population moved to the Wet Zone of the south-east where agriculture could be sustained by regular rainfall.

For these reasons it is not possible to arrange the capitals in a strict chronological order, but it goes something like this:

380BC-AD993	Anuradhapura (with interruptions)
477-495	Sigiriya
993-1293	Polonnaruwa (with interruptions)
1272-1284	Yapahuwa
12th century	Panduvasnavara
1232-1284	Dambadeniya (on and off)
1371-1597	Kotte
1469-1815	Kandy

This list by no means tells the whole story. For instance, between 1029 and 1055 seven kings, refugees from Polonnaruwa, ruled from the southern fastness of Rohana. That seven kings should rule in so short a period indicates instability. Rohana itself, when not being used by the northern kings, was a more less independent state. Other less important centres were used from time to time. In addition Jaffna was capital of a northern (Tamil) kingdom from the 13th century until it was conquered by the Portuguese in 1620.

THE CULTURAL TRIANGLE

The area bounded by Kandy, Anuradhapura, and Polonnaruwa is known as the **Cultural Triangle**. These three places, and the other sites in the triangle, encapsulate two and a half millennia of Sri Lanka's history. Most of the major sites (some of the active Buddhist monasteries are self-supporting) are administered from the Cultural Triangle Office at the Ministry of Cultural Affairs, 212 Bauddhaloka MW, Colombo 7, (Tel 01-587 912). They sell the **Cultural Triangle Permit** for $35 which gives entry to the museum in Kandy, Nalanda, Sigiriya, Polonnaruwa, and Anuradhapura. This is quite a saving, as each of the three main sites costs $15. The one problem with the permit (and the individual tickets) is that they are valid for one day only, you cannot make one visit in the evening and another the following morning. The Colombo office also sells very reasonable handbooks and books on Sri Lankan painting.

It is usual, for reasons of convenience, to visit the ancient cities from Kandy, and in the order in which they are described here. This means, however, that you see the three most important places (Anuradhapura, Sigiriya, and Polonnaruwa) out of chronological order. There is a lot to be said for starting from Anuradhapura, as then you progress towards the later and better preserved buildings.

KANDY TO DAMBULLA

Kandy, the last capital of an independent Sinhalese kingdom, is the usual starting point for exploring the ancient capitals. It is worth allowing some time for the journey from Kandy to Dambulla. Aluvihara, and Nalanda in particular, justify a visit.

MATALE

Matale is a bustling town in the centre of a cattle raising area. It gained a place in history for the part it played in the rebellion of 1848. This was a relatively minor affair (especially in the context of 1848 as the Year of Revolutions) which marked the last armed opposition to British rule. When the British had assumed the government of all Ceylon in 1815 they had promised to maintain government support for Buddhism, very much as an established religion; over the years, however, this support had been eroded as a result of Christian evangelical pressure on the Colonial Office in London. The rebellion was soon put down, a process greatly aided by the new roads the British had built, as much for this reason as to serve the rapidly growing plantation economy. The same root cause, a perceived threat to traditional religion from insensitive Christian zealots, was to be the main cause of the Great Indian Mutiny nine years later. The **Matale Rebellion memorial** stands in the town park.

The **Sri Muthumariamman Thevasthanam** Hindu temple follows the common South Indian pattern of a walled enclosure with multiple shrines inside. A pillar to the right of the entrance bears a moon (a motif borrowed from local Buddhism) on it, and below a set of scales signifying, here as elsewhere, justice. The main shrine is dedicated to Parvati; she is the wife (or a feminine aspect) of Shiva and, as usual for a Shiva shrine, Nandi the bull stands in front.

There are several other shrines, notably one of Vishnu reclining on a snake whose five heads shade him from the sun. Outside on either side are Hanuman the monkey-faced god and Durga. Durga (and the more gruesome Kali) are also feminine aspects of Shiva, representing his destructive side. Unusually in this case Durga has angel's wings. This shrine is frequented by women praying for a child. The corrugated asbestos roof may keep the ground cool enough to walk on but is hardly a thing of beauty. The temple cars are of more interest than the temple itself. The woodwork is ornately carved, the lower parts varnished and the upper brightly painted. The cars are used to carry the deities in a huge procession on 11th March.

The hilltop ruins above Saxton Park are of Fort Macdowall, named after the British commander in the war of 1803.

Arrival and departure. Matale is 24km north of Kandy. For most of the way the road is in appalling condition (and less than attractive) though work was just starting in early 1998. The train takes a nicer route past the **Hunas Falls** and, if you are going just to Matale and Aluvihara, is a much better bet. Bus (Nos 593, 594, 636) from Goods Shed bus-stand in Kandy.

Accommodation. The *Rest House* (066-3239) is probably the best bet, around $10 for a double with bath.

ALUVIHARA

For the first four hundred years or so of Buddhism all the teachings of Buddha and the commentaries on them were passed down orally. Shortly after Buddha's death in 486BC a great convocation of monks was held at Rajagriha (present day Rajgir in Bihar, North India). Ananda, one of Buddha's disciples, recited all the Buddha's teachings, and the five hundred other monks present committed this one form to memory. The same process was followed for the monastic regulations. Human memory being what it is (this is a huge volume of work), and the fact that no set language was specified, soon led to inconsistencies, not helped by the differing interpretations of newly emerging sects. Then a variety of disasters, some natural, some man-made, like an invasion from South India, sowed the seeds of doubt. Accordingly in the reign of Valagamba (89-77BC) a council of monks was held at Aluvihara (Silver Monastery) to commit the Buddhist Canon to writing. Thus the Therevada tradition, written in Pali (an international language for Buddhists in the way that Latin was for Christians), was preserved in a pure form. More than 500 senior monks worked at this task for years. The monastery library was destroyed when British troops pursued a notorious rebel here in 1848, and restoration work is still being carried out.

Steps from the road lead up to the site of a monastery founded by Vattagamini Abhaya some time in the first century BC. Two **cave temples*** are approached through an impressive cleft in the rock. Inside the first is a large reclining Buddha and another seated in meditation posture and a row of six in the teaching mudra. The ceiling paintings have the look of fabric hangings. Steps lead up under what looks like a Portuguese belfry. The antechamber of the second cave temple is illustrated showing the unpleasant fate awaiting sinners in hell. The people stuck on a thorny tree are adulterers, and what the one next door has done to deserve impalement is anyone's guess. Above the door to the inner shrine a woman emerging from a lotus symbolises heaven; one side is a sun and on the other a moon and rabbit. Inside are a large reclining Buddha and several more in meditation mudra.

A path through a smaller gap in the rocks takes you to the workshop; the foundation stone was laid by Prince Sihanouk of Cambodia, symbolic of the strong links between the countries following Therevada Buddhism. The guide will give you a quick demonstration on preparing the palm leaf pages, and cutting and inking the text. You can see the monks at work only by prior arrangement. The caves here are not on the same scale as Dambulla, but they are off the tourist track and much quieter.

Arrival and departure. 2km north of Matale. Many buses pass, or use a three-wheeler from Matale.

North of Aluvihara the road crosses from the Wet Zone to the Dry, and also one gets the last real views of the mountains. Numerous **spice gardens** and a few **batik works** line the road starting only a kilometre or two past Aluvihara. It is worth knowing that most of these 'spice gardens' grow only enough to show you, otherwise they are just sales outlets for commercially produced spices. Some places will give you a good run-down on the medicinal aspects of the herbs, which is very interesting, but you need to know what the stuff would cost you in an ayurvedic pharmacy in town — usually half. All the places along this road are geared to package tours, and they know as well as we do that such people are in a hurry and tend to have more money than sense.

NALANDA

Nalanda was the site of a large Buddhist monastic university in Bihar, North India. At the height of its importance (fifth to twelfth centuries AD) it was the leading Buddhist place of learning in the world holding, according to legend, ten thousand students.

Sri Lanka's Nalanda is a little more modest. Strategically placed between Kandy, Polonnaruwa, and Anuradhapura, King Parakramabahu I (1153-1186) built a great fort and other buildings here, though these have long since vanished. One temple, the **Nalanda Gedige****, a contemporary of the fort, has survived and is a most unusual structure.

Although built as a Buddhist gedige (home of a Buddha image) this is to all intents and purposes identical with the eighth century Pallava temples of Mahabalipuram in Tamil Nadu, South India. The material is a crystalline limestone, rather than the brick properly specified for a gedige, and has eroded rather badly. On either side of the steps you can just make out makaras. The steps into the mandapa are held up by dwarves, and elephants are on either side. Above, two more elephants shower Gajalakshmi, the goddess of wealth. The pillars and pilasters of the mandapa have chaityas (the omega symbol of a Buddhist monastery) at the top; above would have been capitals and cross beams to support a roof of some kind. Above the door of the shrine are two seated Buddhas and five pasadas. In the shrine is a standing Buddha in the blessing mudra, a fold of his robe over his left arm. The remains of a similar figure is beside it. Ganesh stands guard on one side, another Hindu figure too eroded to identify on the other. The section of the roof outside repeats the chaitya theme, only one of the two end figures, Kuvera (the god of wealth) remains. More chaityas appear on the plinth, and the keen-eyed will detect a little erotic sculpture, most unusual on a Buddhist shrine.

Beside the gedige is a brick stupa. The usual circular plan on a square base, it had been pretty well destroyed by treasure hunters before 19th century restoration. The bo-tree has grown from a cutting of the tree in Anuradhapura brought here in 1985. The original approach to the enclosure was by a flight of steps on the east side, marked by four vertical stones which would have reinforced a superstructure of some kind.

The ruins of the gedige had received sporadic maintenance work since 1895, though it remained in poor condition, one of the main problems being tree roots destabilising what was left of the structure. Excavation had unearthed not only missing elements of the gedige but parts of other buildings also. Then, in the 1970s the Mahaveli hydro-electric scheme involved creating a large lake on the site. The decision was made to completely rebuild the temple on a raised plinth 7m/23ft above its original level. This huge jigsaw puzzle proved far more difficult than reconstructing a complete building, but the result is almost an improvement on the original, an attractive temple surrounded by water. Best of all the tourist groups have yet to discover it.

Information. *Nalanda* by P.L. Prematilleke (Rs35) available from the Central Cultural Fund office, 212 Bauddhaloka MW, Colombo 7, is a thorough description and has illustrations of the gedige in its original location and being rebuilt.

Arrival and departure. 25km north of Matale. The gedige is 1.5km from the main road; this is a relatively shady walk, but the only refreshments are a water tap and perhaps some bananas.

Accommodation. *Rest House* opposite the lane to the gedige. An iron cannon testifies to the short-lived British garrison here after the Matale rebellion of 1848.

Eating and Drinking. You are probably not meant to eat in the temple precincts, but there are quiet, shady places to picnic.

WAHAKOTTE

A number of Portuguese prisoners were held in this area during the reign of King Senerath (1604-1635). This is still a Catholic community, and the church has statues dating from the 17th century. Some of these probably came from a Catholic church in the Bogambara area of Kandy which was demolished by Vimaladharmasuriya II (1687-1707). The statues were kept in the royal treasury until the reign of Kirti Shri Rajasinha (1747-1781) who handed them over to the church.

Arrival and departure. 11km north-west of Nalanda.

DAMBULLA

In a rock cleft above Dambulla are Sri Lanka's premier **Buddhist cave**

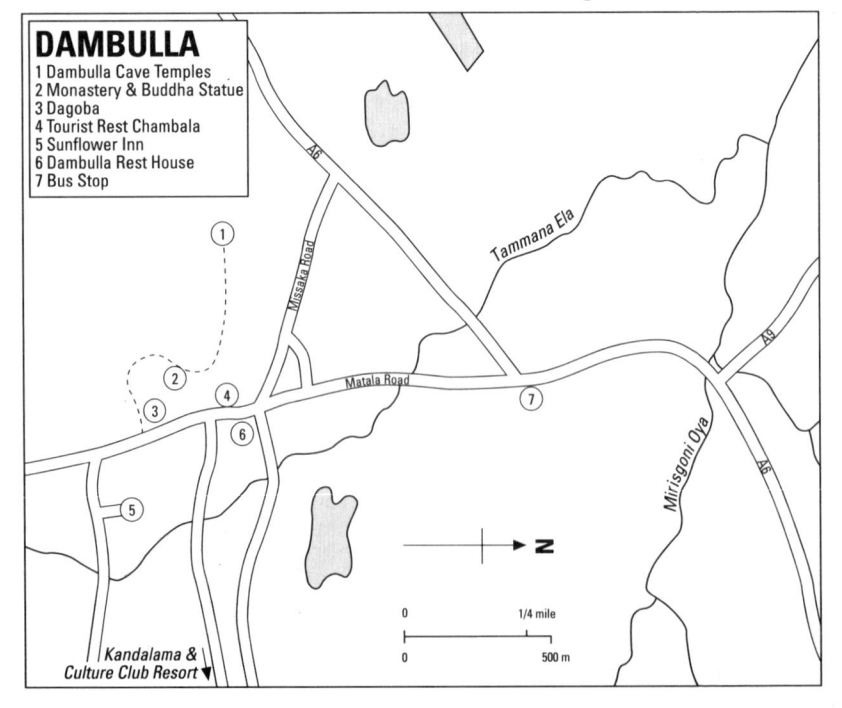

DAMBULLA
1 Dambulla Cave Temples
2 Monastery & Buddha Statue
3 Dagoba
4 Tourist Rest Chambala
5 Sunflower Inn
6 Dambulla Rest House
7 Bus Stop

temples***. Despite their popularity as a place of pilgrimage the caves have a serene atmosphere set off by their spectacular setting. In the caves are multiple Buddha figures and wonderful wall and ceiling paintings, the latter including hundreds and hundreds of Buddhas.

There is evidence (stone tools and so on) of the caves having been inhabited in prehistoric times. Later they are thought to have been used as shrines for pre-Buddhist deities. When Buddhism took root in the second century BC they were occupied by Buddhist monks. In 90BC Vattagamani Abhaya (or Valagambahu - same man) fled Anuradhapura when the Tamils took it and found refuge here with his court. He is said to have started the tradition of pilgrimages to the caves in thanks for his return, fourteen years later, to Anuradhapura.

The caves receive their first mention in the Mahavamsa in the time of Vijayabahu I (1055-1110). He evicted the Tamils from Anuradhapura, and celebrated by building a new capital at Polonnaruwa and restoring numerous old temples, including those of Dambulla. It is recorded that King Nissanka Malla (1187-1196) gilded many of the statues and covered the temple with gilded plates. By the 17th century the caves were in very poor condition and received extensive restoration from King Senerath (1604-1635). Painting of the eyes was left to the end of the work and marked by great celebrations attended by the king, three queens, and three princes.

Further restoration was carried out by Kirti Sri Rajasinha (1747-1781), and he built a new temple in the gap between Cave 2 and Cave 4. Some time in the 19th century, strangely enough there is no record of when, a storeroom was converted into a fifth cave temple.

Exploring

The caves are open 0700-1100 and 1200-1900. The entrance is by the large dagoba on the main road, not the white gateway. Tickets (Rs200) from the administration block, though you will be lucky to find anyone selling them before 0730. To the left, at the foot of the hill, a new building is going up as the base for a 61m/200ft high Buddha due to be completed for the new millennium. A model of this can be seen in the administration block. Steps climb 100m/330ft past frangipani trees to a terrace with five caves. Photography inside the caves is emphatically not allowed; in the entrance hang films removed from transgressors' cameras.

Cave 1 is the Devaraja-Viharaya. Devaraja is a form of Vishnu as Lord of the Gods. He is a protector of Buddhism and used his divine power for the construction of these temples. Doratupalas stand beside the entrance, the makara-toranas above are peacocks with monsters' heads. The principal figure is a large reclining Buddha with flowers, said to be lotuses, painted on his feet in place of the usual chakras. Near the feet are seated and standing Buddha figures, and that is all you can see at the moment. Up by the head Vishnu and other figures are hidden behind a brightly painted wooden screen opened only at poya times. The ceiling and wall paintings have been badly affected by water and the smoke from incense and oil lamps, but are still very beautiful. The doors here are the type that would have been fitted to the Nalanda gedige. Beside the cave is a blue-painted Vishnu shrine and, over to the left, a bo-tree. Now take the steps up into a long cloister.

Cave 2 is the Maharaja-Viharaya (Cave of the Great King) and the largest at 53m long, 23m wide, and 7m high. Entering the first door the five Buddhas facing you are in the advising mudra. Above this entrance is a ceiling painting of the Buddha in teaching mudra. Going left from here the first standing Buddha is in the blessing mudra, his robe held up by his left arm. The two Buddhas with the right palm outwards are teaching, the one with his arms crossed on his chest is in thinking mudra. The two Hindu figures are the blue Upulvan (a local form of Vishnu) and the gold Saman, another local god closely associated with Buddhism; behind are murals of Kataragama with his peacock and Ganesh above his mouse. The paintings are all modern, probably 18th century, but may be copies or restorations of ones dating from the 11th or 12th centuries. There are perhaps 1500 images of Buddha.

At the end are five seated Buddhas increasing in height according to the headroom. The figure before the second entrance represents Vattagamani Abhaya (103-77BC), the first king to beautify this cave. On the ceiling above is a long narrative painting relating Buddha's life on earth. The Buddhas at the top signify the twenty-four annunciations; the easiest scenes to pick out are Buddha meditating under the bo-tree and dying. The eight stupas represent the building of memorials and the distribution of relics, and at left bottom is the first Buddhist council held at Rajgir in modern day Bihar in northern India. Beside this a large Buddha in witness mudra with his right hand touching the earth is surrounded by demons trying to distract him from achieving enlightenment; the demon king Mara directs operations seated on his multi-tusked elephant. Opposite this second door is a group of five figures which are the main focus of worship; the central Buddha still has traces of the gilding reported to have been applied by King Nissanka Malla. The figures on either side are Mahayana boddhisatvas, that to the left having lion-faced ear lobes. Walking round the back of this group gives a clue to where the pictures on court cards come from.

Continuing round from the second door two of the Buddhas on the dagoba are shielded by three-headed cobras; this is the snake king Mucalinda who shaded Buddha the sixth week after his enlightenment. On the ceiling above, having failed with the demons, Mara tries out Buddha with his comely daughters, and fails again. Just after the first door is a standing Buddha then a huge reclining one. Right in the corner, hidden by a large Buddha, is King Nissanka Malla. After that a succession of seated Buddhas (and just one standing) goes all the way round to the starting point. Holy water drips through the roof into a large bowl; the supply is said to survive even the worst drought. Murals continue behind the statues right under the fold of the hill. These depict major events in the development of Buddhism in Ceylon, but are too poorly lit to see. This and the space behind the figures of the south wall constituted an ambulatory.

Few of the figures in these caves are stone, most are brick or wood plastered over. Looking closely you can see where termites have had a go at the wood. A common feature is the flame on the head of each statue. Buddha figures always have some symbol on the head, even if it appears only to be a topknot, signifying enlightenment; this is the Sri Lankan form.

The ceiling really is intriguing, looking like the roof of a tent. Apart from the paintings detailed above much of it is taken up by countless repetitive Buddhas; otherwise large areas are done in geometrical designs which heighten the effect of hanging fabric.

Cave 3, the Maha Alut Viharaya (New Great Temple) arrived on the scene only in the 18th century, the work of Kirti Sri Rajasinha (1747-1781). As you enter the makara-torana of the central Buddha figure merges into the ceiling. To the right from the door are two seated Buddhas. The floral decoration on the wall would look at home in a Mughal building, and behind the Buddhas is what appears to be the plan of a garden with a square lake having an elephant's head at the centre of each side. The next figure is King Rajasinha, and behind him are courtiers carrying bunches of flowers and a gold sword. Two large maitreya Buddhas are on the ceiling and, apart from some patterned areas, the rest is hundreds of identical seated Buddhas. At the feet of the reclining Buddha is a white marble Buddha in witness mudra with his right hand touching the ground; this is of Burmese origin and said to have been found in the jungle.

Cave 4 is the Pascima Viharaya. The name means western temple, though in fact the much later Cave 5 has taken this position. This is a small but pleasing cave, its main Buddha facing east towards the sunrise. The dagoba was popularly believed to contain the jewellery of King Valagamba's queen, and has been damaged in the recent past by optimistic morons.

Cave 5 is the Devana Alut Viharaya (Second New Temple). This is the latest of the series, having been converted from a storeroom. The main image is a large reclining Buddha made, like the others, of brick plastered over. Murals include a group of three by the reclining Buddha's feet; the central dark one is Vishnu, the right Kataragama with his peacock, and the left Bandara (another local deity). To the left of the door is a mural of a noble carrying lotus flowers, perhaps the man who endowed the temple; above are details of restoration work in 1915.

These caves are living places of worship. Fifty monks live beyond Cave 5, and worship in the caves early in the morning. A much larger number of monks used to live in the 73 cave shelters which dot this area.

Walk back along the terrace to admire the views; photography is permitted out here. The monkeys are unaggressive, but will grab anything put down. Running along above the caves is a dripstone to prevent water running round the curve of the rock into the caves. The Lion Rock of Sigiriya can be seen from various points on the walk up. You are not allowed to climb to the top of the hill, at 550m above sea level, as this would mean walking over Buddha, a stricture obviously not applying to goats!

The best times to visit are early morning or late afternoon to avoid the tour groups. The latter has the advantage of a great sunset, hundreds of swallows twittering around, and the sound of monks chanting far below.

Information. *Golden Rock Temple of Dambulla* (Rs105) by Anuradha Seneviratna, available from Cultural Fund office, Ministry of Cultural Affairs, 212 Bauddhaloka MW, Colombo 7 is exhaustive.

Practical Information

Arrival and departure. 72km north of Kandy, 25km from Sigiriya. Buses to Sigiriya (½hr), Kandy (2hrs), Polonnaruwa (2½hrs), Anuradhapura (2½hrs), and Colombo (4hrs). Long distance buses, except from Kandy, stop at the road junction 2.5km north of the caves. Any bus towards Kandy will take you down there, or use a three-wheeler.

Accommodation (STD Code 066)
Rest House (CHC), Kandy Road. Tel 8299 or 01-503 497 (Colombo). SWB $13 DWB $18 incl. Rest. Bar. Large rooms with fan and nets. Nice veranda. Well managed, good western food, ask for cheaper Sri Lankan menu if you prefer.
Chambala Hotel, Kandy Road. Tel 84488. DWB $7-10. Rest. Bar. Under construction when visited, should be good. Large garden with view to hills.
Tourist Rest Chambala, 121 Kandy Road. Tel 84488. DWB $4. Rest. Rooms clean but basic with small bathrooms.
Sunflower Inn. DWB $4. Rest. Simple rooms but clean.

Two expensive, but very good, hotels are in the jungle nearby: *Culture Club Resort* (Tel 83500 or Colombo 01-683 378) and *Kandalama* (Tel 83475 or Colombo 01-333 071), the latter designed by Geoffrey Bawa.

SIGIRIYA

Sigiriya, was one of the shortest lived of Sri Lanka's old capitals having a heyday of a scant twenty years. Here King Kassapa I (473-491) built a spectacular and impregnable palace on top of a rocky outcrop. Beautiful formal gardens were laid out around the base of the hill, and the hill itself was adorned with murals. The entrance to the palace was through the mouth of a huge lion, the city's name deriving from Simha-giri, Lion Mountain, though some think the second element to be *giriya* meaning throat.

Kassapa's aim was to reproduce on earth the palace of Kubera, the god of wealth. He certainly achieved something very lavish, though the legend that it was all built in seven years stretches credulity. One interesting point about Sigiriya is that it was virtually a secular capital; there were monasteries, of which very little remains, but nowhere on the scale of Anuradhapura and Polonnaruwa.

History

King Dhatusena I (459-473), who ruled from Anuradhapura, had two sons. The elder, Kassapa, though not of noble birth, was by far the more capable of the two. When his father announced that the younger son Mogallana, who was the son of a princess and appears to have been something of a wimp, was to succeed him Kassapa rebelled. In 477 he imprisoned his father and drove out Mogallana to India. Needing a secure new capital he built Sigiriya. He subsequently killed his father for refusing to tell him where the state treasure was hidden. The legend goes that Dhatusena offered to show Kassapa the treasure if he could have one last bathe in Kalawewa Tank; there he poured sparkling water through his hands and told Kassapa that was his treasure. This was not what Kassapa wanted to hear, so he walled up his father and left him to die. The ensuing civil war lasted eighteen years. Kassapa's fortress capital of Sigiriya never fell, but in the end he tired of the constant warfare. Deciding on one final trial of strength with Mogallana, who had enlisted the aid of a Tamil army, he met him in battle outside the fort in 495, and lost. Sigiriya was handed over to monks and never used again as a palace. The monks left in 1155 and, apart from brief military use by the kingdom of Kandy in the 16th and 17th centuries, Sigiriya reverted to jungle until rediscovered in 1828.

Mogallana was by no means the only Sinhalese prince to seek Tamil military assistance; as many other people have found getting rid of mercenaries is much more difficult then employing them.

Exploring

Planning

The Lion Rock which forms the base of the citadel and royal palace of Sigiriya is a huge lump of gneiss, the quartzitic stone forming most of Sri Lanka, which rises sheer from the surrounding country. An east-west axis was drawn through the centre of the summit level and everything else laid out symmetrically around this.

West and east of the rock were large walled and moated enclosures and, beyond the eastern one, a further rampart enclosing the city. The western enclosure covers an area 900m by 800m (72ha/178 acres); once thought to have been an aristocratic enclave, it is now known to be purely the royal gardens. To the east of the rock is a smaller enclosure, about 700m by 500m (35ha/86 acres), which had only one permanent building, a pavilion on a rock. This obviously could not have been the working class area it is sometimes described as, and appears to have had a ritual purpose. Outside this area the outer ramparts enclosed a rectangle 1500m by 1000m which constituted a residential enclave.

Around the base of the rock is an inner royal precinct in the shape of an irregular ellipse. This comprises terraced gardens with various pavilions and rock shelters covering around 15ha.

The fortifications and gardens***

Walking from the Rest House round the south-western corner of Sigiriya you can stroll along the outer wall and see a short surviving part of the outer moat. The geometrical precision of the inner moats is reminiscent of the lake at Versailles. This is also a great place for bird watching; there can't be many places where you would see pied and blue kingfishers on the same tree. Entry is over the inner moat and through the rampart.

The ceremonial entrance to the city followed the east-west axis straight to the Lion Rock and crossed the outer moat and wall before joining the road from the Rest House. The inner moat is 25m wide and 4m deep and, having crossed that, the path traverses the inner defences. To the right is a newly excavated small water garden. The many tanks and attendant pavilions are all done in brick, though some of the tanks are bottomed with quartz limestone. The buildings had tiled roofs and possibly formed a cool summer palace. This is probably later than the main works, and there is evidence of alterations as late as the 13th century. There may well be a matching garden the other side of the path.

Passing through a large gatehouse you enter the main water garden. This is effectively an island between four tanks and, with the buildings at either end, measures 175m by 110m. Much restoration has been done recently with UNESCO help. The layout is that of a walled Persian charbagh (*char* = four + *bagh* = garden), a walled quartered garden with a gate in the centre of each wall. This design is commonly found in Mughal pleasure gardens and tombs like the Taj Mahal. This garden, of course, predates the Taj Mahal by more than 1000 years. It equally predates Islam, which came to regard such gardens

SIGIRIYA

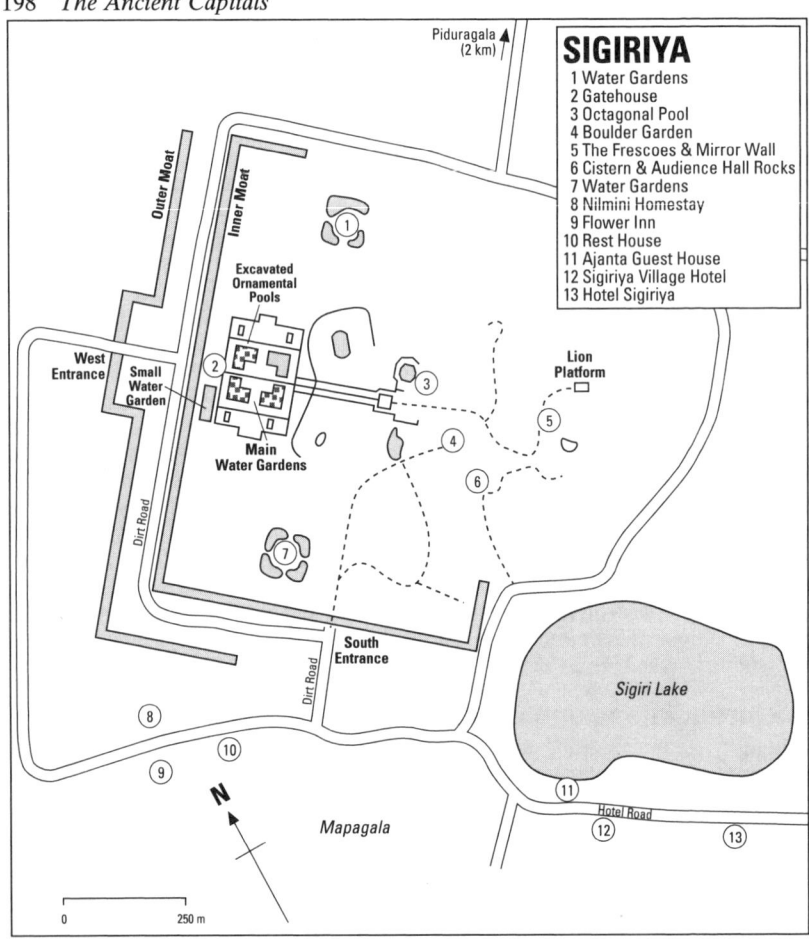

1 Water Gardens
2 Gatehouse
3 Octagonal Pool
4 Boulder Garden
5 The Frescoes & Mirror Wall
6 Cistern & Audience Hall Rocks
7 Water Gardens
8 Nilmini Homestay
9 Flower Inn
10 Rest House
11 Ajanta Guest House
12 Sigiriya Village Hotel
13 Hotel Sigiriya

as representations of Paradise (indeed our word paradise may well come from the Persian pardes meaning a park or enclosure). Whatever, this is probably the oldest surviving garden of its kind. Three of the ponds have been excavated and display their brick linings, that to the north-east is to be left, for the moment anyway, in its as-found state.

Pass through another gate, and long tanks with waterways and little cascades, again recently excavated, flank the path. The fountains, made from perforated limestone are now working again after nearly fifteen centuries; all that was necessary was to clear out the conduits. Note the cisterns. Beyond the waterways, on either side, is a large island, partly natural, in a moat contained by stone walls. These moats are reservoirs for the tanks of the main water garden. Pavilions stood on both islands, and are said to have constituted a summer palace. Having to incorporate huge boulders these have a more landscape look than the rest of the rather formal gardens. Further out again is another pair of charbagh islands awaiting excavation.

The final water garden, on a higher level, marks the transition from the planned garden to the naturalistic boulder area. It incorporates a much smaller charbagh garden; to the left is an octagonal pool dwarfed by a huge boulder, and with the remains of a 'bathing pavilion', and to the right a rectangular pool. All of the water gardens, the defence moats, and the artificial Sigiriya Lake to the south are connected by underground conduits, with the lake being the summit level and the supply for all the other works. The engineering had to be of a high order as water is scarce in this Dry Zone.

The Boulder Garden**

This was constructed around and from the huge boulders at the foot of the massif. Local people and tour guides (who should know better) may tell you that the notches on the rocks were to hold candles on Poya days; in fact they are footings for brickwork, and the holes were for wooden posts. Together they indicate that almost every boulder had some sort of building on top. The overall effect must have been rather like a Japanese garden.

Twenty or so caves and rock shelters are located in this area. Some of the shelters are dated by donatory inscriptions to the period spanning the third century BC to the first century AD. In other words, they predate the building of the gardens and palace, and the move of the monastery to Pidurangala (see below). After the death of Kassapa they resumed their original function when the monk Mahanama (uncle of Mogallana) moved here from Lake Kalawewa. The caves provided both chapels and living accommodation for the monks, and were originally enclosed by side and front walls which have mostly disappeared. An important feature of these caves (which will be seen in many other places) is the dripstone ledge to prevent water running down the rock into the cave.

The caves were plastered and painted, and faint traces remain in a few of them, notably of apsaras in cave 15. Some of these shelters were in use up to the 12th or 13th century, and painting apparently continued up till then. Traces of ceiling painting have survived in the Cobrahood Cave (cave 9); an inscription dates this to the second century BC.

The most impressive remains here are the so-called audience hall and ritual bath. A huge boulder has been flattened and finely finished to form the floor of a building, and a throne 5m long cut from the living rock. Beside this is a cave, again finely finished and with a throne. Traces of painting remain on the ceiling. On top of the rock above, again levelled off, is a large cistern, partly cut from the rock and partly built up with huge slabs of stone. It is said that this was an audience hall of King Kassapa, but is far more likely to have had a purely religious use, the two thrones representing Buddha and forming a focus for the monks' devotions.

The boulder garden leads into the third and final garden form at Sigiriya, the terraced gardens. These were formed by building rubble retaining walls. The boulder and terrace gardens have received the least attention so far from archaeologists. Further excavation should provide a better idea of the original layout.

The Frescoes and Mirror Wall***

The ascent from the boulder garden starts between two huge rocks leaning together. The steps lead up to a long almost level walkway.

At this level of the Lion Mountain is the rock face containing Sigiriya's famed frescoes. This extraordinary artistic effort once covered an area 140m long and 40m high and stretched around the rock past the Lion Staircase. Not for nothing has it been called the largest picture gallery in the world. Today only a tiny fraction remains to remind us of this past glory. Unlike most Sinhalese or Indian murals these have no narrative content. Despite many theories there is no really convincing explanation for what the figures represent. They are not obviously deities; whether they were apsaras (most plausible), or Kassapa's wives, or just done for the aesthetic hell of it we shall probably never know. Nor do we know whether these figures are representative of the whole or just an isolated part of it. What we can say is that these paintings are of a distinct Sri Lankan style, livelier and more naturalistic than their Indian contemporaries at Ajanta and elsewhere.

From the top of the spiral staircase (made in Cornwall!) look right over the desk; the first woman is holding a temple flower in her left hand and is contemplating a lotus bud. The next figure lower down has two lotus buds and a water lily in her left hand and a temple flower in the right. According to a local guide she has a maiden breast and body compared with the first which has a full, grown up breast. Both look equally well endowed. You only get one go at fresco painting, once the paint is on the wet plaster it's on, and here you can see a first attempt at the headdress. In the first pair above that the right one is lighter skinned and the left wears a choli blouse. Of the second pair the right apsara holds a flower in one hand whilst her left nipple plays peek-a-boo; on the left girl of the pair the initial go at the left nipple was in the wrong place. Directly below the girl in the red choli had the outline of a third hand above her breasts before the artist changed his mind. She holds a bowl of flowers and her companion has a large lotus flower. The last pair is badly mutilated, the legacy of mindless vandalism in 1967. Restoration of the others was carried out by an Italian expert, but this was beyond repair.

Beyond (this part of the gallery is at present closed) are five more paintings; the rather faded colours look more natural than those which have been restored. One of the women has an African look, supporting the idea that the paintings may illustrate the king's harem. The one pair that you can see is interesting in that the left figure is painted in a hollow; the artist manages not only to compensate for distortion, but (and you can't test this) the eyes appear to be looking at you whichever side of her you stand.

The painters had to work from bamboo scaffolding set up on the terrace below. The iron loops give an idea of how precarious access was before the present gallery was built. They are a relic of Victorian exploration, though the first archaeological commissioner HCP Bell actually had himself hauled up on a seat from above. The intriguing thing is how did Kassapa and others see them?

The word fresco, incidentally, is often misused for the more general mural meaning any wall painting. These, unlike the murals at Ajanta, are true frescoes in that they were painted on wet plaster and in places you can see the thickness of this. The firm bonding this creates is one reason these have lasted longer than Ajanta's better protected murals.

Below the frescoes the walkway was protected by a wall coated with plaster including lime, beeswax, and egg whites. This was burnished to such a shine that it became known as the Mirror Wall. After Kassapa's death Sigiriya became a place of pilgrimage, and the frescoes obviously made a powerful impression on visitors over the years. They composed little verses and inscribed them on the wall; over 700 of these graffiti, mostly sixth to 14th century, have been deciphered.

It is important to distinguish between original graffiti and later vandalism. Just after the tenth yard mark (above an elephant and by a human figure's left ear) is a neatly done bit of Sinhalese script surrounded by the original polish of the wall. Looking at an acute angle up the wall from here you can see other surviving patches of polish.

Other, and unique, evidence of the impression the paintings made is that terracotta replicas 10cm/4in to 20cm/8in high have been found in some of the excavated sites. These may have had a devotional purpose, but equally may have been sold as souvenirs to take away. Opposite the 60 yard mark you can see plaster and paint on the rock splashed from the cave above.

Further on, looking down from the iron gangway, you see the foundations of a guardroom and, above it, a large boulder on props. It is said, rather fancifully, that it could have been dropped to block the entrance. It seems more likely that the idea was to prevent it falling of its own accord, taking with it the building which once stood on top. Pausing for breath at the top of the steep flight of steps look back to see a groove all the way up above the steps, this helped to support a roof.

The Lion Platform**

When you arrive on the Lion Platform have a look at the brickwork of the paws; you can distinguish between the old narrow bricks and the modern ones used for repairs. Now retreat to the back of the platform for a clear view (and some peace and quiet), and try to visualise a lion, head-on, 14m/46ft high. Niches in the rock above each paw provided a key for the bricks which formed the lion's head and shoulders and indicate its outline. The whole structure was plastered and painted to give a realistic appearance, and must have been visible for miles. It is assumed that a timber framework inside supported steps up to the level of those cut into the rock.

This lion was the most important part of Kassapa's plan and had a number of symbolic meanings. The lion was the emblem of the kings of Lanka, and they traced their descent from it. Its size was a statement of Kassapa's power and wealth. As an entrance to the palace it was designed to impress, and entering it implied submission. Seen in peace after the crowds have gone it all reminds one of Ozymandias 'Look on my works ye mighty and despair'.

Before advancing towards the staircase glance over to your right. The wire cage was made to protect archaeologists from the swarms of wild bees that used to frequent and, according to legend, protect Sigiriya. The foundations belong to three pavilions that once stood here, each having guardstones and moonstones at the entrance. The iron stairway which replaces the lion is something else, seeming to hang in mid-air. When it joins the rock it follows the course of the original stairway. The recesses you see in the stone up here were not the actual steps. Stone slabs fitted into the recesses and were supported from below by brickwork, in its turn supported by the lower grooves in the rock. It is assumed that another mirror wall protected the steps and that the grooves above were for a canopy.

The Palace***

The plateau on top of the rock is 200m above the plain and 360m above sea level. It covers 1.5ha/3¾ acres, but it is very hard to make out much of the **palace**. You arrive at the summit near a couple of small tanks cut from solid rock, and a little further is the highest part of the palace. We know that this was part of the inner palace but not its precise function. It is nice to think of an open pillared pavilion here to make the most of the stunning location.

A north-south paved path divides the higher inner palace (for the royal family) from the lower outer one (for guards and service staff). Facing east is a stone throne with the holes for pillars to support a canopy of some kind, and what a view! The large tank marked the boundary between the outer palace and the lower terraced gardens. Great flights of steps, both rock-cut and structural, lead down to the water. The most interesting view of the palaces is from the south eastern corner near the big tank where the multiple brick terraces have the look of a middle eastern ziggurat, or stepped pyramid. It's worth reflecting that all the brick and limestone (and there was far more than we see now) had to be hauled up here. Walking back from here suggests that the palace must have been a real labyrinth.

The whole summit was excavated at the end of the 19th century, and among the finds was a jar containing over a thousand Roman coins, proof of Lanka's importance on the trade routes of the ancient world.

Never mind all the history and architecture (not that any is left), the top of the Lion Rock is for the views and the sheer fun of getting there.

Other things

The **museum** is not wildly interesting, but has very well made bricks and other terracotta items including water pipes.

Look out for roofed tree platforms along the road from Dambulla; these are for farmers to guard their crops from the wild elephants still quite common in this area. Fires are burnt, and you may hear the explosion of firecrackers during the night. A friendlier elephant lives under a tree at the edge of the lake by the Hotel Sigiriya sign.

Practical Information

Information. The site opens at 0600, and this is the best time for coolness, peace and quiet, and clarity of air. Perversely the ticket office does not open until 0700 so, unless you have a Cultural Triangle pass, buy a ticket the night before. Sigiriya is better not visited at weekends and especially on public holidays.

Shopping. Brass shop opposite Hotel Sigiriya. Wood carving workshop and retail shop next to the police station on same road. There is no post office or bank.

Arrival and departure. 25km by bus from Dambulla (½hr). Bus direct from Kandy Goods Shed bus-stand (3hrs). Taxi from Dambulla Rs500 or less.

Accommodation (STD Code 027)

Sigiriya Village Hotel. Tel/Fax 066-84716. DWB A/C $60/90. Rest. Bar. Rooms in bungalows secluded in the trees of a lovely garden. Deluxe rooms have mini-bar, courtyard, and lily pool. Good menu and wine list (crab Rs650, lobster Rs900, other prices average). Tennis court, swimming pool. Ayurvedic treatment and massage centre.

Hotel Sigiriya. Tel/Fax 025-4811. DWB $50 Rest. Bar. Super views of the rock from the restaurant and bar. Reasonably priced food. Swimming pool (Rs150 for non-residents).

Rest House (CHC). Tel 066-8324 or 01-503 497 (Colombo). DWB $23. Rest. Bar. Great location with views of the rock from the verandah. Good food, breakfast Rs150, rice and curry Rs150.

Nilmini Homestay. Tel 610 819. DWB $7. DR $3. (Only two rooms). Rest. Fan and nets in rooms. Breakfast Rs97, lunch and dinner Rs125-225.

Flower Inn. DWB $7. Rest. Fan and nets. Nice garden, good place to stay. Breakfast Rs150, three course evening meal Rs200.

Ajanta not recommended. There are several other places to stay along the road from Dambulla to Sigiriya, but really only useful if you have your own vehicle. Buses from Sigiriya finish at nightfall, and three-wheelers and taxis, if available, double their prices after that.

Cool drinks are sold on the Lion Platform, very necessary. Before whingeing about the price consider how they get there.

Further Afield

Pidurangala** is the 320m/1050ft hill visible to the north of Sigiriya. *Pidu* means offering and *rangala* is jungle. The story goes that monks were living on Sigiriya when Kassapa decided to build his palace there. So he constructed the new caves, a temple, and a large brick stupa here in the jungle and offered them to the monks. This was explained to us by a teacher in the Sangharama, the school for young monks, at the foot of the hill. The youngsters are obviously happy and have a lot of fun, though their curriculum is gruelling. They have to learn Pali (the language of the ancient Buddhist texts), Sanskrit (notoriously difficult), Sinhalese, and English. The teacher himself is interesting; after a career and raising a family he took the Buddhist equivalent of sannyas and came to teach here. He is unpaid, living on his pension.

Walking or taking a three wheeler round from Sigiriya you come to the Sangharama. Crossing the yard and climbing the steps by a spreading bo-tree you find a white building in which is a **cave temple** housing a large reclining Buddha. Figures of Vishnu, with a dark face, and the local god Saman stand in a glass case. The murals are good, but the ceiling is most attractive. A central rosette of eight geese with their necks entwined and the rest resembling a cloth hanging. Girls on the murals outside have an embonpoint to make the Sigiriya maidens very envious! The **stupa** is nearby.

Steps lead up from the right of the cave temple and soon give way to a rough path. A large overhang, now occupied by swallow and little mud wasp's nests, provided the roof for ten caves. These have mostly disintegrated, but in the last is a reclining Buddha 12.5m long. Construction is of brick covered with cement and plaster. Damage to the head and feet is said to have been done by treasure hunters. A reclining Buddha is a dying Buddha, and there would be less attractive places than this to pop your clogs. Past here a pool has been cut in the solid rock. A bit of a scramble at the top of the path brings you out by the huge balanced rock visible from the summit of Sigiriya. You can clearly see the queues crawling up the Lion Rock, and the sense of superiority from the peace and isolation are good enough reasons for the climb. The trees at the summit hide the remains of a stupa built by Kassapa.

Arrival and departure. Pidurangala is 2km from Sigiriya. There will be no transport back to Sigiriya unless you have kept a three-wheeler waiting. If your Sigiriya ticket is current you can take the short cut straight through the gardens at the foot of the rock. Do not walk back in the dark, wild elephants are a real danger.

Mapagala is the 245m hill to the south of Sigiriya. It has the walls and ruins of a palace possibly dating to the time of Kassapa. Mapagala is 500m from the rock but of minimal interest.

SIGIRIYA TO POLONNARUWA

A dirt road runs from Sigiriya to Morageswewa on the Habarana-Polonnaruwa road. There is no public transport, and you are supposed not to take hire cars along such roads. It should be fun for the intrepid who have hired trail bikes. The *Trekkers' Guide to Sri Lanka* details the 27km walk from Sigiriya to Minneriya, said to be possible in 9hrs.

HABARANA

Habarana is a crossroads town. A friendly little place, it makes a useful base for the Cultural Triangle for those who quickly tire of unpacking and packing. The Buddhist temple has some interesting paintings, and there is a good view from a rock by the tank. You can do an **elephant safari** from The Lodge (see below), two hours costs $30 per person. A kilometre or so out of town on the Anuradhapura road you often see elephants in the little river being scrubbed down with a bit of coconut husk.

Arrival and departure. Habarana's railway station (3km out of town on the Trincomalee road) is the nearest to Dambulla and Sigiriya.

Accommodation (STD Code 066).
   The Lodge. Tel 8321. Fax 01-447 087. DWB A/C $10/13. Rest. Bar. Super gardens. Buffet dinner Rs492 incl, a la carte dishes around Rs200 (+20%). Swimming pool, billiards room. Beautifully done, but your companions will all be package tourists.
   The Village. Tel 8316. Fax 01-447 087. SWB $35 DWB $40. Rest. Bar. Rooms in cottages with verandahs and wicker furniture. Swimming pool (non-residents Rs100), tennis court, boats, fishing in the lake. Meals average prices, main courses Rs150-200, beer Rs197 incl. Recommended. The Lodge and The Village are a short distance out of town on the Dambulla road.
   Rest House (CHC), at crossroads. Tel 8355. DWB $10. Rest. Bar. Good food (usual Rest House menu), charming staff, and a very pleasant place to stay.
   Habarana Inn, Dambulla Road. SWB $8 DWB $9. Rest. Bar. Breakfast Rs130, rice and curry Rs200, beer Rs110. Clean rooms, nice small hotel.
   Good cheap rice and curry place just the Dambulla side of the crossroads.

MINNERIYA GIRITALE SANCTUARY

This wildlife sanctuary, covering 1600sq km, encompasses the huge Minneriya Wewa tank. This has a perimeter of 32km/20miles and was constructed by King Mahasena (274-301). Like the rest of the irrigation system it fell into disrepair after the abandonment of Polonnaruwa around 1300, and was not restored until 1903. Giritale tank, of more modest proportions, forms part of the boundary of the sanctuary. Bird life over the tanks may include the Ceylon fish-owl or a sea eagle.

Two good hotels make Giritale an alternative base for Polonnaruwa (for the well heeled).

Arrival and departure. 12km from Polonnaruwa on the Habarana road.

Accommodation (STD Code 027).
Royal Lotus Hotel. Tel 6316. Fax 01-449 790. Rest. Bar. SWB/DWB A/C $60.
Giritale Hotel. Tel 6311. Fax 01-449 790. SWB A/C $40 DWB A/C $45. Rest. Bar. Both these places overlook Giritale tank and have swimming pools.

There are cheaper places to stay, but it seems pointless when there are good inexpensive places in Polonnaruwa.

POLONNARUWA

The two great long-term capitals of Sri Lanka were Anuradhapura and Polonnaruwa. The date of the founding of Polonnaruwa is not known, but there was a settlement of some kind here, named Pulatthi or Pulastipura, in the reign of King Mahasena (274-301), and the extensive remains of irrigation works date from then. Another name, Toparé, derives from the Topawewa tank. Polonnaruwa's significance is strategic. It commands the crossings of the Mahaveli River, which were important in both the internal trouble between Anuradhapura and Mahagama in the south and as a protection against the Tamils. Initially Polonnaruwa was a royal residence, the first palace having been built in 368AD. It became a capital only in the mid-eighth century.

For a long time the jungle protected Polonnaruwa from the Tamils based in Jaffna, but it was captured by the Chola king Rajahrajah in 993. In 1056 it was recaptured by Vijayabahu I (1055-1110), and this heralded a golden age. Most of the buildings date from the reign of Parakramabahu (1153-86). Tamil pressure remained, however, and Polonnaruwa was abandoned in 1288 when the Sinhalese kings retreated to Dambadeniya. This may well have been due to a breach in the tank rather than direct Tamil action.

Southern group

This consists of just two monuments 1.5km/1mile down the bund of the Topawewa, a pleasant cycle in the early evening. Alternatively have lunch and a swim at one of the hotels opposite.

The **Topawewa tank** is the work of King Parakramabahu I (1153-1186). Part of its area was already occupied by three smaller tanks, the work of earlier Anuradhapura kings. Raising the bunds created a lake so large (2500ha/9¾ sq miles, and holding 134 million m^3/29,480 million gallons of water) that it is often called the **Parakrama Samudra** (Parakrama's Sea). The tank is fed by canal from the Amban Ganga, a tributary of the Mahaveli, Sri Lanka's largest river, but like others the tank fell into disrepair. Complete restoration to its original size was completed only in the 1950s. The tank is clean, and an evening swim from the Rest House steps is very refreshing. The bird life is interesting, and the tank full of fish, mostly small but good eating. The fishermen can be persuaded to take you out in their outrigger canoes.

The **Potgul Vihara** (Library Monastery) stood to the south of a royal garden along the tank. Its centre is a circular building dating from the 10th century, although tradition makes it much older. This was a place of monastic study, and is said to have held the most sacred texts. The walls are almost 4½m/15ft thick at ground level. The roof was presumably rounded like a dagoba, though not a true dome as all the bricks are horizontal showing a corbelled construction. A dagoba stands in each corner of the square plinth mirroring the northern Indian panchayata temple with its four corner chapels.

The **statue of Parakramabahu** (so-called) is a superb piece of sculpture 3½m/11½ft high and dating, it is thought, from the ninth century. An alternative theory makes it the sage Pulasti after whom the city was called Pulastipura. There is similarly argument over what the figure is holding. It could be a palm leaf book, which would tie in with the sage theory and its position near the library or, if you reckon the statue is of Parakramabahu, it could be the yoke of kingship. Whatever, it used to appear on old pattern Sri Lankan bank notes. At present it has an ugly scaffolding over it and barbed wire in front, making it impossible to photograph.

Rest house group

These buildings date from the time of Nissanka Malla (1187-1196) who was too vain to use the second-hand palace already built by Parakramabahu. They stand in a field (once called Dipuyyana, or island garden) beside the lake, access being behind the bo-tree outside the Rest House. Water buffaloes roam, and the area is popular with washermen and local people bathing and swimming. With the possible exception of the Council Chamber these buildings are of limited interest, though at least entry is free.

Below the level of the lake were the **royal baths**. The other side of the tank (now empty) is the bathhouse lined with stone. The sluices here allowed the other buildings to be surrounded by water, and perhaps to fill the moat around the city wall. Above stands the foundation of a circular building.

The **ruin** may mark the site of the funeral pyre of Nissanka Malla. It is of brick and still has the remnants of fine white plaster and painting.

The **palace of Nissanka Malla** was also of plastered brick construction and had two upper storeys of wooden construction. Compare the shape of the bricks here with the modern ones of the rebuilt Council Chamber.

The **Council Chamber** of Nissanka Malla is the most northerly building. Originally of stone it was reconstructed in brick in the 19th century incorporating the remaining fragments of stone; the moulded bricks follow the original lines. The lower part of the plinth had a frieze of elephants, a few can still be seen on the lake side. The main entrance is on the north side, on the left are three of the lions which formed the upper frieze, and above them are lion makaras. The pillars and capitals are held together by mortise and tenon, the tenons on top of the capitals once located the roof beams. At the far end is a

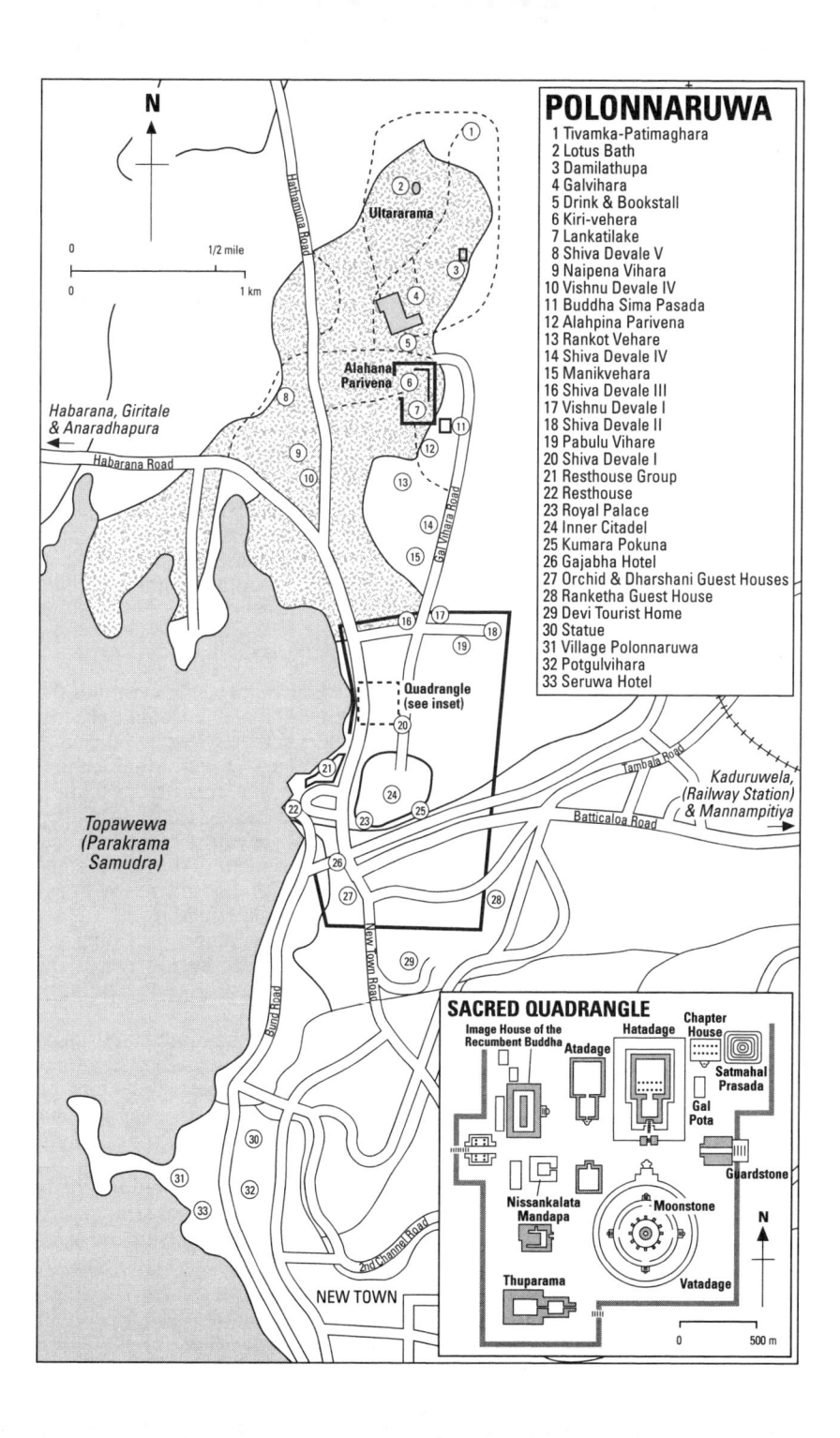

POLONNARUWA

1. Tivamka-Patimaghara
2. Lotus Bath
3. Damilathupa
4. Galvihara
5. Drink & Bookstall
6. Kiri-vehera
7. Lankatilake
8. Shiva Devale V
9. Naipena Vihara
10. Vishnu Devale IV
11. Buddha Sima Pasada
12. Alahpina Parivena
13. Rankot Vehare
14. Shiva Devale IV
15. Manikvehara
16. Shiva Devale III
17. Vishnu Devale I
18. Shiva Devale II
19. Pabulu Vihare
20. Shiva Devale I
21. Resthouse Group
22. Resthouse
23. Royal Palace
24. Inner Citadel
25. Kumara Pokuna
26. Gajabha Hotel
27. Orchid & Dharshani Guest Houses
28. Ranketha Guest House
29. Devi Tourist Home
30. Statue
31. Village Polonnaruwa
32. Potgulvihara
33. Seruwa Hotel

SACRED QUADRANGLE

- Image House of the Recumbent Buddha
- Atadage
- Hatadage
- Chapter House
- Satmahal Prasada
- Gal Pota
- Guardstone
- Nissankalata Mandapa
- Moonstone
- Thuparama
- Vatadage

large stone lion with inscriptions on either side, a fine piece of work but suffering the erosion to which this stone is prone. This replaces the throne in the form of a lion which is now in Colombo Museum. According to the chronicles the heir to the throne, the kings ministers, army commanders, regional governors, and so on stood in a rigid pecking order. The names of some are recorded in the inscriptions on the pillars.

A **pleasure pavilion** stands on a small island. It is completely overgrown, but a few pillars stick up.

Another small **pavilion** stands in the lake just south of the Rest House. A new **Archaeological Museum** is being built beside the road.

THE ANCIENT CITY

The main **ruins of Polonnaruwa***** are the other side of the main road, and one can walk through the Rest House group to the entrance. North of the entrance part of the outer wall of the city runs between the road and the lake. The whole area of the Citadel and monasteries is forested and a peaceful haven for wildlife. A lot of clearance and landscaping work has been done in recent years, enhancing the pleasure of wandering around the imposing and beautiful reminders of a glorious past.

The Inner Citadel

The Citadel is a fortified area close to the lake which marked the centre of the old city. Within this is a smaller (10ha/25 acre) inner citadel. Turning right just after the check point you pass a tall inscribed stone, and then through the main gate of the inner citadel, which contains the **Palace of Parakramabahu I** (1153-1186), the Vejayanta Pasada. The central keep is a large brick building, parts of the walls still standing two storeys high and having traces of plaster and painting. The holes in the walls were for floor beams, and the vertical grooves up to first floor level for stone reinforcement. Above that the brickwork gets thinner, and varying reports speak of two or seven upper storeys of wood. In front of this was an audience hall. Surrounding all this are the tiny rooms typical of an eastern palace. Other buildings, providing the palace infrastructure, extended on all sides and enclosed the courtyard. The inside and outside would have been plastered all over and brightly painted, a bit hard to imagine now.

You cross the large palace courtyard to the other main building, the **Council Chamber** of the same king. The stone base of this has a frieze of elephants in a variety of poses. The steps have two sets of moonstones and elephant makaras. The next level has friezes of lions and then dwarves. The forty columns are supported by dwarves and are finely carved.

The **Kumara Pokuna** or Royal Bath is the other side of the city wall from the Council Chamber. The water arrived through a pair of gargoyles either side of the steps. This is always called the Royal Bath, but it does seem strange that it should be so far from the residential part of the palace, and outside the walls. Beside it is a pavilion on two levels. This presumably had a light roof, the socket holes for supports can be seen.

A grey stone temple stands a little outside the gate of the Inner Citadel. The **Shiva Devale I** dates from the Pandya occupation of the early 13th century. Construction is entirely of finely cut stone in South Indian style; all the

Buddhist buildings, by contrast, are of brick or a combination of brick and stone. Looking closely you can see how the tight fit of the stones was achieved by bevelling the stone away from the mating lines; a similar technique to that used in Central and South America. The bottom halves of two guardian figures stand by the doorway, and in the shrine is a rather battered yoni-lingam. Bronze images from the interior are now in Colombo Museum. Around the back of the shrine is a couple of long-bearded figures, possibly Agni, the fire god from before the development of Shiva and Vishnu. This temple is popularly known as Dalada Maligawa from its supposed temporary use as a home for the Tooth relic. It is possible that this temple was never finished; a lot of stones have lumps on them, presumably to help with handling, and which would have been chiselled off later.

The Sacred Quadrangle

The **Thuparama** is not a dagoba as the thupa would suggest, but an image house. This is a brick building with tremendously thick walls. The outside has friezes, pilasters, and niches done in moulded brick and plastered, and now very eroded. The roofs of the front and central chambers have collapsed (a little of the latter remains to show the method of construction), but the shrine has a unique vaulted dome and tower. The brick base in the shrine was for a large Buddha seated in the meditation pose. He faced east and small windows provided indirect light. The inner doorway is much higher than the outer one so that you could see his face from the threshold and make obeisance. The other images in the shrine were brought here from where they were found in the jungle; most are made of quartzitic limestone which glitters in candlelight. Exit was through a doorway in the right of the nave (which shows how thick the walls are); one could not turn one's back on Buddha, and this reduced the distance to walk backwards. This building is older than the others, probably dating from the reign of Vijayabahu I (1055-1110).

The **Bodhighara**, whatever it was, is of no interest.

The **Nissankalatamandapa** 'in which he listened to the chanting of protective religious texts' is surrounded by a three bar Buddhist railing similar to that used for many stupas. Eight unique and sinuously beautiful pillars take the form of lotus stems and have capitals of lotus flowers. One wonders if the pillars were inspired by the 'thrice-bent' posture of some Buddhist statues. A small dagoba stands in the middle of the plinth.

In the **Image House of the Recumbent Buddha** you can just about make out in a wavy line of bricks the shape of the Buddha and his pillow.

The **Atadage** was the Tooth Relic Shrine of Vijayabahu I. This was a multi-storeyed building. The rough pillars would have been reinforcement buried in the brick walls, whilst the well finished ones were free standing inside the temple.

The **Hatadage** was the Tooth Relic Shrine of Nissankamalla. A lot of confusion surrounds the popular names for these two shrines; they translate literally 'house of eight' and 'house of sixty'. The former is said to relate to the number of relics kept there, and the latter to the number of days it took to build, but there seems little to back up either theory.

This building was of composite brick and stone construction; the upper level, presumably of brick, was less durable than the stone. As with the present arrangement in Kandy, the Tooth Relic was kept on the upper floor. On the outside geese are incised in the stones, and a frieze runs around the top. There are long inscriptions on the right of both the outer and inner entrances. Note the moonstone and two Hindu figures shaded by snakes. In the first hall, fronting the steps are three inscribed slabs which somebody went to a lot of trouble to break up. The tooth relic shrine was a pillared hall, the stone lining neatly fitted in a rather random fashion. Note how the Buddha statue here lines up with one in the Vatadage which is framed by the doorways.

From the Hatadage one crosses to the **Vatadage** which is the best preserved monument at Polonnaruwa. An inscription to the effect that it was erected by Nissanka Malla is likely to be untrue, being more probably the work of his predecessor Parakramabahu I. The superb moonstones have no bulls as by this time Hindu influence had made them too holy to be stepped on. Guardstones are both sentinels and auspicious symbols; these are mature forms and very Indian in style. The main figure is a nagaraja (snake king) shaded by a seven headed cobra. He has a punkalasa (cornucopia) in one hand and a branch in the other. The two dwarfs at his feet are Padma with the lotus and Shankar with the conch shell, attendants of Kubera, the god of wealth. Dwarves on the risers support the steps. The outer terrace has holes for three concentric rings of pillars; fragments of pillars and their capitals lie on the terrace. The stone balustrade around the relic chamber is of four petalled temple flowers, and there are lotuses on the moulding below.

Four stone doorways, aligned to the cardinal points, lead into the interior, that on the west having the flowers done in better detail. The vahalkadas facing out of the doorways are unusual for their smooth heads. The circular wall is of tiny and rather irregular bricks, once plastered over. Many of the paving stones have a chaitya symbol. In the centre is a brick dagoba which would have housed the relic. Two circles of octagonal pillars stood around the dagoba; together with the outer rings and the walls they would have supported a wooden roof.

This is a very pleasant place to sit in the shade and relax for a while before continuing the tour. From the outside the combination of brick and stone puts one in mind of the Albert Hall.

Beside the Hatadage is the **Gal Pota** (Stone Book), a huge slab of rock 8m by 1.8m (26ft by 6ft) weighing 25 tonnes. On each end elephants shower Lakshmi, and a continuous row of geese runs right round the edge. On the upper face is the longest rock inscription in Sri Lanka. The twenty-four lines are largely a puff for the boastful Nissanka Malla, and also tell how the stone was brought the 96km/60 miles from Mihintale by elephants using wooden rollers. The stones at Stonehenge are bigger and came much further, and they didn't have elephants!

Behind that a shrine called the **Chapter House** has a single lotus stem pillar.

The **Satmahal Prasada** is a seven storeyed relic house (*sat* = seven + *mahal* = palace or temple) possibly influenced by Far Eastern architecture, but not dissimilar to Indian towers.

Going down the steps for a cold drink, glance back at the unusual guardstone.

More dagobas and temples

The **Pabulu Vihara** (Coral Shrine) is a brick dagoba, the third largest at

Polonnaruwa, still with fragments of the cement facing. Shrines surround the dagoba. Not very interesting but in a nice woodland setting.

The track continues to the 11th century **Shiva Devale II**. This is the oldest building at Polonnaruwa which can be dated definitely (from its Tamil inscriptions), and dates from a time of Chola dominance. It is stone built in the South Indian Thanjavur (Tanjore) style. As usual for a Shiva temple Nandi the bull sits in front. The remaining part of the roof in the hall shows the massive pieces of stone used. In the shrine is a plain lingam in a square yoni.

It is worth having a look at the northern gate of the Citadel and its complex of guardrooms. The walls have a wide step inside the parapet, which was once much higher, and there is a moat outside. These were serious fortifications.

The gate out of the citadel is flanked by two Hindu temples. The **Vishnu Devale I** on the right, with its statue, dates from the 12th century. On the other side is the **Shiva Devale III** which still has a yoni and lingam at its base. It is conjectured that the Hindu shrines in the citadel were used by royalty as an adjunct to their Buddhist worship. Many of those outside were used for purely Hindu worship by people of lower rank.

The **Manikvehara** is a monastery most of which dates from the eighth century. The main elements are the stupa, the stone base of which has a frieze of cheerful lions, an image house, and a Bodhi tree all located on a sacred terrace. The buildings and cells north of the terrace may well have been a hospital, a pair of forceps was found when the site was excavated. This monastery, though, is of no great interest if time is short. The four pillars nearby belong to a small building having an inscription of Nissanka Malla.

Another Hindu temple, the brick **Shiva Devale IV**, stands beside the road.

The Alahana Parivena

The next buildings are all part of a large monastic university, the Alahana Parivena (Monastery of the Burning Ghat), built by Parakramabahu I. The name derives from the location near the royal cremation ground. Many of the small stupas scattered around will have held relics of the royal family, others those of prominent monks. The whole complex covers 80ha/198 acres, and some years ago only a fraction of it had been fully excavated. Much of the site was concealed by a thick layer of debris and overgrown by jungle. This has now been cleared with UNESCO aid, and the layout is much plainer. Interesting artefacts were also found.

The **Rankot Vehera** has a huge stupa (55m/180ft in diameter and 61m/200ft high) built, according to an inscription, by Nissanka Malla in the Anuradhapura style. Unlike some this stupa is not all brick; the centre and outer shell are, and the space between is filled with earth. Surrounding it are chapels with statues of Buddha. The chapels at the cardinal points have no entrances. A broad avenue leads to the north and the next places described, you can use this or return to the road.

From the road the path passes a large bathing tank for the monks, and then heads between two small stupas to the large one.

The **Kirivehera** (White Shrine) was possibly built by one of Parakramabahu's wives, Queen Subhadra. The stupa derives its name from the outer coating of lime plaster. It appears, almost uniquely, to have kept its original shape despite several restorations over the years. It is, in fact, an architectural throwback as vahalkadas make a reappearance on it after a gap of hundreds of years.

The **Lankatilaka*** (Glory of Lanka) was the main image house of the monastery. A brick structure, 52m/170ft by 20m/66ft, it was built by Parakramabahu I. The now headless Buddha inside (once 14m/45ft high) was designed as an integral part of the building and uses just the same materials; it symbolises the move away from the abstract dagoba to the use of images of the Buddha. The roof has gone, but the walls are 17m/56ft high.

By the entrance steps are guard stones similar to those of the Vatadage. Behind are complicated makaras composed of elephants, crocodiles, and other beasts. The pilasters of the entrance arch are finely fluted and plastered, on the left one is the remains of a large Hindu figure. The great height of the entrance, once arched, was necessitated by the need to see the Buddha's head from the threshold. Of the pillars in the side aisles only one is at full height, and its capital indicates the position of the first floor. There is an ambulatory behind the Buddha so that one can circle it as one would a stupa. In the ceiling of the side exit are remains of the painting which once covered most of the building. The stucco relief on the outside of this north wall gives us an idea of how these buildings looked when complete.

This truly magnificent building is contemporary with the great cathedrals of Europe, and its soaring accentuation of the vertical symbolises the same reaching for heaven.

Facing the Lankatilaka is a matching multi-pillared mandapa, perhaps a music hall.

The third main element of the Alahana Parivena, with the Lankatilaka and the Kirivehera, was the **Buddha Sima Pasada**, the chapter house. This is a large and complex building which now appears as a square pillared hall surrounded by a quadrangle of monks' cells. The hall is raised above the courtyard, and all four entrances have moonstones, that in the west entrance is especially good. In the centre is a raised platform, and around it a hall with a multiplicity of well finished pillars, then there are cells, and finally the outer walls of very substantial brickwork. The thickness suggests that it was designed to support several upper storeys of brick, and probably wooden ones above that. We have no way of knowing just how high the building was, but the chronicles tell of similar buildings with up to twelve storeys. Clearly it was very impressive indeed.

The central hall was a meeting place for the monks. It was customary for the monks to meet on every new and full moon day to recite the code of conduct and then confess their transgressions. This process was led by the abbot and other senior clerics from the central dais. It is assumed that the floors above provided accommodation.

The courtyard would have been a colourful and lively scene. Buddhist monks were taught to declaim their teachings loudly as they strode up and down. The courtyard is surrounded by cloistered monks' cells; these were commonly of two storeys, and may well have been here. Whilst simple the living accommodation was well thought out. Adjoining a smaller chapter house behind the Kirivehera and Lankatilaka can be seen the bath and toilet arrangements.

Admire the view from the eastern exit of the Buddha Sima Pasada, then descend the steps and follow a narrow path to the **Gopala Pabbata**. This is a rock from which four caves have been cut, one having five Buddha images hewn from the solid rock. Another has a Brahmi inscription showing that monks were using this site in the fifth century AD.

The scale of the Alahana Parivana is staggering, everywhere you look there are more remains, shrines, stupas, and tanks. Returning now to the road, the cluster of buildings by the tank provides refreshments, and there is also a bookshop with Cultural Triangle publications. The tank shows on a small scale how the earth bunds of the Dry Zone reservoirs were built.

The Galvihara

A short walk from the eastern bank of the tank is the **Gal Vihara** (Stone Shrine), also known as the Kalugal Vihara or Black Stone Shrine. Three huge figures carved from one piece of gneiss represent Buddha sitting, standing, and reclining. To the left a 5m/16ft high Buddha meditates on a lotus throne. Behind him are triple toranas and a halo of flames. The turrets above the toranas probably show how the tops of the buildings here would have looked. They resemble the rathas of Mahabalipuram in Tamil Nadu which have survived because they are carved from solid stone. This statue, unfortunately, now has a gruesome shelter over it. A smaller image of the meditating Buddha sits in a cave between this and the next large statue.

The standing figure, identified in the past as the monk Ananda (note the staff), is the finest of the three. The position of the arms is very unusual and the whole composition looks back to Greek influence.

The reclining Buddha is a truly beautiful work, note especially the details of the head and pillow and the chakras on the feet. This was once thought to represent the death of Buddha with the disciple Ananda in attendance. It is now thought that the three figures represent Buddha's life: the seated figure in meditation, the standing figure bringing the message of enlightenment, and the recumbent figure representing Mahaparinirvana, the death of Buddha and hence the end of his mission.

These statues indicate the appearance of their contemporaries, such as that in the Lankatilaka, which were done in brick and plaster. Holes in the rock for timbers, and the foundations in front, suggest that each of the statues had its own enclosure. Excavation also revealed the site of a monks' refectory. There is a good view from the nearby rock. These statues are a magnificent piece of work, enhanced by the grain of the rock. There is no doubt that, as a work of art, they are far more pleasing as they are than when enclosed and separated. The indentations in your rock grandstand show where slabs have been split off. The twigs you see under the two large boulders (and elsewhere) are apparently a little joke - they hold the rocks up.

The Outer Garden

The last three groups of buildings are known as the Uttararama, the outer garden, as they were the last main buildings at Polonnaruwa. The Galvihara is actually part of this monastery. The monastery is also known as the Jethavanarama. This alternative name derives from the Jethavana monastery at Sravasti (present day Saheth-Maheth near the Nepalese border in the Indian state of Uttar Pradesh) where Buddha is said to have lived and preached for twenty-five years. This is no great distance from his birthplace at Lumbini.

The **Damilathupa** (or Damala Maha Seya) was constructed by Tamil (Damala) prisoners of war under the direction of Parakramabahu I who had defeated a Pandya army. The intention was that this should be the largest stupa at Polonnaruwa. A retaining wall 200m/656ft in diameter was built around a natural hillock. The space between the two was filled with rubble, but the indications are that it never reached its full intended height. At some later date, when deterioration and plants again made it look like a natural hill, a small dagoba was built on top. Excavation work is going on here.

The **Lotus Bath** is 7.6m/25ft in diameter and takes the form of a lotus, the five steps representing the five rows each of eight petals. Fed by an underground channel, it may have been a ritual bath for use before entering the Tivanka Pilimage. There are believed to many more similar baths scattered around the monasteries.

The **Tivamka-patimaghara** (or Tivanka Pilimage) is the main image house of the Uttararama. It follows the same general pattern as the Lankatilaka but is far better preserved. The roof and upper walls had collapsed, and when the wreckage was cleared in 1866 beautiful frescoes were found. Extensive restoration is now taking place, the whole image chamber having been rebuilt.

The usual guard figures and makaras stand at the entrance. This was a three storeyed building, pillars in the first hall defining the position of first floor. The magnificent frescoes, in the style of Sigiriya and the Indian cave temples at Ajanta, depict the Jataka tales (stories of Buddha's life) and his previous incarnations. It is the intention to restore the huge Buddha image which is in the thrice-bent (tivamka) position. Again there is an ambulatory behind the image. Steps in the thickness of the wall lead up to an outside ambulatory where small windows look on to the Buddha's head. These steps are very narrow, forcing you to go up sideways and thus not turn your back to Buddha. Good views from the top including the dagoba at Dimbulagala. In the side exit doorway is an illustration of the image house complete.

The exterior was also painted in a decorative rather than a narrative fashion, but little trace of this remains. There is some lovely detailing, however, especially behind the image chamber where the dwarves are at their genial liveliest. One old guide book refers coyly to a 'yoni being fertilised by a bee' but it eluded me.

A lot of people fail to see the Tivamka-patimaghara simply because it is so far out. It ranks, however, with the Galvihara and the Lankatilaka as one of Polonnaruwa's outstanding monuments. Unmissable and getting even better as restoration proceeds.

Odds and ends

The **Naipena Vihara** is a misnomer as this is actually a Vishnu temple. Naipena means cobra hood, images of Vishnu frequently depict him shaded from the sun by a seven-hooded cobra. Huge chunks of bonded brick, suggesting the scale of the structure, lie by the shrine. Many fine bronze statues were found when this site was cleared. Whilst the Shiva temple next door is still used for worship the only likely activity here is a game of coarse cricket.

The **Shiva Devale** is, like the Naipena Vihara, of limited interest. Over the road is yet another Shiva Devale, stone this time, and ditto.

To the south, and between the main road and the lake, are two more buildings. **Priti Danaka Mandapa** means 'the reception chamber which brings joy', perhaps because asylum could be claimed here. The **Minneri Dewala** is a Buddhist temple despite its Hindu name, but both are hard to find and of little interest.

The offices used to be the **Museum** which is at present defunct.

Practical Information

Shopping. A large and lively market takes place around the post office area on Tuesdays.

Local transport. The ruins are very spread out, and for the northern part at least some kind of transport is essential. We found it best to do the citadel area on foot in the morning and then hire a bike (Rs75-100) or a three-wheeler (Rs300-350) to see the rest. A man at the entrance hires out bicycles, he asks Rs150 and has to be beaten down; several guest houses also have them for hire from Rs75 upwards.

Arrival and departure. Bus from Kandy (4hrs), Dambulla (2½hrs), Habarana, or Anuradhapura (3hrs). All buses arriving in Polonnaruwa pass through the old town, where the ruins and accommodation are, before going to the new town and Kaduruwela. When leaving there is better chance of a seat in Kaduruwela than when the bus reaches the old town.

The train station at Kaduruwela, 4km from the old town and ruins, is currently the terminus of the Batticaloa line. At present two trains a day serve Polonnaruwa, but only the most dedicated rail enthusiast would bother. It takes 7½hrs to get to Colombo with a change at Gal Oya, or 10hrs to Anuradhapura with changes at Gal Oya and Maho Junction. Mind you, there are worse ways of spending a day.

Accommodation

Accommodation (STD Code 027)

Seruwa Hotel (CHC). Tel 2411. SWB/DWB A/C $23. Rest. Bar. Standard Rest House menu, breakfast Rs150, dinner $8. Overlooks lake. Swimming pool (Rs100 to non-residents).

The Village Polonnaruwa. Tel 541 198. Fax 541 199. SWB A/C $12 DWB A/C $15 (all incl.). Rest. Bar. Set dinner menu which changes every day Rs360incl. A la carte average prices. Bar area round a central garden, a good place for a drink for non-residents. Swimming pool (free to non-residents who buy a meal or drink). This and the Seruwa are in the same compound opposite the southern group of monuments, 1.5km down the tank bund from the Rest House.

Rest House. Tel 2299 or 01-503 497 (Colombo). DWB $23. Rest. Bar. Great location on the lakeside, the dining room actually built out over the lake, you could fish while having breakfast. The terrace is a great place for a cold beer or a pot of tea, and a swim. Pleasant old-fashioned rooms with new bathrooms. Super staff, food not up to the usual standard.

Gajabha Hotel. Tel 2394. DWB $7/10/12. Rest. Bar. Pleasant garden. Breakfast Rs120, main courses Rs150. Very good food, open to non-residents.

Ranketha Guest House. Tel 2080. DWB $8. Clean rooms. Breakfast Rs175, curry and rice with chicken Rs200.

Devi Tourist Home. Tel 3189. SWB Rs350 DWB $5. Rest. Free pick-up from bus stand, it is a 15-20 minute walk into town. You could not meet a nicer family. Bicycle hire Rs75 per day.

Darshani Guest House. SWB $3 DWB $5. Rest. Basic clean rooms. Breakfast Rs100, Curry and rice Rs175.

Samudra Guest House. DWB $4. Rest. Basic clean rooms with nets and fan. Breakfast Rs80, rice and curry Rs75. International phone calls. Hires bikes at Rs75 per day.

Orchid Guest House. Tel 3720. DWB $3. Rest. Basic clean rooms. Breakfast Rs75, curry and rice Rs100.

Further Afield

DIMBULAGALA

Dimbulagala is a hill in the jungle 534m/1752ft high. One of the odder features of colonialism is the way that natural features were named after some fancied resemblance to a familiar object. This hill was known as Gunner's Quoin, presumably because someone thought it looked like the wedge used to elevate a cannon. A Buddhist monastery stands at the foot of the hill, and a dagoba on a crag high above.

The monastery's new temple has two fine wooden images at the upper level, one of Buddha with his hand raised in blessing, the other of Maitreya. The capitals of the pillars comprise four lions, the emblem of the Emperor Ashoka (and of the state of India). Behind is a complex of cave temples with colourful tableaux, the most vivid of Buddha's temptation by demons led by a blue multi-armed Mara on his elephant. The portrait and statue are of the leader of the community who was killed by terrorists. Towards the lower dagoba is a Hindu shrine with, in its four niches, images of Ganesh, Kataragama, Vishnu, and Shiva.

The walk up to the hilltop dagoba is pleasantly shady (when in doubt follow the line of lamp standards), but will give you a whole new perspective on sweating. At the top the octagonal shrine has a huge footprint of Buddha watched over by Saman and an elephant holding a lotus flower. Pilgrims throw coins on the foot; that and the grid design rather irreverently reminds one of a roulette table. You can clamber down from in front of the main dagoba to a cleft in the rock with a figure identified by its trident as Shiva. In the basement of the dagoba is a large wheel of life with hell at the bottom (note the devil with his big black book) and heaven at the top, and the various stages in between. The central rosette shows the progression from school through meditation to being a monk and then total renunciation of the world. Up in the dagoba are a large bell and, above that, images of Buddha and Maitreya.

A further hour's walk from the summit dagoba leads to a bathing pool fed by hot springs, you would need a three-wheeler driver prepared to act as guide. Further round the base of the hill are numerous rock hermitages and, off the road back to Mannampitiya, an archaeological site. The area from Gunners Quoin to Kokagala, west of Mahaveli, was inhabited by Veddhas.

Frankly, only the views justify this excursion, and you can get equally good ones much more easily.

Mannampitiya is a Tamil village which produces baskets and cane furniture.

Arrival and departure. 25km from Polonnaruwa. A three-wheeler costs Rs400-500 for the round trip; the road is in fair condition but subject to delays at checkpoints. Bus to Mannampitiya on the main A11 south-east from Polonnaruwa, then change for Dimbulagala which is 10km away. The road skirts the hill, and you get off at a T-junction with a couple of cool drinks stalls. A very early start is advisable if bussing.

MEDIRIGIRIYA

The vatadage in the remains of **Medirigiriya monastery**** is one of the finest of its kind. Its peaceful rural surroundings make it well worth a visit.

Park under a bo-tree and walk up past a lotus pond with good bird life to the first building which is an image house enshrining three standing Buddhas and two seated ones. In front of them is a huge stone altar slab for flower offerings.

Another image house next door has the brick foundation of a large reclining Buddha. In front is a stone medicine bath like a sarcophagus.

The vatadage, a circular image house, was built around a small and very old (probably pre-Christian era) dagoba towards the end of the seventh century AD by King Agbo IV. The approach is by a flight of steps to a square landing at the same level as the vatadage. This is separate from the round platform of the vatadage to symbolise the transition from earthly life to nirvana. You will have noticed how most stupas are built on a square base; here the same transformation from a square or rectangular form to a circular one is achieved in a different way. Urns on pillars flank the bridge.

Outside the vatadage is a broad stone pavement, a missing section of this showing an earlier brick structure. A three-railed balustrade cut in low relief and set on a lotus border surrounds the shrine, the main brick structure of which has disappeared. The octagonal pillars set in this balustrade have lions on their capitals. The traditional four entrances have a seated Buddha facing out of each, reminiscent in a way of the watchful eyes on Nepalese stupas. Another two rings of pillars have dwarves on the capitals, makes a change from them being at the bottom.

The rock opposite has another stupa (and a good view of the vatadage). Facing the vatadage is a finely finished stone platform. The gateway leads to a small bathing tank, a cave, and the scant remains of the monastery which once supported these shrines.

Medirigiriya is a popular place of pilgrimage at poya time but otherwise totally quiet and very beautiful, but it will now cost you $8.

Arrival and departure. 30km north of Polonnaruwa. This is an hour's drive by taxi, a scenic pastoral run but very potholey. This journey is difficult by bus. The vatadage is 3km out of town, and three-wheelers wait at the bus stop.

Eating and Drinking. Cold drinks available in Medirigiriya village, but you would need to bring a picnic, and a lovely place for one.

POLONNARUWA TO ANURADHAPURA

Unless the security position has improved, making it possible to visit Batticaloa and the east coast, it is now necessary to backtrack via Habarana. You have a choice between the short road route to Anuradhapura or the slower and very circuitous railway. In either case there is scope for interesting detours off the beaten track.

RITIGALA STRICT NATURAL RESERVE

This reserve is centered on the 766m/2512ft Ritigala-kanda (Ritigala Peak). This most attractive looking hill has its own micro-climate, being much cooler and having a better rainfall than the surrounding plains. This makes it a happy hunting ground for the botanist. Wild orchids grow in profusion, and there are other species unique to Sri Lanka and even to this hill.

This is also an interesting place historically. Ritigala is the Aritthagiri of the Ramayana; when Hanuman discovered where Sita was being held captive he jumped from here to India to tell Rama. There are numerous archaeological remains: a number of monasteries, one dating from the second century BC, a large bathing tank for the monks, and the remains of their scattered austere cells. All very beautiful and rarely visited.

The British actually planned to take advantage of the healthy location by building a sanatorium here; luckily nothing came of the plans, and Ritigala is left unspoiled for the hill-walker, botanist, and archaeologist.

Information. The monastic remains are described in great detail in *Ritigala* (Rs37) available from the office of the Central Cultural Fund, 212 Bauddhaloka MW, Colombo 7.

Arrival and departure. Track (8km/5miles) from the village of Galapitagala, near the 8mile or 13km marker from Habarana on the main road to Anuradhapura, frequent buses pass.

KALAWEWA

This large tank (the name means Black Water) was first built by Dhatusena (455-473). This was a major undertaking, the bund being 10km/6miles long and 15m/50ft high. It was restored by Parakramabahu I in the 12th century and again by the British in the 19th century, though the water level is now less high. The tank harnesses two rivers and covers 18sq km/7sq miles. Later restoration of the Yoda Ela canal means that the Kalawewa again fulfils its purpose of supplying water to Anuradhapura, 86km/54miles away, and many villages along the way. This canal was an outstanding feat of engineering for its time; over the first 30km the fall in level is less than 1cm per kilometre. From the top of the bund, travelling south from Kalawewa town and just past the first sluice, you can glimpse over the trees to the right the head of the Aukana statue and its dagoba.

AUKANA

Here is a 12m/39ft high **statue of Buddha*****, probably the finest in Sri Lanka. Approaching the statue note the guardstone with nagaraja, the snake king, on it. This statue, unlike the reliefs at at Buduruvagala, is carved in the round. A legend relating to its carving is told in the description of the Sasseruwa statue below. The statue faces east, and is at its best at sunrise as its name, which means sun-eating, might suggest.

For years there was controversy over its date, with estimates ranging from the fifth to twelfth centuries AD. Stylistically some of the detailing, notably the eyes and lips, suggest a date around the ninth century, but the profile, 'barrel-like stomach', and disproportionate arms and neck belong to two centuries earlier. The matter was finally settled in 1952 by the discovery of an inscription dating it beyond much doubt to the eighth century AD. The sirispata, the hand-like (or sometimes flame-like) shape on the head which represents rays emanating from Buddha, does not belong to the statue and was put there in the 19th century. This was one of the causes of confusion over the date, as the sirispata came into fashion only in the mid-fifth century.

Another odd thing is that this statue is usually described as being in abhaya mudra, a pose in which the outward facing palm signifies fearlessness. Yet, looking at the statue, one clearly sees the right hand sideways in asisa mudra, the blessing position.

The image house presumably once extended as far as the foundation walls. The new brick shelter, believed to resemble the original in profile, dates from 1976. At the time of writing there are concerns about the shelter collapsing and damaging the statue. Apparently it was built with inferior bricks and, because no one bothered to remove trees growing on it, it is suffering severe water penetration. Various departments are wrangling about how to take it down and who will pay. It can only be an improvement.

Information. *The Avukana Buddha* (Rs60) by Chandra Wikramagamage is available at the site.

Arrival and departure. Occasional direct bus from Dambulla (30km), otherwise change in Kekirawa (20km) (also a bus from Habarana to here), on the main road from Dambulla to Anuradhapura. Failing that get off at the end of the Kalawewa bund and walk 2½km. Station at Kalawewa (5km from statue), and also a railway halt near the statue, though only slow trains stop.

SASSERUWA

Here is another 12m high **Buddha statue*** more or less contemporary with that at Aukana, though uncompleted. The statue was the centre of a scattered community of forest hermits, and is in abhaya mudra. Despite inferior artistry this statue is somehow friendlier, even more religious, than that at Aukana. The setting is peaceful and beautiful.

Two legends are told of this statue. The first is that when the visible cracks appeared the king gave up and started again at Aukana, which is why this is not quite finished. The second story is that the king set two masons, one the master and the other his apprentice, to work at the same time on the two statues. As the master neared completion of the Aukana statue, the apprentice was dismayed how much better it was than his effort here and gave up. You will note, for instance, how the folds of the robe are just grooves rather than in relief as at Aukana.

Returning down the steps, a path to the right leads to a **cave temple** with some attractive unrestored wall and ceiling paintings. You should be able to recognize the themes by now. Note how termites have attacked the plaster under the paint. In a second cave behind this is a large reclining Buddha. Following the ambulatory behind it you can see how the whole figure is covered with a layer of cloth and then the folds of the robe added. In a small cave beside this, more Hindu than Buddhist, an old monk tells fortunes. Note the benchmark in one of the steps.

Arrival and departure. 11km west of Aukana, mostly on unmade country roads; the signs say Reswehera rather than Sasseruwa. Very, very occasional bus.

Accommodation. The family at the house across the tank from the statue will provide space on their floor overnight. Take your own food, and tip them Rs100-200 in the morning.

YAPAHUWA

Between 1273 and 1285 Yapahuwa was the capital of the kings of Sri Lanka whilst the Tamils held Polonnaruwa. As a fallback capital this was a comparatively modest affair, though in strength the fortifications almost matched those of Sigiriya, a sign of the times. By this time the Tooth Relic had become a symbol of sovereignty, and a fine temple was built for it in the palace precinct. The Tamils plundered Yapahuwa (the Good Mountain) in 1285 and captured the Tooth, Parakramabahu III only getting it back from India by becoming a vassal of the Pandya kings.

The entrance to Yapahuwa is through a double wall and moat. Inside a flight of very steep decorated steps leads up to an **ornate porch***. These steps are an interesting mixture of influences. The pair of lions which stand guard have a very Chinese look, and the staircase has been likened to those on the Khmer pyramids of Cambodia, monuments themselves Indian influenced. Around the base of the temple, you need to detour to see it properly, is a frieze depicting a procession - dancers, musicians, acrobats, and women with fly whisks. In the facade of the entrance, above the window openings, are carvings of Gajalakshmi being showered by two elephants, between makara-toranas, this Hindu imagery is symbolic of Buddhist tolerance. This building shows Dravidian influence, but what was it? Nobody knows for sure; it may have been the Dalada Maligawa, shrine for the Tooth Relic, or it may just have been an upper part of the palace.

And the porch, in truth, is all there is to see. No more than the foundations of the building itself survive. It is possible to climb the rock from here and, in the opinion of some people, the view is better than that from Sigiriya.

The royal palace area is at the foot of the steps. Directly in front is the audience hall, but again only the foundations of this and the palace itself remain. The museum (closed Saturday) has one of the pierced stone windows from the porch of the building at the top of the steps but is otherwise hopeless. A cave temple has modern paintings on all the usual themes.

Yapahuwa is an easy detour off the Colombo-Anuradhapura road if you have your own transport; whether it is worth the effort on public transport is doubtful.

Arrival and departure. On the main road from Anuradhapura (70km) to Kurunegala (51km). 4km east of Maho Junction station; it has its own halt, but few trains stop.

Accommodation. Archaeological Department Circuit House. Looks a very nice place to stay and absolutely peaceful.

ANURADHAPURA

This is a town of ancient foundation. Ptolemy, the Greek geographer (AD 90-168), mentions Anouragrammon, but Anuradhapura was already old if we are to believe the date of 440BC quoted by the Mahavamsa. The same source says that the town was founded by the Vijaya dynasty. The fact that the same kings founded Lanka as a Sinhalese state gave it a powerful symbolism. The name probably derives from the star Anuradha which represents a divinity of light. This figure was analogous to the Indo-Aryan Mithra, the Roman Mithras, and the Hindu Mitra, the latter a Vedic god ruling over the daylight hours. This is the start of a fascinating red herring trail through bull worship to the modern Russian word *mir* meaning peace. Alternatively, and far simpler, Anuraddha was a disciple of Buddha who was present at his death and memorised part of his teaching.

Anuradhapura's closeness to southern India meant that from its earliest days it was fought over by the Sinhalese and a variety of Tamil invaders. Despite this there were long periods of stability and prosperity when prodigious building works were undertaken. This was indeed a large and wealthy city, it being said that 1000 men were employed just to maintain and clean the streets.

Anuradhapura was a living city until around 1200, though the kings had finally moved their seat to Polonnaruwa in 993.

Anuradhapura's lifeblood

As told in the story of the conflict between Kassapa and his father (see Sigiriya) water is true wealth in this dry area. In fact, the whole northern civilisation depended on irrigation, and Anuradhapura is surrounded by the tanks which supplied its lifeblood. The **Basavak Kulam** and **Bulan Kulam**, at the heart of the monastery area, are thought to be as old as the city. The **Tissa Wewa**, to their south, is the work of King Devanampiya Tissa (250-210BC). The far larger (1200ha/3000 acres) **Nuwara Wewa** to the West is later, perhaps second century AD. The way in which Anuradhapura's water was supplied from the Kalawewa 86km/54 miles away is described on p218.

The collapse of the irrigation system led eventually to the total abandonment of Anuradhapura. Even in the Dry Zone things grow fast, and the once grand city disappeared under jungle. The work of clearing the ruins began as early as 1840 when the government rather grudgingly voted £40 for the purpose. More recently a lot of continuing assistance from UNESCO has seen really worthwhile renovation work taking place

Southern dagobas and monasteries

The **Mirisavati Dagoba** dates from around 100BC. After King Dutthugamani had thrashed the Tamil King Elara he celebrated by disporting himself (with, it's said, his harem) in the Tissa Wewa. Here he stuck in the ground his lucky spear which contained holy relics. Later it was found impossible to move the spear, so the king built this dagoba to enshrine the relics. It was in its time the largest of its kind, over 60m/200ft high. Its present form, smaller than the original, stems from restoration by Kassapa V, one of the last kings of Anuradhapura, in the 10th century AD. A statue of Dutthugamani stands in the modern chapel. The dagoba has been rebuilt recently by the Buddhist Society. Numerous remains of the associated monastery stand all around, the refectory notable for the food trough which held a thousand helpings, but this is not the most exciting of dagobas.

The name implies that the **Tissa Wewa** tank was built by King Devanampiya Tissa (250-210BC), but there was probably already a smaller tank here when he started work. The water now comes from the Kalawewa, over 80km/50 miles away, a remarkable achievement described on p000. The 210ha/450 acres tank provided water for the city and for irrigation, as it still does. Piped water systems were in use in Sri Lanka by the first century AD.

South from the Tissawewa Rest House runs the **King's Pleasure Garden**, with the remains of sundry pavilions, tanks, and the irrigation arrangements. The one thing of real note is the frieze of elephants at play in a lotus pond, a rare secular sculpture.

King Tissa founded a monastery, the Issaramana (place for ascetics), on the banks of his tank. The name has been corrupted over the years, and one of the few parts remaining is the **Isurumuniya Gala****. This rock-cut temple is probably the oldest extant Buddhist temple in Sri Lanka. The steps up and the platform have been reconstructed from various bits and pieces excavated on the site. The main image of a seated Buddha meditating is much later than the cave, probably ninth or tenth century.

Looking over the side of the platform you see a very strange figure of a seated man with his horse peering over his shoulder. This is a Pallava work of the seventh or eighth century representing Aiyanar, a South Indian god who protects villagers; the god is in a nonchalant pose called 'kingly ease' (*maharajajahlila*). Aiyanar is associated with elephants, and they appear below him, that on the right of the cleft having a very jolly expression. And you can amuse yourself trying to lob a coin into the niche above him. In the tank below are shoals of fish. The cleft in the rock and the sculptures are reminiscent of the great carving at Mahabalipuram in southern India and, indeed, belong to the same school and period.

Behind the rock a path and steps lead up to the bund of the Tissa Wewa. On the back of the rock itself are two dripstones, presumably to protect long-vanished murals or monk's shelters. You can climb the rock to see two Buddha's footprints (and more on a slab), and you get a view of the Tissa Wewa.

The modern temple has a large reclining Buddha and murals depicting the development of Buddhism in Sri Lanka. The famous sculpture of the 'Isurumuniya lovers' is in the small **Archaeological Museum****. It is not known who is depicted in this lovely work; legend claims it is Saliya, King Dutthagamani's son, who gave up the throne for his commoner lover Ashokamala. Whilst most probably of Sri Lankan origin it is in the North Indian Gupta style of the sixth century AD. Behind the museum is a modern monastery.

The **Vessagiriya** (Mountain of Wisdom), which was part of the Issaramana, is a huge rock-cut monastery which was once home to 500 monks. Most of the

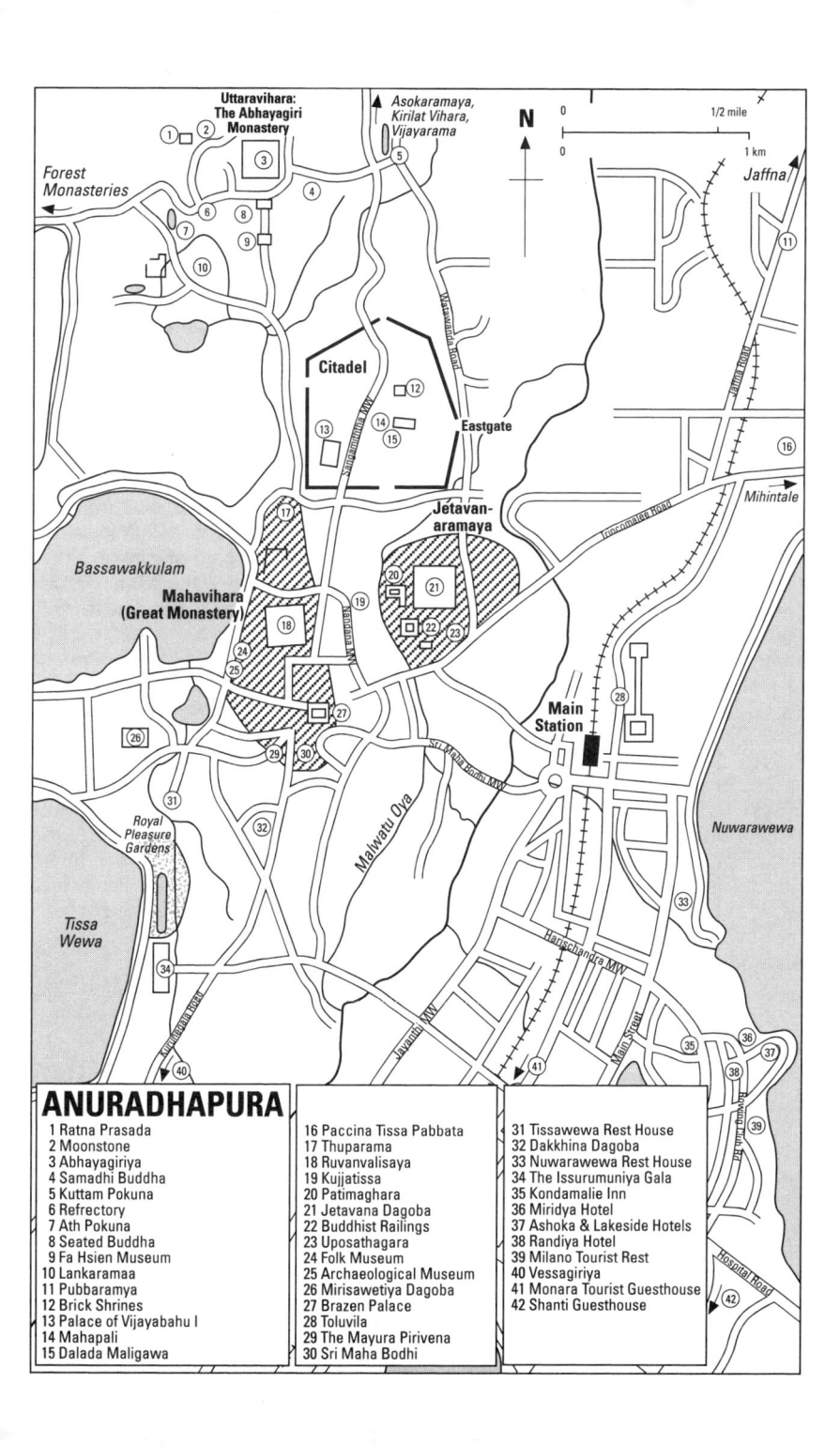

ANURADHAPURA

1 Ratna Prasada
2 Moonstone
3 Abhayagiriya
4 Samadhi Buddha
5 Kuttam Pokuna
6 Refectory
7 Ath Pokuna
8 Seated Buddha
9 Fa Hsien Museum
10 Lankaramaa
11 Pubbaramya
12 Brick Shrines
13 Palace of Vijayabahu I
14 Mahapali
15 Dalada Maligawa
16 Paccina Tissa Pabbata
17 Thuparama
18 Ruvanvalisaya
19 Kujjatissa
20 Patimaghara
21 Jetavana Dagoba
22 Buddhist Railings
23 Uposathagara
24 Folk Museum
25 Archaeological Museum
26 Mirisawetiya Dagoba
27 Brazen Palace
28 Toluvila
29 The Mayura Pirivena
30 Sri Maha Bodhi
31 Tissawewa Rest House
32 Dakkhina Dagoba
33 Nuwarawewa Rest House
34 The Issurumuniya Gala
35 Kondamalie Inn
36 Miridya Hotel
37 Ashoka & Lakeside Hotels
38 Randiya Hotel
39 Milano Tourist Rest
40 Vessagiriya
41 Monara Tourist Guesthouse
42 Shanti Guesthouse

massive trimmed stones have been taken for later buildings, and there is little to see.

The **Dakkhina Dagoba** stands over the cremation place of King Dutthagamani (161-137BC). His ashes, which were found inside, are now in the Museum. It was built fifty years or so after his death and considerably enlarged a century or so later. The carved column in front is one of a pair that stood in front of each of the four vahalkadas at the cardinal points and represents a tree of life. This dagoba was thought at one time, for no obvious reason, to be a monument to Elara, the Tamil usurper who captured Anuradhapura in 145BC and was defeated in single combat by Dutthagamani. Elara fulfilled the Buddhist concept of a just king who ruled (for forty years) by spiritual force rather than armed might. Dutthagamani gave him an honourable funeral, but not this dagoba.

Mahavihara

The **Basawakkulam** tank is one of the earliest irrigation works in Sri Lanka, at least 2400 years old. The royal palace and pleasure gardens on its banks were turned by King Devanampiya Tissa into a monastery to guard and revere the sacred Bodhi Tree. Pilgrims still bathe in the tank. In time the Mahavihara became the leading monastery of Sri Lanka and the staunchest supporter of Therevada, the true path.

Sri Maha Bodhi***. This bo or Bodhi (Enlightenment) tree, actually a pipal or Indian fig, was grown from a cutting of the tree in Bodhgaya (in northern India) under which Buddha achieved enlightenment. The cutting was brought here by the Emperor Ashoka's sister Sanghamitta in the third century BC. Strictly speaking it wasn't a cutting as that would have been sacrilege, so they had to rely on a miracle to remove a branch.

When the parent tree was destroyed in the seventh century by a king of Bengal who was a Shiva fanatic seeds were taken from here back to Bodhgaya. By contrast, South Indian invaders revered the tree as much as the local Buddhists. Most of the Bodhi trees in South-East Asia have grown from the seeds of this tree. The walled enclosure was built in the 18th century to protect the tree from elephants. For a long time this was the only part of Anuradhapura not concealed by thick jungle.

The tree is said to be the oldest documented tree in the world. It is the responsibility of the Minister of Agriculture, and the guardians trace their descent from those appointed by King Tissa. After all the other beautiful bo-trees this is a bit of an anticlimax. The original tree, as distinct from the ones around it which have grown from its roots, is a rather straggly affair supported by an iron frame. It is completely inaccessible on a platform 3m/10ft above the public terrace and surrounded by a modern gold railing.

This is, nevertheless, the holiest place in Sri Lanka and always busy with pilgrims. Having generally avoided attacks on holy places, the Tamil Tigers showed their true Marxist colours when they were responsible for the massacre of 146 pilgrims here in May 1985.

The **Mayura Pirivena** (Peacock Palace) is actually a fourth century monastery for senior clerics. It is marked only by a few columns bearing friezes of dwarves.

The **Archaeological Museum**** (0800-1700 except public holidays) has a lot of good stuff. Most notable are the lavatory stones decorated with representations of the rich and comfortable monasteries that ascetics could thus literally pee and crap on. Really worth seeing is the model of a vatadage complete with its wooden roof, the only way to visualise how these circular image houses looked in their heyday. The Cultural Triangle ticket office is here.

The **Folk Museum** (0900-1700 except public holidays) covers local life.

These museums, and the Fa Hsien, are all sited in the Sacred Area of controlled entry. This means that if they are closed (as for a public holiday) when you visit the monuments you cannot visit them the following day without paying again.

The **Loha Pasada*** (Brazen Palace) was never really a palace at all; it began life in the third century BC as a meeting place for the monks who tended the Bo-tree. Two centuries later King Dutthagamani rebuilt it as a nine-storeyed residence for the same monks; it took its popular name from the copper plates used for its roof. In the centre was an empty ivory throne, symbolic of Buddha in the days before images of him. The throne was inlaid with gems and a gold sun, perhaps an inspiration for the royal throne of Kandy now in Colombo Museum. The Mahavamsa gives us a good description of this building, but it burnt down only fifteen years after completion, the upper floors being of wood. All that remains today are the 1600 pillars of the ground floor, and many of these do not belong to the original building, the result of restoration by Parakramabahu I in the 12th century.

Dutthagamani also began the **Ruvanvalisaya*** in 144BC to commemorate his victory over Elara and the Tamils. The site had been chosen by Mahinda and marked by a column of King Tissa a hundred years before. Dutthagamani laid the foundation bricks himself, but the dagoba was still unfinished when he fell seriously ill. His brother Saddhatissa, who was to succeed him, created a mock-up of bamboo and cloth that Dutthagamani could glimpse from his sickbed and thus die contented. He then continued the work, finishing it in 137BC.

The stupa contained the largest collection of Buddha's remains, and this makes it still the most revered of all the dagobas in Sri Lanka. Dutthagamani had commissioned a bo-tree with a silver trunk, gold leaves, and gems and coral for fruit and also a golden Buddha on a solid gold throne for the relic chamber. The conical top, representing an umbrella, was surmounted by a ruby as big as a man's fist. The monument was the first to be built in the water bubble shape, but the profile has changed over the years assuming its present form during restoration early in the 20th century. At the same time the ruby (long since plundered) was replaced by a large rock crystal from Burma. The dagoba is surrounded by a stone terrace supported by an elephant wall, appropriate as much of the heavy construction was done by elephants. The diameter at the base is 80m/262ft and the height 53m/174ft. The statue on the terrace is definitely that of a king, and it is nice to think that it may be Dutthagamani.

The **Thuparama**** was the first dagoba in Sri Lanka, hence its name which means simply 'the stupa'. Having converted King Tissa to Buddhism, Mahinda complained that they had nothing as a focus for their worship. So a monk was sent to the Emperor Ashoka who gave them one of Buddha's shoulder blades and his alms bowl. The bowl went to Mihintale, and a 'heap of paddy' shaped dagoba was built here for the bone, making it a very holy place. The dagoba was rebuilt as a vatadage in the seventh century, and then completely rebuilt again in a bell shape in the 19th century. How much, if any, of the original structure remains is unclear. The triple row of pillars is a relic of the vatadage stage, having supported its conical roof.

The **Kujjatissa Pabbata** stands between the Thuparama and the Jetavana Monastery in an attractive woodland setting. The present structure is a brick dagoba of the eighth century. Legend has it that Dutthagamani buried the ashes of his respected enemy Elara here.

The Jetavanaramaya

It is tempting to think of Buddhism as a calm reflective religion in which adherents simply get on with the quest for enlightenment and truth. In fact, like every other religion it is, and always has been, riven by dissent. Nor is this simply a difference between Hinayana (or Therevada) and Mahayana; Therevada itself has at least three major sects. A large number of dedicated individuals in a hierarchical organisation can easily become politicised, and the power thus developed was a factor kings had to consider. Sri Lanka has always been a stronghold of Therevada Buddhism, but there were times when kings found it expedient to create a Mahayana counterbalance. The Jetavanaramaya (Jetavana Monastery) was founded by King Mahasena (274-301AD) for precisely such reasons. Concurrently the Mahavihara monastery was pillaged (the land for the Jethavana was taken from its gardens) and its monks dispersed.

As with the Jetavana monastery in Polonnaruwa the name comes from the monastery founded by Buddha himself at Sravasti (modern Saheth-Maheth near Lucknow in northern India), and where he lived and taught for twenty-five years.

The **Jetavana Dagoba***** was built by Mahasena as the centre of his new monastery. In the circumstances it is not surprising that he should set out to build something really impressive. The dagoba was originally 120m/400ft high overall, on a diameter of 100m/327ft. When it was built it was the highest brick structure in the world, and surpassed in volume only by two of the pyramids in Egypt. Nor is what you see the whole story, the brick foundations go down 8½m/28ft in places to support the massive weight, as revealed by recent excavation.

The monks of the Mahavihara did not take the appropriation of their garden without a fight, and actually hid in tunnels under the building site to delay work, a technique used by present-day road protesters in Britain.

The dagoba is set in the usual square sand court oriented to the cardinal points, and the terrace has a high retaining wall once decorated all the way round with elephants. Straight in front from the main entrance (in the east) you can see different layers of brick. The lower and outer is the latest; above that, with string courses, is an earlier layer. Also here is a standing stone with the figure of a king shaded by a five-headed cobra. On top, the square section is done in imitation of the fence around a grave; above that is a cylinder, the stem of the tapering series of umbrellas.

Look back as you leave the dagoba. It is big. One of those little calculations beloved of Victorian guide books tells how it contained enough bricks (not far short of 100,000,000) to build a wall 10ft (3m) high from London to Edinburgh (a good 640km/400 miles).

The dagoba is now being conserved, as opposed to rebuilt, as part of a

UNESCO programme. This includes work in the future on outlying buildings of the Jetavana Monastery, worth having a snuffle round.

The monastery has two other outstanding buildings. The first was the **Patimaghara**, or image house, to the west of the dagoba. The image house of a monastery ranks with the Bo-tree in sanctity, second only to the dagoba. Little of the image house remains above ground, but the 8m/26ft high door posts give an idea of its scale. There are conflicting ideas about the Buddha image; the usual thing would be for it to be made in brick and plaster. Here, however, limestone may have been used, there being evidence of its having been destroyed by fire. This may have been simply for the purpose of destruction or to produce cement. Either way the size of the lotus pedestal suggests that the statue was around 12m/39ft high.

The Bo-tree site here is not known for certain, but it may have been in what is called the **Buddhist railing site***, to the south of the dagoba. This is an area 43m by 34m enclosed by a three-railed stone fence on top of a stone plinth. Actually, these Buddhist fences always are three-railed because they represent the Three Gems of Buddhism (Triratna): Buddha himself, his teachings, and the Samgha or order of monks. The building inside was enlarged by stages, and the multiple pillars indicate that it was multi-storeyed.

A short distance from here is the **Uposathaghara**, the Chapter House which was also the place where the monks recited the rules of the order and made their confessions. The details are essentially the same as for the Chapter House in Polonnaruwa.

The Citadel

Dividing the southern monasteries from the northern ones is the citadel of the secular city. This area, 1.6km/1mile by 1.2km/¾ mile, was surrounded by a moat and strong wall, the latter 5m/16ft thick and probably at least as high. Archaeological evidence, at a depth of up to 9m/30ft, shows that this site was inhabited at least as far back as 500BC.

The road north from the Ruvanveli Dagoba, Sanghamitta MW, cuts through the southern wall of the citadel, though missing the gate, and passes between the palace and its gatehouse. The **Palace of Vijayabahu I** was a late attempt to keep Anuradhapura alive as a royal city, being built after Vijayabahu had defeated the Cholas in 1070. By this time, however, most of Anuradhapura was a sacked, burned, and depopulated ruin. Vijayabahu continued to rule from Polonnaruwa, so this palace was really just a royal outpost rather than a seat of government. The two usual guard stones at the entrance are of high quality, and there are traces of the frescoes which once richly decorated the walls, but little of real interest. It is assumed that the remains of earlier palaces lie under this one.

The **Mahapali** is an alms hall which functioned as both a canteen and stores depot for the monks. Such buildings were stocked by a tithe of produce brought into the city; this was collected at the city gates and also provided part of the king's income. In the alms hall the rice went into the large stone trough where any monk could fill his begging bowl. A sixth century king had donated a bronze rice boat, but this was melted down by a later king to pay his soldiers. The large **step-well** nearby provided drinking water.

The Tooth Relic, one of Buddha's teeth, was brought to Sri Lanka from Kalinga (modern-day Orissa on the east coast of India) in 313AD for safekeeping as a resurgent militant Hinduism started to threaten Buddhism there. The remains of its temple, the **Dalada Maligawa** are authenticated by an inscription. This temple dates from the fourth century AD, and it seems probable that it was the first in the succession of Tooth Relic Temples in Sri Lanka. The pillars suggest that this was a building of at least two stories, and the assumption is that, as in Kandy where the Tooth Relic is now enshrined, it was kept on the upper level. The Tooth used to be taken from here in procession to the Abhayagiri for public exhibition, and one can think of this as the origin of the modern Perahera.

North of the Mahapali and Dalada Maligawa is a pair of **brick shrines**, maybe sixth century AD, of similar design. One of these is one of the very few buildings at Anuradhapura still to stand above ground level. It thus gives us some slight idea of what the other buildings may have looked like.

The road north from the Jetavana Dagoba, Watawandana Road, passes the **East Gate** of the citadel. This has been excavated recently, and displays the strength of the fortifications. You can visit this as you return from the northern monasteries.

Uttaravihara

Uttaravihara means Northern Monastery, and this was the largest of the five major viharas. Before Buddhism became preeminent in Sri Lanka there was a Jain monastery here. The Jains are a religious group, virtually unknown outside India, who have had a curiously parallel existence with Buddhism. Jainism was founded at much the same time and in much the same place as Buddhism, and has very similar iconography. Both began as ascetic monastic orders only later acquiring the trappings of religions. There is even conjecture that Mahavira, the founder of Jainism, and Buddha met.

One of the Jain monks made the mistake of blowing a raspberry at King Vattagamani Abhaya as he fled the Tamil invaders of Anuradhapura. When Vattagamani regained his kingdom fourteen years later he dealt condignly with the monk and replaced the Jain monastery with a Buddhist one. Vattagamani spent part of his wilderness years at the Rawana Ella Temple (see p175).

The five thousand monks of the Abhayagiri saw themselves as Therevada, but Mahayana and Tantric Buddhism were both taught there. This caused the strictly orthodox monks of the Mahavihara, who were, after all, the people who wrote the history, to describe them as heretics.

The **Abhayagiri***** (Abhaya's mountain or Mountain of safety) is a dagoba which takes its name from the king who founded the monastery and giri, a rock or hillock. At least two stories are told to explain the dagoba. One of Vattagamani Abhaya's queens was too ill to take flight during the Tamil invasion and stayed here rather than slow down the rest of the royal family. And, one guesses, came to a sticky end. Fa Hsien, on the other hand, says that when Buddha planted his footprint on Adam's Peak his other foot was here.

The dagoba is the second largest in the world, being 107m/351ft in diameter and 75m/246ft high, though it is thought at one time to have been well over 100m high. It was first built by King Gajabahu I (114-136), enlarged in the fourth century AD, and last restored by Parakramabahu I in the 12th century.

At the southern entrance the guardian figures, attendants of Kubera, have become shrines in their own right. A pair of urns, symbolising plenty and prosperity, stand on either side at the top of the steps. These lead down to a large square enclosure, and then up to the broad stone circular pavement. The southern half of this has been restored with an inner ring of white limestone. The western vahalkada and a strip of brickwork have also been restored recently. There is an unusual moonstone here, and a lovely bo-tree stands nearby. The northern gateway has been restored, but the vahalkada is still in a jigsaw puzzle state. The circular altar has a lotus in the centre, and lying here are parts of a large octagonal column from the top of the dagoba.

By the road is a seated **Buddha figure**, badly weathered. This is not to be confused with the Samadhi Buddha, but would have been equally attractive. Dating from the seventh century, it is in the vitakka posture, an early stage in meditation.

The **Refectory*** has one of the largest rice troughs. Monks were obliged to eat before midday, and preparing and serving this amount of food must have been quite a task. Five thousand monks, the trough is said to hold enough for 5,800, had to help themselves from here; the smaller trough is presumably for vegetable curry. A stone sundial kept track of time, and saw to it that stragglers went hungry.

As in many religions, ritual bathing is important in Buddhism. Five thousand monks, the population of the Abhayagiriya alone, needed a large supply of water. Hence the **Ath Pokuna** (Elephant Pond) which, despite its name and size (equivalent to six Olympic swimming pools), certainly was not for elephants. Conduits, at least one of which still works, brought water from nearby tanks; the cistern out-take in the south-western corner supplied water to smaller bathing tanks. Since it also supplied the refectory it is debatable whether it was itself a bathing tank. The walls are designed to minimise the erosive effects of wavelets.

The **Lankarama** (Garden of Lanka) is a vatadage dagoba marking the place where King Vattagamini Abhaya (alias Walagambha, 103 & 89-77BC) escaped from the five Tamil princes invading his capital. He built this in gratitude after his restoration. Three rings of pillars supported the conical roof. This was probably the centre of its own monastery, rather than being part of the Abhayagiriya.

The **Fa Hsien Museum*** is named after the Chinese monk (c338-c422) who visited India and Sri Lanka in search of holy texts. His account of this fifteen year trip, he had to walk over the Himalayas, provides much of our knowledge of early Buddhism. Built by the Chinese, this is very informative.

The ruins of the **Ratna Prasada*** (Gem Palace) have been referred to as Elephant Stables or the Queen's Palace. It was in fact the main chapter house of the Abhayagiri monastery, having been built by King Mahinda II in the eighth century. This was a multi-storeyed building constructed, like so many others, on the foundations of a much older one. The real reason for coming here is to see the guardstone, reckoned the best in Sri Lanka. This follows the usual form of a nagaraja carrying lotus flowers and a flowering branch, symbols of peace and prosperity. Peace could be elusive, however. The Ratna Prasada was a place of sanctuary, and some of the king's ministers, in dispute with him, had taken shelter here. The king's bodyguard broke in and killed them, only to be followed by an angry mob who scaled the high walls and dealt summarily with them in their turn.

Moonstones are a common feature on the threshold of religious buildings in Sri Lanka and unique to this country. Probably the best of all can be seen in the remains of an **image house*****, a building sometimes inaccurately referred to as Mahasena's Palace or the Queen's Pavilion. This building dates from the eighth or ninth century, and stands on older foundations. The approach is between two side chapels. The moonstone as a whole represents the progress from samsara, the cycle of death and rebirth, to nirvana, the escape from that cycle. The outer ring is the flames of desire. Conquering that you have a ring of animals representing the four sorrows of birth, disease, old age, and death. The next ring is of vines and leaves meaning a clinging to life. The bar-headed geese are Hamsa which symbolise the unity at the heart of all creation; they have another significance in that, like Buddha, they leave home and security to travel great distances. After a scroll comes the lotus, the symbol of escaping ignorance and achieving enlightenment, the way to nirvana. The lotus also represents Buddha as it forms his throne. Although well preserved and beautifully carved, the animals lack variation compared with other stones. Behind the moonstone, which is usually covered by an ugly guard, characterful dwarves support the steps. The guardian figures and makaras have gone, but the two attendants of Kuvera and a pair of lions stand at the top of the steps.

The **Samadhi Buddha**** is a third or fourth century AD statue representing Buddha in a state of deep meditation (samadhi) after achieving enlightenment. This statue, and the three battered companions behind, would have been placed under a Bodhi-tree facing the cardinal points. The statue is weathered, but obviously was very beautiful. Traces indicate that it was painted, and it may have had gems for eyes. It is not enhanced by the ugly modern canopy, and the railing is not much better.

The **Kuttam Pokuna***** (Twin bath) of the eighth century was for the monks' ritual ablutions. Built on solid rock, these are stepped tanks allowing use at different water levels. Urns, pots of plenty, flank the flights of steps. The construction is of well finished stone throughout, so this is one of the very few things at Anuradhapura you see in its original form. At the far end of the smaller pond is the supply system. Water is fed into the central settling tank to trap sediment, then over a lip into an outer tank, and finally through a lion-headed gargoyle into the tank. Beside this is a superb naga, or snake, stone. Frogs and terrapins inhabit the tanks. The *kuttam* bit is the same Tamil word, implying together, as appears in catamaran, a couple of tree trunks (*maram*) lashed together.

The western monasteries

These were forest monasteries built near the city's cremation grounds (as inauspicious to Buddhists as to Hindus), and used by groups of ascetic monks. All Buddhist monks make a vow of poverty, but these pamsa-kullikas (cemetery robes) took things a stage further, making their clothes from scraps of cloth taken from corpses.

The plainness of these monasteries was intended to match the ascetic inspiration of the inmates, but they were, nevertheless, built on a large and expensive scale. The interior layout is of double meditation pavilions surrounded by a cooling moat. The other notable feature is the urinal stones.

And elsewhere

There are several other monasteries to the north and east of the Abhayagiri. They were much smaller, for up to five hundred monks, and, following the same Mahayana sect (plus a bit of Tantrism), probably tributary to the Abhayagiri. They all follow the same pattern, with the now familiar four major elements (dagoba, bo-tree, image house, and chapter house) on a raised platform.

The huge **Nuwarawewa** tank grew to its present size over the centuries, the work of many kings. It is 7km/4½miles across and up to 12m/39ft deep. It is fed from the even larger Nachcheduwa tank and the Kalawewa (see p218).

The **Pubbaramaya** follows the plan mentioned above. Note how the monks' accommodation is arranged symmetrically around the platform, but that the main buildings appear misaligned. They were actually carefully sited according to an esoteric tantric formula. The monastery is surrounded by a moat and has a hot water bathhouse outside this to the south. The Pubbaramaya is located just off the main Jaffna road.

The **Paccina-Tissa Pabbata Vihara** stands between the Nuwarawewa and Pulliyankulam tanks by the Mihintale road. It was founded by King Jettatissa I (263-273), who was famous for his skill as an ivory carver, and follows the usual pattern. One of the earliest of its kind, it is not well preserved.

The **Toluvila** is the ruins of another monastery near the station.

North of the Twin Ponds of the Abhayagiri are three more monasteries, **Asokaramaya**, **Kiribat Vihara**, and **Vijayarama**. These three places are more for peace and quiet than any religious or archaeological interest.

Anuradhapura can seem a little disappointing after Polonnaruwa and Sigiriya. With the sole exception of the huge dagobas everything is similar to Polonnaruwa but less well preserved and less attractively sited. Anuradhapura is a long way out and, unless you are determined to see everything, time is better spent at Dambulla, Sigiriya, and Polonnaruwa.

Festivals. Snana piya at Sri Maha Bodhi in April. Poson poya, the June full moon, is a huge celebration of the bringing of Buddhism to Sri Lanka.

Practical Information

Information. *Anuradhapura* (Rs70) is available from the Central Cultural Fund office at 212 Bauddhalokha MW, Colombo 7. Passes from there or from the ticket office at the Archaeological Museum in Anuradhapura.

Arrival and departure. Bus to Kandy (A/C 3hrs, ordinary 4hrs), Polonnaruwa (3hrs), Colombo (5hrs). Train from Colombo (6hrs), also Kandy changing at Polgahawela. Wait for the main station, not Anuradhapura New Town.

Local transport. The remains are very spread out, and a bicycle is the best way of getting around. Most hotels arrange hire at about Rs125 per day. Shuttle bus between two bus-stands.

Accommodation (STD Code 025).
Miridiya Hotel, Rowing Club Road. Tel/Fax 22112. DWB A/C $24/29 +20%. Rest. Bar. Lunch/dinner buffet Rs300 incl. Main courses Rs200, omelettes Rs90, soup Rs50. Beautiful garden runs down to lake. Swimming pool open to non-residents.

Nuwarawewa Rest House, Rest House Road. Tel 22565 Fax 22112. SWB/DWB A/C $37.50. Rest. Bar. Nice gardens and good staff, but lacks character of the Tissawewa Rest House. Swimming pool.
Tissawewa Rest House. Tel 22299 Fax 23265. SWB/DWB $27.50 SWB/DWB A/C $35. Rest. No bar as it is in the holy area. Old building of great character with nice gardens and verandah. Perfectly located in the heart of the ancient city. Guests can use the pool at the Nuwarawewa Rest House.
Randiya Hotel, Rowing Club Road. Tel/Fax 22868. SWB $11 DWB $14 + $3 for A/C. Rest. Bar. Most attractive place, rooms in cottagey style. Nice garden. Curry and rice Rs100. A la carte starters Rs90, main courses Rs175. All +20%.
Ashoka Hotel, down road beside Miridiya. Tel 22753. DWB $10. Rest. Bar. Plain rooms of a good size, clean but could do with a little work. Some have balconies overlooking lake. Breakfast Rs225, lunch/dinner RS345-410, beer Rs124 all plus 18%.
Milano Tourist Rest, 596/40 JR Jaya MW. Tel 22364. Rest. Bar. A pleasant place to stay, but beware of flexible pricing. Proper rate should be $5-7 for the smaller rooms and $7-8 for the larger rooms. If they try to charge more there are plenty more nice places.
Kondhamalie Hotel, 42/388 Harischandra MW. Tel 22029. DWB $8. Rest. Bar. Breakfast Rs90. Omelettes Rs50, rice and curry Rs190, western dishes Rs225 all +10%. New block spotless and complete with Laura Ashley curtains.
Lakeside/Lake View, past Ashoka. Tel 23111. DWB $7. Rest. Appears very scruffy, and you would need a periscope to see the lake.
Shanthi Guest House, 891 Mailagas Junction. Tel 22515. DWB $5 with net. Rest. Breakfast Rs125, rice and curry lunch or dinner Rs75-100, all +10%. Bicycles Rs100 per day.
Monara Tourist Guest House, 63 Freeman Mawatha. Tel 23043. SWB/DWB $4. Rest. Needs a lick of paint but quite acceptable.

Eating and Drinking.
Nothing much except two Chinese. *Swan*, 310/1 Harishchandra Mawatha and *Nanking*, also Harischandra Marg. Note that the food at the *Miridiya Hotel* is very reasonable.

Excursions

Induarane

This is a Buddhist meditation centre where a banyan tree has been trained into a beautiful arbour. Benches are placed inside for meditation. The monkeys obviously reckon it has been done to make a climbing frame for them. In a shed at one corner, at the end of a meditation path, is a timely reminder of mortality, symbolising the path through life to death. All are welcome here the only cost being a contribution towards the monks' food.
Arrival and departure. On the main road between Anuradhapura and Mihintale.

MIHINTALE

Mihintale, previously Mahindatale (Mahinda's Hill), is one of the holiest places in Sri Lanka as the various memorials commemorate the meeting of King Tissa and the Buddhist monk Mahinda in 243BC, the event which led to Buddhism taking root in Sri Lanka.

Mahinda was one of the missionaries sent out by his brother the Emperor Ashoka of India. Along with his sister and four monks he landed here after a miraculous journey from India. After conversion the king gave him the Mahavihara site at Anuradhapura for his monastery, but Mihintale always remained a place of pilgrimage.

The legend is that Tissa was hunting in the forests below Mihintale when he saw a stag feeding. Thinking it unfair to shoot it like that he put it to flight and then followed. The stag fled up the hill, and Tissa pursued it to the top where he heard someone calling his name. There stood Mahinda and his followers.

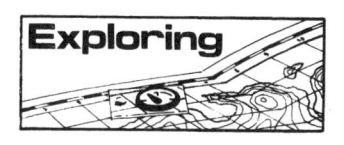

Exploring

Around town

Walking from the roundabout towards the hill a row of **modern statues** on the right commemorates the pioneers of Buddhism in Sri Lanka. Behind them is a pleasant small park. One then passes through a mango grove planted in the last century.

The **museum** is, unfortunately, all too typical of Sri Lankan museums, lacking in both imagination and information. In the entrance is a reconstructed relic chamber from a dagoba and several stone reliquaries of different kinds. Other finds, which had eluded the tomb robbers, include crystal items and a lovely little set of the four animals found on moonstones. Note the photographs of relic chamber paintings with a very Gauguinesque look.

As in medieval Europe hospitals were connected to religious establishments, and the devout gained merit by financing them. The **hospital** here was founded by King Sena II (853-857). The ruins take the form of cloistered cells around a courtyard with a shrine of some kind in the centre. In one corner is a carved stone medicine bath. The adjoining courtyard has several rooms, one with a large stone bath and another a stone mortar.

To the left at the foot of the steps are the remains of a quincunx **vihara**. Entry to the walled enclosure is through a gatehouse. The five shrines have some guardstones and makaras, but are worth only a very quick glance.

The holy hill

The impressive flights of broad steps up the **holy hill***** were restored in the 19th century. There is a total of 1850 to the top. One climbs under a canopy of frangipani trees to the first platform, from where steps to the right lead to the **Kantakacetiya**, a dagoba dating to before Christian era. The circumference is 130m and the height originally about 30m, the brick once covered by a thick layer of lime plaster. The dagoba was damaged first by treasure hunters and then by the jungle but still has its four vahalkadas at the cardinal points. These have some fine carvings, each devoted to one of the four moonstone animals.

Off to the left from another platform a little higher an indistinct path leads

MIHINTALE

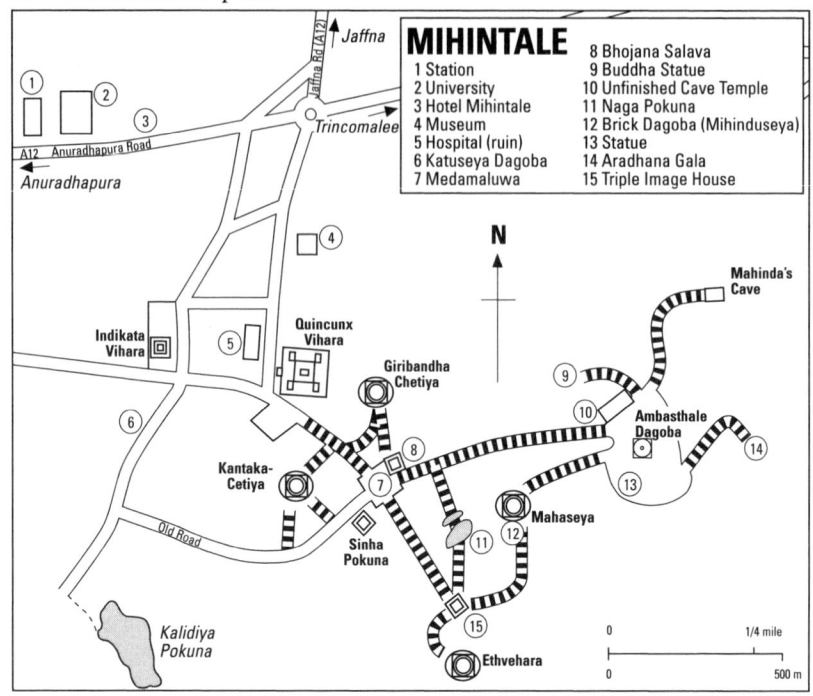

1 Station
2 University
3 Hotel Mihintale
4 Museum
5 Hospital (ruin)
6 Katuseya Dagoba
7 Medamaluwa
8 Bhojana Salava
9 Buddha Statue
10 Unfinished Cave Temple
11 Naga Pokuna
12 Brick Dagoba (Mihinduseya)
13 Statue
14 Aradhana Gala
15 Triple Image House

to the remains of the **Giribandha Chetiya** and **Kiri Vihara**. This path forms an alternative route to the Medamaluwa, but the ruins are of very limited interest.

At the top of the next flight a gatehouse leads into a large walled compound, the **Medamaluwa**, which was the major monastery. The walls are a rubble core with a thin facade of well fitted stone. Turning right from the entrance is a good view of the Kantakacetiya, probably as much as you need to see of it. To the left of the entrance is the **Bhojana Salava**, the monks' refectory, the various buildings around a central courtyard. The smaller of the two stone troughs for the monks' food has corrugations in the bottom and a flat surface at one end for grinding spices; grooves allowed them to be washed into the trough. The larger trough is huge and beautifully hollowed inside, a bit like a dug-out canoe. Water supply and drainage arrangements are visible, including part of an overhead aqueduct which brought water from the Naga Pokuna.

Next to the refectory take the steps up between two small dagobas to the **Dhatage** or relic house. The two stone tablets over 2m high were placed here by King Mahinda IV (975-991). These lay down the rules of the house and a daily routine for the monks. At the back of the enclosure is the chapter house, a meeting place for the monks, its roof supported by 64 pillars. Returning from the summit we sat under one of the magnificent trees here. One of the guides raced over to warn us that a cobra had been seen there the previous day. We moved. There is road access to the Medamaluwa level for the idle.

The steps continue past a large rock inscription much eroded to the **Ambastala Maluwa**, the level where the famous meeting took place. Shoes off and pay the Rs50 entry fee here. The place where Mahinda and Tissa actually met is marked by a bell-shaped dagoba, the Selacetiya or **Ambasthala** (mango tree). First built in the first century BC the original shape has been lost in subsequent enlargement and restoration. The pillars for a wooden roof are in the style of the seventh century AD. The brass-railed enclosure on the south side and its footprint mark where Mahinda stood. A statue opposite (with its head detached) is said to be of King Tissa, but is more likely a boddhisattva.

The large white Buddha statue above was bought by pilgrims' donations and completed in 1986. Below this a cave temple was roughed out in perhaps the twelfth century but curtailed by war, which is unfortunate as it would have been most unusual. Cave temples hollowed out of solid rock are common enough in India; in Sri Lanka the normal technique is to build a wall beneath an overhang. The smaller Buddhas come from Thailand.

The clamber up to the **Aradhana Gala**, Mahinda's point of arrival, is well worth it for the views. Take care, the steps and rails are slippery in morning dew. Less rewarding is the rough path a long way down to Mahinda's cave and his stone couch.

Unless you plan to go straight down again pick up (but do not wear) your shoes for the climb to the summit. The **Mahaseya**, the Great Dagoba, was built to house the ashes and a lock of the Buddha's hair which Mahinda brought with him. This was completely rebuilt in the 1960s. In the modern temple the reclining Buddha is propped up on one elbow rather than the usual pillow and, for some reason, the right foot is longer than the left. The view is tremendous.

Beside the Mahaseya are the remains of the **Mahinda Seya**, a dagoba enshrining relics of Mahinda. This was recovered from its own debris and the jungle only in 1949. Various relics and other items were found inside. The altars at the cardinal points have the Buddha's footprints.

From here a reasonably distinct path leads down to a **triple image house**. A flight of steps, guarded by a pair of elephants, leads up to the **Eth Vehara** (Elephant Monastery). This really is quite a climb, but the views from the small dagoba at the summit are stunning, notably of the dagobas at Anuradhapura. At 309m/1014ft above sea level this a good deal higher than Mihintale hill itself, and you have an aerial view of all the monuments there.

Having returned to the triple image house, the path ahead leads straight down to the Medamaluwa. To the right of that steps go up to the **Naga Pokuna**, a largely natural pool guarded by a five-headed cobra. The old story of King Tissa bathing here is probably bunk, and it is even less likely that the small pool was for the queen. The Naga Pokuna was a reservoir for the monastery, and the small pool a settling tank. The drain hole of this is inhabited by a large real snake. The path continues to rejoin the main steps down the hill.

Below the Medamaluwa is the **Sinha Pokuna**, or Lion Bath. The frieze includes the usual lions, elephants, and dwarves and, more unusually wrestlers, this having been a national sport. The spout looks like a sea-lion.

Other attractions

One can continue down this road, noting the rock on the right with a line of holes, the first step in splitting off a slab. Turn left at the bottom and walk 250m along the road.

The **Kaludiya Pokuna***, Bath of Black Water, is a lovely quiet place. A monastery was constructed on the banks of this natural looking tank in the tenth century AD. This would be a perfect place for a picnic brunch after climbing the hill. Under a large rock is a refined cave dwelling complete with windows and door; many of the monks' hermitages would have looked like this.

Walking back into town you pass the **Katuseya dagoba** on a well finished stone base and the **Indikatu Vehara**.

Festivals. Not surprisingly Poson Poya, celebrating the bringing of the Buddhist message to Sri Lanka, is a big event here.

Arrival and departure. Mihintale is 13km east of Anuradhapura, bus or three-wheeler is the best bet. A new railway line provides an erratic service from Anuradhapura.

Accommodation (STD Code 025).
Hotel Mihintale. Tel 6599. DWB A/C $31/35. Rest. Bar. Beautifully designed and maintained (run by Ceylon Hotels Corporation). Good reasonable food. A quiet and civilised place to stay.
Retiring Rooms at the station and a *Rest House* near the crossroads in town.

Further Afield

ANURADHAPURA TO COLOMBO
KURUNEGALA

This was the capital of Lanka for the first quarter of the 14th century, and used by Parakramabahu IV when the Tamils had taken Polonnaruwa. Marco Polo was one of its distinguished visitors. It is said that Kurana is an old Sinhalese word for elephant, hence elephant rock, but this may be fancy.

From the small lake you can see Etagala (Elephant Rock), Ibbagala (Tortoise Rock), and several others, all named after animals. The she demon who once lived in the lake resented the animals drinking away her habitat during a drought and turned them into stone. You have a good view over the town from Elephant Rock.

Another legend connected with the lake relates how Vathimi Bandara, a Muslim prince who had usurped the throne, came to a sticky end. He was lured to a throne on Elephant Rock and given a golden chalice of holy water. The drums rolled, ropes were pulled, and the throne on hidden rollers went whizzing into the lake. They say the chalice reappears on Esala full moon nights bobbing on the lake, but anyone who tries to retrieve it is bound to go mad.

The clock tower doubles as a war memorial.

Arrival and departure. On the railway line from Anuradhapura (2½hrs) to Colombo (1½hrs), also to Kandy but with an awkward connection at Polgahawela Junction. Station 15min walk from town centre. For Kandy and the Cultural Triangle the buses are a better bet; the bus-stand is in the town centre.

Accommodation. The *Old Rest House*, or Rajapihilla Rest House, (Tel 22299) is in the town centre and said to be noisy. The best bet is the *New Rest House*, or Ranthaliya Rest House, (Tel 22298) in a good location on the banks of the lake.

Eating and Drinking. Try *Diva Dahara Hotel*, on North Lake Road, which overlooks the lake.

RIDIGAMA VIHARA

The Silver Monastery was founded by Dutthagamini around 100BC, and takes its name from a local silver lode. The present building is 18th century, built by Kirti Sri Rajasimha (1747-82), the king of Kandy. Excavation has revealed door frames carved and inlaid with ivory and an altar with Delft tiles given by a Dutch governor. Some of these depict Christian scenes, unusual but not unique, as you can see similar ones in at least one place in India (Jaipur).

Arrival and departure. 20km north-east of Kurunegala near Ibbagamuwa, difficult by bus.

PANDUVASNAVARA

The ruins of this ancient city and monastery are of extremely limited interest.

Arrival and departure. Between Chilaw on the west coast and Kurunegala, bus services from Chilaw to Wariyapola and Kurunegala.

DAMBADENIYA

Dambadeniya was briefly the capital of Lanka during the 13th century. From here in 1240 Parakramabahu II launched his successful attack on the Tamils.

The ruins of the Temple of the Tooth and a dagoba are picturesque. A modern temple stands at the foot of an unclimbable rock face; it is said that prisoners were kept on the rock and that the steps were the attempt of one to escape.

Arrival and departure. 30km south-west of Kurunegala, again difficult by bus.

The East

Emergency Repairs

The east of Sri Lanka, like the north, has traditionally been Tamil territory. A large part of the Muslim population, many of them of Malay origin, also lives there. As a result the area has suffered at least as much as the North in the civil war. As in the language issue the government has exacerbated matters. Irrigation from the huge Gal Oya Valley Scheme opened up hundreds of thousands of acres of former jungle to farming. With typical insensitivity the government resettled large numbers of landless Sinhalese on the land. The Tamils allege this has been done with the deliberate intention of changing the balance of the population, so the government would have an excuse (as if they needed one) for digging their heels in over the granting of any degree of autonomy. The difficulty, all political considerations aside, is that the Sinhalese are the traditional peasant farmers of Sri Lanka and the people in the growing population who most need land. The British, in fact, had started the process back in the 19th century as soon as they began, albeit on a much smaller scale, to restore old irrigation works. As in most such situations, there are no easy answers.

The east coast of Sri Lanka boasts some of the island's best beaches, diving, and surfing. Several resorts were developed before the troubles started in the 1980s; these, and the national parks were the only reason for visiting the east, the towns of Trincomalee and Batticaloa being of decidedly limited interest.

Season. The north-east monsoon causes heavy rain in November and December, and the sea remains quite rough during January and February. The coast is at its best from April to August.

Safety. In early 1998 it was safe to visit Trincomalee, Uppuveli, and Nilaveli only. Other places are described for information only. The situation is liable to change either way, and you should take responsible advice before travelling (see p.40). Your embassy and the tourist information offices will always err on the side of caution; the police and military may well lean the other way.

TRINCOMALEE

Trincomalee, usually shortened to Trinco in conversation, is an anglicised version of the Tamil Thirukonamalai, meaning sacred hill of the sun.

Trincomalee has one of the world's finest natural harbours, and this has long made it the target of invaders. Looking just at the european era the Dutch took it from the Portuguese (who had arrived rather late in their time in Sri Lanka in 1622) in 1639 and lost it to the French in 1673, but got it back the following year. The English grabbed it in 1782 but were evicted by the French later that year, and they gave it back to the Dutch the following year. The British seized it in 1795, and the Peace of Amiens in 1802 confirmed their tenure.

King Parakramabahau I (1153-1186) used Trinco to launch his invasion of Burma, and whilst the Dutch held Galle and Colombo this was Kandy's access to the sea. British and Danish merchant shipping (the Danes had a colony at Tranquebar in Tamil Nadu until they sold it to the British in 1845) first used Trincomalee in 1650 as part of their Indian coastal trading operations. With the demise of the Kingdom of Kandy in 1815 Trincomalee became primarily a naval base rather than a commercial harbour. Nelson, who visited Trinco as a young midshipman, praised it as 'the best harbour in the world'. The town has no real significance beyond the naval base, land communications are poor as they always have been, and the economic success of the harbour had no effect on the hinterland.

Trincomalee's finest hour came in the Second World War. The main British naval base in the Far East was Singapore. This fell in February 1942 as the Japanese swept through the British, Dutch and French eastern empires in 1942 wiping out the scratch naval forces confronting them. The Japanese then sent a force of four battleships and three aircraft carriers into the Indian Ocean. They raided Colombo, Trincomalee, and Madras and sank a lot of shipping in the Bay of Bengal. Among their victims were the aircraft carrier HMS

Hermes, which was sent out of Trincomalee with no aircraft to defend itself, and the two cruisers HMS Cornwall and HMS Dorset. More by luck than judgment the main British fleet of elderly battleships avoided contact (and probable annihilation) and withdrew to East Africa. The defences of Colombo and Trincomalee had however destroyed quite a few Japanese carrier planes which could not be quickly replaced, and the fleet therefore withdrew probably feeling it had achieved its aims.

Strategically the Japanese had no interest in India or Sri Lanka. They had Burma's oil, and their other aim (as it remained until mid-1944) was not further conquest but cutting off the supplies to China that went through Calcutta and Chittagong via the Assam railways to the Burma Road. One of the best ways of doing this would have been to take Ceylon or, for that matter, Madagascar, but it seems that that was never part of their plan. In due course Trincomalee and its associated air base at China Bay became a factor in the Japanese downfall.

Exploring

Fort Frederick was built originally by the Portuguese who, as in Galle, took advantage of geography by building a strong wall across a narrow isthmus. The fort was later strengthened by the Dutch and acquired its present name from the Duke of York when the British took over in 1803. The fort maintained its importance, albeit as a seaward defence rather than a landward one, until 1945. The latest works date from that time, and it is said that the modern 6" guns would still work if the British had not taken the breech blocks with them. Many older guns are on display inside.

The present gatehouse is dated 1676. Entry rarely presents a problem for foreigners, though you may have trouble getting a vehicle in. Inside, the British military buildings, typical of their practical tropical architecture, are largely unspoiled. The catch is that the fort is intensively garrisoned by the Sri Lankan army and, whilst they are very tolerant, a serious study of the fortifications or weapons would require an arrangement with either the Defence Ministry or the officer commanding.

Wellesley Lodge is named after Arthur Wellesley (later Duke of Wellington) who stayed here in 1800. The old story that he fell ill and thus missed catching a ship which sank with all hands off Aden does not hold water. Wellesley was indeed in Trincomalee organising an expeditionary force against either Batavia (the Dutch) or Mauritius (the French) according to the changing whim of his brother Richard who was Governor-General of India. (A third brother Henry was also in India at this time). When it was decided to use the force to attack Napoleon in Egypt a more senior officer was put in command over Wellesley. Piqued, he headed for Bombay to equip the force and then wangled a posting back to Mysore where he enhanced his already outstanding reputation.

At the furthest point of the fort is the **Konesvaram Temple** in modern Dravidian style and one of the five most sacred Shiva shrines in Sri Lanka. It is built on the site of a temple the Portuguese destroyed in 1622 for material to use in the defences. The **views** from the high ground are good, and that is about it.

There is little else to see around town. Somewhere there is meant to be an

Archaeological Museum, and St Stephen's Cemetery may be worth a browse.

That said Trincomalee town is, to put not too fine a point on it, a dump. One hesitates to be too harsh considering what the town and its people have had to endure over the last fifteen years, but it simply has nothing to offer the average traveller. If you have a specific interest to justify a visit we suggest you stay out at Uppuveli and keep your stay as short as possible.

Arrival and departure. Bus (2hrs) or train (3hrs) from Habarana, both originating in Colombo. At present there is only one train a day, and the station staff in Trinco are less than helpful. A railcar was glimpsed peeping out of its shed at Trinco station. At the time of writing the direct road from Trinco to Anuradhapura is not open, and buses travel via Habarana.

Accommodation. There are *Railway Retiring Rooms* (Tel 026-22271), a rather grim *Municipal Rest House* (Tel 026-22562), and sundry cheap hotels.

Eating and Drinking. You could try the *Chinese Eastern* near the Clock Tower or *Rainbow Hotel*, 322 Dyke Street, for fast food.

The **British War Cemetery** at Sampalthivu (6km from town centre on the road to Nilaveli) is beautifully kept, and the charming old custodian will tell you all you need to know. As in all such graveyards there is no discrimination by rank, race, or religion, and servicemen and women of many other nations are buried here. These war cemeteries are always poignant places, so many young lives lost so far from home. The more so here. As if one needed another reminder of the evil futility of war some of the gravestones bear the marks of recent fighting.

You may be allowed to take the **ferry** across the harbour and Koddiyar Bay to **Mutur** and travel on to the lighthouse on Foul Point. Nearby is **White Man's Tree** with a memorial to Robert Knox, nineteen years a captive in Kandy and author of *An Historical Relation of Ceylon* (see p251).

In **Tampalakaman Lagoon** is found the window pane oyster (placuna placenta). In many parts of the Far East the translucent flat shells of these molluscs were used in windows in place of glass; a few are still seen in Goa, though we have yet to spot one in Sri Lanka. The pearls from these oysters are no use for jewellery, but were ground up as lime for use in superior paan.

Kanniya (10km/6miles from Trinco) has seven hot springs sacred to Buddhist, Hindu, and Muslim alike. A dagoba, Vishnu temple, and mosque stand nearby. The Hindu legend is that Ravana struck the ground here with his spear when in a rage.

BEACH RESORTS
UPPUVELI

Uppuveli is a beach resort 5km north of Trincomalee. The beach may not be as good as Nilaveli, but the convenience of being closer to town and transport compensate. The area between the beach and the town where people displaced from the countryside have been resettled is grim.

Accommodation. *Club Oceanic* (Tel 026-22397) is a top class resort hotel, and should do a cheap deal like the Nilaveli Beach, though prices will rise sharply if stability returns. The *Pragash Garden* (026-21705) is said to be good.

NILAVELI

Before the troubles Nilaveli was a fairly well developed tourist resort. The beach is pleasant and faces out to Pigeon Island. The coral reefs offshore provide good snorkelling and scuba diving, though the currents can be dangerous for swimming off the beach.

The position in early 1998 was that while it is safe to visit Nilaveli few if any independent travellers do so. It is not our job to make a difficult situation worse, but the novelty of having a whole resort complex to oneself wears off very quickly. The drive out from Trincomalee is depressing; neglected land and hundreds of derelict buildings. The first step in counter-insurgency is to deny the guerillas contact with the local people from whom they can expect (or extort) food and cash, and this is the result. Getting back to Trincomalee without your own transport is problematical, see below.

Arrival and departure. 17km from Trincomalee. Buses are subject to frequent and stringent security checks, and in any case the hotel is near enough a kilometre from the main road. A three-wheeler from town or station (Rs250-300) is a much better idea. You are completely cut off at Nilaveli, and security can make it hard for a three-wheeler to come out of town to pick you up. The chances of local transport are slight.

Accommodation. Only the *Nilaveli Beach Hotel* (Tel 026-22071) is open. Room rates are an absolute bargain, comfortable doubles starting at $5. Rest (good). Bar. Swimming pool.

Shahira Hotel is closed and semi-derelict.

Eating and Drinking. No alternative to the Nilaveli Beach Hotel which, unless you are very careful, makes it look much less of a bargain.

PASSEKUDAH

This was the main package tourist resort on the east coast, though with only three large hotels it was hardly overdeveloped. A number of budget places to stay had been set up on **Kalkudah Bay** just to the south. The great advantage of these places was the beaches, sheltered from dangerous currents and rough seas by a reef.

Arrival and departure. Passekudah is roughly 70km south of Trincomalee and 30km north of Batticaloa. Bus or train to Valachchenai on the main road between the two, then local transport.

BATTICALOA

The Portuguese left the two ports of Trincomalee and Batticaloa in the hands of the kingdom of Kandy until very late in their presence in Ceylon, seizing them in 1628. Only eleven years later the Dutch, invited in by the Kandyans, took Batticaloa and, under the terms of their treaty, handed it back to Kandy. The Dutch had expelled the Portuguese from Ceylon altogether by 1658, and from then on were looking for an excuse to control the whole coastline. One of the main incentives was British attempts to set up trading posts on the east coast and thus threaten the Dutch monopoly in spices. The opportunity came with a rebellion against the King of Kandy. The Dutch helped to suppress it and, since they were in the area anyway, grabbed the ports, Trincomalee in 1665 and Batticaloa in 1668. The outer walls of their **fort** can be seen near the Rest House.

There is singularly little else of interest in Batticaloa, but mention must be made of its **singing fish**. Batticaloa is surrounded by a lagoon and, at certain times of year, notably full moons, a weird sound emanates from the water. The locals reckon it comes from a shellfish and, whilst there are plenty of other theories, nobody has resolved the matter one way or another.

Arrival and departure. Batticaloa is the terminus of the railway line from Gal Oya Junction through Polonnaruwa, but at present no passenger services run beyond Polonnaruwa, so it's a bus from Kandy (4½ hrs), or Colombo. The road from Trincomalee is unlikely to be open.

Accommodation. You could try *Sunshine Inn*, 118 Bar Road (over tracks from station), which has a garden, or *Beach House Guest House*, near the lighthouse. Also the *Rest House*, and *Railway Retiring Rooms* (Tel 065-2271) at the station.

GAL OYA NATIONAL PARK

The Gal Oya river was dammed in the 1950s to form a lake of 78sq km/30sq miles. Apart from hydro-electric power this lake irrigates over 1000sq km/ 250,000 acres of cleared jungle, now some of the most productive farmland in Sri Lanka. The land, and the associated new towns and villages, are largely populated by Sinhalese, formerly a small minority in this area, and a major cause of grievance to the Tamils. The lake is surrounded by hills and, when the park is open, boat trips and fishing are possible.

The 260sq km/100sq miles around the lake has been made a national park mainly to house the wildlife which lost its habitat with the clearances. Elephants and buffalo can be seen. The town at the foot of the dam, and the main access to the lake, is Inginiyagala.

Arrival and departure. A difficult journey on public transport, in the unlikely event of the park being open, with multiple changes of bus.

Accommodation. *Inginiyagala Safari Inn* (Tel 063-2499 or Colombo 91805) run tours in the park. Also a Rest House in Inginiyagala and a lodge at Ekgal Oya (a smaller tank outside park).

ARUGAM BAY

In the early 1990s Arugam Bay became a popular budget resort with several good places to stay. Ever since, access and safety have been problematical. The latest news we have is that you are allowed to visit, but that it is boring. There is a lack of other people, and nothing to do but lie on the beach, thought the surf is said to be very good.

Pottuvil, a couple of kilometres to the north, is the nearest town. It has a somewhat unsavoury reputation for attracting western paedophiles.

Arrival and departure. The road south from Batticaloa is unlikely to be open, which means you have to take a bus from Badulla or Wellawaya to Pottuvil; it may be necessary to change in Monaragala. The alternative is to change buses in Buttala for Kataragama and the south coast.

Accommodation. The *Stardust Beach Hotel* (Tel Colombo 01-323 021), south of the lagoon mouth, is Danish owned and runs trips to Yala East National Park. *Arugam Bay Hilton* (no relation)is cheap, and there are very cheap cabanas to be found.

Excursions

The **Lahugala-Kitalan National Park** is a small sanctuary set up in 1980. The large Mahawewa tank attracts many water birds. The park is part of a scheme to provide elephants with a migratory route between the Gal Oya and Yala parks. Elephants can be seen at the water in the August to October dry season. A real oddity is the climbing perch which migrates across dry land in search of water as the small pools dry up.

The park is on the main road from Monaragala to Pottuvil, and there is a park bungalow.

Near the park is the **Magul Maha Vihara**, the ruins of an ancient monastery, the vatadage and dagoba of which have been reclaimed from the jungle in recent years. It is said that Queen Viharamahadevi, mother of the great King Dutthagamani, was married here.

Kudimbigala Bird Sanctuary is 25km south of Arugam Bay via Panama; the bird life is excellent in May and June. Further south is **Yala East National Park**, home to many wild elephants. There are bungalows at Tunmulla and Okanda, reservations through Wildlife Conservation Department, 82 Rajamalwatta Road, Battaramulla, Colombo, Tel 433 012. Take your own bedding and food.

THE NORTH

It seems highly unlikely that it will be safe to visit this area of Sri Lanka in the foreseeable future. The following brief description is just for the record.
First, a warning. Westerners, especially anyone with a journalistic or media background, may find themselves offered a trip to northern Sri Lanka by various Tamil organisations. This is most likely to happen in Madras (Chennai) in India. The aim is to keep alive the myth of a separate Tamil state. This may sound like the opportunity for a little adventure, but you would be very foolish to accept. Entering a war zone, especially in the company of guerillas, is unwise. The straits between India and Sri Lanka are patrolled heavily and, after some nasty surprises, the Sri Lankan Navy is likely to open fire on unauthorised shipping without warning.

THE JAFFNA PENINSULA

By the 13th century AD Jaffna was the centre of a Tamil kingdom. Part of the population was of long-established settlers from India, augmented by invaders and mercenaries who decided to stay on. Others who had been settled in the irrigated area withdrew to Jaffna as the irrigation system fell into disrepair. The Portuguese coveted Jaffna as it commanded the trade connections with the Malabar Coast of India; their degree of control grew in the latter part of the 16th century until, in 1591, they were able to put a puppet on the throne. The kingdom finally came to an end when the Portuguese captured Jaffna in 1621. In turn, Jaffna was to become their final stronghold in Ceylon, the Dutch winkling them out in 1658 after a bitter siege.

Jaffna has again been the scene of ferocious fighting in the last fifteen years. Jaffna is the centre of the Tamil secessionists and was for years under the control of the Tamil Tigers, who claimed to have set up a provisional government. Jaffna town was retaken by government troops at the end of 1995. Control has been slowly extended to the rest of the peninsula. A major advance from the south aims to crush remaining insurgents in the middle. Unfortunately Sinhalese nationalists fail to understand that a military victory in the field will bring neither peace nor a cessation of acts of terrorism.

The Jaffna Peninsula is to all intents and purposes a large island at the top end of Sri Lanka. The Tamils have been established here for at least two thousand years and form the great majority of the population. You may well hear less well educated Sinhalese calling the Tamils interlopers. In fact they have probably been here just as long as the Sinhalese themselves. One suspects that the scorn, often tinged with barely suppressed envy, with which the Sinhalese (just like his fellow Aryans in northern India) regards the Dravidian

Tamil, stems from a mute admission of the Tamils' industriousness and application.

Population density in the peninsula is about the highest in Sri Lanka. Despite its lack of rainfall the resourceful local farmers have dug deep wells and made the area green and productive. It is especially famous for its mangoes.

The main access to the Jaffna Peninsula is by **Elephant Pass**, a causeway built where wild elephants used to wade over. The crossing is of obvious strategic value, and has frequently been the scene of vicious fighting in recent years.

There was little in **Jaffna town** to interest the foreign visitor in the first place and, by all accounts, huge damage has been done, and much of the population has drifted away. The **Dutch fort** was the finest in the East, surpassing even their headquarters at Batavia (now Jakarta) in Java. Its 22ha/54 acres on a star plan encompassed the Groote Kerk and a fine house for the governor. The outer defences were completed only four years before the British took it over in 1796. It has been used as a strongpoint by both the Indian and Sri Lankan armies (the only real fighting it has ever seen) and badly damaged as a result.

Arrival and departure. The railway line north from Anuradhapura currently terminates at Vavuniya, 140km from Jaffna.

Excursions

There are good beaches near Jaffna, notably **Palm Beach** on the north coast. **Point Pedro**, the northernmost point of the island, is marked by a lighthouse. Beyond Jaffna Peninsula is a number of islands, some connected by causeways, others by a ferry. **Kayts Island** has a Dutch fort described, surely fancifully, as a miniature Chateau d'If. On **Karaitivu Island** opposite is the Hammenhiel Fort; the Dutch thought of Ceylon as ham-shaped, and this bent-over top end was logically its heel. **Delft**, named after the Dutch town, means a ferry trip. This windswept island, very lightly populated, is home to herds of wild ponies, thought to be descended from Portuguese and Dutch stock. Smaller islands nearby are important places of pilgrimage for both Buddhists and Christians.

ADAM'S BRIDGE

Sri Lanka is virtually joined to India by Adam's Bridge (or Rama's Bridge), a string of islands and sandbanks. This was in fact negotiable on foot until the 15th century AD when especially violent cyclones swamped some islets and deepened the water between them. The first name stems from the Muslim belief that Adam crossed to Sri Lanka this way after his expulsion from the Garden of Eden. The Ramayana, on the other hand, tells how Hanuman placed the islands to help Rama cross to rescue Sita.

The Sri Lankan end of the chain is Mannar Island, a bleak and arid place. The town of **Mannar** has a well preserved Dutch fort and, in it, a church with Portuguese tombstones. 30km further on, at the tip of the island, is **Talaimannar**. In peaceful times this was the terminal for the short ferry ride to Rameswaram in India. The ferry was the only reason anyone visited this area, and there seems little prospect of the service being restored in the foreseeable future. Talaimannar is the terminus of the currently non-operational railway line to Madawachchi Junction and from there through Anuradhapura to Colombo.

GLOSSARY

abhaya-mudra	Buddha figure in 'fearless' posture
apsara	heavenly nymph
arrack	spirit distilled from toddy
Aryans	Indo-European peoples of northern India, to whom the Sinhalese are related
avatar	one of the nine guises in which Vishnu has come to earth
Avelokiteshwara	'all-seeing', 'compassionate', the most important of the Boddhisatvas
Ayurveda	traditional medical system
bhikku	Buddhist monk
bhumisparsha-mudra	Buddha in earth-witness pose
Bo/Bodhi-tree	fig tree under which Buddha achieved enlightenemnt
Boddhisatva	a Buddha to come, see p35
Buddha	title meaning The Enlightened One
bund	embankment, dam
Burghers	Sri Lankans of mixed descent
cetiya, chaitya	Buddhist chapel or dagoba
chakra	wheel device with various meanings
chena	slash and burn nomadic cultivation
chatta, chhattri	umbrella, mark of respect and symbol of Buddha
Chola	dynasty and empire (10-14th centuries) based on Thanjavur, Tamil Nadu
choli	skimpy blouse worn with a sari
coir	coconut fibre for mats and so on
Culavamsa	Sinhalese chronicle (13th century) following on from Mahavamsa
dagoba	hemispherical Buddhist memorial
devale	temple of one of the Hindu guardians of Buddhism, see p201
dhamma	Buddhist personal law (like Hindu dharma)
dhyana	meditation, hence dhyani-mudra
dhyani-mudra	Buddha in meditation pose
doratupala	guardian figure at entrance to building
Dravidian	South Indian
Gajalakshmi	Lakshmi being showered by two white elephants
gedige	Buddhist image house, properly of corbelled brick
gopuram	highly ornamented gateway to Hindu temple
Goyigama	most important Sinhalese caste in Sri Lanka, farmer-landlords
Hanuman	the monkey-faced demi-god who helped Rama rescue Sita in the *Ramayana*, a patron of learning and medicine
Hinayana	literally lesser vehicle. Therevada (qv) is the preferred term

Glossary

isvaram	one of the five holiest Shiva shrines in Sri Lanka
jaggery	coarse brown sugar from palm sap (good!)
Jataka	literally birth or incarnation, tales of Buddha's earlier lives
JVP	Janatha Vimukthi Peramuna (People's Liberation Army), a fiercely left-wing, anti-Tamil nationalist group, now a political party
Karava	fishemen caste
karma	the law of cause and effect
Kataragama	pre-Buddhist warrior deity, analogous to the Hindu Skanda, guardian of Buddhism
Kartikkeya	North Indian form of Skanda
kolam	masked dance drama
kovil	Tamil Hindu temple
Krishna	eighth incarnation of Vishnu
Kubera	monstrous god of wealth and the dead (like Pluto), head of the Yakshas
Lakshmi	Vishnu's wife, the goddess of good fortune (with four arms) or beauty (with two)
lingam	stylised phallus, the emblem of Shiva
LTTE	Liberation Tigers of Tamil Eelam, the dominant Tamil militant group
madrasa	Islamic school
maha	great
Mahavamsa	chronicle of the Sinhalese people up to sixth century (continued by Culavamsa)
Mahavishnu	lord of the elephants, an early Sri Lankan god
Mahayana	literally great vehicle, layman's branch of Buddhism
maidan	open space, parade ground
Maitreya	the Buddha to come
makara	mythical beasts guarding buildings
makara-torana	as above, in the form of an arch
mandapa/mandape	many pillared hall, usually in front of a temple shrine
MW (Mawatha)	street
moksha	literally release (from the cycle of death and rebirth), enlightenment
moonstone	(1) symbolic semi-circular threshold (2) semi-precious stone
mudra	hand position signifying an activity
Murugan	pre-Hindu Tamil deity, associated with Skanda
nag/naga	snake, sometimes a snake deity
Natha	supreme god of ancient Lanka
Nirvana	what the enlightened achieve after moksha, a state of perfect knowledge, of neither being nor not being
ola	palm leaves prepared for writing
paan	areca nut and betel leaf chew
paddy	growing rice
Pali	early Indo-European language spoken by Buddha and used for Buddhist scriptures
Pallava	dynasty and empire (AD400-890) based on Kanchipuram in Tamil Nadu
Pandya	dynasty and empire (AD500-1310) based on Madurai in Tamil Nadu
Pattini	pre-Hindu virgin goddess of rivers, also of smallpox,

	analagous to Maryamman and Shitala
perahera	lively Buddhist religious procession
pilimage	Buddha image house
poya	full moon day each month, public holiday
rajah	king
Rama	seventh incarnation of Vishnu, hero of the *Ramayana*
ratha	chariot of the gods
Ravana	demon king of Lanka and kidnapper of Sita, an embodiment of evil whom Vishnu came to Earth (as Rama) to destroy
Saman, Samanta	old Lankan god, associated with Shiva, said to be a Maitreya
Samgha	the community of Buddhist monks
sannyas	renunciation of all worldly things
seya	variant of cetiya, a dagoba
Shiva	one of the two main Hindu gods; destoyer, creator, and teacher of priests
sinha	lion
Sita	wife of Rama, a form of Lakshmi
Skanda	South Indian name for the god of war, one of the sons of Shiva and Parvati
Sri	Mr, also a general honorific
stupa	dagoba
Subramanian	another South Indian form of Kartikkeya
tank	reservoir
Therevada	the earliest form of Buddhism in which Buddha is an ideal rather than a god, the dominant form in Sri Lanka and South-East Asia
three-wheeler	two-seat scooter rickshaw
thupa	variant of stupa, dagoba
toddy	alcoholic drink of fermented palm sap
torana	archway, entrance
tuk-tuk	baby talk for three-wheeler
UNP	United National Party
Upulvan	early Hindu god, protector of Sri Lanka, associated with Varuna and possibly Uranus
urinal stone	perforated sculpted stone so an ascetic monk could pee on the image of a cosy monastery
vahalkada	feature on dagoba at cardinal points
varna	colour, the Indian term for caste
Varuna	early Hindu god, regulator of the heavens and oceans
vatadage	circular Buddha image house
Veddha	aboriginal, literally means archer
vel	trident or lance of Shiva
Vibhushana	younger brother of Ravana; exiled for disobeying his brother, he helped Rama to rescue Sita
vihara	Buddhist monastery
Vishnu	one of the two main Hindu gods; the preserver, has come to earth in nine forms (avatars) including Buddha
VOC	Vereenigde Oostindische Compagnie, the Dutch East India Company
Yaksha	demon, according to tradition original inhabitants of Sri Lanka
yoni	receptacle for lingam, female fertility symbol

PLACE NAMES

ārāma	monastery, park	oya	large stream
deniya	paddy field under a hill	pitiya	park
duwa	island	pura	town (Sinhalese)
ela	stream	puram	town (Tamil)
gaha	tree	tara, tota	port (or ford if inland)
gala	rock or hill	tale	tank, lake (Sinhalese)
gama	village	turai	port (or ford if inland) (Tamil)
ganga	river	uttar	north
kanda	mountain	vila	pond (Sinhalese)
kulam	tank, lake (Tamil)	vilei	pond (Tamil)
maha	great	watte	garden
nuwara	city	wewa	tank, lake (Sinhalese)

BIBLIOGRAPHY

Adikaram, E.W. *Early History of Buddhism in Ceylon*. 1946.
Archer, W.G. & Paranavitana, S. *Ceylon: Paintings from Temple Shrine and Rock*. New York Graphic Soc, Paris 1958.
Ariyatane, D.H. *Gems of Sri Lanka*. Felix Press, Colombo 1976.
Banks, John & Judy. *A Selection of the Birds of Sri Lanka*. Banks. [Also other wildlife titles].
Arumugam, S. *Ancient Hindu Temples of Sri Lanka*. Colombo 1982.
Barlas, Robert & Wanasundera, Nanda P. *Culture Shock: Sri Lanka*. Kuperard, London 1994.
Bell, Bethia N. & Heather M. *H.C.P. Bell: Archaeologist of Ceylon & the Maldives*.
Beny, Roloff. *Island Ceylon*. Thames & Hudson, London 1971.
Bond, Thomas. *Wild Flowers of the Ceylon Hills*. OUP, 1953.
Brohier, R.L. *Changing Face of Colombo 1505-1972*. Lake House, Colombo 1972.
Seeing Ceylon. Lake House, Colombo 1965.
Clarke, Arthur C. *Off the Reefs of Taprobane*. 1957. *View from Serendib*. Random House, New York 1977.
Cook, E.K. *Geography of Ceylon*. 1939.
Coomaraswamy, Ananada K. *Medieval Sinhalese Art*. Pantheon, New York 1956. *Myths of the Hindus and Buddhists*. Dover, London 1967.
Cordiner, James. *A Description of Ceylon etc.* 1807. Reprinted Tisara Prakasakayo, Colombo 1983.
Dasanayake, M. *The Kandy Esala Perahera; Asia's Most Spectacular Pageant*. Ranco Publishers, Colombo 1977.
Davis, Peter & Cannon, Teresa. *Aliya - Stories of the Elephants of Sri Lanka*.
Deraniyagala, S.U. *The Prehistory of Sri Lanka (2 vols)*. Dept of Archaeological Survey of Sri Lanka, Colombo 1992.
de Lanerolle, Nalini. *A Reign of Ten Kings*. CTB, Colombo 1990.
De Silva, Colin. *The Winds of Sinhala, The Founts of Sinhala, The Fires of Sinhala*. Panther, London 1982-87. [Trilogy of novels].
De Silva, Dr K.M. *A History of Sri Lanka*. OUP, Bombay 1981.
De Zoysa, Neela & Rahem, Rhyana. *Sinharaja: A Rain Forest in Sri Lanka*. March for Conservation.

Dissanayake, J.B. *Say it in Sinhala.*
Dissanayake, T.D.S.A. *The Agony of Sri Lanka: An In Depth Account of the Racial Riots of 1983.* Swastika Ltd, Colombo 1983.
Geiger, W. *Culture of Ceylon in Medieval Times.* Harrassowitz, Wiesbaden 1960. *Mahavamsa.*
Godakamburre, C.E. *Architecture of Sri Lanka.* Dept of Cultural Affairs [Monograph], Colombo 1963.
Goonatilleke. *Masks and Mask Systems.*
Goonetileke, Hai. *Lanka, their Lanka.* Navrang, New Delhi 1984. [Anthology of foreigners' views - sounds good]
Goonetilleke, D.C.R.A. *The Penguin New Writing in Sri Lanka.* India 1992.
Gunesekhara, Ramesh. *Monkfish Moon.* Penguin, London 1992. *Reef.* Penguin, London 1994.
Handbook for the Ceylon Traveller. Studio Times Publications, Colombo 1983.
Henry, G.M. *A Guide to the Birds of Ceylon.* OUP & K.V.G. De Silva, Kandy 1978.
Hulugalle, H.A.J. *Ceylon.* Oxford 1949.
Jayawardene, Kumari. *Ethnic & Class Conflicts in Sri Lanka.* Centre for Social Analysis, Colombo.
Kautzsch, Eberhard. *A Guide to the Waterfalls of Sri Lanka.* Tisara Prakasakayo, Dehiwala 1983.
Keble, W.T. *Ceylon, Beaten Track.* Lake House, Colombo.
Keyt, George. *Folk Stories of Sri Lanka.* Lake House, Colombo 1974.
Knox, Robert. *An Historical Relation of Ceylon.* Tisara Prakasakayo, Colombo.
Kotagama, Sarath & Prithviraj. *A Field Guide to the Birds of Sri Lanka.* Wildlife Heritage Trust of Sri Lanka.
Kotelewala, Sir John. *An Asian Prime Minister's Story.* 1956.
Little, D. *Sri Lanka: the Invention of Enmity.* US Inst of Peace Press, Washington 1994.
Ludowyk, E.F.C. *The Modern History of Ceylon.* Praeger, New York 1966. *The Story of Ceylon.* Faber, London 1962.
McGowan, William. *Only Man is Vile: The Tragedy of Sri Lanka.* Picador, London 1993.
Malangoda, K. *Buddhism in Sinhalese Society 1750-1900.* Berkeley 1976.
Maloney, Clarence. *Peoples of South Asia.* Holt, Rheinhart & Winston, New York, 1974.
Mendis, G.C. *Early History of Ceylon.* 1940.
Mitton, G.E. *The Lost Cities of Ceylon.* John Murray, London 1951.
Moore, M.P. *The State and Peasant Politics in Sri Lanka.* London 1985.
Munro, Ian. *Marine and Freshwater Fishes of Ceylon.* Australian Dept of External Affairs, Canberra 1955.
Nanarama, Ven Matara Sri. *The Seven Stages of Purification and the Insight Knowledges.* Buddhist Publications Society, Kandy 1983.
Navaratnam, C.S. *A Short History of Hinduism in Ceylon and Three Essays on the Tamils.* 1964.
O'Ballance, Edgar. *The Cyanide War: Tamil Insurrection in Sri Lanka 1973-88.* Brassey's (UK), London 1989.
Obeyesekere, R. & Fernando, C. (eds). *An anthology of modern writing from Sri Lanka.* Tucson 1981.
Ondaatje, Michael. *Running in the Family.* Picador, London 1983.
Parker, H. *Ancient Ceylon.*
Perera, H.R. *Buddhism in Ceylon Past and Present.* Buddhist Pubn Soc, Kandy 1966.
Piyadasa, L. *Sri Lanka: The Holocaust and After.* Marram Books, London 1984.

Bibliography

Ponnambalam, Satchi. *Sri Lanka: The National Question and the Tamil Liberation Struggle*. Zed Books, London 1983.
Qureshi, I.H. *The Muslim Community of the Indo-Pakistan Sub-Continent 610-1947*. OAP, Karachi 1977.
Rahula, Walpola. *What The Buddha Taught*. Gordon Fraser, London 1967 (reprint 1982). *History of Buddhism in Ceylon*. 1959.
Ratnapala, Nandesena. *Sinhalese Folklore, Folk Religion and Folk Life*. Sarvodaya Research Institute, Colombo 1980.
Raven-Hart, R. *Ceylon: History in Stone*. Lake House, Colombo 1973.
Reynolds, C.H.B. (ed). *An Anthology of Sinhalese Literature of the 20th Century*. London 1987.
Robinson, Francis (ed). *Cambridge Encyclopaedia of India, Pakistan*. Cambridge 1989.
Ryan, Bryce. *Caste in Modern Ceylon: The Sinhala System in Transition*. Rutgers UP, New Jersey 1953.
Sansoni, Barbara. *Viharas and Verandahs*. Ranco Publishers, Colombo 1980.
Sitwell, Sacheverell. *The Red Chapels of Banteai Srei*. Weidenfeld & Nicholson, London.
Sivaratnam, C. *Origin and Development of the Hindu Religion and People*. Ranco Publishers, Colombo 1980.
Spittel, R.L. *Far Off Things*. CAC Press, Colombo. *Savage Sanctuary*. Colombo Book Centre, Colombo 1953. [Novel about Veddhas]. *Vanished Trails: The Last of the Veddhas*. Associated Newspapers of Ceylon, Colombo 1961.
Still, John. *Ancient Capitals of Ceylon*.
Stutley, Margaret & James. *Dictionary of Buddhism*. *Dictionary of Hinduism*. Routledge Kegan Paul, London 1977.
Thorana Guide to Sri Lanka. Lever Brothers Cultural conservation Trust, Colombo 1979.
Thornton, E.M. & Niththyanantham, R. *Sri Lanka: Island of Terror*. Eeelam Research Organisation, London 1984.
Tillakaratne, Miniwan P. *Customs and Ceremonies of Sri Lanka*. Sri Satgura Publishers, Delhi 1986.
Tomlinson, Michael. *The Most Dangerous Moment: The Japanese Assault on Ceylon 1942*. Tisara Prakasakayo, Dehiwala 1976 (Third revised 1993).
Trekkers' Guide to Sri Lanka. Trekkers Unlimited, Colombo.
Tresidder, A.J. *Ceylon: Resplendent Isle*. 1962.
Vijayatunge, J. *Grass for my Feet*. Howard Baker, London 1935. [Village life].
Weerakoon, P. *Sri Lanka's Mythology*. Samayawadhava, Colombo 1985.
Welbon, Guy R. *Religious Festivals in South India and Sri Lanka*. Manohar, New Delhi 1982.
Wijesekera, Nandadeva. *Veddhas in Transition*. M.D. Gunasena, Colombo 1964. *Heritage of Sri Lanka*. Archaeological Society of Sri Lanka, Colombo 1984.
Williams, H. *Ceylon: Pearl of the East*. 1952.
Wirz, Paul (tr Doris B. Pralle). *Kataragama, the Holiest Place in Ceylon*. Lake House, Colombo 1966.
Woodcock, Martin. *Handguide to Birds of the Indian Sub-Continent*. Collins, London.
Woodhouse, I.G.O. *Butterfly Fauna of Ceylon*. Govt Press, 1942.
Woolf, Leonard. *Growing: An Autobiography*. Hogarth, London 1961. *The Village in the Jungle*. 1st 1913. OUP, Madras (pb) 1987. [Novel].

PERIODICALS
Official Handbook of Sri Lanka. Ceylon Tourist Board, Colombo. Quarterly.
This Month in Sri Lanka. Spectrum Lanka Ltd. Colombo. Monthly.

INDEX

accommodation ... 56
Adam's Bridge ... 246
Adam's Peak ... 161
Ahangama ... 118
Ahungalla Animal Park ... 103
airport tax ... 40, 43
Alawwa ... 137
Aluthgama ... 101
Alutnuwara (Mahiyangana) ... 160
Aluvihara ... 190
Ambalangoda ... 104
angling ... 63, 164
antiques ... 70
Anuradhapura ... 221
architecture ... 33
art galleries ... 62
Arugam Bay ... 243
ATMs ... 45
Aukana ... 218
Avissawella ... 185
Ayurveda ... 101, 174

Badulla ... 178
baggage ... 46
Baker Falls ... 169
Balana ... 140
Bambarakanda Falls ... 182
Bandarawela ... 174
Bat Cave ... 181
batik ... 69, 103, 190
Batticaloa ... 242
beaches ... 64, 96, 104, 115
Belihul Oya ... 171, 182
Bentota ... 102
Beruwela ... 101
bird watching .. 129, 130, 132, 169, 205, 244
black market ... 45
blowhole ... 125
Bogawantalawa ... 161
Bogoda bridge ... 179
books ... 37, 63, 128
Brief Gardens ... 102
Buddha images ... 35
Buddhism ... 27
Buduruvagala ... 180
Bundala National Park ... 129
bus travel ... 53

canals ... 95
canoeing ... 64
car hire ... 53
cashew nuts ... 137
caste (Buddhism) ... 29
caste (Hinduism) ... 31
changing money ... 44
Chilaw ... 99

children ... 75
Christianity ... 32
cigarettes ... 61
cinema ... 65
civil war ... 19
climate ... 14
Colombo ... 78
costs in Sri Lanka ... 44
credit cards ... 45
Cultural Triangle Office ... 89, 148, 188
currents (warning) ... 64, 94, 106
cycling ... 56

dagoba ... 33
Dalhousie ... 161
Dambadeniya ... 237
Dambulla ... 192
dance ... 66
Dedigama ... 137
Delft Island ... 246
Demodera Loop ... 178
devale (definition) ... 149
Devinuwara ... 123
Devon Falls ... 163
Dikwella ... 123
Dimbulagala ... 216
Dinawar ... 123
disabled travellers ... 75
Diyaluma Falls ... 181
Diyatalawa ... 174
Dodanduwa ... 108
Dondra Head ... 123
doratupala ... 34
dress ... 46
drinking ... 60
driving licence ... 43
drugs ... 73, 75
drums ... 121
Dry Zone ... 11
Dunhinda Falls ... 179

eating ... 58
economy ... 22
electricity ... 75
Elephant Orphanage ... 138
Elephant Pass ... 246
elephants ... 131, 138, 181, 204
Ella ... 175
embassies (foreign in SL) ... 77
embassies (Sri Lankan abroad) ... 42

fauna ... 62
festivals ... 51, 67, 96, 122, 134, 151, 231
fire walking ... 134
flora ... 62
food ... 59
footprints of Buddha ... 162

254 Index

Galle ... 108
Gal Oya National Park ... 243
Gampola ... 160
gardens ... 81, 102, 137, 156, 168
gems ... 69, 183
geography ... 11
geology ... 11
Ginigathena Pass ... 186
golf ... 64, 164, 186
government ... 25
Goyambokka ... 125

Habarana ... 204
Hakgala Botanical Gardens ... 168
Hambantota ... 127
Handapanangala ... 181
Hanguranketa ... 159
Hanwella ... 186
Haputale ... 171
Hatton ... 160
health ... 70, 73
Henerathgoda Botanic Gardens ... 137
Hikkaduwa ... 104
Hinduism ... 29
history ... 15
horse racing ... 66, 164
Horton Plains ... 168
hotels and guest houses ... 56
Hunas Falls ... 189
Hunnasgiriya ... 160

Induruwa ... 103
Inginiyagala ... 243
inoculations ... 71
Internet ... 76
Islam ... 32
Istripura Caverns ... 168

Jaffna ... 245
jewellery ... 69

Kadugannawa ... 140
Kaduwela ... 186
Kalawewa ... 218
Kalkudah ... 242
Kalpitiya ... 100
Kalutara ... 101
Kandy ... 141
Kanniya ... 241
Karaitivu Island ... 246
Karawanella ... 186
Kataluwa ... 118
Kataragama ... 132
Katukurunda ... 101
Kayts Island ... 246
Kelani Valley Railway ... 185
Kelliebedde Tea Factory ... 172
Kitulgala ... 186
Kirinda ... 129
Kirundu Oya Falls ... 160

Knuckles Range ... 160
Koggala ... 117
Kosgoda ... 103
Kudimbigala Bird Sanctuary ... 244
Kurugala Caves ... 182
Kurunegala ... 236

Labookellie Tea Factory ... 163
Lahugala Kitalan National Park ... 244
language ... 36
local transport ... 55

Madampe ... 99
Mahawewa ... 99
Mahiyangana (Alutnuwara) ... 160
mail ... 49
makara (-torana) ... 34
Maligawila ... 181
Manikdiwela ... 159
Mannampitiya ... 217
Mannar ... 246
maps ... 9, 50
Maskeliya ... 161
masks ... 104
Matale ... 189
Matara ... 121
Mawella ... 125
Mawanella ... 140
Medamahanuwara ... 160
media ... 49
Medirigiriya ... 217
meditation centres ... 232
meeting people ... 25
Midigama ... 118
Mihintale ... 233
Minneriya Giritale Sanctuary ... 205
Mirissa ... 120
mobile phones ... 48
money ... 44
moonstones ... 34, 104, 230
motor racing ... 101
motorcycle hire ... 55
mountain biking ... 64
mudra ... 35
Mulkirigala ... 124
murals ... 124
museums ... 62
music ... 65

Nalanda ... 191
name ... 10
Namunkula ... 179
National Parks etc
    Bundala ... 129
    Gal Oya ... 243
    Horton Plains ... 168
    Kudimbigala ... 244
    Lahugala Kitalan ... 244
    Minneriya Giritale ... 205

Peak Wilderness 168
Ritigala 218
Ruhuna 131
Sinharaja 182
Uda Walawe 135
Wilpattu 100
Yala East 244
Yala West 131
Negombo 95
nightlife 66
Nilaveli 242
Nonagama 127
nudity 47
Nuwara Eliya 163

paan 61
painting 35
Panduvasnavara 237
Passekudah 242
Pasyala 137
Pattipola 168
Peak Wilderness Sanctuary 168
Peradeniya Botanic Gardens 156
Perahera (Kandy) 151
phones 48
photography 47, 75, 105
Pidurangala 203
pilimage 34
Pinnewala Elephant Orphanage ... 138
Polhena 120
police 75
politics 21
Polonnaruwa 205
population 22
Pottuvil 243
Puttalam 99

radio 50
rafting 64
rail travel 51
railways, special interest 52, 100, 137,
   178, 185
Ratmalana 100
Ramayana 176, 246
Rawana Ella Rock Temple 175
Ratna Ela Falls 160
Ratnapura 183
religion 26
rest houses 57
restaurants 59
Ridigama Vihara 237
Ritigala Strict Natural Reserve 218
running 64
Ruwanwella 186

St Clair Falls 163
safety 10
salt 99, 128
Sasseruwa 219

season (tourist) 58, 239
serendipity 10
shopping 69, 87, 88
Sigiriya 196
Sinhala (language) 36
Sinhalese (people) 23
Sinharaja Biosphere Reserve 182
Sitavaka 186
spectator sports 66
spice gardens 190
stars 51
steamrollers etc 159
Stilt fishermen 118
swimming 63, 94, 115

Talaimannar 246
Talawakele 163
Talawila 99
Tamil (language) 36
Tamil (people) 23
Tangalla 125
tea processing 172
telegrams 49
television 50
tennis 164
theatre 65
time 76
tipping 45
Tissamaharama (Tissa) 130
tourist offices 76, 88, 96
trekking 64
Trincomalee 239
turtles 102, 103, 108

Udappawa 99
Uda Walawe National Park 135
Unawatuna 114
Uppuveli 241

vahalkada 34
vatadage 34
Veddahs 23
Victoria Dam 159
visas 42

Wahakotte 192
watersports 63, 96, 101, 104, 116
Weherehena Temple 122
Weligama 118
Wellawaya 179
Wet Zone 11
Wewurukannala Temple 123
Wilpattu National Park and Game Sanctuary 100
women in Sri Lanka 24
women travellers 26

yachting 64
Yala East National Park 244
Yala West National Park 131
Yapahuwa 220

Vacation Work publish:

	Paperback	Hardback
The Directory of Summer Jobs Abroad	£8.99	£14.95
The Directory of Summer Jobs in Britain	£8.99	£14.95
Supplement to Summer Jobs in Britain and Abroad *published in May*	£6.00	–
Work Your Way Around the World	£12.95	–
The Good Cook's Guide to Working Abroad	£11.95	–
Taking a Gap Year	£10.99	–
Working in Tourism – The UK, Europe & Beyond	£11.95	–
Kibbutz Volunteer	£8.99	–
Working on Cruise Ships	£9.99	–
Teaching English Abroad	£11.95	–
The Au Pair & Nanny's Guide to Working Abroad	£10.99	–
Working in Ski Resorts – Europe & North America	£10.99	–
Working with Animals – The UK, Europe & Worldwide	£11.95	–
Accounting Jobs Worldwide	£11.95	–
Working with the Environment	£10.99	–
Health Professionals Abroad	£10.99	–
The Directory of Jobs & Careers Abroad	£11.95	£16.99
The International Directory of Voluntary Work	£10.99	£15.99
The Directory of Work & Study in Developing Countries	£9.99	£14.99
Live & Work in Japan	£10.99	–
Live & Work in Russia & Eastern Europe	£10.99	–
Live & Work in France	£10.99	–
Live & Work in Australia & New Zealand	£10.99	–
Live & Work in the USA & Canada	£10.99	–
Live & Work in Germany	£10.99	–
Live & Work in Belgium, The Netherlands & Luxembourg	£10.99	–
Live & Work in Spain & Portugal	£10.99	–
Live & Work in Italy	£10.99	–
Live & Work in Scandinavia	£10.99	–
Travellers Survival Kit: Sri Lanka	£10.99	–
Travellers Survival Kit: Mozambique	£10.99	–
Travellers Survival Kit: Cuba	£10.99	–
Travellers Survival Kit: Lebanon	£10.99	–
Travellers Survival Kit: South Africa	£10.99	–
Travellers Survival Kit: India	£10.99	–
Travellers Survival Kit: Russia & the Republics	£9.95	–
Travellers Survival Kit: Western Europe	£8.95	–
Travellers Survival Kit: Eastern Europe	£9.95	–
Travellers Survival Kit: South America	£15.95	–
Travellers Survival Kit: Central America	£8.95	–
Travellers Survival Kit: USA & Canada	£10.99	–
Travellers Survival Kit: Australia & New Zealand	£10.99	–

Distributors of:

Summer Jobs USA	£12.95	–
Internships (On-the-Job Training Opportunities in the USA)	£16.95	–
Sports Scholarships in the USA	£16.95	–
Scholarships for Study in the USA & Canada	£14.95	–
Colleges & Universities in the USA	£15.95	–
Green Volunteers	£10.99	–

Vacation Work Publications, 9 Park End Street, Oxford OX1 1HJ
Tel 01865–241978   Fax 01865–790885

Visit us online for more information on our unrivalled range of titles for work, travel and adventure, readers' feedback and regular updates:
Web site http://www.vacationwork.co.uk